LIBRARY IN A BOOK

HATE CRIMES
REVISED EDITION

Tom Streissguth

An imprint of Infobase Publishing

Facts On File, Inc.
An imprint of Infobase Publishing
132 West 31st Street
New York NY 10001

Library of Congress Cataloging-in-Publication Data
Streissguth, Thomas, 1958–
    Hate crimes / Tom Streissguth. — Rev. ed.
       p. cm. — (Library in a book)
    Includes bibliographical references and index.
    ISBN 978-0-8160-7365-8 (alk. paper)
    1. Hate crimes—United States. I. Title.
    HV 6773.52.S768 2009
    364.15—dc22   2009013932

Facts On File books are available at special discounts when purchased in bulk quantities for businesses, associations, institutions, or sales promotions. Please call our Special Sales Department in New York at (212) 967-8800 or (800) 322-8755.

You can find Facts On File on the World Wide Web at http://www.factsonfile.com

Printed in the United States of America

MP Hermitage 10 9 8 7 6 5 4 3 2 1

This book is printed on acid-free paper and contains 30 percent postconsumer recycled content.

CONTENTS

INTRODUCTION TO
THE REVISED EDITION

Since the first edition of this book was published in 2003, the subject of hate crimes has significantly changed, especially after September 11 and in response to the issue of immigration reform. As hate crimes debates continue, new legislation offered each year expands the legal definition of hate crimes as well as the statutory authority granted to the federal government to punish crimes of prejudice. As of this writing, the most recent Uniform Crime Reports (UCR) of the Federal Bureau of Investigation, for the year 2006, reports an increase of 8 percent in the incidence of hate crimes nationally. Important aspects of the issue are crimes directed against Muslim and Arab persons, by reason of their religion and ethnic origin, after the terrorist attacks of September 11, 2001, and the ongoing war in Iraq, and the incidence of hate crimes directed against Hispanic and undocumented (illegal) immigrants.

This updated and revised edition presents new background material; an updated chronology of relevant events; recent books, articles, reports, and web sites; updated contact information for organizations and advocacy groups dealing with the issue; and the most recent text of proposed federal legislation. Speeches, articles, and a White House position statement are included to illustrate the positions of supporters and opponents of the law.

PART I

OVERVIEW OF THE TOPIC

CHAPTER 1

INTRODUCTION TO
HATE CRIMES

"Hate crime" as a legal category is a recent invention, but bias-motivated violence has a long history. Since antiquity, humans have been selecting other humans for assault, injury, and murder for their different appearance, color, nationality, language, or religion. Individuals and governments have carried out what would be defined in the 21st-century United States as hate crimes. The Romans murdered Christians; the Nazis persecuted Jews; the 1994 genocide in Rwanda pitted Hutus against Tutsis; Muslims were singled out for imprisonment, rape, and mass execution by Christians in the former Yugoslavia.

For a period of more than three centuries, beginning in the 16th century, Native American tribes were methodically destroyed by Dutch, French, Spanish, and British colonists, and then by American citizens, who had the conquest and cultivation of a new land in mind. The American settlers also carried out extrajudicial executions of those whites holding different political views, an act that came to be known as lynching. The verb *lynch* originates with an 18th-century Virginia planter named Charles Lynch who, with a group of like-minded colonists, would sometimes take the law into his own hands and punish Tories (those who sympathized with the British colonial government), most often by tarring and feathering but also by summary hangings.

Lynching has come to be defined as an execution done outside of the ordinary system of justice. A lynching represents a breakdown of order and a defiance of the law. The victim is chosen either because of a suspected crime, or simply (and most commonly) because of his or her race. No trial is held, and no jury passes sentence. After the American Revolution, lynching became an expedient way to deal with suspected criminals in places where the police authority was weak or nonexistent. On the western frontiers, lynch mobs punished the crimes of horse and cattle stealing, kidnapping, robbery, and murder.

CUSTOMARY PREJUDICE

The English Protestants who made up the majority of North American colonists brought their customary prejudices and habits of mind to the New World. One of the strongest such prejudices was directed against Catholics, who in most areas of the British colonies (with the exception of Pennsylvania and Maryland) were banned outright. Catholics were suspected of conspiring to undermine or overthrow established governments in the name of their church. Despite the fact that Protestants and Catholics shared a common faith, the sectarian rivalry of Europe endured in America, finally abating in the 20th century as the two groups melded into a common nationality and secular culture. The colonies were also a hostile place for Jews, whose numbers in North America remained small through the 18th century. The Jewish communities of New York, Newport, Savannah, and Charleston isolated themselves from the surrounding society, whose members often treated them with contempt as craven usurers and—a prejudice remaining from the medieval age—as the killers of Christ and of good Christians.

Bigotry was not only directed at Catholics and Jews. The British colonies were separated from each other by long distances as well as by important cultural and religious differences. The Dutch of New York and New Jersey strongly distrusted the English Puritans of Massachusetts. Anglicans, who belonged to the national Protestant church of England, disliked the breakaway sect of Puritans as well as the Presbyterians, who hailed from Scotland. The American Revolution brought forth a wide variety of new loyalties and hatreds among the colonists. Support for the revolution was by and large divided along religious differences, with Anglicans opposing the revolt and Baptists and Presbyterians supporting it. The Quakers of Pennsylvania professed pacifism and refused to give their allegiance or military service to either side. For this they were despised and maltreated by members of both factions outside of Pennsylvania. After the Revolution, many Loyalists, who refused to join the movement for separation from England, were driven from the colonies; those who remained saw their property confiscated and their legal rights to sue in court, to vote, to collect debts, and to sit on juries ended. Many colonies required their citizens to swear an oath of allegiance to the new United States; those who refused were relegated to a second-class legal status.

The Revolution did not end the rivalries among the 13 British colonies. Fears of a new monarchy and mistrust of strongly centralized government had great influence on the writers of the U.S. Constitution. The states were allowed to pass and enforce their own laws, but the Constitution also required the states to maintain republican (nonmonarchal) forms of local government, and to grant newcomers from other states the same legal rights as longtime residents. The Constitution also prevented religious tests for public officeholders. By the Bill of Rights—the first 10 amendments to the Constitution—the citizens of the United States were guaranteed freedom of speech, freedom of religious worship, the right to petition, and other rights seen as essential to prevent the return of tyranny and arbitrary rule. The First Amendment was written in part as a check on the government's power to interfere in organized religion.

But many state constitutions read quite differently. Only Protestants were granted full citizenship in some states, and in most places Catholics and Jews were prevented from holding public offices. Public officeholders in New Jersey had to be Protestant, while Massachusetts simply required all officeholders to repudiate the authority of the pope. In addition, the rights and privileges of the federal Constitution did not extend to slaves of African origin or to Native Americans. With no legal or constitutional right to their land, Indian tribes were forced from their homes and driven west, beyond the Appalachian Mountains. Black slaves were kept in bondage, while a provision in the Constitution allowed a period of 20 years (until 1808) before the importation of slaves would be legally ended.

Most Americans considered slavery to be the natural condition for Africans, whom they saw as inferior, half-human beings who were not, and never would be, worthy of constitutional rights and full citizenship. Article IV of the Constitution allowed for the extradition of runaway slaves, who were to be returned to their legal owners. In addition, as the vast majority of slaves lived in the South, the framers of the Constitution took care not to see the southern states gain greater power through congressional representation, which was based on population. For the purpose of representation in the Congress, a slave was counted as only three-fifths of a white inhabitant.

Political rivalries between Federalists and Republicans led to the writing of new laws such as the Alien and Sedition Acts of 1798. By these statutes, all those found to be speaking or writing scandal or treason against the government were subject to fines and imprisonment. Those considered dangerous to the government could be deported from the country. Written and passed by a Federalist-dominated Congress, the Alien and Sedition Acts originated in suspicion toward the new Republican faction, which was seen by Federalists as an atheistic mob that took inspiration from the violent, disastrous revolution that had just taken place in France. In the opinion of many, the acts represented a direct infringement of the Bill of Rights; the laws were repealed during the administration of Republican president Thomas Jefferson.

IMMIGRANTS AND KNOW-NOTHINGS

In his book *Legacy of Hate*, author Philip Perlmutter describes the development of racial, religious, and ethnic bigotry in 19th-century America:

> *When economic depression, labor strife, war or the threat of war developed . . . Americans struck out against the supposed enemy within—alien or radical. Generally, the worse the conditions, the more the vituperation against religious, racial, and ethnic groups, each of whom was charged with inability to assimilate, lowering wage standards, strikebreaking, and taking jobs away from the native-born. . . . The result was an ever-repeating pattern of majority-group members disliking minority ones and the latter disliking each other.*[1]

In the first half of the 19th century, the settlement of the frontier and the expansion of mining and industry called for a permissive immigration policy. Most newcomers arrived from northern Europe, particularly the British Isles, Germany, Holland, and Scandinavia. Later, new groups arrived from Italy, Greece, Austria-Hungary, Russia, Spain, and Poland. Two major immigrant groups developed: northern and southern European. The Old World hatred worsened as these newcomers began competing for jobs and living space. More recent arrivals were targeted by those who had enjoyed a generation or two of citizenship. The cities and settled regions of the country were the scene of violence against immigrants and Catholics from Ireland and southern Europe. New immigrants were feared for their willingness to work for low wages and despised for their unfamiliar social and religious customs, for their strange accents and foreign languages. They often suffered what would today be described as "hate crimes," such as mob assaults, burning of property, random acts of violence, and murder. These attacks took place most often in times of economic distress, when jobs and money were scarce and the public sought out scapegoats for punishment. The response on the part of the authorities was to establish city police departments, which were charged with investigating crime, arresting criminals, and keeping public order.

The formation of the Know-Nothing Party in 1845 resulted from the widespread fear and mistrust of new immigrants, many of whom were escaping a famine then sweeping through the largely Catholic nation of Ireland. The Know-Nothings, whose official name was the American Party, formed lodges, invented secret rituals and handshakes, wrote inflammatory books and pamphlets, and ran for (and in many northeastern states, won) public office. The goal of the Know-Nothings—who considered Protestantism as the true faith of genuine American citizens—was to rid the government and business institutions of all Catholic and foreign influence. The

Know-Nothings suspected Catholics of voting at the direction of their priests and pope, and of plotting to overthrow the American government and replace it with a religious dictatorship, a government controlled from the papal headquarters in Rome.

The Know-Nothings were heartily supported in this program by workers who feared the loss of their jobs and lowering of wages through the influx of cheap laborers. Samuel Eliot Morison, in his *Oxford History of the American People*, describes this period as follows:

> *This wave of immigration enhanced the wealth and progress of the country, yet encountered bitter opposition, as did Asiatics half a century later. Sudden influxes of foreigners with strange ways and attitudes always do that, everywhere. In part, the antagonism was religious, since most of the Irish and many of the Germans were Roman Catholics. . . . The greater number of immigrants, however, only wanted an opportunity to work; but their need for work was so desperate that they cut wages at a time when native-born mechanics were trying to raise their standard of living through the labor unions.[2]*

The result was a series of violent riots and crimes committed against Catholic immigrants in the eastern cities where they congregated. The Irish were attacked in the streets; their homes and churches were vandalized and burned; they were prevented from obtaining work by bigoted employers; they were suspected of carrying disease and bringing crime and the general degradation of public morals. (The bigotry worked two ways, however, as the Democrats enlisted Irish Catholics to intimidate voters inclined to vote the wrong way in presidential and municipal elections.)

The rising resentments and a long-burning conflict over the use of the (Protestant) King James Bible in the public schools brought about an explosion in Philadelphia, Pennsylvania, in May 1844, in which several dozen Catholic homes as well as two Catholic churches were burned to the ground. State militia were called out to restore order, but the Protestant/Catholic riots, the worst religious outbreak in American history, brought the deaths of 30 people.

The Know-Nothings were a largely northern phenomenon, as the southern tier of states had largely been sheltered from new European immigrants. But in the middle of the 19th century, as conflict over slavery intensified between the North and South, African Americans were singled out for violence. The activities of abolitionists in the northern states brought a reaction from those in the South who saw abolitionism as an attack on a valued, traditional way of life, in which each segment of society knew and remained in its proper place.

In an attempt to resolve the thorny issue of slavery in new states and territories, Congress passed a series of compromises. In 1820, Missouri was admitted as a slave state and Maine as a free state; in addition, all territory north of latitude 36 degrees, 30 minutes was closed to slavery. In 1850, another compromise admitted California as a free state, while in New Mexico and Utah the residents were allowed to decide for themselves whether or not to permit slavery. By the 1854 Kansas-Nebraska Act, the residents of these new territories decided on slavery; while Nebraska peaceably banned it, Kansas became the scene of violence, as abolitionists combatted proslavery factions.

Many Southerners, even those who did not own slaves, heartily supported the institution as the best possible for those of African origin, who otherwise would find themselves at the mercy of ordinary employers who would hold them in perpetual bondage through low wages and poor working conditions. Prejudice against blacks persisted in northern states where slavery had been banned since the late 18th century. Black residents were kept strictly apart from whites in public places such as theaters and inns. Black workers could not ordinarily join labor unions. They could not vote and they could not worship in white churches. In the cities, they were restricted to black neighborhoods, which were sometimes attacked by white mobs. By the 1857 Supreme Court decision in *Dred Scott v. Sanford*, black slaves were held to be an inferior class without the normal rights of U.S. citizens. By the Emancipation Proclamation of 1863, President Lincoln freed African Americans from slavery—but only in those states that had seceded from the Union. In July of the same year, the drafting of unemployed laborers for service in the Union army in New York City sparked a riot among workers who opposed the Union cause and feared the loss of their jobs to free blacks. Hundreds of black residents of the city were attacked, beaten, lynched, or burned alive.

After the Civil War ended in 1865, a veteran Southern officer, Nathan Bedford Forrest, met with a group of tradition-minded brothers in Pulaski, Tennessee, to form a secret society that would return the defeated South to the virtues of the past and fight, with any means available, against Reconstruction, northern interference, and the pretensions of newly freed slaves. Members of the group, who rode at night under cover of terrifying masks and robes to commit their mayhem, gave themselves the appropriately obscure name of Ku Klux Klan. Their darkest deed, carried out only after appropriate warning was given, was the kidnapping and hanging of their victims—a lynching in the name of the Old South.

THE ANTI-KLAN LAWS

The Congress that began its session in December 1865 took a hand in the drive to establish universal suffrage. By the Fourteenth and Fifteenth

Introduction to Hate Crimes

Amendments to the Constitution, passed in 1868 and 1870, respectively, all those born or naturalized in the United States were given the right to equal protection and due process of the law. As citizens, blacks were given the right to vote, although they were unable to exercise this right wherever election officials raised barriers such as a literacy requirement. By the Civil Rights Act of 1870, it was made a federal crime for two or more persons to conspire against the right of any citizen to vote.

Southern representatives were forbidden to hold seats in Congress until their states ratified the Fourteenth Amendment. Throughout the South, the reaction to these new laws and to the constitutional enfranchisement of blacks was intensified bigotry and racial violence. A race riot erupted in Memphis, Tennessee, in May 1866, with white citizens rampaging through the city, attacking blacks and those whites seen as sympathetic to the freed slaves. The riot resulted in at least 46 deaths. Another such riot erupted in New Orleans, Louisiana, in July, while the state governor, James Wells, attempted to ensure black suffrage in the state by reconvening the constitutional convention and rewriting the state constitution.

The increasing racial violence in the South was a reaction to the new constitutional amendments, the doctrine of equal protection, the drive for black suffrage, and the imposition of state governments by what was seen as a hostile Republican administration. Fearing racial equality as a threat to their livelihoods, white southerners banded together and singled out their black neighbors for vandalism, floggings, and lynchings.

In response to Klan violence, or white-on-black violence that was not prosecuted in many regions of the South, the federal government passed new laws. The first of these laws, passed in 1870 as 18 U.S. 241, criminalized conspiracies of two or more people to "injure, oppress, threaten, or intimidate any person. . . . In the free exercise of any right or privilege secured to him by the Constitution. . ." The statute did not mention race or prejudice and did not address the issue of bias violence per se. It was instead formulated as a guarantee of the free exercise of constitutional rights, no matter the race, color, religion, or ethnic origin of the criminal or the victim.

A second federal statute, 18 U.S. 242, was more explicit in its language: "Whoever, under color of any law . . . subjects any person . . . to the deprivation of any rights . . . secured or protected by the Constitution or laws of the United States, or to different punishments, pains, or penalties, on account of such person being an alien, or by reason of his color, or race . . . shall be fined . . . or imprisoned." This statute was intended to protect the people from abuses of constitutional rights by public officials, and in particular by police officers, under the guise of enforcing the law.

The next and final piece of postwar civil rights legislation was the Civil Rights Act of 1875, a bill that was debated and amended for several years after its introduction by Senator Charles Sumner in March 1871. By the time the bill was passed, support for sweeping equal rights protection was fading; the Republican administration of President U.S. Grant, which supported the bill, was immersed in a series of scandals and the problems of the 1873 economic financial panic. The Senate finally passed the bill on May 22, 1874, and the Civil Rights Act became law in February 1875. The final language of the bill simply prohibited discrimination in public places, but also provided for federal prosecution in matters that had traditionally been handled by the states. The debate over states' rights and federalism would continue to be a central issue in future civil rights laws and hate-crime statutes.

JIM CROW LAWS

The last federal troops were withdrawn from the South on the order of President Rutherford B. Hayes in 1877, when the era of Reconstruction came to an end. In an attempt to restore some semblance of the old order, the southern state governments passed new "Jim Crow" laws that effectively separated the white and black populations. In his book *The Strange Career of Jim Crow*, historian C. Vann Woodward explains the impetus behind the new segregation laws:

> *The public symbols and constant reminders of [the Negro's] inferior positions were the segregation statutes, or "Jim Crow" laws. They constituted the most elaborate and formal expression of sovereign white opinion upon the subject. In bulk and detail as well as in effectiveness of enforcement the segregation codes were comparable with the black codes of the old regime, though the laxity that mitigated the harshness of the black codes was replaced by a rigidity that was more typical of the segregation code. That code lent the sanction of law to a racial ostracism that extended to churches and schools, to housing and jobs, to eating and drinking. Whether by law or by custom, that ostracism extended to virtually all forms of public transportation, to sports and recreations, to hospitals, orphanages, prisons, and asylums, and ultimately to funeral homes, morgues, and cemeteries.[3]*

The Jim Crow laws adopted in the South were supported by a series of Supreme Court decisions that gradually shifted lawmaking power from the federal government back to the states. Segregation was given the highest legal sanction in 1896 by the Supreme Court's decision in *Plessy v. Ferguson*, which held that segregated public facilities did not violate the equal protection clause of the Fourteenth Amendment, provided that the separate facilities were "equal." The doctrine of "separate but equal" reigned in the South until the civil rights era of the 1960s.

Introduction to Hate Crimes

While Jim Crow laws began the segregation era, the Klan's campaign to restore the pride and customs of the white South was carried out first against freed slaves and their families, and then against African Americans in general. Beginning in the 1890s, the practice of lynching blacks for suspected crimes or insults against white citizens began in earnest. But the Klan had many other ways of enforcing its views. Targets were kidnapped and horsewhipped; their homes were vandalized; they were branded and beaten; and their property was destroyed. Cross burning, the Klan's ceremonious way of threatening its enemies, occurred in front of homes, businesses, and churches, extending the Klan message to an entire neighborhood or community.

The Klan specialty of lynching took place most commonly in the South. Blacks were often targeted for lynching when economic times were hard; they were chosen whenever progress was threatened in the area of civil rights and equality before the law; they were lynched for "unacceptable" behavior, such as defying an employer or whistling at white women. Lynching was carried out by small groups in the middle of the night; it was also attended by large mobs in full daylight.

In the meantime, the late 19th century saw another wave of anti-immigrant bias, directed against Italian Catholics, eastern Europeans (particularly Jews) and, on the West Coast, Asians (Chinese, Japanese, Koreans, and Filipinos) who had been recruited to work in the mines and on the railroads of the western United States. The old prejudices were reinforced by economic rivalry and political turmoil. Eastern Europeans were suspected of fomenting revolution and socialism; Finns were accused of drunkenness; Jews were viewed as greedy and dishonest, although intelligent; Italians were believed to be naturally violent. In 1881, 11 Italian residents of New Orleans were arrested at random and accused of the assassination of a police official, found not guilty, then promptly lynched, after which several hundred Italian residents fled the city.

Asians suffered on the basis of their foreign customs, language, appearance, and religions. Throughout the country, the prevailing view was that Asians could never assimilate in American society and that they would always remain an insular and dangerous foreign element, one that would pose a dire threat to public morals, to established Christian religions, and to the jobs of ordinary laborers. Chinese immigrants were subjected to discrimination, violence, and murder. A mob lynched 22 Chinese residents of Los Angeles in 1871. After the western railroad network was completed, the fear of widespread unemployment and cheap Asian labor was so strong that the Chinese Exclusion Act was adopted in 1882, banning all immigration from China for 10 years. By the Scott Act of 1888, more than 20,000 Chinese workers who had left the country temporarily were forbidden to return, even though they held proper reentry documents. In 1902, the Chinese Exclusion Act was made permanent.

At this time, white Protestant Americans formed the dominant social and political group, particularly in the eastern United States. Feeling what they considered to be "their" country threatened by immigrants, some authors advanced new theories holding Anglo-Saxons and northern Europeans to be the most advanced "races" on Earth, intellectually and morally superior to lesser breeds such as Asians, Africans, Native Americans, and southern Europeans.

One book advertisement of the 1920s sounded the familiar alarm:

Instead of our making Americans of the foreigners among us, in many cases they have imposed their customs and semi-foreign ways on the native Americans. Most thoughtful readers will be astounded, as well as alarmed, to learn what the oldest foreign elements and some of the new immigration groups have done to American institutions and customs in their communities. . . . Upon the solution of the problem depends the future racial, mental, and moral make-up of our people.[4]

Many authors grew alarmed at the fact that these lesser races seemed to be reproducing at a faster rate, and predicted the day would come when the traditional white and Protestant caste that had dominated the United States since the American Revolution would have to submit to new customs, laws, and religions upheld by the new majority—thus threatening personal liberties and the country's constitutional basis.

THE NEW KLAN

World War I, which the United States entered in the spring of 1917, had been seen throughout the United States as an exclusively European affair. The country entered the war on the side of Allies and against Germany only after much debate among federal lawmakers and within the executive branch. Violence and discrimination against Germans took place, while the fear of German espionage prompted the passage of new federal laws in direct conflict with the provisions of the First Amendment. The Espionage Act of 1917 banned all speech tending to obstruct the war effort or give aid and comfort to the enemy. In 1918, the Sedition Act made speech considered disloyal or critical of the government punishable by a long prison term. Certain magazines or newspapers held to be critical or unsupportive of the war effort were banned from the mails by the postmaster, while hundreds of suspected spies (nearly all of them immigrants) were arrested, convicted under the new laws, and imprisoned on New York's Ellis Island, an important entry point for European immigrants. The general fear and disdain of African Americans manifested itself in stricter segregation laws, which spread by a policy of President Wilson into the federal government, in which black employees were restricted to separate facilities.

Meanwhile, a revived Ku Klux Klan spread beyond the South while taking on a broader philosophy. The organization was marketed to the general public by professional publicity agents, who built the Klan into a popular national secret society. The strange costumes, the mysterious rituals, the special vocabulary and titles, and above all the message of "100 percent Americanism" appealed to many people who feared the disruptions of a modernizing world. The Klan stood opposed to what its members saw as the mongrelization of American society by Catholics, Jews, and foreigners generally. In New England, the Klan targeted French Canadian immigrants for random attack. In the Southwest, Klan members harassed Mexicans and Asians.

As new waves of immigrants arrived after World War I, the general fear of immigrants increased along with America's political isolationism. Conflict between whites and blacks continued, and race riots erupted throughout the Midwest. In 1919, when a young black swimmer entered a whites-only area along the shores of Lake Michigan in Chicago, a riot broke out, ending only after two weeks, the deaths of several dozen black and white Chicagoans, and the razing of entire black neighborhoods. Lynching carried out or inspired by the Klan spread from the South to the Midwest.

The rivalry among social and ethnic groups that had long simmered within the United States was given free rein during the Great Depression of the early 1930s and during World War II. Immigrants were again blamed for the economic malaise, and in communities where different ethnic groups came in contact there were frequent scenes of violence. In Los Angeles, Mexicans were randomly attacked on the streets; thousands of Mexican laborers were forcibly repatriated to Mexico.

The declaration of war by the United States after the Japanese attack on Pearl Harbor in December 1941 inspired patriotic fervor across the country. Japanese-Americans were confronted and attacked, particularly on the West Coast, where after Pearl Harbor many people feared an invasion. An entire community of U.S. citizens of Japanese descent was rounded up and interned in California during the war.

Wartime prejudices were not limited to the Japanese. On the East Coast, German Americans were seen as a third column of Nazi sympathizers. Jews, now the target of Germany's murderous Nazi government, heard very strong echoes of the anti-Semitism that was sweeping across Germany and the rest of Europe. Jews were accused of starting the war as an insidious internationalist plot against the United States and its ancestral nations in Europe. Jews serving in the military experienced these prejudices outright. Leonard Dinnerstein, in *Anti-Semitism in America*, reports that:

Jewish chaplains in the services found that a number of their Christian peers also harbored strong prejudices. Some of the ministers denounced Jews as "Godless Communists," believed that there were too many of them in government in Washington, and thought that "all of you Jews are good business executives."[5]

These sentiments did not end with the successful conclusion of the war against Germany and Japan. The campaign against Communist influence in the federal government, which reached a high tide during the 1950s, brought a strong wave of anti-Semitism among a general public fearing an international conspiracy to bring down the United States and its democratic institutions. The fear found its darkest expression in incidents of violence and vandalism directed against Jews and their homes and families.

THE CIVIL RIGHTS ERA

The postwar period also saw the issue of discrimination come to the forefront. In 1948, President Harry S. Truman signed an executive order banishing segregation in the armed forces and in all three branches of the federal government. (Jim Crow laws remained in force in the South long after World War II.) During the Eisenhower administration, the country's political leaders were focused on the outside Communist menace rather than the domestic undercurrent of troubled race relations. Yet segregation of the races did meet with challenges, starting with the decision of the U.S. Supreme Court on May 17, 1954, in the case of *Brown v. Board of Education*, in which the justices unanimously declared that "separate but equal" public education violated the equal protection clause of the Fourteenth Amendment. On May 31, 1955, the Court handed down a decree ordering the implementation of its decision in a "reasonable" time under the authority of federal district courts, which would hear and resolve cases brought on the issue of school desegregation.

This decision sounded the knell for years of protest and violence against the doctrine of racial segregation, as well as intensifying reaction. In Mississippi, "citizens' councils" were formed to defend segregated public facilities. While the federal courts handed down decisions in favor of school desegregation, the citizens' councils spread outside of Mississippi. On the other side, black Americans were organizing with a new sense of urgency and militancy, as described by author Philip Perlmutter:

Civil rights organizations began changing their tactics and goals, with calls made for stressing group rights rather than individual rights; self-interest politics rather than coalitional politics; color-conscious justice rather than blindfolded justice; and preferential treatment rather than equal opportunity.[6]

Introduction to Hate Crimes

A violent reaction began in May 1961, when a group of Freedom Riders, protesting the segregation of interstate buses, were attacked by white mobs in Anniston and Birmingham, Alabama. The state of Mississippi, however, took first place in its determined opposition to desegregation. Historian C. Vann Woodward observed:

> *Mississippi, however, easily maintained its historic priority in racism. . . . Its Negroes lived in constant fear and its whites under rigid conformity to dogmas of white supremacy as interpreted by a state-subsidized Citizens Council. In 1955 three Negroes were lynched, the first in the country since 1951, and one was a fourteen-year-old boy, Emmett Till. No one was punished, nor were any of the lynchers who took another victim in 1959. Less than 2 per cent of the Negroes over twenty were registered voters. Law enforcement was in the hands of bigots, and bigotry was respectable.* [7]

The battle over civil rights in Mississippi reached its climax on the campus of the University of Mississippi at Oxford, where in September 1962 a federal court order paved the way for the enrollment of James Meredith. Governor Ross Barnett defied the order by instructing state police to arrest any federal officials interfering on Meredith's behalf. On October 1, federal marshals who accompanied Meredith into a university dormitory came under attack by mobs of students, with Mississippi state troopers standing by. The general campus riot that followed left two dead and hundreds injured.

Racial violence continued throughout the Deep South. In the spring of 1963, Birmingham, Alabama, police chief Theophilus Eugene "Bull" Connor closed parks, swimming pools, and other public facilities in defiance of court-ordered desegregation. The Southern Christian Leadership Conference (SCLC), under the leadership of the Reverend Dr. Martin Luther King, Jr., convened a series of sit-ins and demonstrations, opposed by the police and furious mobs of white citizens, as well as by Governor George Wallace, a determined opponent of desegregation. On May 11, after a bomb planted by the Ku Klux Klan exploded at the home of King's brother, rioting raged out of control for several days. That fall, Governor Wallace followed the example of Governor Barnett by stationing himself in front of the University of Alabama to block the enrollment of black students. Tension continued as public high schools prepared for their first year of court-ordered desegregation. Although the first week passed in relative calm, the uneasy truce was shattered on September 15, when a bomb exploded at the Sixteenth Street Baptist Church, killing four young black girls.

Such incidents, broadcast nationwide, caused a sense of frustration and outrage among the public at large, and spurred a commonly held view that only action at the federal level would solve the problems of discrimination and racial violence. At the same time, the domination of the country's elite institutions by white Protestants began to end. Edward Brooke became the first black senator since the Reconstruction era; John F. Kennedy, a Catholic, was elected president; Thurgood Marshall became the first African American appointed to the U.S. Supreme Court. Discrimination in legislative representation was effectively ended by the Court in the 1962 decision of *Baker v. Carr*, which held that such representation must be determined without reference to race, sex, economic status, or place of residence within a state. The Twenty-fourth Amendment to the U.S. Constitution banned poll taxes in federal elections.

President Kennedy threw his determined support to passage of a new federal civil rights bill. In June 1963, the White House proposed a sweeping new law, and President Kennedy signed Executive Order 10925, which established "affirmative action" as a principle in which all applicants for government jobs be treated without regard to race, creed, or color. The debate over civil rights law continued until November 22, 1963, the day of Kennedy's death, an event that gave new impetus to the legislation as it was taken up by Kennedy's successor in office, Lyndon Baines Johnson of Texas. In his speeches on civil rights, Johnson would insist on "equality as a result," not just "equality as a right." The next summer, during a presidential election year, the voter registration drive resumed with the arrival of white volunteers from the North. On June 21, three of these northern volunteers—Michael Schwerner, Andrew Goodman, and James Chaney—were arrested, thrown in jail, released, then abducted and murdered. Their bodies were discovered on August 4. The murders gained nationwide press attention; the killing of northerners in Mississippi sounded a faint echo of the terrible war between the states fought a century earlier. The deaths spurred passage of the Civil Rights Act of 1964; in the meantime an extensive investigation was ordered by J. Edgar Hoover, the director of the Federal Bureau of Investigation (FBI), who until that time had been most reluctant to get his agency involved in civil rights cases. The arrest of white suspects in the case marked a change from past practice in the South, where white police and juries had been slow to investigate and prosecute whites for crimes of violence against blacks. (The murder trial that followed this crime ended on October 20, 1967, with the convictions of seven members of the Ku Klux Klan. This was one of the first trials in the nation's history to result in convictions for a violation of civil rights.)

While the 1964 Civil Rights Act banned preferential treatment for minorities, in 1965 affirmative action and other antidiscrimination measures were given a new emphasis. Federal regulations not only banned discrimination by those doing government business but also encouraged affirmative action programs among employers, educational facilities, government agencies, and other institutions. These organizations were urged to actively recruit and prefer members of racial minorities in order to show a proportional number of minorities hired or trained—objective proof of an end to the often-subjective phenomenon of discrimination.

The ongoing battles and the eventual victories of the civil rights movement spawned a new era in American social history. This era was described by authors Valerie Jenness and Kendal Broad in their book *Hate Crimes: New Social Movements and the Politics of Violence:*

> *Early advances by the modern civil rights movement spurred more than awareness, however. They also defined for other constituencies the potential of mobilization. As a model and ground-breaker, the Black struggle . . . facilitated the mobilization of future movements in the United States . . . by sensitizing opinion makers, polity members, authorities, and the wider public to the challenges, promises, and consequences of protest.[8]*

The direct result of this awareness was the founding of new organizations that fought for civil rights for other ethnic and national minority groups, for homosexuals, for women, and for religious faiths. These organizations include the Anti-Defamation League of B'nai B'rith (ADL); the Southern Poverty Law Center (SPLC); and the National Organization for Women (NOW). In addition, the founding of the National Organization of Victim Assistance (NOVA) in 1975 and the National Victim Center (NVC) in 1985 marked the rise of an entirely new criminal justice field, that of victims' rights. NOVA and NVC arranged for the national coordination of local and state victim assistance programs, lobbied for new legislation expanding the rights of crime victims in the justice system, and sponsored a wide range of educational programs designed to make crime victims aware of these rights.

Many of these groups took on the battle against bias violence as one of their most important functions. They used the civil rights movement as a model, and applied their protests, their mobilization of public opinion, and their lobbying efforts to the newly perceived, but in fact ancient, social problem of hate crimes.

HATE CRIME LEGISLATION

The U.S. Congress opened the modern era of hate-crime legislation with a federal statute, 18 U.S. 245, a law passed in 1968 as part of the landmark Civil Rights Act. The law made it illegal to, by force or by threat of force, injure, intimidate, or interfere with anyone who is engaged in six specified protected activities, by reason of their race, color, religion, or national origin. The prosecution of such crimes must be certified by the U.S. attorney general.

This law was an attempt to address the wave of violence that was occurring in response to the civil rights movement. The murders of civil rights workers by their opponents in the South had brought a call for action from legislators determined to see the Civil Rights Act put into full effect. Like the earlier statutes, the law enumerates "protected" activities. These include "enrolling in or attending a public school or university; participating in any benefit, program, service or facility provided by a state or local government; applying or working for any state or local government or private employer; serving as a juror; traveling in or using any facility of interstate commerce, or using any vehicle, terminal, or facility of any common carrier; or using any public facility, such as a bar, restaurant, store, hotel, movie theater, or stadium. . ."

While attention focused on the struggle of African Americans for their civil rights, discrimination was not limited to blacks. Philip Perlmutter outlines the varied ethnic and nationalistic prejudices that have often manifested themselves in recent decades by assaults and killings:

> *Immigrants, particularly illegal ones, were viewed as economic threats. More Blacks than Whites in 1979 believed illegal immigrants deprived them of jobs. . . . Tensions also erupted in Florida between Cubans and Haitians, who believed that "the government gives the Cubans financial assistance to get started, while we get deported." In Hawaii, Filipinos, Puerto Ricans, Koreans, Samoans, and native Hawaiians complained about Japanese being overly represented in government and education. . . . In West Philadelphia, in the early 1980s, Black students assaulted Asian ones for allegedly receiving preferential treatment in schools. In Denver, Mexican-Americans reacted violently to Vietnamese obtaining apartments in a housing project for which they were on the waiting list. In Long Beach, California, resentments and gang wars took place between Mexicans and Cambodians.*[9]

The year 1978 brought the passage of the first state hate-crimes statute, California's Section 190.2, providing for penalty enhancement in cases of murder motivated by prejudice. This law defined four varieties of "protected status": race, religion, color, and national origin. The range of protected statuses increased with the passage of new hate-crimes laws in Washington State in 1981 (ancestry); in Alaska in 1982 (creed and gender); and then in other states for disability, sexual orientation, and ethnicity. By the 1990s, states were extending protected status to age, marital status, membership in the armed forces, and membership in civil rights organizations. Three states and the District of Columbia now have hate crimes based on political affiliation.

In addition, with the passage of time new state laws expanded the range of criminal acts that could be considered as hate crimes, depending on circumstances and evidence: aggravated assault, assault and battery, vandalism, rape, threats and intimidation, arson, trespassing, stalking, and many other acts. Finally, in 1987, new California hate-crimes legislation included "all crimes" as possible hate crimes.

The states have adopted a wide variety of hate-crimes statutes, including penalty enhancement laws for crimes motivated by prejudice; ethnic intimidation, institutional vandalism, cross-burning, and hood-wearing statutes; reporting statutes that require statewide data collection on hate crimes; compensation statutes that provide money awards to victims of bias crimes; statutes providing for civil lawsuits against those convicted of hate crimes; and statutes that provide for parental responsibility when the offender is a juvenile. Each state also must decide on what constitutes a hate crime, which protected attributes (such as race, religion, sexual orientation) a hate crime may be directed against, the range of sentence enhancements, and whether or not prosecutors may ask for hate-crime penalty enhancements when charging defendants under ordinary criminal statutes (such as laws against assault or vandalism). When a conviction is won under such statutes, penalty enhancement may be achieved either by lengthening the sentence or upgrading the "offense category," a method commonly used to determine fines and prison time.

Concurrent with the writing of new hate-crimes laws came the founding of grassroots and nongovernmental organizations (NGOs) seeking to deal with hate crimes on a local level through education, mobilization, and lobbying. This activism was frequently modeled on the civil rights groups that had successfully pushed for equal rights for African Americans in the 1950s and 1960s. The new groups organized crisis intervention, victim assistance, legal services, watch services, street patrols, counseling, and hot lines for those in fear of or experiencing hate crimes.

Among the largest of such organizations were the Anti-Defamation League of B'nai B'rith, the National Gay and Lesbian Task Force, the National Institute Against Prejudice and Violence, and the Southern Poverty Law Center. These groups released statistics, collected with a wide variety of methods, that purported to show hate crimes on the rise. Yet rather than support a consensus for new laws, the statistics often gave rise to further debate over whether the country was actually experiencing a hate-crime epidemic, or whether these and other advocacy groups were merely spinning an issue out of inflated numbers in order to strengthen their presence in the media and among the public.

TROUBLE IN NEW YORK

The multiethnic "melting pot" city of New York paved the way in the handling of hate crimes. In 1980, the New York City Police Department

(NYPD), under its commissioner Robert McGuire, established the Bias Investigation Unit, later renamed the Bias Incident Investigation Unit, or (BIIU). The unit's task was to investigate criminal acts motivated by prejudice against race, religion, or ethnicity (in 1985, this list was expanded to include sexual orientation, and in 1993 to disability). The BIIU also collects and disseminates statistics on hate crimes, provides victim assistance programs, provides a liaison agency between the NYPD and community and interest groups, and conducts training programs for police officers in handling suspected bias crimes. The BIIU became a model for many other big-city police departments over the ensuing 20 years.

While New York's police department developed this response to hate crimes, a troubling death that gave strong impetus to the hate-crimes debate took place in the Howard Beach neighborhood of Queens on December 19, 1986. A white, largely Italian working-class enclave, Howard Beach was typical of many areas of New York City, a place where neighborhood ties were close and those of different social or economic background were seen as unwanted, uninvited outsiders. On that December night, three black men had been driving along Cross Bay Boulevard, a main thoroughfare through Howard Beach, when their car broke down. While wandering through the neighborhood, they stopped at the New Park Pizzeria, where they exchanged taunts with a group of white men. Later, after midnight, the locals returned with weapons—baseball bats and a tire iron—and gave chase. One of the black men, 23-year-old Michael Griffith, ran onto the Belt Parkway and was struck and killed by a speeding car. A year later, assailants Jon Lester, Scott Kern, and Jason Ladone were found guilty of having "recklessly caused the death of another," and a fourth was charged and convicted of assault in a plea-bargain deal. As yet, New York had no statute punishing crimes motivated by racial bias.

While the Howard Beach incident simmered in New York, the debate over the true facts of the hate-crime debate, and the desire for a systematic method of recording hate crimes, brought about passage of the Hate Crimes Statistics Act (HCSA). In 1983, the U.S. Civil Rights Commission had recommended the establishment of a nationwide bias-crime reporting system. In 1985, the Anti-Defamation League and other organizations had asked Congress for a new statute to mandate hate-crime reporting. Vigorously lobbying for the bill were private and public civil rights groups, including the ADL, the American Civil Liberties Union, the Coalition on Hate Crimes Prevention, and the International Association of Chiefs of Police.

One issue arising during the debate over the HCSA was inclusion of gender as a protected status for the purpose of defining hate crime. Few states included gender in their hate-crimes provisions; nor did the ADL include gender as a protected status within the model legislation it created in 1981. Women's groups argued that gender bias is often the basis for crimes of violence such as spousal battery and rape, and that female crime victims are most often victimized by men. They also argued that inclusion of gender bias in the bill would serve its most useful purpose in raising public awareness of the prevalence of gender-motivated crimes.

However, other organizations lobbying for passage of the bill opposed the inclusion of gender bias. Opponents maintained that because violence against women was often motivated within a personal relationship between two individuals, the victim of such violence could not be considered as being selected because of her membership in a group. Also, the broader definition of hate crime to include gender bias would turn the spotlight away from hate crimes motivated by racial or religious prejudice, the concern of organizations such as the ADL and the NAACP.

In their book *Hate Crimes: New Social Movements and the Politics of Violence*, Valerie Jenness and Kendal Broad describe the problems that arose with gender and the HCSA:

> *Prior to the passage of the HCSA, the Coalition on Hate Crimes Prevention contemplated promoting the inclusion of gender as a protected status in the HCSA, but eventually decided against it for a variety of reasons. First, some members of the coalition believed that the inclusion of gender would delay, if not completely impede, the (timely) passage of the HCSA. Second, some members of the coalition argued that the inclusion of gender in the HCSA would open the door for [the protected status of] age, disability, position in a labor dispute, party affiliation, and/or membership in the armed forces provisions. Third, some believed that including gender would make the enactment of the HCSA too cumbersome—if not entirely impossible—since violent crimes against women are so pervasive . . . opponents feared that adding gender as a victim category would simply overwhelm the data collection efforts of law enforcement agencies and human rights organizations that track hate crimes . . . [and that] the large number of crimes against women would overshadow statistics on hate crimes against members of other groups.[10]*

Although the House of Representatives had first passed the bill in 1985, Congress had adjourned before a Senate vote, and debate continued for five more years before the bill's final passage in 1990. An important point of debate was the inclusion of antihomosexual violence in the bill—the HCSA was the first federal civil rights law to mention sexual orientation. Led by Senator Jesse Helms of North Carolina, a group of lawmakers opposed the inclusion of antigay violence in the HCSA and the designation of homosexuals as a "protected group."

A compromise was reached with a passage in the bill that expressed the finding of Congress that "1. American family life is the foundation of

American society. 2. Federal policy should encourage the well-being, financial security, and health of the American family. 3. Schools should not de-emphasize the critical value of American family life." The addition of this language paved the way for passage of the HCSA in 1990 and its final signing by President George H. W. Bush in April 1990.

This seemingly innocuous "reporting statute," which carried no criminal penalties or sanctions for bias-motivated violence, turned out to be a watershed in the field of hate-crimes law. The law gave responsibility to the attorney general for establishing guidelines and collecting data on certain crimes from state and local law enforcement officials—crimes that manifested "evidence of prejudice based upon race, religion, sexual orientation, or ethnicity." The crimes included murder, manslaughter, rape, aggravated assault, simple assault, intimidation, arson, and vandalism. The statistics, which at first were given voluntarily, would be published as part of the Uniform Crime Report (UCR) program of the FBI. In 1991, the FBI issued its *Training Guide for Hate Crime Data Collection* to aid public officials in the collection and reporting of hate-crimes statistics.

For legislators, policy makers, and journalists, the annual UCR represents the nation's crime score—the statistical guidebook to trends in the occurrence and type of crime and, since hate crimes appeared as a new category in the UCR in January 1991, to the issue of hate-crimes legislation. The 1991 report consisted of a single page of statistics on hate crime as recorded in 1991. Data from 32 states and 2,771 law enforcement agencies was presented; a grand total of 4,558 hate crimes were recorded, out of a total of 14 million crimes reported (by 12,805 agencies) in the comprehensive UCR.

At that time, the number of law enforcement agencies actually reporting hate crimes was low—about one in five, and those from mostly urban departments where bias crimes had already been acknowledged as a problem. Gradually, the reporting improved. In 1992, the number of reporting agencies jumped to 6,865, representing 42 states; in that year the number of reported hate crimes increased to 7,466. By the late 1990s, nearly every jurisdiction in the country was involved. In 1999, 12,122 agencies from 49 states reported 7,876 hate crimes. Most of the states had passed laws mandating such reporting, and as the recording of hate crimes became more common, the statistical picture came to be seen as more accurate. The effect of reporting was to make police officers aware of hate crime, and the effect of publishing statistics on hate crime was to provide reinforcement to those demanding action on the issue.

For many, however, the issue of hate crimes was not so cut-and-dried as simply checking a box on a police incident report. Many police departments did not have the time, personnel, or inclination to investigate hate crimes. Some saw the reporting of hate crime as a blemish on their community, and thus underreported it. On the other hand, a high (and inaccurate) reporting of hate crimes sometimes backed up a demand for the hiring of more police officers, or the granting of additional public funds for equipment and salaries. Above it all lay the possibility that the raw numbers could be manipulated—hate crimes could be shown to be "increasing" or "insignificant"—to support or denigrate a certain point of view. The raw statistics of hate crime gradually turned into a debating point for both sides on the overriding issue: whether hate-crimes laws are necessary, effective, or constitutional.

THE CROWN HEIGHTS RIOT

In the meantime, racial tensions continued to simmer in New York. To the north of Howard Beach, in the Brooklyn neighborhood of Crown Heights, there had been longstanding tension between a newer community of conservative Hasidic Jews and a long-established group of African Americans. The two groups separated themselves as much as possible and carried out their disputes in relative peace, most often over the issues of housing and schools. But the rising tension needed only a spark to bring open violence, and that spark was struck on August 19, 1991, when a seven-year-old African-American boy, Gavin Cato, was killed by a car that was part of a Hasidic Jewish motorcade. In the riots that subsequently broke out, a Jewish student, Yankel Rosenbaum, was chased down by a mob and stabbed to death. Rosenbaum identified his killer before dying in a hospital a few hours later.

The Crown Heights riots enveloped the administration of Mayor David Dinkins in controversy. The mayor, an African American, was accused of not doing enough to calm the situation and with instituting a "no arrest" policy that brought about a state of near anarchy. Norman Rosenbaum, the brother of Yankel Rosenbaum, and members of the Crown Heights Jewish community brought suit against the city. The suit was settled under the subsequent administration of Mayor Rudolph Giuliani, who made a public apology and extended a financial settlement to the family.

In the meantime, the criminal trials proceeded. Lemrick Nelson and Charles Price were brought up on criminal charges by the state of New York. Lemrick Nelson, who was 16 years old at the time, was charged in Rosenbaum's murder, while Price was charged with incitement to riot, after being videotaped calling on a crowd to "kill the Jews." Lemrick's attorney argued that he committed the killing in the heat of the moment and without premeditation. The prosecution dismissed this defense, pointing out that others in the mob had not been inspired to murder. But on October 29, 1992, Lemrick Nelson was found not guilty of the murder of Yankel Rosenbaum.

Nelson and Price were then charged in federal court with violating Rosenbaum's civil rights. In 1997, these charges brought convictions; Nelson was sentenced to the maximum 19 years, six months; Price was sentenced to 21 years, 10 months. But the Crown Heights verdict was overturned in January 2002 by the U.S. Second Circuit Court of Appeals. The decision was based on the attempts by District Court judge David G. Trager to select a jury representative of the community—from both a racial and religious standpoint. The appeals court found that such race-based selection of jurors was impermissible. A new trial was ordered, and in April 2003, a trial of Nelson began in Brooklyn's federal court. This time Nelson admitted to the killing but claimed he committed the murder while drunk and not because of anti-Semitic views.

Through the 1990s, the hate-crime debate continued in New York City, a kaleidoscopic, often balkanized metropolis that has centuries of experience with violence between rival nationalities, religions, and interest groups. Many murders, assaults, arsons, and other crimes were quickly transformed into political debates, in which politicians seeking support from one group or the other either characterized or dismissed the act in question as a hate crime. These debates involved high civic officials: city and borough council members, the mayor, the commissioner of police, and public and private organizations. In turn, the hate-crimes debates in New York, the nation's media capital and a place where local events can be magnified to national proportions, rippled across the United States, bringing the subject of hate-crimes laws sharply into focus for the public and for legislators.

THE SUPREME COURT AND HATE CRIMES LAW

A series of decisions made by the U.S. Supreme Court supported the expansion of criminal and civil penalties for discrimination and bias-motivated violence. In the 1987 decision of *Shaare Tifila Congregation v. Cobb*, the Court allowed the members of any ethnic group to sue for compensation and punitive damages under the provisions of the 1866 Civil Rights Act.

In the same year as the passage of the HCSA, an incident occurred that resulted in one of the Supreme Court's most far-reaching judicial decisions over hate crimes. It was an act of petty vandalism that happened in the evening of June 21, 1990, in the front yard of Mr. Russ Jones, a new black resident of a mostly white East Side neighborhood of St. Paul, Minnesota. Hearing a noise from his front yard, Jones looked out to see a small cross, made from two broken sticks of furniture, burning in front of his house.

Seventeen-year-old Robert Viktora was arrested and charged with violating St. Paul's Bias-Motivated Crime Ordinance. The ordinance banned the display of any "symbol, object, appellation, characterization, or graffiti" that "arouses anger, alarm, or resentment in others on the basis of race, color, creed, religion, or gender." Adopted in 1982, the ordinance went beyond the ADL model statute, which punished bias-motivated crimes against persons or property, to punish bias-motivated *expression*, which would be treated as a misdemeanor synonymous with "disorderly conduct." The law was amended in 1989 to include burning crosses, a traditional emblem of the Ku Klux Klan, and Nazi symbols such as the swastika. The charge against Viktora was the first prosecution brought by the city under the ordinance.

Arguing that the law violated the First Amendment, Viktora's attorney, Edward J. Cleary, appealed the conviction in Ramsey County Juvenile Court, where Viktora was originally convicted. The judge agreed with Cleary and the conviction was overturned. The court cited an opinion rendered in a 1989 U.S. Supreme Court case, *Texas v. Johnson*, in which the Court ruled that Dallas could not outlaw flag burning solely for the unpalatable sentiments it expressed. In the same way, St. Paul could not outlaw cross burning on the grounds that the expression was racist, unpleasant, or socially unacceptable.

St. Paul then appealed to the Minnesota Supreme Court, which upheld the conviction and stated that cross burning was not an expression that deserved free-speech protections. This decision was based on the "fighting words" verdict reached by the U.S. Supreme Court in 1942 in the landmark case of *Chaplinsky v. New Hampshire*, which held that expression that tends to incite disorder is not protected by the First Amendment. Finding that cross burning was a comparable act, the Minnesota Supreme Court decided it was also not protected by the Constitution, and upheld the conviction of Robert Viktora.

The U.S. Supreme Court reversed this decision on June 22, 1992, in a unanimous decision. The Supreme Court found the law too broad, but the justices split on whether cross burning was a form of speech that should be protected by the First Amendment. Four justices (White, Blackmun, Stevens, and O'Connor) took the position that the law could be struck down as it was overbroad; five (Scalia, Thomas, Souter, Kennedy, and Rehnquist) took the position that the law unconstitutionally singled out specific expressions on the basis of their content. This majority argued that laws passed against expression cannot select certain viewpoints and not others for prohibition. The five-to-four vote was split along "conservative" and "liberal" lines in the Court.

Writing about *R.A.V. v. City of St. Paul*, columnist Nat Hentoff, a frequent commentator on First Amendment issues, described the case as follows:

> It was the First Amendment, not cross-burning, that powered this case. At issue was a municipal ordinance so overbroad that its effect, if adopted by other cities and states, would have chilled the speech, both verbal and symbolic, of large numbers of protesting citizens.[11]

WISCONSIN V. MITCHELL

A second landmark Supreme Court decision was reached in 1993 with *Wisconsin v. Mitchell*. The case arose out of an assault that took place in Kenosha, Wisconsin, on October 7, 1989, when a group of African-American youths, enraged by a scene in the movie *Mississippi Burning*, attacked and beat a white youth, nearly killing him. One of the defendants, Todd Mitchell, had been convicted of aggravated battery and charged under Wisconsin's statute 939.645, which provides for "penalty enhancement" when the accused selects a victim for a crime based on the victim's "race, religion, color, disability, sexual orientation, national origin or ancestry of that person." The evidence for conviction under the statute was not a criminal action, but instead Mitchell's choice of words just before the attack took place: "Do you all feel hyped up to move on some white people? . . . You all want to f—k somebody up? There goes a white boy; go get him."

The enhanced sentence was challenged all the way to the U.S. Supreme Court on the grounds that it represented a constitutional ban on free speech. The defendants, and the many briefs that were filed in this case on their behalf, claimed that the Wisconsin statute was broadly unconstitutional in the same manner as the St. Paul city ordinance that was struck down in *R.A.V. v. St. Paul*. But on June 11, 1993, the nine justices unanimously upheld the sentence and therefore passed a favorable verdict on all similar penalty-enhancement statutes in the United States. In the Court's opinion, ". . .Whereas the ordinance struck down in *R.A.V.* was explicitly directed at expression, the statute in this case is aimed at conduct unprotected by the First Amendment." Since the decision of *Wisconsin v. Mitchell*, the Supreme Court has not found it necessary to certify any further cases for argument on the subject of penalty-enhancement statutes.

STATE HATE-CRIMES STATUTES

Through the early 1990s, as state legislatures wrote new hate-crime statutes, and as law enforcement began recording, investigating, and prosecuting hate crimes, criminal and appeals courts throughout the country faced the task of interpreting the new statutes. There were a wide variety of legal challenges to hate-crimes law: vagueness and arbitrary arrest and prosecution in violation of the Fourteenth Amendment; unconstitutional restriction of free speech and opinion in violation of the First Amendment; and denial of equal protection before the law, also in violation of the Fourteenth Amendment, as the statutes singled out certain ethnic, religious, and other groups for preferential protection as victims of crime.

In 1992, a series of decisions—including the U.S. Supreme Court opinion in *R.A.V. v. St. Paul*, the Ohio Supreme Court decision on that state's ethnic intimidation law in *Ohio v. Wyant*, and the Wisconsin Supreme Court's overturning of the earlier appeals court decision in *Wisconsin v. Mitchell*—found hate-crimes laws to be overbroad and an unconstitutional restriction of speech. These decisions, most of which cited *R.A.V. v. St. Paul* in their support, found that those accused of hate crimes were being punished not for conduct, but for opinion and motive. These decisions cast the future of hate-crimes legislation into serious doubt on constitutional grounds.

Over the next few years, however, statutes similar to Wisconsin's penalty-enhancement law withstood nearly all the legal challenges presented to them in state courts. By the late 1990s, hate-crimes legislation grew increasingly standardized across the country, as the courts moved away from the basic constitutional issues and delivered more focused instruction on what constituted punishable behavior on the part of hate-crime offenders. Nevertheless, hate-crimes law still had its vociferous critics, who maintained that such statutes remained vague, redundant, and unconstitutional. The debate continued as new federal legislation was proposed increasing the range of offenses punishable as hate crimes.

THE VIOLENCE AGAINST WOMEN ACT

After the passage of the HCSA, women's groups frustrated in their efforts to include gender bias in the definition of hate crime began lobbying Congress for a new bill specifically targeting such crimes. The lobbying effort won a sympathetic hearing on Capitol Hill, and the effort to draft a new bill specifically targeting gender-based hate crimes emerged in 1990, the year of the HCSA's final passage. Senator Joseph Biden, who introduced the Violence Against Women Act (VAWA), stated in Judiciary Committee hearings in 1992 that:

> *Title III [of the VAWA] seeks to put gender-motivated bias crimes against women on the same footing as other bias crimes. Whether the attack is motivated by racial bias or ethnic bias or gender bias, the results are often the same. The violence not only wounds physically, it degrades and terrorizes, instilling fear and inhibiting the lives of those similarly situated.[12]*

The new law was included in an omnibus bill known as the Violent Crime Control and Law Enforcement Act, which passed the House and Senate in 1993 and then was signed by President Bill Clinton. Title I of the

VAWA provided for a budget of $300 million for special units of police and prosecutors and public-safety measures, such as lights and security cameras. Title III of the act allowed plaintiffs to bring civil suit against defendants for violence motivated by gender, even if no prior criminal complaint or conviction existed. Title IV dealt with campus security measures for women; Title V provided for training programs on the issues of gender-motivated violence for state and federal judges.

HATE CRIMES GAIN NATIONAL PROMINENCE

Hate crimes took an ever-increasing share of news headlines through the mid-1990s. In Fayetteville, North Carolina, three Fort Bragg soldiers were charged with the bias-motivated slaying of an African-American couple in December 1995. At the same time, newspapers were reporting a rash of church arsons, as well as vandalism of synagogues, across the South. Congress responded to these acts with the Church Arson Prevention Act of 1996, which prohibited " . . . intentional defacement, damage, or destruction of any religious real [tangible] property because of religious, racial, or ethnic characteristics of that property, as well as intentional obstruction by force or threat of force or attempts to obstruct any person in the enjoyment of their free exercise of religious beliefs."

The rising prominence of the issue inspired widespread discussion and analysis of hate crimes and the psychology of hate-crimes perpetrators among academics. Surveys showed that the incidence of hate crimes tends to rise with difficult economic conditions or with dramatic changes of the socioeconomic makeup of affected neighborhoods. In addition, racist speech and discourse on the Internet, talk radio, and in the media can prompt what the academics called a "climate of hate," in which racial tensions are rising and a single confrontation or incident between members of different racial or religious groups can spark a wave of bias-motivated violence. The sharp rise of hate crimes in the early 1990s was put down to an economic recession and competition from foreign producers; the issue of immigration, especially immigration from Latin America and the Caribbean; and certain nationally prominent incidents such as the beating of black motorist Rodney King by several Los Angeles police officers in March 1991. The riots that followed the acquittal of the L.A. officers in April 1992 provided further evidence that bias-motivated violence endangered entire communities, not just individual victims.

In 2008, the continuing weakness in the economy may have spurred increasing activity among long-dormant hate groups, including the National Socialist Movement, the National Alliance, the Posse Comitatus, and the Ku Klux Klan. These groups are particularly strong in industrial states of the Midwest, where the weakening economy has had the harshest effect. As unemployment rises, competition for scarce jobs breeds resentment of those seen as unfairly competing. The unemployed provide a fruitful pool of recruits for the Klan and other groups that were virtually inactive and losing members in more prosperous times. The Southern Poverty Law Center noted also that the number of hate groups rose in 2007, to 888 from 844 in 2006.[13] Some of the groups cited, however, are vigorously protesting this characterization. The Federation for American Immigration Reform (FAIR) claimed that its appearance on the SPLC's list of hate groups was nothing more than a fund-raising tactic by the SPLC as the group suffered a drop in donations, also due to the weakening economy. Rather than a "hate group," FAIR sees itself as a forum for debating ideas on immigration reform and an advocate for an end to illegal immigration.

JAMES BYRD AND HATE-CRIMES LAW IN TEXAS

On June 7, 1998, while driving their pickup truck along a dirt road in Jasper, Texas, three white men—Shawn Allen Berry, Lawrence Brewer, and John King—picked up a black hitchhiker, James Byrd, Jr. The three men beat Byrd, chained him by the ankles to the back of the pickup truck, and dragged him along two miles of the road, killing him and dismembering the body. On July 7, the three men were indicted on a charge of first-degree murder. John King was convicted of murder and kidnapping on February 23, 1999, and sentenced to death. Lawrence Brewer was found guilty of murder, although on the witness stand he had claimed to be only a bystander to the crime. He was also sentenced to death. Shawn Berry was found guilty as well but was spared the death penalty.

The death of James Byrd touched off a long dispute over hate-crimes legislation in Texas. The debate revolved around a proposed law known as the James Byrd, Jr., Hate Crimes Act, a penalty-enhancement law that would have affected anyone convicted of a crime against race, religion, or sexual preference. The statute would have enhanced certain categories of crimes, although not first-degree felonies or capital murder. For vandalism, the law would have enhanced a Class C misdemeanor, which in Texas carries a maximum fine of $500 and no prison sentence, to a Class B misdemeanor punishable by a maximum fine of $2,000 and up to six months in prison.

The bill had vehement supporters and opponents. Opponents argued that the proposed bill would violate the legal principle of equal protection and confer special rights on certain classes of citizens. They also argued that

Texas already had a hate-crimes statute. This law, passed in 1993 in response to vandalism against Texas synagogues, set down enhanced penalties for those convicted of crimes against members of "a group."

Supporters of the new bill believed this statute was too vague and largely ineffective in fighting bias crimes. In their opinion, the new law improved on the old one by specifying broad categories such as race, religion, and sexual orientation, giving prosecutors a better focal point for investigation and prosecution of bias crimes. They also pointed out that by avoiding the naming of any group such as Jews, African Americans, or homosexuals, the James Byrd, Jr., Hate Crimes Act avoided the constitutional bans against unequal protection of the laws. In 1999, the bill passed the Texas House but was killed in a Senate committee. In early 2000, the bill again came up for a hearing before the Texas House Judicial Affairs Committee. During this hearing, Stella Byrd, the mother of James Byrd, testified about the crime and pleaded with lawmakers to pass the bill as a testament to her son. Opponents brought their witnesses forward as well. A retired air force major challenged the bill and demanded that hate crimes against members of the military be included.

A change in membership on the Senate committee, giving Democratic members a four-to-three majority, helped its chances in 2001. The Senate committee, chaired by Senfronia Thompson, a Democrat and a sponsor of the bill, finally approved the bill.

In "The Hate Debate," an article in *Texas Monthly* discussing the Texas hate-crimes bill, author John Spong succinctly described the hate-crimes debate as follows:

> *Most lawmaking involves familiar questions of politics and policy, matters that are worth fighting over but are nevertheless well removed from basic ideas of what kind of society we want and what role our laws should play in shaping it. There is a certain amount of government intrusion when the state sets a speed limit or requires cars to be inspected, but it does not have the same impact as a law that says society disapproves of a certain thought or belief, or one that says that some victims need more protection than others from similar crimes. Hate crimes laws seem to draw just these sorts of lines, which is one reason they stir up so much emotion. At issue are two of the most elemental principles of American law, free speech and equal protection of the laws—the kind of things that first-year law students argue about among themselves in the first week of law school.*[14]

MATTHEW SHEPARD

A second high-profile hate-crime case began on October 6, 1998, when Matthew Shepard, a gay University of Wyoming student, was beaten, tied to a fence post, and left for dead outside Laramie, Wyoming. Following the assault, the state of Wyoming indicted Russell Henderson and Aaron McKinney for aggravated robbery, kidnapping, and attempted murder. When Shepard died five days after the incident, Henderson and McKinney were both charged with first-degree murder, a charge that can bring the death penalty in Wyoming. At the time of the indictments, Wyoming did not have a hate-crimes statute.

In the months between Shepard's murder and the trial of Henderson and McKinney, the crime sparked a nationwide debate on the issue of hate crimes. Competing demonstrations were held in state capitals and in Washington D.C., with one side calling for tougher and more comprehensive hate-crimes legislation and the other protesting the same.

The trial of Russell Henderson began on March 24, 1999. The defendant pled guilty to the charges of kidnapping and murder and was given a sentence of two consecutive terms of life in prison. McKinney, whose trial began on October 11, 1999, attempted to defend his actions by reason of panic induced by Shepard's homosexual advances. The judge barred this defense, however, and McKinney was found guilty of felony murder (and acquitted of premeditated murder). Through the intercession of the parents of Matthew Shepard, McKinney was spared the death penalty and sentenced to life in prison without parole.

The Matthew Shepard murder brought the spotlight onto another aspect of hate crimes: violence directed against individuals on the basis of their sexual orientation. Although the inclusion of such acts in the legal definition of "hate crime" was contested through the 1990s, many state and federal statutes have been adopted or expanded to include them. In the same way, crimes that involve prejudice against the disabled have been added, state by state, to the legal definition.

In the late 1990s, the introduction of new hate-crimes legislation became an annual event in the U.S. Congress. The Hate Crimes Prevention Act of 1998 would have expanded federal jurisdiction over hate crimes by allowing federal authorities to investigate all hate crimes, and not just those in which the victim was exercising a federally protected right such as the right to vote, attend a public school, and so on. The legislation also expanded the definition of hate crimes to include those committed over gender, sexual orientation, and disability. The new law died in committee, however, while the debate over the necessity for new hate-crimes legislation continued.

In March 1999, Representative John Conyers of Michigan introduced the Hate Crimes Prevention Act of 1999. The new law would have expanded the definition of hate crimes to include those committed against homosexuals. With more than 200 cosponsors and support from both political parties, the bill passed the Senate in July 1999, but failed in the House of Representatives.

THE YEAR 1999

Hate crimes again took the national spotlight in 1999. On February 19, 1999, a gay man named Billy Jack Gaither was murdered by Charles Monroe Butler and Steven Mullins in Sylacauga, Alabama. Both of the killers were given life sentences.

Over the Fourth of July weekend of 1999, white supremacist Benjamin Smith went on a shooting rampage in Illinois and Indiana. The spree began in West Rogers Park, a mostly Jewish Chicago neighborhood, on the evening of Friday, July 2, 1999, when Smith opened fire on Dr. Michael Messing and his 16-year-old son Ephraim. Both men escaped unhurt. But Smith was not finished. Later he drove to Skokie, a Chicago suburb, where he opened fire on Ricky Byrdsong, an African-American and former Northwestern University basketball coach, killing Byrdsong immediately. He then drove to the suburb of Northbrook, where he shot an Asian-American couple he found in a car.

The rampage continued on the next day, Saturday, July 3. Smith shot and wounded an African-American man in the state capital, Springfield, then shot a black minister in Decatur. He then drove to the campus of the University of Illinois in Urbana, where he fired on a group of Asian-American students, injuring one of them. On Sunday, July 4, Smith arrived in Bloomington, Indiana, where he opened fire on a group of Korean Americans while they were leaving Sunday church services. One of the targets, an Indiana University student, was killed. Smith fled the scene in a stolen car as the local police gave chase. When finally stopped and cornered, Smith killed himself.

Another rampage occurred a month later in Los Angeles. On August 10, 1999, Buford Furrow began shooting at a Jewish community center, then killed Joseph Ileto, a Filipino postal worker. Furrow surrendered the following day and was charged by a federal grand jury with five separate hate crimes.

On March 1, 2000, Ronald Taylor, an African American, killed three white men and wounded two others in Wilkinsburg, Pennsylvania. Taylor was arrested and charged with murder, arson, aggravated assault, and "ethnic intimidation."

HATE CRIMES AND THE ELECTION OF 2000

The spree of bias crimes in 1999 brought hate crimes to the fore during the 2000 presidential election. The hate-crimes issue followed Texas governor George W. Bush as he entered the race. The NAACP called on its members to work against Bush for his opposition to the hate-crimes statute in Texas, opposition that the NAACP largely blamed for the defeat of the bill. A television commercial, showing a chain being dragged behind a pickup truck, alluded to the Byrd crime and suggested that Bush was insensitive to black voters and to the issue of bias violence against African Americans.

Governor Bush was finally declared president by the U.S. Supreme Court after a bitterly contested vote recount in the state of Florida. Early the next year, the momentum within the Texas legislature began to swing back in favor of the James Byrd, Jr., Hate Crimes Act. With the unanimous support of Democratic representatives in the Texas House of Representatives, the bill passed the House on April 24, 2001, by a margin of 87 to 60. An editorial in the *Dallas Morning News* on May 2 urged the Texas senators to pass the bill:

> *Opponents mischaracterize the issue when they claim that hate crimes legislation distinguishes one victim from another. It is more truthful to say that what is being differentiated are not the victims but rather the crimes. Not all crimes are equal. What separates them are not just the varying degrees of damage and human suffering they cause but also whether those damaged or made to suffer are individuals or a whole group of people.*
>
> *When a person is attacked because of the essence of who he is, the attacker intends to do harm that goes beyond the individual victim. The perpetrator intends to send a message—a violent one—to others who share the same characteristic: You could be next.*
>
> *Now, the Texas Senate has a chance to send a message of its own—that this sort of intimidation will not be tolerated.*[15]

On the next day, the Senate committee passed the bill 5 to 1, and on May 7, the bill passed the Senate by a vote of 20 to 10, despite the addition of amendments by Senator Florence Shapiro intended to derail the legislation. When the bill was returned to the House, it was passed by a vote of 90 to 55, and on May 11, Governor Rick Perry signed the bill.

THE HATE-CRIMES DEBATE

Sociologists, criminologists, psychologists, and journalists have all added their considered opinions to the discussion on hate crimes. All acknowledge the existence of such acts, and many have suggested what inspires such crimes. A few generally agreed-upon points have emerged.

First, hate crimes by and large are committed by individuals, not groups. The existence of "hate groups" may play an important role in the thought and motivation of hate-crime perpetrators, but if the leaders of such groups direct a conspiracy to commit a hate crime they risk a civil lawsuit and very heavy financial punishment. (The most prominent example is the White Aryan Resistance, a neo-Nazi organization headed by Tom Metzger, which was subject to a multimillion-dollar judgment in the wake of a race-motivated murder in Portland, Oregon.) Second, hate crimes are the acts of the young, and more particularly the young male. Such perpetrators often act out of boredom, peer group pressure, and a desire to prove themselves through an act of violence committed against a despised group.

What are the motivations? One is resentment over the perceived threat of a different class of people to another group's success and standing in the community. Such resentment arrives when blacks move into a white neighborhood, when immigrants appear in the workplace, or when women or homosexuals march or protest against discrimination. Prejudice is sometimes given a legal stamp of approval, such as when the U.S. Congress passed the Chinese Exclusion Act of 1882. At this time, Chinese laborers made up a majority of foreigners brought into the United States for work on the western railroads; when railroad construction began to slow, American-born citizens saw a threat to their jobs and clamored for the government to close the immigration gates.

The success of immigrants can be deeply resented by those who have long-established roots in the community, and whose prejudice and antagonisms are aroused when an economic threat is perceived. Such was the case for Hispanic victims of hate crimes, who in the late 1990s made up the largest single ethnic group victimized when an ethnic prejudice was involved. Violence against Hispanic immigrants in the southern tier of the United States, and particularly in California, Florida, and Texas, has given rise to what many local law enforcement officials are reporting to the FBI as hate crimes. The legal status of the victim—as a resident alien, naturalized citizen, or undocumented alien—often makes no difference to the perpetrator.

Another spark for the commission of a hate crime may be a perceived slight or injury by a member of the targeted group. A tense or violent encounter between two individuals may lead to a thirst for retribution or revenge on some randomly selected stranger, who represents the enemy only through his or her appearance. The same may occur when a national or international event, and in particular a war, commences and a certain ethnic group becomes identified with a national enemy. During the two Gulf wars between Iraq and U.S.-led coalitions of European and Arab allies, Arab Americans have been subject to increased violence and harassment throughout the United States.

The perpetrator of hate crimes is most often not a habitual offender or career criminal. In the American Psychological Association report entitled *Hate Crimes Today: An Age-Old Foe in Modern Dress*, the authors found that: "Most hate crimes are carried out by otherwise law-abiding young people who see little wrong with their actions. Alcohol and drugs sometimes help fuel these crimes, but the main determinant appears to be personal prejudice, a situation that colors people's judgment, blinding the aggressors to the immorality of what they are doing."[16]

Alcohol or drugs may influence an individual or group to simply leave aside the normal social inhibitions and allow fears and anger to come to the surface, inspiring an act of violence. Hate crimes range from such random acts, to premeditated injury inflicted on a chosen individual, to those perpetrated by what criminologists term the "mission offender," an individual who carries out a crusade, sometimes carefully planned, against the hated group.

THE ROLE OF LAW

The essential debate over hate crimes revolves around the necessity, effectiveness, and constitutionality of hate-crimes statutes. Those supporting hate-crimes laws explain that such laws are a necessary defense of public order, which is threatened more seriously when prejudice is involved. According to the Anti-Defamation League, an organization that saw its model legislation widely adopted by the states: "Hate crimes demand a priority response because of their special emotional and psychological impact on the victim and the victim's community. . . . By making members of minority communities fearful, angry, and suspicious of other groups—and of the power structure that is supposed to protect them—these incidents can damage the fabric of our society and fragment communities."[17]

Another argument for hate-crimes laws claims it as a logical extension of widely accepted laws that prohibit discrimination based on race, gender, religions, nationality, and so on. Nadine Strossen, in "Yes: Discriminatory Crimes," a 1993 article published in the *American Bar Association Journal*, explains this viewpoint as follows:

> *[The] fundamental distinction between protected thought and punishable conduct is central to both free speech jurisprudence and anti-discrimination laws. . . . Anti-discrimination laws long have prohibited discriminatory acts that would not otherwise be illegal—for example, refusing to hire someone—because of society's consensus that such discriminatory acts cause special harms, not only to the immediate victim but also to the racial or other societal group to which the victim belongs, and to our heterogenous society more generally. Why, then, shouldn't the law treat discriminatory criminal acts more severely than other criminal acts?*[18]

Opponents see the demands of certain groups for legal protections and civil rights as inspiring a backlash among those who oppose such protections. They also view hate-crimes laws as a cynical tool of politicians seeking to curry favor with the voters. James Jacobs, a prominent opponent of hate-crimes laws, states in *Hate Crimes: Criminal Law and Identity Politics:*

> *Politicians have fully endorsed the existence of a hate crime epidemic. Passing laws denouncing hate crime provides politicians with an opportunity to decry bigotry. They can propose hate crime legislation as a quick-fix solution that's cheap and satisfying to important groups of constituents.*[19]

As for legal principles, opponents believe that punishing prejudicial beliefs, no matter how obnoxious they may be, violates a fundamental constitutional right to freedom of expression and belief. In his article "Should Hate Be a Crime?" Jacobs responded as follows:

> *To fragment criminal law into specialized laws recognizing a moral hierarchy of motives and offender/victim configurations will have little, if any, crime-control benefit, while carrying serious risks for race relations and social harmony. . . . The new hate crime laws both reflect and contribute to the politicization of the crime problem and the criminal justice process, especially around issues of race, and thereby exacerbate social divisions and social conflict.*[20]

CHALLENGES TO HATE-CRIMES LAWS AFTER SEPTEMBER 11, 2001

The long-term effects of the devastating terrorist attack of September 11, 2001, may well extend to the nation's laws and criminal justice system. On that morning, 19 hijackers, all of them Muslims, commandeered four passenger jetliners in the eastern United States, disabled the pilots and crew, and used the planes as guided missiles against targets that to them symbolized American power, imperialism, and arrogance. One plane crashed into the Pentagon in Washington, D.C., and two others hit and destroyed the twin towers of the World Trade Center in New York City. A fourth plane, in which the passengers apparently overcame the hijackers, crashed in rural Pennsylvania before reaching its target. Approximately 3,000 people were killed in the attacks.

Almost immediately after the attacks took place, they were attributed to the al-Qaeda terror network masterminded by Osama bin Laden, a Saudi exile who ran the organization from a headquarters in Afghanistan. In the wake of the attacks, Arab Americans became the target of violent assaults, and in some cases outright murder—crimes unquestionably motivated by the bias of the perpetrator against the nationality or appearance of the victim. Virulently anti-Arab statements and proclamations appeared on the Internet, while government officials, including President George W. Bush, called for calm and tolerance. While the panic and shock over the September 11 attacks slowly subsided, occasional violence continued. An assailant shot and killed an Indian gas station owner in Mesa, Arizona. A gunman in a ski mask fired more than 20 shots at Hassan Awdah, a Yemeni native and U.S. citizen, in Gary, Indiana. Awdah was saved by a thick screen of bulletproof glass. The Islamic Institute of New York received daily threats against its 450 students. The incidence of "profiling," or selective questioning or investigation of individuals according to their race or nationality, also became commonplace. In Providence, Rhode Island, while searching for terrorists on an Amtrak train, police removed and questioned a group of 10 people who appeared to be of Arab descent.

In its 2005 report "Unequal Protection: The Status of Muslim Civil Rights in America," the Council on American-Islamic Relations (CAIR) documented 141 "actual or potential" incidents of anti-Muslim violence, an increase of 52 percent from the 93 cases documented in 2003. The report also noted a decrease in incidents of workplace discrimination, Internet harassment, and complaints involving government agencies. California was the source of 20.17 percent of all complaints, followed by New York, Arizona, Virginia, Texas, Florida, Ohio, Maryland, New Jersey, and Illinois.[21]

The post-9/11 trouble was not limited to Muslims. In June 2003, just after the invasion of Iraq by the United States, a Boston-area pizza deliveryman named Saurabh Bhalerao was robbed, beaten, stabbed, stuffed into a trunk, and dumped along the side of a road. The attackers, mistaking the Hindu Bhalerao for a Muslim, shouted "Go back to Iraq!" On many occasions, Sikh men, who have South Asian ancestry and customarily wear turbans and beards, have been mistaken for Muslims and assaulted. There is a long history of acts of violence and taunting against Sikhs in New York City, where many Sikhs hold publicly visible jobs that make them an easy target. But the Sikhs also have a vigorous defender in the Sikh Coalition, which works actively with the New York City Police Department and its Hate Crimes Task Force in investigating these incidents.

IMMIGRATION AND HATE CRIMES

Although Arab Americans and Arab immigrants found themselves the target of assaults after September 11, 2001, anti-immigrant bias in general also targeted Latino residents of the United States, whether "documented" (with legal papers and valid visas) or "undocumented" (without visas and thus illegally present and often working). In its latest Uniform Crime Report, documenting the incidence of hate crimes in the year 2006, the FBI reported a 35 percent rise in anti-Latino violence, 816 incidents in 2006 compared with 595 in 2003. The 2006 hate crimes report cited 1,305 incidents motivated by national origins, with 62.8 percent of those with an anti-Hispanic bias and 37.2 percent "other."

A good deal of the violence was perpetrated by white-supremacist and neo-Nazi groups, who found a new issue to exploit. In the attempt to recruit new members and attract funds and publicity, these groups and several hundred others are focusing on the immigration debate, border security, a perceived threat from Mexico, and the jobs taken and public services used by Hispanic Americans. For example, in June 2004, Casey Nethercott was convicted for an attack on two Salvadoran immigrants in Hebbronville, Texas. Nethercott belonged to Ranch Rescue, one of many ad-hoc militias and volunteer groups that claim to protect farms and border areas of the United States from illegal immigrants.[22] The Southern Poverty Law Center, which tracks such groups, counted a total of 800 active racist groups operating in the United States, a 33 percent increase from 2000.[23]

The debate over immigration law and the presence of undocumented Hispanic immigrants has brought about a new flash point for bias crime violence. Such violence peaks when political debate sharpens around proposed new federal laws, such as the Comprehensive Immigration Reform Act of 2007 (which failed to pass in June of that year after a month of national controversy). The Anti-Defamation League documented several dozen anti-immigrant incidents in the first half of 2008. Among the groups it identified as sponsoring anti-immigrant activities were the Emigration Party of Nevada, the National Alliance, and the successor groups to the Ku Klux Klan.

THE JENA SIX

The most recent hate-crimes report, contained within the 2006 FBI Uniform Crime Reports, lists 7,722 hate crimes, a rise of 7.8 percent over the previous year. Of these, 51.8 percent were motivated by race bias, 18.9 percent by religion, 15.5 percent by sexual orientation, 12.7 percent by ethnicity/national origin, and 1.1 percent by disability. The most common crimes listed on the report were intimidation and vandalism, followed by simple and aggravated assault. By fall 2007, 45 states and the District of Columbia had hate-crime statutes, while 31 states and the District of Columbia had statutes establishing hate crime as a civil cause of action in addition to creating a criminal penalty for this offense. The District of Columbia and 27 states had reporting statutes requiring law enforcement to collect hate-crime statistics.

Despite the passage of new hate-crime statutes and active prosecution of these cases, the Jena Six case again raised the specter of discrimination and unequal justice. The story began in August 2006, when students at the Jena, Louisiana, high school hung nooses from a tree in a school courtyard. The nooses were promptly taken down by school authorities, who in their later investigation concluded that the students who carried out the act had done so as a prank, and not with the intent to intimidate or threaten anyone. The students responsible were given two-week suspensions.

Although a federal investigation ensued, as did a congressional hearing, the "prank" was not prosecuted as a hate crime, as the perpetrators were not adults. Nevertheless, rising racial tensions that fall erupted in confrontations and fights between white and African-American youths. On December 4, Justin Barker, a white teenager, was assaulted by six black teenagers and sent to a local hospital. The six perpetrators were arrested and charged with attempted murder in the second degree, with five of the six to be prosecuted as adults.

The Jena Six case was of local interest only until "alternative" magazines and then the BBC and the *Chicago Tribune* picked up the story in the spring of 2007. Soon the town of Jena was the focus of stories and opinion pieces in the national print and broadcast media, with many commentators noting, in their view, disproportionate charges against white and African-American students involved in the incidents. The controversy culminated in a march on September 20, 2007, in which several thousand demonstrators walked peacefully through Jena to protest what they viewed as another example of racial injustice in the Deep South. The Jena Six case resulted in various plea bargains, reduced charges, and appeals, several of which continued into summer 2008.

HATE-CRIMES LAW IN THE 21ST CENTURY

Many countries have enacted hate-crimes laws. A rising tide of immigration into Europe has brought about increasing tension between ethnic groups. In response France passed a hate-crimes law in 2003, writing penalty enhancement into the law for crimes against nationality, race, religion, or sexual orientation. Denmark enhances penalties for crimes based on a racist motive. The United Kingdom punishes threats and insults that the victim perceives as motivated either by racial or religious prejudice or by bias against nationality or sexual orientation. Canada punishes crimes motivated by bias against race, national origin, language, color, religion, sex, age, disability, sexual orientation, "or any other similar factor," and it also has a law against inciting hatred, or advocating or promoting genocide, against any "identifiable group." Opponents of hate-crimes laws in the United States often cite the Canadian example as evidence of how these laws endanger First Amendment protections of free speech, even (or in particular) speech that would be considered obnoxious or intolerant by a reasonable observer. Although a handful of U.S. states have prosecuted hate-crime cases on the basis of "intimidation"—presumably verbal intimidation—rather than physical violence, very few lawmakers in the United States propose an imitation of the Canadian example.

Kyrgyzstan takes the hate-crimes law a step further, making it the basis for a wide range of legal restrictions that in the United States would be struck down as unconstitutional. Kyrgyzstan has written an antidiscrimination clause into its constitution as well as its national law. The law bans incitement to discrimination or hatred against anyone based on nationality, race, or religion; membership in any group that advocates racial discrimination; the public expression of offensive ideas; and discrimination in a business transaction, such as selling a product or service. No complaint on the part of the victim is necessary for a public prosecutor to take action on these grounds.

In the United States, the issue of hate crimes continues to be debated in Congress, where some version of an expanded federal hate-crimes law is introduced every session. In May 2007, the House of Representatives passed the Local Law Enforcement Hate Crimes Prevention Act of 2007 (LLE-HCPA), H.R. 1592, also known as the Matthew Shepard Act. The bill, which has been reintroduced in every Congress since 1999, would expand the existing law to include crimes motivated by a victim's actual or perceived gender, sexual orientation, gender identity, or disability. It would also end the requirement that the victim must be taking part in a federally protected activity, such as attending school or voting. In its 2007 version, the bill called for federal authorities to prosecute a hate-crimes case even if state authorities have not moved forward with charges, or have refused to prosecute a crime as a hate crime. The 2007 bill earmarked an additional $10 million in federal funds to aid local prosecution of hate crimes. In answer to critics who claimed the revised hate crimes law would have a chilling effect on free speech, the bill also made specific the requirement that it cannot be interpreted to restrict First Amendment rights of free speech or free association: "Nothing in this Act, or the amendments made by this Act, shall be construed to prohibit any expressive conduct protected from legal prohibition by, or any activities protected by the free speech or free exercise clauses of, the First Amendment to the Constitution."[24]

At congressional hearings held in April 2007, opponents and supporters of the bill exchanged eloquent defenses of their positions. Those opposing the bill made their case by arguing that extending protection to selected groups was unconstitutional; those supporting claimed that a rise in antihomosexual violence demanded some kind of response and preventive action at the federal level. The legislators also heard the testimony of a 16-year-old Mexican American, David Ritcheson, the victim of a particularly brutal crime that took place on April 22, 2006, in Spring, Texas. Two high school students beat and tortured Ritcheson, who was stripped, burned with cigarettes, sodomized with a PVC pipe, burned with bleach, and left for dead overnight. Ritcheson survived but spent more than three months in the hospital and went through more than 30 reconstructive surgeries in the 15 months following the attack. Although witnesses testified that the attackers had used racial slurs during the beating, the crime was not prosecuted either by state or federal authorities as a hate crime. Instead, Ritcheson's attackers were convicted of aggravated sexual assault and both given life sentences.

Ritcheson spoke of the need for federal prosecution of hate crimes when state resources or laws fail to recognize such crimes as bias motivated acts. "I was fortunate to live in a town where police had the resources, the ability and the will to effectively investigate and prosecute the hate violence directed against me. But other bias crime victims may not live in such places. Local prosecutors should be able to look to the federal government for support when these types of crimes are committed. Most importantly, these crimes should be prosecuted for what they are: hate crimes."[25]

At the same hearings this position was answered by opponents of the bill, who pointed out the life sentences handed down to Ritcheson's attackers and noted the penalties would not have been any more severe under a hate-crimes statute. In declaring his opposition, Representative Louie Gohmert of Texas invoked the very recent mass shooting at Virginia Tech: "The new hate crime bill creates a vague, ambiguous Federal offense that sends a message that random, senseless acts of violence, possibly like yesterday at Virginia Tech, are far more preferable in society than the same violent actions with a motive."[26]

Despite Gohmert's opposition, the House of Representatives passed the bill in May, while another version passed the Senate in September 2007. The two bills have not been reconciled. Meanwhile the White House threatened a veto on the part of President George W. Bush, maintaining there was no need for expanded federal enforcement: "State and local criminal laws already provide criminal penalties for the violence addressed by the new Federal crime defined in section 7 of H.R. 1592, and many of these laws carry stricter penalties. . . . There has been no persuasive demonstration of any need to federalize such a potentially large range of violent crime enforcement, and doing so is inconsistent with the proper allocation of criminal enforcement responsibilities between the different levels of government."[27]

Nonetheless, on August 14, 2008, President Bush signed into law the Higher Education Opportunity Act, which mandates improved hate-crime data collection on college campuses. The new law came 10 years after Congress amended the Higher Education Act to require colleges and universities to report hate-crime statistics to the federal Department of Education. According to some observers, campus hate crimes were underreported, as several categories of crimes were not included in the reports. The 2008 law makes the data provided to the Department of Education consistent with the categories and reporting methods of the FBI's Uniform Crime Report.

CHALLENGES TO THE LAW

As of April, 2009, 31 U.S. states had pressed ahead with an expansion of their hate-crimes laws to include sexual orientation, and the Michigan legislature was debating a similar bill that would also designate intimidation of the disabled, cross-burning, or the hanging of a noose as a hate crime. The judicial fate of such hate-crime laws at the state level is uncertain, however, as demonstrated by a Pennsylvania case decided in 2008.

The case arose from an incident in 2004 during Outfest, an annual gay pride rally in Philadelphia. Demonstrators from Repent America staged a protest during the event, and a potentially violent confrontation broke out between protesters and Outfest marchers. When they refused to obey a police order to disperse, 11 members of Repent America were arrested. The charges against them included criminal conspiracy, obstructing a highway, disorderly conduct, and a violation of the state hate-crime statute banning ethnic intimidation. A recent state law had added sexual orientation and gender identity to the state's "ethnic intimidation" law. As amended, state law defined ethnic intimidation as "malicious intent" toward, among other characteristics, sexual orientation.

Although the city eventually dropped the charges against the protesters, Repent America pursued a case against the city, alleging that the police had violated their civil rights and that the hate-crimes statute was unconstitutional. The Pennsylvania hate-crime bill had originated as a law against vandalism, and it was later altered into an expansion of the state's hate-crimes statute; the Repent America protesters argued that passage of the bill had violated the state constitution's provision against altering a bill and changing its original purpose during debate and passage through the legislature. The Commonwealth Court of Pennsylvania agreed with the Repent America protesters, holding that the amended legislation violated the state constitution. On July 25, 2008, the Supreme Court of Pennsylvania agreed with the Commonwealth Court, overturning the state hate-crimes law.

Even as the constitutionality of new hate-crimes laws came under scrutiny in several states, economic issues—including inflation, energy prices, unemployment, mortgage foreclosures, and credit-market turmoil—took precedence in the print and broadcast media. With the proposed federal law stalled in Congress, the hate-crimes issue faded from public view during the presidential election season of 2008. Democratic candidate Barack Obama came out in favor of new hate-crimes law but rarely touched on the issue, or on the more general topic of racial discrimination, in his speeches and position statements. Republican candidate John McCain, who has consistently voted against any new federal hate-crimes law, avoided the topic while attempting to distance himself from the identical position of President George W. Bush.

Though the hate-crimes debate has been largely overshadowed by other national concerns, legislators continue to debate proposed extensions and innovations in the law. Whether or not homosexuals should be covered by a comprehensive law that considers them as a protected group is an important point of contention. In addition, lawmakers are considering new laws that would extend hate-crimes protection on a federal level to the disabled. A ban on employment discrimination has already been written into federal law as the Americans with Disabilities Act (ADA), and a vigorous "disabilities rights" campaign has inspired a variety of new laws and ordinances at the local level. Should such protection be extended in the form of a new federal statute criminalizing bias-motivated assaults against the disabled? Such questions will certainly continue to be raised in the public forum and addressed in U.S. legislatures and courts in the coming decade.

In their article "Examining the Boundaries of Hate Crimes Law," authors Valerie Jenness and Ryken Grattet summarize the moral principles underlying such an extension of hate-crimes laws:

> . . . [criminals] often expect—with good reason—that the criminal justice system will share the view that such victims are unworthy of vigorous enforcement of the law. The stereotypes and biases upon which these views are based are, in turn, residues of historical relations of subordination, inequality, and discrimination, which criminals capitalize upon and reinforce. Moreover, like the school-yard bully who preys upon the small, the weak, and the outcast, crimes against the disadvantaged are increasingly understood to possess a distinct moral status and evoke particular policy implications.[28]

Those arguing against this extension of hate-crimes laws to the disabled maintain that protected status will set off disabled persons from the rest of society, further isolating them and reinforcing society's rejection and indifference. In turn, say opponents, such isolation will breed further bias crimes, committed by those who see the disabled as vulnerable prey, and bring about the opposite effect intended by any new law.

The creation of new protected-status groups lies at the heart of much current public policy debate over hate-crimes laws. On one side, supporters, citing the country's history of bigotry and racism, call for a redress of past grievances and discrimination. They call upon lawmakers to live up to the original promises of the Declaration of Independence and the Constitution, to allow citizens "life, liberty and the pursuit of happiness" and to bring about "equal justice for all." The creation of new laws is seen as one possible remedy for the problem of crimes motivated not by greed or malice, but by prejudice—a pernicious moral component that affects society as a whole, and thus should be more severely punished.

On the other side are those who protest at the fragmentation of society into distinct groups, each with its own claim to certain rights and legal redress. Opponents view this process as a threat to the historic ideals of the United States, in which people of all backgrounds should be considered American citizens first, and members of ethnic and socioeconomic groups second, with all living under a common law.

---

[1] Philip Perlmutter, *Legacy of Hate: A Short History of Ethnic, Religious, and Racial Prejudice in America*. Armonk, N.Y.: M. E. Sharpe, 1999, p. 58.

[2] Samuel Eliot Morison, *The Oxford History of the American People*. New York: Oxford University Press, p. 481.

[3] C. Vann Woodward, *The Strange Career of Jim Crow*. New York: Oxford University Press, 1955, p. 7.

[4] Advertisement for *World's Work* Magazine, in *Outlook*, November 7, 1923, p. 427.

[5] Leonard Dinnerstein, *Anti-Semitism in America*. New York: Oxford University Press, 1994. p. 138.

[6] Perlmutter, p. 192.

[7] Woodward, pp. 173–174.

[8] Valerie Jenness and Kendal Broad, *Hate Crimes: New Social Movements and the Politics of Violence*. New York: Aldine de Gruyter, 1997, p. 24.

[9] Perlmutter, pp. 203–204.

[10] Jenness and Broad, pp. 142–143.

[11] Quoted in Cleary, Edward J., *Beyond the Burning Cross: The First Amendment and the Landmark R.A.V. Case*. New York: Random House, 1994, p. xiv.

[12] Jenness and Broad, p. 147.

[13] David Crary, "Hate Crimes Linked to Immigration Debate," CommonDreams.org News Center. Available online. URL: http://www.commondreams.org/archive/2008/03/10/7587. Posted on March 10, 2008.

[14] John Spong, "The Hate Debate." *Texas Monthly*, April 2001, p. 64.

[15] Editorial, *Dallas Morning News*. May 2, 2001, p. 14A.

[16] American Psychological Association, *Hate Crimes Today: An Age-Old Foe in Modern Dress*, p. 2.

[17] Anti-Defamation League, "Hate Crimes Laws: Introduction." Available online. URL: http://www.adl.org/99hatecrime/intro.html. Downloaded on May 30, 2001.

[18] Nadine Strossen, "Yes: Discriminatory Crimes." *American Bar Association Journal,* May 1993, p. 44.

[19] James Jacobs and Kimberly Potter, *Hate Crimes: Criminal Law and Identity Politics.* New York: Oxford University Press, 1998, p. 52

[20] Jacobs, James, "Should Hate Be a Crime?" *The Public Interest,* vol. 113, Fall 1993, p. 14.

[21] "The Status of Muslim Civil Rights in the United States 2005." Council on American-Islamic Relations. Available online. URL: http://www.cair.com/CivilRights/CivilRightsReports/2005Report.aspx. Accessed on August 25, 2008.

[22] "Extremists Declare 'Open Season' on Immigrants: Hispanics Target of Incitement and Violence." Anti-Defamation League. Available online. URL: http://www.adl.org/main_Extremism/immigration_extremists.htm?Multi_page_sections=sHeading_4. Accessed on August 25, 2008.

[23] "How Immigration Is Rousing the Zealots," Jeffrey Ressner, *Time,* May 29, 2006. Available online. URL: http://www.time.com/time/magazine/article/0,9171,1198895,00.html. Accessed on August 25, 2008.

[24] From the full text of the Local Law Enforcement Hate Crimes Prevention Act. Available online. URL: http://thomas.loc.gov/home/gpoxmlc110/h1592_eh.xml. Accessed on August 25, 2008.

[25] "Hate Crime Victim Testifies Before Senate Judiciary Committee." Anti-Defamation League. Available online. URL: http://www.adl.org/Civil_Rights/Ritcheson.asp. Accessed on August 26, 2008.

[26] "Rep. Robert C. Scott Holds a Hearing on Hate Crime Prevention." Access My Library. Available online. URL: http://www.accessmylibrary.com/coms2/summary_0286-30346506_ITM. Accessed on August 26, 2008.

[27] "Statement of Administration Policy: H.R. 1592, Local Law Enforcement Hate Crimes Prevention Act of 2007." The White House. Available online. URL: http://www.whitehouse.gov/omb/legislative/sap/110-1/hr1592sap-h.pdf. Accessed on August 25, 2008.

[28] Valerie Jenness and Ryken Grattet, "Examining the Boundaries of Hate Crime Law: Disabilities and the 'Dilemma of Difference.'" *The Journal of Criminal Law and Criminology,* vol. 91, no. 3, Spring 2001, p. 598.

CHAPTER 2

THE LAW OF HATE CRIME

FEDERAL LEGISLATION

Many legal scholars trace the origins of modern hate-crime legislation to federal statutes passed just after the Civil War. The new laws were intended to put in place an evenhanded and colorblind system of justice, as supposedly guaranteed by the Fourteenth Amendment, end the vigilante "justice" dispensed by the Ku Klux Klan, and end the arbitrary and discriminatory arrests, trials, and convictions of former slaves in the South. The first of these statutes, 18 U.S.C. (United States Code) Section 241, banned conspiracies to deprive citizens of their rights secured by the Constitution:

> *If two or more persons conspire to injure, oppress, threaten, or intimidate any inhabitant of any State, Territory, or District in the free exercise or enjoyment of any right or privilege secured to him by the Constitution or laws of the United States, or because of his having so exercised the same; or*
> *If two or more persons go in disguise on the highway, or on the premises of another, with intent to prevent or hinder his free exercise or enjoyment of any right or privilege so secured;*
> *They shall be fined under this title or imprisoned not more than ten years, or both; and if death results from the acts committed in violation of this section or if such acts include kidnapping or an attempt to kidnap, aggravated sexual abuse or an attempt to commit aggravated sexual abuse, or an attempt to kill, they shall be fined under this title or imprisoned for any term of years or for life, or both, or may be sentenced to death.*

The second of these statutes, Section 242, is directed at public officials, such as police and judges, who deprive citizens of their constitutional rights "under color of any law." It states:

> *Whoever, under color of any law, statute, ordinance, regulation, or custom, willfully subjects any inhabitant of any State, Territory, or District to the*

deprivation of any rights, privileges, or immunities secured or protected by the Constitution or laws of the United States, or to different punishments, pains, or penalties, on account of such inhabitant being an alien, or by reason of his color, or race, than are prescribed for the punishment of citizens, shall be fined not more than $1,000 or imprisoned not more than one year, or both; and if bodily injury results shall be fined under this title or imprisoned not more than ten years, or both; and if death results shall be subject to imprisonment for any term of years or for life.

The statutes did not mention protected groups or statuses, or punish crimes committed on the basis of prejudice. In modern times, these statutes have most often been enforced against public officials such as the police. For example, in 2007 a police lieutenant of the Rusk County Sheriff's Office in Henderson, Texas, was convicted of violating this statute for striking, throwing to the floor, and jumping on a handcuffed suspect during an interrogation at the sheriff's office in 2006. In perhaps the best-known case involving this charge, Section 242 was used in prosecuting the Los Angeles police officers accused of beating black motorist Rodney King in 1991.

THE CIVIL RIGHTS ACT OF 1968

A new law passed within the Civil Rights Act of 1968, 18 U.S.C. Section 245, was enacted during a turbulent era in which federally protected civil rights became an important focus of new laws. This law deals specifically with the criminal offense of interfering with a person's enjoyment of a federally protected right on the basis of their race, color, religion, or national origin. These protected rights are listed as follows:

A. Voting or qualifying to vote, qualifying or campaigning as a candidate for elective office, or qualifying or acting as a poll watcher, or any legally authorized election official, in any primary, special, or general election;

B. Participating in or enjoying any benefit, service, privilege, program, facility, or activity provided or administered by the United States;

C. Applying for or enjoying employment, or any perquisite thereof, by any agency of the United States;

D. Serving, or attending upon any court in connection with possible service, as a grand or petit juror in any court of the United States;

E. Participating in or enjoying the benefits of any program or activity receiving Federal financial assistance.

The act further protects those who are:

A. Enrolling in or attending any public school or public college;
B. Participating in or enjoying any benefit, service, privilege, program, facility or activity provided or administered by any State or subdivision thereof;
C. Applying for or enjoying employment, or any perquisite thereof, by any private employer or any agency of any State or subdivision thereof, or joining or using the services or advantages of any labor organization, hiring hall, or employment agency;
D. Serving, or attending upon any court of any State in connection with possible service, as a grand or petit juror;
E. Traveling in or using any facility of interstate commerce, or using any vehicle, terminal, or facility of any common carrier by motor, rail, water, or air;
F. Enjoying the goods, services, facilities, privileges, advantages, or accommodations of any inn, hotel, motel, or other establishment which provides lodging to transient guests, or of any restaurant, cafeteria, lunchroom, lunch counter, soda fountain, or other facility which serves the public and which is principally engaged in selling food or beverages for consumption on the premises, or of any gasoline station, or of any motion picture house, theater, concert hall, sports arena, stadium, or any other place of exhibition or entertainment which serves the public. . .

Traditionally, Title 18, Section 245 has been the statute used to prosecute those who commit "hate crimes." Yet the number of crimes actually prosecuted by the Justice Department stood at 37 in the decade after 1991. The burden of proof for federal prosecutors is high: They must prove that the crime occurred because of the victim's membership in a protected group and because he or she was engaging in the protected activity. In addition, the U.S. attorney general must certify in writing that a prosecution would be in the public interest. In effect, the statute has turned over the prosecution of hate crimes to state and local law enforcement. For this reason, the Hate Crimes Prevention Act was proposed in 1999 to make federal prosecution of hate crimes an easier task; but as of March 2009, several expanded versions of the law had been proposed but not passed.

ADL MODEL LEGISLATION

An important basis for modern hate-crimes legislation was a model statute created by the Anti-Defamation League in 1981. Although the Anti-Defamation League was founded to combat anti-Jewish bias, the ADL's model statute uses general language to cover hate crimes against any and all religions, as well as crimes against individuals based on their race, religion, national origin, sexual orientation, or (as of a 1996 amendment) gender. The model statute also criminalizes vandalism against houses of worship, churches, cemeteries, schools, and community centers; creates a cause of action for civil lawsuits aimed at perpetrators of hate crimes; provides for the payment of punitive damages in these civil actions; and provides for the liability of parents for the actions of their minor children. According to the ADL, "Expressions of hate protected by the First Amendment's free speech clause are not criminalized. However, criminal activity motivated by hate is subject to a stiffer sentence."

The "penalty-enhancement" concept that lies at the heart of the ADL model was upheld by the U.S. Supreme Court decision in the case of *Wisconsin v. Mitchell*, which occurred in June 1993. As of 2008, every state except Arkansas, Georgia, Indiana, South Carolina, and Wyoming had passed some form of bias-motivated violence law.

THE HATE CRIMES STATISTICS ACT

Originally sponsored by Representative John Conyers (D-Mich.) and Senator Paul Simon (D-Ill.), this federal statute was signed into law by President George H. W. Bush in April 1990 and codified as 28 U.S.C. 534. It requires the U.S. attorney general, head of the Department of Justice, to collect information from law enforcement agencies on the occurrence of crimes that "manifest evidence of prejudice based on race, religion, sexual orientation, or ethnicity," and to publish these statistics each year. The specified crimes include homicide, nonnegligent manslaughter, forcible rape, assault, intimidation, arson, and vandalism of property. The attorney general was given the task of setting the guidelines for collecting the data; at the time of passage, Attorney General Richard Thornburgh delegated this task to the FBI, a Justice Department agency. The FBI publishes its findings each January as *Hate Crimes Statistics*, a subsection of the Uniform Crime Reports (UCR). To assist local law enforcement agencies with the job of determining if a hate crime had occurred within their jurisdictions, and how to report it, the FBI issued a *Training Guide for Hate Crime Data Collection* in 1991. This guide states that a hate crime has occurred when "some evidence" demonstrates that the prejudices "in part" motivated the accused.

The first statistics published under the Hate Crimes Statistics Act appeared in January 1993 and covered the calendar year 1991. At the time, compliance with the act amounted to less than 20 percent of all state and local law enforcement agencies (2,771 agencies in 32 states, out of about 16,000 agencies in all that participated in the Uniform Crime Reports). Although the Hate Crimes Statistics Act expired on December 31, 1994,

Louis Freeh, then FBI director, ordered that the data-collection efforts continue. In the meantime, through the 1990s, states were passing statutes that mandated hate-crimes data collection. In addition, the Justice Department instituted the National Incident Based Reporting System (NIBRS), a more comprehensive crime-reporting system that integrates bias motivation as a factor. The new laws and procedures, as well as the growing awareness of hate crimes as an important law enforcement issue, brought the participation by 1999 to well over 90 percent.

The Hate Crimes Statistics Act represented an attempt by federal lawmakers to provide some clarity to an issue clouded by partisan wrangling and debate. While advocacy groups pushed for tougher laws on bias-motivated crimes, opponents of hate-crime law raised the issues of constitutional freedom of speech and opinion, as well as vagueness of the laws and the additional burden placed on police and prosecutors. Although well-intentioned, the Hate Crimes Statistics Act has been only partially successful in its original goal. Private advocacy groups are still providing their own statistics, which in many cases include bias-motivated "incidents," which have an element of prejudice but do not rise to the level of prosecutable crime. Such statistics often clash with those provided by the Uniform Crime Reports. In addition, local law enforcement agencies may avoid reporting true hate crimes out of fear of damaging community reputation.

By the Violent Crime Control and Law Enforcement Act of 1994, data collection was extended, as of January 1, 1997, to hate crimes against those defined as "disabled."

FURTHER FEDERAL MEASURES AGAINST HATE CRIME

Hate crimes remained a prominent topic of news headlines and public debate in the early 1990s, and as a result further initiatives were undertaken by Congress. As part of the Juvenile Justice and Delinquency Prevention Act of 1992, the states were required to include hate-crimes prevention as part of their plans to combat juvenile delinquency. The Office of Juvenile Justice and Delinquency Prevention (OJJDP), part of the Department of Justice, also was mandated to make a national survey of juvenile hate-crime offenders.

The Hate Crimes Sentencing Enhancement Act was passed as Section 28003 of the Violent Crime Control and Law Enforcement Act of 1994. It affects the guidelines to be followed by the U.S. Sentencing Commission, which is charged with setting penalty levels for those found guilty of federal crimes. The commission must provide an "enhancement" of no less than three offense levels for hate crimes, defined as a crime against persons or property motivated by the victim's actual (or perceived) race, color, religion, national origin, ethnicity, gender, disability, or sexual orientation. The predicate crimes—which must take place on federal property—were specified as murder, nonnegligent manslaughter, forcible rape, aggravated assault, simple assault, intimidation, arson, and destruction, damage, or vandalism of property.

The Violence Against Women Act of 1994 was passed as Title IV of the Violent Crime Control and Law Enforcement Act of 1994 in September 1994. It provides that "all persons within the United States shall have the right to be free from crimes of violence motivated by gender," and sets down criminal penalties for those who commit violent acts after traveling across state lines and while violating a protective order. By Title III, the law also creates a "cause of action," or a basis for a civil lawsuit in which a plaintiff can recover monetary damages: "A person (including a person who acts under color of any statute, ordinance, regulation, custom, or usage of any State) who commits a crime of violence motivated by gender . . . shall be liable to the party injured, in an action for the recovery of compensatory and punitive damages, injunctive and declaratory relief, and such other relief as a court may deem appropriate."

The bill also allocated federal funds for education, crisis centers, hot lines, victim services, and law enforcement training.

CHURCH ARSON PREVENTION ACT

A rash of church burnings during the early 1990s prompted Senator Edward Kennedy (D-Mass.), Senator Lauch Faircloth (R-N.C.), Representative Henry Hyde (R-Ill.), and Representative John Conyers (D-Mich.) to sponsor the Church Arsons Prevention Act. The law was intended to assist local and federal investigations in cases of vandalism and arson against houses of worship. It was passed on July 3, 1996.

The Church Arson Prevention Act created the National Church Arson Task Force (NCATF), charged specifically with investigating cases of arson against churches. The NCATF coordinates federal prosecutors and local law enforcement agencies in these investigations.

The Church Arson Prevention Act of 1996 enhanced a 1988 statute that made vandalism causing more than $10,000 damage against church property a federal crime. It allowed a sentence of death if a death, kidnapping, or aggravated sexual assault resulted from a violation. For noncapital offenses, it set a statute of limitations of seven years. It also allowed for loan guarantees for rebuilding damaged property.

HATE CRIMES PREVENTION ACT

Since the passage of Title 18, Section 245, lawmakers have introduced new statutes targeted at more specific aspects of bias-motivated crimes, such as church arsons and violence against women. Yet because the original law set a high burden of proof on federal prosecutors, the investigation and prosecution of hate crimes fell in large part to local law enforcement. Through the 1990s, while the UCR documented more than 50,000 hate crimes, the federal government brought only 37 cases under the hate-crimes law codified as 18 U.S.C. 245.

In the late 1990s, lawmakers introduced new bills to remedy what they perceived as an important yet toothless federal law. In 1997, the first Hate Crimes Prevention Act (HCPA) was introduced as H.R. 3081, amending 18 U.S.C. 245, in the 105th Congress. The bill failed to pass, and so it was reintroduced as H.R. 1082 in 1999. The law, slightly amended and renamed the Local Law Enforcement Enhancement Act, and attached as an amendment to the National Defense Authorization Act for fiscal year 2001, was passed by the Senate by a vote of 57 to 42 on June 20, 2000. In the House of Representatives, however, the bill did not emerge for a final roll-call vote, instead becoming the focus of a variety of arcane parliamentary procedures. After the Senate passage, supporters in the House of Representatives forced the House to vote on a nonbinding motion that "instructed" the leaders of the House to accept an identical version to that passed in the Senate. This motion passed by a vote of 232 to 194, with 41 Republicans joining 191 Democrats in support. But a conference committee of House and Senate members voted to kill the motion, ending any hope supporters had of bringing the bill to a House vote.

When and if passed by the House of Representatives, the bill would expand the role of the federal government in hate-crimes prosecution; it would also expand the meaning of "hate crime" to include those committed on the basis of (perceived or actual) gender, sexual orientation, or disability. It would provide technical, forensic, prosecutorial, or any other form of assistance to state and local law enforcement officials in cases of crimes that are considered hate crimes under state law, or that: (a) constitute a crime of violence; (b) constitute a felony under state law; and (c) are motivated by bias based on race, color, religion, national origin, gender, disability, or sexual orientation. The Local Law Enforcement Enhancement Act authorizes the attorney general to grant up to $100,000 to local law enforcement for hate-crimes investigations; it also authorizes grants to train local law enforcement officers in identifying, investigating, prosecuting, and preventing hate crimes.

The act requires the Justice Department to certify that reasonable cause exists to believe the crime was motivated by bias, and to certify that a federal attorney has determined that a state does not have jurisdiction, has requested the Justice Department to assume jurisdiction, and/or does not object to the Justice Department assuming jurisdiction. The law also includes those crimes in which the state has completed prosecution and which the Justice Department wishes to prosecute.

Opponents argue that the legislation is vague and unconstitutional. Supporters state that it would simply strengthen existing local laws by making federal prosecution a backup to local law enforcement when such action is requested by local prosecutors and investigators.

The new hate crimes bill came under debate in the Senate on January 3, 2001, when it was reintroduced with a concurrent resolution by Texas representative Sheila Jackson-Lee. The resolution expressed "the sense of the Congress regarding the need to pass legislation to increase penalties on perpetrators of hate crimes." Nevertheless, the bill remained stalled, with opponents blocking any effort to bring it to a final floor vote. In 2002, the reintroduced bill was subject to a filibuster (parliamentary delay) in the Senate, a tactic that succeeded in delaying Senate passage in that year. In September 2002, Representative Conyers introduced a rarely used discharge petition. If a simple majority (or 218 members out of the total 435) of members of the House sign such a petition, the Speaker of the House (at the time, Dennis Hastert, R-Ill.) must call a vote. By October 2, 2002, the petition had 165 signatures.

Like its predecessor, Local Law Enforcement Hate Crimes Prevention Act of 2007, H.R. 1592, proposed to expand the hate crime law to include crimes based on sexual orientation, gender identity, or disability. The bill also set out to end the caveat that the victim had to be engaged in a federally protected activity, provide for more funding to state and local agencies to investigate hate crimes, and add hate crimes against transgender victims to the statistics kept by the FBI. The bill passed by a vote of 237 to 180 in the House of Representatives on May 3, 2007, and was then introduced into the Senate on July 11, 2007, as S. 1105. In an attempt to prevent an ultimate presidential veto, the bill's Senate sponsors attached it to the Defense Reauthorization Act. Caught up in the debate over troop withdrawal from Iraq, the bill languished until September 27, 2007, when the Defense Authorization Act passed the Senate by a vote of 60 to 3. In December, however, the hate crimes provisions were removed from the defense authorization bill (which was subsequently signed). Through December 2008, S. 1105 remained in committee.

STATE LEGISLATION

Since the passage of the post–Civil War statutes, the states have followed the lead of federal legislators in enacting their own civil rights and hate-crimes laws. State laws provide the true focus of the hate-crimes debate, as it is on the state level that the vast majority of hate-crimes laws are prosecuted. Most of these laws increase the sentence of a convicted criminal, or provide a mandatory minimum sentence, if the evidence shows a certain specified crime was motivated "because of" or "by reason of" a certain specified prejudice. Relying on the phrase "because of" allows prosecutors to muster a case regardless of the perpetrator's racist beliefs—simply convincing a jury of racist motive surrounding a single act is sufficient to gain a conviction.

The crimes may vary from state to state (the ADL model statute, on which many state hate-crimes laws are based, covers the crimes of intimidation and harassment). They may include murder, assault, aggravated assault, manslaughter, rape, robbery, kidnapping, arson; they may include misdemeanor offenses such as intimidation, trespassing, menacing, or criminal mischief. The specified prejudices in the various state hate-crimes laws include bias against race, color, religion, national origin, gender, personal appearance, sexual orientation, disability, union membership, age, service in the armed forces, marital status, political views, or position on abortion.

What most legal scholars consider as the original modern state hate-crime statute was passed in 1987 by California and is closely modeled on the federal civil rights law passed in 1968. The California statute reads: "No person, whether or not acting under the color of law, shall by force or threat of force, willfully injure, intimidate, interfere with, oppress, or threaten any other person in the free exercise or enjoyment of any right secured to him or her by the constitutional laws of this state or by the Constitution or the laws of the United States because of the other person's race, color, religion, ancestry, national origin, or sexual orientation."

By 2008, and with the federal hate-crimes bill stalled in Congress, 31 U.S. states had expanded their hate-crimes to include sexual orientation as a protected class. In addition, the Michigan legislature was debating a similar bill that would also designate intimidation of the disabled, cross-burning, or the hanging of a noose as a hate crime. As of mid-2008 these state-level hate-crime laws were beginning to be tested in the courts.

LEGISLATIVE STRATEGIES OF THE STATES

In their book *Making Hate a Crime*, scholars Valerie Jenness and Ryken Grattet have identified five distinct legal strategies used by the states in their new hate-crimes statutes. These strategies were devised in the 1980s, when many state hate-crimes laws first came into existence. The first harkens back to the earliest form of such federal legislation: criminalizing the "interference" with the exercise of civil rights, as defined in the federal or state constitutions, because of the victim's real or perceived race, national origin, religion, and so on. The second legal strategy involves creating a freestanding statute that creates an entirely new category of criminal act, such as ethnic intimidation, harassment, or malicious behavior, committed on the basis of prejudice.

"Coattailing" statutes simply add a new hate-crimes dimension to preexisting laws. By this strategy, the ordinary crime of assault, for example, can be doubly prosecuted as a hate crime if there is sufficient evidence to show that it was committed by reason of ethnic or religious prejudice. A parallel strategy is to amend a preexisting statute to reclassify crimes committed on the basis of prejudice. Most states set down categories for crimes (Class 1 misdemeanor, Class 2 misdemeanor, and so on) based on their severity or the circumstances surrounding the crime. These two legal strategies—coattailing and modification—are the easiest to write and enforce, as they do not set down new categories of crime that may or may not be struck down by the courts as unconstitutional.

A final and important legal strategy is penalty enhancement, which increases the sentence for certain crimes that have been found to be bias crimes. The penalty enhancement may bring a longer sentencing range on conviction, or it may increase the offense category. The penalty-enhancement strategy was put to the test in the case of *Wisconsin v. Mitchell*, in which a penalty-enhancement statute was brought to the U.S. Supreme Court and upheld in June 1993. The law in question, Wisconsin statute 939.645, first defines hate crimes as those committed "in whole or in part because of the actor's belief or perception regarding the race, religion, color, disability, sexual orientation, national origin or ancestry of that person or the owner or occupant of that property, whether or not the actor's belief or perception was correct."

In general, the penalty enhancement approach has proven to be the most popular method of writing state hate-crimes legislation, along with "coattailing" ethnic intimidation laws. The penalty enhancement strategy, given the favorable decision in *Wisconsin v. Mitchell*, also has passed constitutional muster. Modifying previously existing laws and criminalizing interference with civil rights are the least used options in writing new hate-crime laws.

SUMMARY OF STATE LAWS AND REGULATIONS REGARDING HATE CRIMES

The following list summarizes the various forms of hate-crimes laws passed by state legislatures through June 2008.

Age: The following states have criminalized bias-motivated actions inspired by prejudice against the victim's age: District of Columbia, Iowa, Louisiana, and Vermont.

Bias-Motivated Violence and Intimidation: In all, 45 states and the District of Columbia have passed statutes punishing bias-motivated violence and intimidation: Alabama, Alaska, Arizona, California, Colorado, Connecticut, District of Columbia, Delaware, Florida, Hawaii, Idaho, Illinois,

Iowa, Kansas, Kentucky, Louisiana, Maine, Maryland, Massachusetts, Michigan, Minnesota, Mississippi, Missouri, Montana, Nebraska, Nevada, New Hampshire, New Jersey, New Mexico, New York (limited to aggravated harassment), North Carolina, North Dakota, Ohio, Oklahoma, Oregon, Pennsylvania, Rhode Island, South Dakota, Tennessee, Texas, Utah, Vermont, Virginia, Washington, West Virginia, and Wisconsin.

Civil Action: Thirty-one states and the District of Columbia have provisions for civil action (lawsuits seeking monetary damages) arising from bias-motivated crimes: Arkansas, California, Colorado, Connecticut, District of Columbia, Florida, Georgia, Idaho, Illinois, Iowa, Louisiana, Maine, Massachusetts, Michigan, Minnesota, Missouri, Nebraska, Nevada, New Jersey, North Carolina, Ohio, Oklahoma, Oregon, Pennsylvania, Rhode Island, South Dakota, Tennessee, Texas, Vermont, Virginia, Washington, and Wisconsin.

Data Collection: Twenty-seven states and the District of Columbia have passed statutes mandating the collection of hate-crime statistics by local law enforcement agencies: Arizona, California, Connecticut, District of Columbia, Florida, Hawaii, Idaho, Illinois, Iowa, Kentucky, Louisiana, Maine, Maryland, Massachusetts, Michigan, Minnesota, Nebraska, Nevada, New Mexico, New Jersey, Oklahoma, Oregon, Pennsylvania, Rhode Island, Texas, Virginia, Washington, and West Virginia.

Gender: The following 28 states and the District of Columbia have passed laws providing criminal penalties for violence motivated by bias against the victim's gender: Alaska, Arkansas, Arizona, California, Connecticut, District of Columbia, Hawaii, Illinois, Iowa, Louisiana, Maine, Michigan, Minnesota, Mississippi, Missouri, Nebraska, New Hampshire, New Jersey, New Mexico, New York, North Carolina, North Dakota, Pennsylvania, Rhode Island, Tennessee, Texas, Vermont, Washington, and West Virginia.

Institutional Vandalism: The following states, 42 in all, and the District of Columbia have laws criminalizing institutional vandalism, acts of arson, or other property crimes motivated by bias: Alabama, Arizona, Arkansas, California, Colorado, Connecticut, District of Columbia, Delaware, Florida, Georgia, Hawaii, Idaho, Illinois, Indiana, Kansas, Kentucky, Louisiana, Maine, Maryland, Massachusetts, Michigan, Minnesota, Mississippi, Missouri, Montana, Nebraska, Nevada, New Jersey, New Mexico, New York, North Carolina, Ohio, Oklahoma, Oregon, Pennsylvania, Rhode Island, South Carolina, South Dakota, Tennessee, Texas, Virginia, Washington, and Wisconsin.

Interference with Religious Worship: Twenty-one states and the District of Columbia have passed laws criminalizing interference with religious worship: Arkansas, California, District of Columbia, Florida, Idaho, Maryland, Massachusetts, Michigan, Minnesota, Mississippi, Missouri, Nevada, New Mexico, New York, North Carolina, Oklahoma, Rhode

Island, South Carolina, South Dakota, Tennessee, Virginia, and West Virginia.

Law Enforcement Training: Fourteen states have passed statutes that mandate training in dealing with hate crimes for law enforcement personnel: Arizona, California, Connecticut, Illinois, Iowa, Kentucky, Louisiana, Massachusetts, Minnesota, New Jersey, New Mexico, Oregon, Rhode Island, and Washington.

Mental or Physical Disability: Thirty-two states and the District of Columbia criminalize bias-motivated violence on the basis of disability or handicap: Alabama, Arizona, Alaska, California, Colorado, Connecticut, District of Columbia, Delaware, Florida, Hawaii, Illinois, Iowa, Kansas, Louisiana, Maine, Massachusetts, Minnesota, Missouri, Nebraska, Nevada, New Hampshire, New Jersey, New Mexico, New York, Oklahoma, Pennsylvania, Rhode Island, Tennessee, Texas, Vermont, Washington, and Wisconsin.

Political Affiliation: The District of Columbia and four states have passed laws making it a crime to commit violence inspired by political prejudice: California, District of Columbia, Iowa, Louisiana, and West Virginia.

Race, Religion, or Ethnic Group: Forty-four states and the District of Columbia have passed laws criminalizing crimes committed because of bias against race, religion, or ethnic group: Alabama, Alaska, Arizona, California, Colorado, Connecticut, District of Columbia, Delaware, Florida, Hawaii, Idaho, Illinois, Iowa, Kansas, Kentucky, Louisiana, Maine, Maryland, Massachusetts, Michigan, Minnesota, Mississippi, Missouri, Montana, Nebraska, Nevada, New Hampshire, New Jersey, New Mexico, New York, North Carolina, North Dakota, Ohio, Oklahoma, Oregon, Pennsylvania, Rhode Island, South Dakota, Tennessee, Texas, Vermont, Virginia, Washington, West Virginia, and Wisconsin.

Sexual Orientation: The following 31 states and the District of Columbia specify sexual orientation as a category protected by hate-crimes statutes: Arizona, California, Colorado, Connecticut, District of Columbia, Delaware, Florida, Hawaii, Illinois, Iowa, Kansas, Kentucky, Louisiana, Maine, Maryland, Massachusetts, Minnesota, Missouri, Nebraska, Nevada, New Hampshire, New Jersey, New Mexico, New York, Oregon, Pennsylvania, Rhode Island, Tennessee, Texas, Vermont, Washington, and Wisconsin.

CANADIAN LEGISLATION

The strict laws on "hate speech" in Canada—at both national and provincial levels—have been resisted in the United States. The Bill of Rights of the United States has its analog in the "Charter of Rights and Freedoms," enacted as part of Canada's Constitution Act of 1982. It was in effect for just a few years before the landmark case of *R. v. Keegstra* was decided in the Supreme Court of Canada in 1990, and thus Canada's free-speech protections have not been established as an inviolable principle in the manner of the First Amendment to the U.S. Constitution. An investigation by the Canadian authorities (specifically, in most cases, provincial human rights commissions) into political opinions considered obnoxious or intolerant is a fairly common occurrence—one that would presumably draw scathing editorial comment and media attention in the United States. Such tribunals may investigate extreme views of the right as well as the left, such as in the case of Sunera Thobani, a university professor from British Columbia who was asked to appear before a public authority and defend a diatribe against American foreign policy.

Observers of expanded hate-crime laws in the United States see potential for the same practice in the United States as new hate-crime legislation expands the categories of protected groups to include homosexuals. In fall 2008, the effort to move new amendments to the hate-crimes law went forward despite President Bush's veto threat. In September, supporters attempted to append the legislation to the defense reauthorization bill for fiscal year 2009. In addition, several U.S. states have instituted laws that, in effect, bar discriminatory treatment—not just crimes of violence—under the category of hate crime.

Yet many political leaders and opinion makers in the United States, some of whom did not support earlier hate-crime legislation, are now advocating Canada's example, albeit in a slightly different form. The change of view can be traced to the terrorist attacks of 2001, which resulted in a campaign to ease constitutional protections on free speech in the interest of protecting the nation from harm. Newt Gingrich, a prominent conservative spokesman and former Speaker of the U.S. House of Representatives, has joined several like-minded public figures in favoring a narrowing of First Amendment protections to exclude the advocacy of "radical Islam." This position is founded on the idea that speech and writing in favor of terrorist acts, and the radical philosophy that underpins them, can justifiably be approached as a threat to the nation's survival.

Opponents of expanded hate-crime laws in the United States see a danger in the Canadian example: that it effectively chills the constitutional principle of free speech. They cite an incident in Philadelphia, where 75-year-old Arlene Elshinnay was arrested for disrupting a gay pride gathering and holding up a sign saying "Truth is hate to those who hate the truth." Opponents also point out the direct effect of Canadian law on public expression, such as radio broadcasts produced by Focus on the Family, a U.S. group with a subsidiary in Canada. On religious grounds, the group makes a public stand against expansion of civil rights that would extend protections to homosexuals. However, Focus on the Family also carefully edits its broadcasts to conform with Canadian hate-speech law, deleting generalizations that might be construed as ascribing malicious intent to any identifiable group. Another group, MM Outreach Ministries, voluntarily gave up its license to operate in Canada, finding intolerable Canada's effective ban on the criticism of religious beliefs and practices by any group that opposes them. Canada's proximity and its distinctly friendly relationship with the United States ensure that its legal stance on hate crimes will continue to have an impact on U.S. opinion, and occasionally U.S. practice, regarding hate crimes.

COURT CASES

The cases below were decided in a variety of jurisdictions, including the U. S. Supreme Court, federal appeals courts, state supreme courts, and state appeals and criminal courts. Each has some bearing on hate-crimes law, setting a precedent either for the prosecution of crimes or in deciding the constitutionality, on either a state or federal level, of hate-crimes statutes. In addition, one Canadian case is included to illustrate that country's contrasting legal framework with respect to hate crimes and freedom of expression.

The principal questions involved in hate-crimes litigation include the following:

- Do hate-crimes statutes punish opinion, in violation of the First Amendment; are they unconstitutionally vague or overbroad, or do they have a chilling effect on the exercise of free (protected) speech? Are hate-crimes laws an unconstitutional regulation of speech based on its content?
- Do hate-crimes laws punish motive and/or intent rather than conduct?
- Do hate-crimes statutes violate the Fourteenth Amendment and the doctrines of equal protection and due process? Do they lead to arbitrary enforcement, or do they mandate preferential treatment for minority groups?
- Must hate-crimes statutes punish only criminal conduct, motivated by racism, homophobia, anti-Semitism, and so on, and not expression and/or opinion?
- In passing and enforcing hate-crimes laws, do legislators and the courts have a valid motive in maintaining public order and preventing the more serious social injuries that result from hate crimes?

Supreme Court Cases

In general, the broad constitutional issues were decided by the U.S. Supreme Court in the early 1990s, in the cases of *R.A.V. v. St. Paul* and *Wisconsin v. Mitchell*. These decisions set the general constitutional boundaries for hate-crimes legislation in the states, where the vast majority of hate crimes are prosecuted. Later state court decisions refined hate-crimes jurisprudence, setting precedent on more specific issues raised by hate-crimes law.

CHAPLINSKY V. NEW HAMPSHIRE
315 U.S. 568 (1942)

Background

Walter Chaplinsky, a member of the Jehovah's Witnesses, was distributing religious tracts on the streets of Rochester, New Hampshire, in 1940. Several people complained of a disturbance to City Marshal James Bowering, telling the marshal that Chaplinsky was denouncing all organized religion as "a racket." Although the marshal allowed Chaplinsky to continue his lawful activities, he later arrested Chaplinsky as disorder began to occur. Chaplinsky then turned on the marshal and addressed him as follows: "You are a God damned racketeer . . . a damned Fascist and the whole government of Rochester are Fascists or agents of Fascists."

Chaplinsky was convicted in the municipal court of Rochester, New Hampshire, for violation of New Hampshire's Chapter 378, §2, which states that "No person shall address any offensive, derisive or annoying word to any other person who is lawfully in any street or other public place, nor call him by any offensive or derisive name, nor make any noise or exclamation in his presence and hearing with intent to deride, offend or annoy him, or to prevent him from pursuing his lawful business or occupation." The conviction was appealed in New Hampshire Superior Court on the grounds that the statute represented an unconstitutional abridgement of free speech, freedom of the press, and freedom of religious worship, in violation of the First and the Fourteenth Amendments to the Constitution. But Chaplinsky was again found guilty, a judgment that was affirmed by the New Hampshire Supreme Court. In early 1942, the case reached the U.S. Supreme Court.

Legal Issues

The New Hampshire statute had been construed by the state courts to apply only to those words which might cause an immediate breach of the peace. Chaplinsky charged that the law was an infringement of speech, of the press, and of freedom of worship. The state of New Hampshire argued that the spoken word per se is not always protected by the constitution, such as in cases of obscenity, slander, and in this case "fighting words." In its opinion, the New Hampshire Supreme Court wrote that "the statute . . . does no more than prohibit the face-to-face words . . . whose speaking constitutes a breach of the peace by the speaker—including 'classical fighting words', words in current use less 'classical' but equally likely to cause violence, and other disorderly words, including profanity, obscenity and threats."

Decision

On March 9, 1942, the Supreme Court handed down its opinion. It first dismissed Chaplinsky's argument that the New Hampshire law impinged on freedom of the press or of religious worship, as it was only Chaplinsky's spoken word that brought the arrest and conviction. The written opinion states that "The spoken, not the written, word is involved. And we cannot conceive that cursing a public officer is the exercise of religion in any sense of the term."

The Court then affirmed the New Hampshire Supreme Court decision, holding that the state statute complied with due process and did not impinge upon constitutionally protected speech. In their opinion, the justices found that "even if the activities of the appellant which preceded the incident could be viewed as religious in character, and therefore entitled to the protection of the Fourteenth Amendment, they would not cloak him with immunity from the legal consequences for concomitant acts committed in violation of a valid criminal statute. . . . There are certain well-defined and narrowly limited classes of speech, the prevention and punishment of which have never been thought to raise any Constitutional problem. These include the lewd and obscene, the profane, libelous, and the insulting or 'fighting' words—those which by their very utterance inflict injury or tend to incite an immediate breach of the peace. . . . Argument is unnecessary to demonstrate that the appellations 'damned racketeer' and 'damned Fascist' are epithets likely to provoke the average person to retaliation, and thereby cause a breach of the peace."

Impact

The case of *Chaplinsky v. New Hampshire* would have far-ranging influence, down to the writing and enforcement of hate-crimes laws 50 years later. In effect, the justices held that certain speech, which can be characterized as "fighting words," is not protected by the Constitution on the grounds that it tends to cause a breach of the peace. When writing and litigating hate-crimes laws, legislators and prosecutors would draw on this opinion to support their contention that racist or otherwise biased language is not always protected by the constitution, and that such speech can make up an important element of a hate crime—either as evidence of intent or motive, or as a crime in itself. Ironically, the Supreme Court would never again use the precedent set down in 1942 to support the prohibition or repression of speech.

Hate Crimes

R.A.V. v. CITY OF ST. PAUL, MINNESOTA
505 U.S. 377 (1992)

Background

On June 21, 1990, Russell Jones, an African-American resident of the predominantly white Dayton's Bluff neighborhood of St. Paul, Minnesota, found a crudely made burning cross in the front yard of his home. A 17-year-old, known in court documents as R. A. V. (Robert Anthony Viktora), was charged with violation of St. Paul's bias assault law, section 292.01. Not certain of an assault conviction in this case, the city prosecutor then amended the charge to the bias disorderly conduct law, or Section 292.02, which specifically mentions cross burning. The ordinance, which had been adopted in 1982 by the St. Paul City Council in reaction to a wave of bias violence and vandalism, provided that:

Whoever places on public or private property a symbol, object, appellation, characterization or graffiti including, but not limited to, a burning cross or Nazi swastika, which one knows or has reasonable grounds to know arouses anger, alarm or resentment in others on the basis of race, color, creed, religion or gender commits disorderly conduct and shall be guilty of a misdemeanor.

Viktora's attorney challenged the city ordinance on the grounds that rather than punishing criminal conduct, it punished constitutionally protected expression. The trial court dismissed the charges on the ground that the ordinance was substantially overbroad and impermissibly content based. The city appealed in turn, and the Minnesota Supreme Court then reversed the lower-court decision. It rejected the overbreadth claim because the phrase "arouses anger, alarm or resentment in others" had been construed in earlier state cases to limit the ordinance's reach to "fighting words" within the meaning of the 1942 Supreme Court decision in *Chaplinsky v. New Hampshire*, in which "fighting words" were defined as a category of expression not protected by the First Amendment. The Minnesota Supreme Court also concluded that the ordinance was not impermissibly content based because it was narrowly tailored to serve a compelling governmental interest in protecting the community against bias-motivated threats to public safety and order. The case was then certified to the U.S. Supreme Court.

Legal Issues

Viktora's attorney maintained that his client's conviction under the St. Paul ordinance should be overturned, as the ordinance prohibits speech and expression protected by the First Amendment. Attorneys for St. Paul argued that the law may ban certain expressions, in particular "fighting words," or expressions designed to arouse a violent reaction, and that St. Paul had the right to pass such a law in the interest of protecting the community against a threat to public order. Viktora's attorney responded that although certain speech may be proscribed by the law, the law cannot discriminate in such speech, in other words, it cannot select the expression of certain ideas (such as racism) and not others as crimes that merit punishment.

Decision

In its decision of June 22, 1992, the Supreme Court did not put cross burning in the same criminal category as "fighting words," finding that "The [St. Paul] ordinance is facially invalid under the First Amendment." The opinion read, in part: "A few limited categories of speech, such as obscenity, defamation, and fighting words, may be regulated. . . . However, these categories are not entirely invisible to the Constitution, and government may not regulate them based on hostility, or favoritism, towards a nonproscribable message they contain [e.g., racist opinion]. Thus the regulation of 'fighting words' may not be based on nonproscribable content. It may, however, be underinclusive, addressing some offensive instances and leaving other, equally offensive, ones alone, so long as the selective proscription is not based on content, or there is no realistic possibility that regulation of ideas is afoot." The Court found that the ordinance "imposes special prohibitions on those speakers who express views on the disfavored subjects of 'race, color, creed, religion or gender' . . . St. Paul's desire to communicate to minority groups that it does not condone the 'group hatred' of bias motivated speech does not justify selectively silencing speech on the basis of its content." While the First Amendment grants freedom of speech and expression, in a few instances such expression may be regulated by the common interest in public order and morality—a test that this particular ordinance did not meet.

The members of the Supreme Court agreed unanimously on the decision, but a minority of justices disagreed with the legal reasoning given in the Court's opinion. Writing for this minority, Justice Harry Blackmun described "the possibility that this case . . . will be regarded as an aberration—a case where the Court manipulated doctrine to strike down an ordinance whose premise it opposed, namely, that racial threats and verbal assaults are of greater harm than other fighting words. I fear that the Court has been distracted from its proper mission by the temptation to decide the issue over 'politically correct speech' and 'cultural diversity,' neither of which is presented here."

Impact

In *R.A.V. v. St. Paul*, a landmark case in the history of hate-crimes law, the U.S. Supreme Court decided, in effect, that St. Paul had prosecuted Robert Viktora under the wrong law. "Let there be no mistake about our belief that burning a cross in someone's front yard is reprehensible," the opinion concluded. "But St. Paul has sufficient means at its disposal to prevent such behavior without adding the First Amendment to the fire." Although trespassing, vandalism, disorderly conduct, and arson may all be punished by city ordinances, such acts could not, in the future, be punished solely on the basis of their racist content. All similar city ordinances banning racist messages, placards, displays, and the like, were held to be unconstitutional, and those opposing hate-crimes laws were bolstered in their opinion that ordinary laws against criminal behavior would have to be sufficient without referring to racial, ethnic, or religious prejudice. In the future, states and cities seeking to set penalties for "hate crimes," which by definition are those inspired by the perpetrator's dislike of certain groups or certain types of people, would have to write or revise their laws with *R.A.V. v. St. Paul* in mind.

WISCONSIN V. MITCHELL
508 U.S. 476 (1993)

Background

On October 7, 1989, in Kenosha, Wisconsin, several African-American youths gathered after viewing *Mississippi Burning*, a film about the deadly violence that occurred in Mississippi during the 1960s. Angered by a scene in the film in which a white man beats a black boy, and seeing a white youth on the street, the petitioner Todd Mitchell roused his companions: "You all want to f—k somebody up? There goes a white boy; go get him." Mitchell then counted to three and the group ran towards the white youth, beat him unconscious, and stole his shoes. The victim survived the beating but remained in a coma for four days afterward.

Mitchell was convicted of aggravated battery in Kenosha County Circuit Court. The two-year sentence was then enhanced because, as the jury found, Mitchell had intentionally selected the victim based on the victim's race. According to the Wisconsin penalty enhancement formula, such an act carries a maximum punishment of seven years in prison. In this case, the defendant was sentenced to four years.

Mitchell appealed, arguing that Wisconsin's penalty-enhancement statute violated the First Amendment. The Wisconsin Court of Appeals decided against the appeal, but the Wisconsin Supreme Court reversed this decision, holding that the statute punishes "what the legislature has deemed to be offensive thought." The Wisconsin Supreme Court also found that bringing evidence of the defendant's prior speech ("There goes a white boy; go get him") would have a "chilling effect," that is, a fear of prosecution based solely on one's expressed ideas, and that the statute "punishes the subjective mental process." The decision of the Wisconsin Supreme Court was then brought to the U.S. Supreme Court.

Legal Issues

The case of *Wisconsin v. Mitchell* put all state penalty-enhancement statutes, the most commonly prosecuted form of hate-crimes laws, under the legal microscope. Mitchell's attorney argued that Wisconsin's penalty-enhancement law punished bigoted thought and not conduct. The state argued exactly the opposite—that Mitchell's "conduct" of directing his companions to beat the victim was punished, and then enhanced because of his discriminatory motive in committing the assault, and that such conduct had nothing to do with his rights to free expression under the First Amendment. Looming in the background as an important precedent was the decision of the U.S. Supreme Court in the case of *R.A.V. v. St. Paul*, reached a year earlier, in which the Court struck down a city ordinance banning any "symbol, object, appellation, characterization, or graffiti" tending to arouse "anger, alarm or resentment . . . on the basis of race, color, creed, religion, or gender. . ."

By long legal precedent, the "conduct" of assault cannot be considered as "expression" protected by the First Amendment. In addition, the practice of penalty enhancement has been found constitutional, and by state and federal laws a wide range of possible enhancements can be passed on defendants for a wide variety of criminal acts. But the abstract beliefs of a defendant cannot be taken solely into consideration—thus, a white racist found guilty of murder cannot see his penalty enhanced solely because of his bigoted beliefs (*Dawson v. Delaware*, 503 U.S. 159 1992). The Supreme Court now had to decide in what manner such beliefs could be the basis for penalty enhancement.

Decision

In its decision of June 11, 1993, the U.S. Supreme Court reversed the decision of the Wisconsin Supreme Court and held that Mitchell's First Amendment rights were not violated by the application of the penalty-enhancement provision in sentencing him. The opinion read, in part:

> *In determining what sentence to impose, sentencing judges have traditionally considered a wide variety of factors in addition to evidence bearing on guilt, including a defendant's motive for committing the offense. While it is equally true that a sentencing judge may not take into consideration a defendant's abstract beliefs, however obnoxious to most people, the Constitution does not erect a per se barrier to the admission of evidence concerning one's beliefs and associations at sentencing simply because they are protected by the First Amendment.*

Nothing in R. A. V. v. St. Paul *compels a different result here. The [St. Paul, Minnesota] ordinance at issue there was explicitly directed at speech, while the one here is aimed at conduct unprotected by the First Amendment. Moreover, the State's desire to redress what it sees as the greater individual and societal harm inflicted by bias-inspired conduct provides an adequate explanation for the provision over and above mere disagreement with offenders' beliefs or biases.*

The U.S. Supreme Court disagreed with the Wisconsin Supreme Court in finding that the penalty enhancement law had no chilling effect on free speech. "The prospect of a citizen suppressing his bigoted beliefs for fear that evidence of those beliefs will be introduced against him at trial if he commits a serious offense against person or property is too speculative a hypothesis to support this claim. Moreover, the First Amendment permits the admission of previous declarations or statements to establish the elements of a crime or to prove motive or intent, subject to evidentiary rules dealing with relevancy, reliability, and the like."

Impact

The *Wisconsin v. Mitchell* decision gave the states broad legal authority to write and pass penalty-enhancement statutes for criminal conduct inspired by prejudice. While the constitutionality of laws that simply punish thought or expression remain in serious doubt after *R.A.V. v. St. Paul*, the constitutionality of laws enhancing punishment for conduct based on prejudice was recognized. This decision remains a controversial one, and hate-crimes laws are still being challenged on the basis that they violate the First Amendment. Yet nearly every such challenge in state supreme courts to penalty enhancement has been defeated, with the judges citing the U.S. Supreme Court as their authority and *Wisconsin v. Mitchell* as their precedent.

BRZONKALA V. MORRISON
120 S. CT. 1740 (2000)

Background

The case of *Brzonkala v. Morrison* began in October 1994, at Virginia Polytechnic University, when student Christy Brzonkala accused two other students, Antonio Morrison and James Crawford, of raping her in a dormitory room. Brzonkala filed a claim under the university's sexual assault policy, and at the subsequent hearing Morrison was found guilty and handed a two-semester suspension (insufficient evidence was found to convict Crawford). Brzonkala then took the case to the U.S. District Court for the Western District of Virginia, seeking damages from Morrison and Crawford under Section

13981 of the Violence Against Women Act of 1994, which allows for victims of gender-motivated violence to sue for compensatory and punitive damages. The defendants moved to dismiss the case on the grounds that Brzonkala had failed to state a claim for damages, and that Section 13981 was an unconstitutional exercise of congressional power under the commerce clause (Article 1, Section 8 of the Constitution) and the enforcement clause (Fourteenth Amendment, Section 5); the district court agreed and dismissed the suit.

This decision was reversed by the U.S. Court of Appeals for the Fourth Circuit, which found that the statute in question was constitutionally legitimate. At a subsequent rehearing, the appeals court reversed itself. The case was granted certiorari by the U.S. Supreme Court on September 28, 1999.

Legal Issues

The case of *Brzonkala v. Morrison* was the test for the constitutionality of civil lawsuits brought by victims of gender-motivated violence. The Supreme Court had to decide whether Section 13981 of the Violence Against Women Act of 1994, specifically its section dealing with redress in civil court, was constitutional under the commerce clause or the enforcement clause. Those arguing for constitutionality held that violence against women deters them from interstate travel and business, and thus interferes with commerce; that violence against women is a growing national problem that has an important economic impact and that calls for federal legislation; and that the commerce clause does not strictly limit such legislation to economic activities. Since not all states have passed laws addressing gender-based violence, women in those states are deprived of their Fourteenth Amendment right to equal protection of the laws, and thus Congress should have the power to pass federal legislation addressing the issue.

Those opposed to the law under which Brzonkala originally sued stated that the commerce clause is indeed limited to economic activities, and that the Violence Against Women Act has nothing to do with interstate commerce. In addition, since the Fourteenth Amendment deals with acts of state governments and public authorities, the acts of private individuals cannot be legislated against by its authority.

Decision

By a 5-4 decision, the U.S. Supreme Court justices held that the commerce clause does not permit the civil redress section of the Violence Against Women Act, as the act regulates criminal and not economic activity, and such activity does not substantially affect interstate commerce. The majority also agreed with the argument that the Fourteenth Amendment deals with discriminatory conduct by state agencies, and that Brzonkala's lawsuit involves private individuals and thus is invalid under the amendment.

The dissenting justices agreed with the argument that Congress had established that crimes against women were having a substantial economic impact (including costs to the public incurred by the criminal justice system). The dissenters also opined that the decision on whether criminal activity has such an impact rests with Congress and not with the Supreme Court.

Impact

With the *Brzonkala v. Morrison* decision, the Supreme Court struck down a key provision of the 1994 Violence Against Women Act, thus invalidating a federal law allowing civil redress for victims of bias-motivated violence. Although the decision was deplored by some women's rights groups, several commentators pointed out that very few such lawsuits had been initiated since the law was passed, and that civil litigation in such cases is usually meaningless, as most defendants have few assets to collect.

APPRENDI V. NEW JERSEY 120 S. CT. 2348 (2000)

Background

On December 22, 1994, the petitioner, Charles C. Apprendi, fired several shots into the home of an African-American family and made a statement, which he later retracted, that he did not want the family in his neighborhood because of their race.

Legal Issues

Apprendi was charged under New Jersey law with second-degree possession of a firearm for an unlawful purpose, which carries a prison term of five to 10 years. The charge did not refer to the state's hate crime statute, which provides for an enhanced sentence if a trial judge finds, by a preponderance of the evidence, that the defendant committed the crime with a purpose to intimidate a person or group because of, inter alia, race. After Apprendi pled guilty, the prosecutor filed a motion to enhance the sentence. The court found by a preponderance of the evidence that the shooting was racially motivated and sentenced Apprendi to a 12-year term on the firearms count. In upholding the sentence, the appeals court rejected Apprendi's claim that by the due process clause of the U.S. Constitution, a finding of bias must be proved to a jury rather than decided by a judge. The New Jersey Supreme Court affirmed the lower court's decision.

Decision

On June 26, 2000, the U.S. Supreme Court held that the Constitution requires that any fact that increases the penalty for a crime beyond the prescribed statutory maximum, other than the fact of a prior conviction, must be submitted to a jury, and proved beyond a reasonable doubt.

The Supreme Court opinion read, in part:

(A) The answer to the narrow constitutional question presented—whether Apprendi's sentence was permissible, given that it exceeds the 10-year maximum for the offense charged—was foreshadowed by the holding in Jones v. United States *that, with regard to federal law, the Fifth Amendment's due process clause and the Sixth Amendment's notice and jury trial guarantees require that any fact other than prior conviction that increases the maximum penalty for a crime must be charged in an indictment, submitted to a jury, and proved beyond a reasonable doubt. The Fourteenth Amendment commands the same answer when a state statute is involved.*

(B) The Fourteenth Amendment right to due process and the Sixth Amendment right to trial by jury, taken together, entitle a criminal defendant to a jury determination that he is guilty of every element of the crime with which he is charged, beyond a reasonable doubt. . .

Impact

The complex decision in the *Apprendi v. New Jersey* case, although only indirectly concerned with hate-crimes law, may have far-reaching implications in the nation's criminal justice system. The case has spawned hundreds of new cases and appeals, based on the initial failure of the courts to submit penalty-enhancement evidence to juries. Defendants in capital cases have asked for additional appeals on this basis, and drug cases have been reopened so that evidence of the amount of controlled substance can be determined by a jury and not by a judge, which was the practice in circuit courts. In general, *Apprendi* means that sentencing schemes in which a state permits a judge to pass a sentence beyond the statutory maximum, based on his own findings of the evidence, are now unconstitutional.

Federal/State/Criminal Court Cases

COMMONWEALTH OF MASSACHUSETTS V. POOR AND TILTON
MASSACHUSETTS COURT OF APPEALS
467 N.E.2D 877 (1984)

Background

On August 30, 1982, Mrs. Regina Campbell, a black woman, moved into an apartment at the Snug Harbor housing project in Quincy, Massachusetts. Bradley Poor, a white male, lived nearby with his wife and children at

30 Taffrail Road. Poor's brother-in-law John Tilton, also white, often stayed with Poor's family, although he was not a resident of the project. On September 9, 1982, around 9:00 P.M., Mrs. Campbell and her children returned home after visiting a relative. She stopped at her back step to talk to a neighbor. As they were talking, an explosion blew out the front living room window. There was no direct evidence of exactly what caused the explosion and fire. Shortly before the explosion, the defendants were observed near the scene and, within a few seconds of the explosion, running away from the smoking window. After an investigation the defendants were arrested and charged with various crimes in connection with the incident.

Legal Issues

The jury in the criminal trial found Poor and Tilton guilty of willfully throwing or placing explosives at or near persons or property and "interference with the civil rights of persons." It was the Commonwealth's theory that the crimes were racially motivated and that the defendants were engaged in a joint enterprise at the time the crimes were committed. During the trial, a Commonwealth witness testified that a few days before the explosion she heard Poor say to Tilton, "Well, why don't they just kill all the n——s." There was no response from Tilton. The judge ruled that the statement was admissible as evidence because it was "relevant as to the knowledge that Tilton might have had as to Mr. Poor's racial attitude" and that it was "material to show what each knew of the other's attitude toward . . . black residents." On appeal, Tilton argued that the admission of the statement against him was an error because Poor's statement had no relevance to the case against him.

Decision

The Massachusetts Court of Appeals noted that out-of-court statements of joint criminal venturers are admissible if made during the pendency of the criminal enterprise and in furtherance of it. The court held that the admission of this evidence was harmless in light of earlier testimony that about an hour before the explosion Tilton was heard to say, "The only way to get these f——g n——s out of here is to burn them out." The court also found that the judge did not err in admitting evidence of an earlier explosion which was relevant to show that the defendant possessed, or had access to, the means to commit the crime. Also, the court held that the defendant was not prejudiced by testimony by a witness that a few days before the bombing she had heard the codefendant, speaking to the defendant, make violent remarks against blacks—the judge's action in permitting the jury to consider this testimony against the defendant could not have prejudiced him in light of earlier testimony about the defendant's similar remarks.

Impact

The decision in the case of *Massachusetts v. Poor and Tilton* was reached several years before the modern era of federal and state hate-crimes legislation. It set an important precedent, however, in concluding that the racial views and opinions expressed by defendants—even when not made during the commission of a crime—are admissible as evidence supporting a guilty verdict on a civil rights charge.

NEW YORK V. GRUPE
NEW YORK CITY CRIMINAL COURT
532 N.Y.S.2D 815 (1988)

Background

A witness described the defendant, Peter Grupe, striking his victim while shouting ethnic slurs, including, "Is that the best you can do? I'll show you Jew b——d." Grupe was charged with aggravated harassment in the second degree (Penal Law 240.30 [3]) in that he allegedly made the assault while shouting ethnic slurs. Prior to this incident, the New York legislature had rewritten the criminal code to classify bias-motivated harassment as a Class A misdemeanor, punishable by up to one year in jail, while such conduct not motivated by bias remained a noncriminal offense punishable by up to 15 days.

Legal Issues

The relevant statute reads, "A person is guilty of aggravated harassment in the second degree when, with intent to harass, annoy, threaten or alarm another person, he . . . strikes, shoves, kicks, or otherwise subjects another person to physical contact, or attempts or threatens to do the same because of the race, color, religion or national origin of such person." Grupe moved to dismiss the charge on the ground that the statute violated his rights to freedom of speech and equal protection of the laws under the First and Fourteenth Amendments of the U.S. Constitution.

Decision

On August 17, 1988, Grupe's motion was denied. The New York City Criminal Court's opinion stated that "No First Amendment issue is raised since the intent of the statute is to prohibit violence and physical intimidation based upon bigotry. Even if defendant's behavior were considered expressive, violent demonstrations are not protected under the First Amendment, and constitutional guarantees of freedom of speech do not prevent states from punishing 'fighting words,' those by which their very utterance inflict injury or tend to incite an immediate breach of the peace. There is a compelling governmental interest in penalizing bias-related violence which is unrelated to the suppression of free expression, and the statute is narrowly drawn to apply only to those situations involving acts of violence or physical intimidation. . . . Furthermore, there is a rational basis for the Legislature to have concluded that the measure was necessary to redress past discrimination."

Impact

This decision drew on the landmark Supreme Court case of *Chaplinsky v. New Hampshire*, which found that "fighting words," or those intended to elicit a violent reaction, are not necessarily protected by the First Amendment. It paved the way for courts to find that certain expressions of bigotry, racism, and prejudice, like "fighting words," are prima facie evidence that a hate crime has been committed. When such expressions are made in the course of a crime such as a murder or assault, they may serve as grounds for separate hate-crime charges or penalty enhancement on ordinary criminal charges, as set down in the new state statutes and local ordinances. The issue of the constitutionality of such laws and prosecution would eventually be resolved by the U.S. Supreme Court decision in the case of *Wisconsin v. Mitchell*.

STATE OF OHIO V. WYANT
OHIO SUPREME COURT
624 N.E.2D 722 (1992)

Background

On the evening of June 2, 1989, David Wyant and his relatives were camping in Ohio's Alum Creek State Park. The adjoining campsite had been rented to Jerry White and his girlfriend, Patricia McGowan. White and McGowan are black; everyone in the Wyant party was white. Sometime between 10:30 and 11:45 P.M., White went to park officials to complain of loud music coming from the Wyant campsite. A park official went to site L-16 and asked Wyant to turn off the radio. Wyant complied.

Fifteen or 20 minutes later the radio came on again, and White and Mc-Gowan heard racial epithets and threats made in a loud voice by Wyant. Specifically, Wyant was heard to say: "We didn't have this problem until those n——— moved in next to us," "I ought to shoot that black moth-erf——," and "I ought to kick his black a—." White and McGowan complained to park officials and left the park.

Wyant was indicted and convicted on one count of ethnic intimidation, Ohio statute 2927.12, predicated on aggravated menacing, and sentenced to one and one-half years' imprisonment. The court of appeals affirmed the conviction. The case was then appealed to the Ohio Supreme Court.

Legal Issues

The Ohio statute set down enhanced criminal penalties for "aggravated menacing," "menacing," "criminal damaging or endangering," "criminal mischief" when motivated "by reason of the race, color, religion, or national origin of another person or group of persons." Although all these actions are punishable under ordinary criminal statutes, the Wyant case raised the question of whether an additional crime or penalty enhancement can be set down for a defendant's motive. In criminal law, motive can be presented as evidence of guilt, but normally is not punishable by itself, as it is considered thought and not conduct. Wyant's attorneys maintained that the statute violated the U.S. Constitution as well as the state constitution, which guarantees the freedom to "speak, write, and publish . . . sentiments on all subjects."

Decision

The Ohio Supreme Court found on August 26, 1992 that R.C. 2927.12 violated both the U.S. and Ohio constitutions. The court reversed the decision of the court of appeals, vacated Wyant's sentence on the conviction for ethnic intimidation, and remanded the case for sentencing on the charge of aggravated menacing. Part of the opinion in the case read: "Once the proscribed act is committed, the government criminalizes the underlying thought by enhancing the penalty based on viewpoint. This is dangerous. If the legislature can enhance a penalty for crimes committed 'by reason of' racial bigotry, why not 'by reason of' opposition to abortion, war, the elderly (or any other political or moral viewpoint)? If the thought or motive behind a crime can be separately punished, the legislative majority can punish virtually any viewpoint which it deems politically undesirable . . . applying these principles, we believe that the government is not free to punish an idea, though it may punish acts motivated by the idea. It may also punish unprotected speech expressing the idea."

Impact

In this case, the Ohio Supreme Court decided that Ohio's penalty enhancement law created a "thought crime," an unconstitutional restriction of speech and opinion. However, in the wake of the U.S. Supreme Court's decision in *Wisconsin v. Mitchell*, the case was vacated by the Supreme Court and remanded to the Ohio Supreme Court for reconsideration. This court would subsequently reverse its earlier decision, keeping alive the constitutional confusion and legal debate over hate-crimes law.

Hate Crimes

STATE OF OREGON V. SHAWN WAYNE HENDRIX
SUPREME COURT OF OREGON
838 P.2D 566 (1992)

Background

The defendant entered a store with several codefendants, who were in possession of weapons. After the codefendants observed that the store employees spoke little English, they made statements concerning the race and ethnic origins of the employees, and all defendants then proceeded to beat the victims while continuing to make the statements. The defendant was then convicted of first-degree intimidation under Oregon statute 166.165(1)(a)(A), which states that "Two or more persons acting together commit the crime of intimidation in the first degree, if the persons: Intentionally, knowingly, or recklessly cause physical injury to another because of their perception of that person's race, color, religion, national origin or sexual orientation. . ."

Legal Issues

Hendrix appealed the criminal court decision on the grounds of insufficient evidence, claiming that the state had failed to prove beyond a reasonable doubt that he had acted because of his perception of the victims' race or national origin. He also claimed that each defendant must have specific intent to act on prejudiced motive, and that since, according to testimony in the case, he had not made prejudiced statements before the criminal act, he could not be convicted under the statute in question. A state appeals court affirmed the conviction, and the case was appealed to the Oregon Supreme Court.

Decision

The Oregon Supreme Court affirmed the appeals court decision on August 27, 1992. The opinion read that "from [the defendant's conduct], the trier of fact reasonably could find beyond a reasonable doubt that defendant acted because of his perception of the victims' race or national origin." The justices agreed with the defendant that he had to have specific intent, and that such intent must be proven beyond a reasonable doubt. But the court also found that the evidence was sufficient to find that the defendant did indeed have the identical, biased intent of his codefendants in the case.

Impact

This decision upheld Oregon's ethnic intimidation statute, finding that those committing a hate crime in concert with others, although perhaps not

74

found to have prejudiced motives or intent themselves, may be found guilty of committing a bias-motivated crime.

MICHIGAN V. DAVID ALLEN RICHARDS, JR.
MICHIGAN COURT OF APPEALS
509 NW 2D 528 (1993)

Background

On May 7, 1990, Richards confronted and threatened an African-American couple while they were attempting to move out of their apartment. The threats included the following: "black motherf——r"; "black sons of b—— s"; "half-breed baby"; "[I'll] whip your black a—"; "[I'll] kill [your] n——r-loving whore." Richards pounded on the victims' door and said that he had a gun with him and had "shot motherf——s before." He also threatened to destroy the couple's property.

The victims made a couple of trips back and forth, and at one point Richards, his girlfriend, and another male approached the victims' vehicle. Richards's male companion had a stick, and the victims decided to drive off after Richards threatened to shoot them. The police arrived shortly thereafter, and Richards continued to shout racial epithets after he saw the police.

On October 2, 1990, a jury convicted Richards of ethnic intimidation (Michigan statutes 750.147b and 28.344(2)). On February 14, 1991, he was sentenced to one to two years of imprisonment. He then appealed the constitutionality of the ethnic intimidation statute.

Legal Issues

The defendant made what would become the standard objections to Michigan's ethnic intimidation statute: that it is overbroad because it sweeps protected speech within its reach; that it has a chilling effect on the speech of others; and that it is vague by not setting reasonably clear guidelines to prevent arbitrary prosecutions.

Decision

In its opinion of November 2, 1993, the Michigan Court of Appeals held that the U.S. Supreme Court's *Wisconsin v. Mitchell* decision disposed of the defendant's constitutional challenge based on the First Amendment. The appeals court judges wrote that "The Supreme Court opined that a defendant could be punished for a discriminatory motive because 'motive plays the same role under the Wisconsin statute as it does under federal and state antidiscrimination laws.'" Furthermore, the court concluded that the Wisconsin statute was aimed at conduct unprotected by the First Amendment.

With respect to Richards's vagueness argument, the court held that "a Michigan statute may be challenged if it is so indefinite that it confers unstructured and unlimited discretion on the trier of fact to determine whether an offense has been committed." In this case, the court found that the statute did not give unlimited discretion: "The statute is satisfied when there is evidence of an underlying predicate criminal act committed because of racial animosity. These elements are very clear and definite."

Impact

This decision took place in the immediate wake of the Supreme Court's *Wisconsin v. Mitchell* opinion and was one among hundreds of state-level cases that cited the Supreme Court in upholding ethnic intimidation statutes and hate-crimes convictions. As in many other such cases, the Michigan court drew a parallel between hate-crimes statutes and antidiscrimination laws, turning aside the argument that hate-crimes laws unconstitutionally punish speech. In the years to come, this argument would become one of the most common justifications for similar decisions across the country.

MISSOURI V. JASON THOMAS VANATTER
MISSOURI SUPREME COURT
869 SW 2D 754 (1994)

Background

On July 9, 1990, Jason Vanatter was arrested and charged with burning a wooden cross on the front porch of the Church of Christ, an African-American church in West Plains, Missouri. The state charged Vanatter with committing the crime of ethnic intimidation "in that defendant knowingly damaged the property of the Church of Christ, West Plains, to wit: the front porch of the Church of Christ located at Washington Avenue, Missouri by burning a wooden cross next to said porch."

Legal Issues

On October 14, 1992, Vanatter filed a motion to dismiss the charge, alleging that the ethnic intimidation statute under which he was charged (Missouri statute 574.093) violated the First Amendment to the U.S. Constitution and Article I, Section 8 of the Missouri Constitution. Relying on the U.S. Supreme Court decision in *R.A.V. v. St. Paul*, the trial court found that Section 574.093 violated the First Amendment and dismissed the ethnic intimidation charge against the defendant on January 22, 1993. The State of Missouri appealed, contending that the statute is constitutional and citing another Supreme Court case, *Wisconsin v. Mitchell*, in support of the statute's constitutionality.

Decision

On January 25, 1994, the Missouri Supreme Court affirmed the original conviction in this case, holding that "Crimes committed because of the perpetrator's hatred of the race, color, religion or national origin of the victim have the obvious tendency to ignite further violence by provoking retaliatory crimes and inciting community unrest. . . . The legislature of this state has determined that the commission of various crimes with a motive relating to the victim's race, color, religion, or national origin should be classified as ethnic intimidation and carry strict penalties." The court agreed that the Missouri statute is more similar to that upheld in *Wisconsin v. Mitchell* as it requires criminal conduct that is subject to criminal sanction and is not afforded First Amendment protection.

Impact

This case brought the two landmark Supreme Court hate-crimes decisions—*R.A.V. v. St. Paul* (which struck down a hate-crimes law) and *Wisconsin v. Mitchell* (which upheld one)—into close contention. The lawyers and justices in the Missouri case had to walk a very fine line in arguing and then deciding whether the defendant's conduct or thought was actually being punished. The final decision cited not only actual arson damage to the property in question but also the state's compelling interest in preventing further outbreaks of violence after a hate crime has been committed. By this time, the *Wisconsin v. Mitchell* decision was gaining precedence in state court decisions regarding hate crimes, which as a result were tending toward uniformity of language and successful prosecution.

STATE OF FLORIDA V. RICHARD STALDER
SUPREME COURT OF FLORIDA
630 SO.2D 1072 (1994)

Background

Herbert Cohen and a friend, Denise Avard, went to Richard Stalder's home on April 14, 1991, to retrieve Avard's earrings. Stalder assaulted Cohen and maligned his Jewish heritage. When Stalder answered the door, he stated, "Hey Jew boy, what do you want?" Cohen replied that he was looking for Avard's earrings. Stalder then started to yell statements to the victim about his Jewish descent, at one point pushing Cohen.

Stalder was charged with violating Section 784.03(1), Florida Statutes (1989) (simple battery) for pushing Cohen, and the penalty was subject to reclassification pursuant to Section 775.085(1) (Florida's hate-crime enhancement statute) from a first-degree misdemeanor to a third-degree felony.

Legal Issues

Stalder contended that Florida's hate-crime enhancement statute is both vague and overbroad and punishes pure thought and expression in violation of the First Amendment of the Constitution. The trial court granted Stalder's pretrial motion to dismiss the enhancement charge, adopting Stalder's argument that the statute violates the free-speech clause. The state appealed, contending that Section 775.085 is neither unconstitutionally vague nor overbroad—the statute simply enhances punishment for those crimes that are committed because the victim has one of several identified characteristics. It was the State's position that the statute punishes criminal action, not speech, and thus does not implicate the First Amendment.

Decision

On January 27, 1994, the Florida Supreme Court agreed with the state and upheld Stalder's conviction.

Impact

The two sides in this case were litigating not just constitutional issues but also the question of how severe hate-crimes penalty enhancements can be. The outcome was positive for those favoring tough hate-crimes laws. In its decision, the Florida Supreme Court accepted the state's argument that bias motivation can turn an action normally punishable as a misdemeanor into a felony.

NEW JERSEY V. VAWTER AND KEARNS
NEW JERSEY SUPREME COURT
136 N.J. 56 (1994)

Background

On May 13, 1991, a person or persons spray painted a Nazi swastika and words appearing to read "Hitler Rules" on a synagogue, Congregation B'nai Israel, in the town of Rumson, New Jersey. On that same night the same person or persons also spray painted a satanic pentagram on the driveway of a Roman Catholic church, the Church of the Nativity, in the neighboring town of Fair Haven.

Stephen Vawter and David Kearns were charged with four counts of putting another in fear of violence by placement of a symbol or graffiti on property, a third-degree offense; four counts of defacement; two counts of third-degree criminal mischief; and two counts of conspiracy to commit the offenses charged in counts one through 10, under New Jersey statutes 2C:33-10 (Section 10) and Section 11, New Jersey's hate-crimes laws.

Section 10 reads as follows: "A person is guilty of a crime of the third degree if he purposely, knowingly or recklessly puts or attempts to put another in fear of bodily violence by placing on public or private property a symbol, an object, a characterization, an appellation or graffiti that exposes another to threats of violence, contempt or hatred on the basis of race, color, creed or religion, including, but not limited to[,] a burning cross or Nazi swastika. A person shall not be guilty of an attempt unless his actions cause a serious and imminent likelihood of causing fear of unlawful bodily violence."

Section 11 provides that "A person is guilty of a crime of the fourth degree if he purposely defaces or damages, without authorization of the owner or tenant, any private premises or property primarily used for religious, educational, residential, memorial, charitable, or cemetery purposes, or for assembly by persons of a particular race, color, creed or religion by placing thereon a symbol, an object, a characterization, an appellation, or graffiti that exposes another to threat of violence, contempt or hatred on the basis of race, color, creed or religion, including, but not limited to, a burning cross or Nazi swastika."

At their trial, the defendants moved to dismiss counts one through eight of the indictment on the ground that Sections 10 and 11 violate their First and Fourteenth Amendment rights under the U.S. Constitution. In denying defendants' motion to dismiss the first eight counts of the indictment, the trial court held that Sections 10 and 11 were violations of their constitutional right to free speech. The state appealed this decision, and the New Jersey Supreme Court then addressed the defendants' constitutional challenge to the New Jersey statutes.

Legal Issues

The basic legal issue at stake was the circumstance under which speech, more specifically, the expression of a threat, can be prosecuted as a criminal act. The state of New Jersey argued that because Sections 10 and 11 regulate only threats of violence, a class of speech that has been found unprotected by the Constitution, the laws fall within the first exception for content discrimination, in which an entire class of speech can be held as illegal.

Decision

On May 26, 1994, the court found that Sections 10 and 11 do not increase the penalty for an underlying offense because of a motive grounded in bias; rather, those sections make criminal the expressions of hate themselves, particularly in view of the fact that New Jersey already had statutes proscribing conduct such as criminal mischief, defacement of property, placing of symbols, arson, and trespass.

Impact

The New Jersey court's decision struck down Sections 10 and 11 of the state's criminal code as regulating expression protected by the First Amendment: "We conclude that sections 10 and 11 are content-based restrictions. In adopting those sections the Legislature was obviously expressing its disagreement with the message conveyed by the conduct that the statutes regulate." The court also found that even if Sections 10 and 11 were construed to proscribe only threats of violence, another problem would arise: the statutes proscribe threats "on the basis of race, color, creed or religion." Under the Supreme Court's ruling in *R.A.V. v. St. Paul*, that limitation makes the statutes viewpoint discriminatory and thus impermissible. Although a statute may prohibit threats, it may not confine the prohibition to threats based on their objectionable content. Because Sections 10 and 11 limit their scope to the topics of race, color, creed, and religion, the statutes were found unconstitutional.

Ayers v. Maryland
Maryland Court of Appeals
645 A.2d 22 (1994)

Background

On the evening of March 2, 1992, John Randolph Ayers, age 22, and a friend, Sean Riley, age 20, were at Ayers's home, in the Aspen Hill section of Silver Spring, Maryland, assembling a shed in the backyard and drinking beer. They worked on the shed until about 10:30 P.M. Later, they discussed an incident of racial confrontation that had occurred at an area 7-Eleven store several nights earlier, an incident in which Ayers was involved. Ayers and Riley left Ayers's house at 2 A.M. on March 3 to look for black people to beat up. They soon observed two black women walking on Georgia Avenue. They stopped their vehicle and began walking behind the women. After the women began to run, the two men chased them. The women separated.

Riley chased one of the women, Myrtle Guillory; Ayers chased the other, Johnnie Mae McCrae. Guillory testified at the trial that as she ran she looked back, saw Ayers grab McCrae and heard McCrae scream. She testified that as Riley chased her, he yelled repeatedly, "I'm going to kill you, you black b——h." She said Riley grabbed her from behind, but she got away when he was distracted by a passing car. Guillory said she ran toward the home of David Davis, a friend. When Guillory reached Davis's yard, she began screaming for help. She ran up to the porch and began banging on the door. Davis opened the door and Riley fled. McCrae testified that as she ran from Ayers, she fell, and Ayers grabbed her by the back of her coat collar and dragged her into the woods. She said that he began "banging her head" and told her he was going to kill her.

Ayers was found guilty of assault, assault with intent to maim, kidnapping, conspiracy to commit a racially motivated crime, and committing a racially motivated crime in violation of Maryland statute section 470A (b)(3)(i). He was sentenced to 10 years for conspiracy to commit a racially motivated crime against Guillory. He was further sentenced to 10 years for assault with intent to maim McCrae (the assault conviction was merged into the aggravated assault conviction); 30 years for kidnapping McCrae; and 10 years for committing a racially motivated crime against McCrae. The court directed that the sentences run consecutively, for a total of 60 years.

Legal Issues

Ayers appealed his conviction, arguing that Section 470A violates the First and Fourteenth Amendments to the U.S. Constitution because that part of the statute which prohibits harassment of someone because of race, color, religious beliefs or national origin is unconstitutionally vague and overbroad. He also argued that the "harass" prong of the statute is a content-based regulation of speech that cannot be justified by the state, maintaining that the state could better advance its interest in deterring bias-motivated crime by instead enacting a penalty-enhancement statute.

Ayers also contended that the trial court erred in allowing irrelevant and prejudicial evidence (the 7-Eleven incident) to be introduced against him. He argued that the evidence of the February 29 incident at the 7-Eleven store was prejudicial because of the danger of it being considered as indicative of a propensity on his part to commit a racially motivated crime. Ayers claims also that there was legally insufficient evidence to convict him under Section 470A because the only evidence that his acts of March 3 were racially motivated came from his accomplice, Riley. Consequently, Ayers suggested that his conviction violates a longstanding rule that a person may not be convicted upon the uncorroborated testimony of an accomplice.

Ayers also argued that the court abused its discretion in sentencing him to 60 years imprisonment, asserting that the sentence was so oppressive as to constitute cruel and unusual punishment under the Eighth Amendment to the Federal Constitution and Articles 16 and 25 of the Maryland Declaration of Rights.

Decision

In its decision of July 21, 1994, the Maryland Court of Appeals found that Ayers was convicted of committing several distinct crimes in addition to the conviction under Section 470A. Because Ayers did not challenge the evidence that supported those convictions, he was found guilty of not only committing the underlying crimes but also of committing them "because of [the victim's] race." The court concluded that Ayers lacked standing to challenge the statute facially on the basis that the harassment prong of Section 470A is vague and overbroad. In addition, the court held that the evidence of Ayers's participation in the February 29 altercation at the 7-Eleven store (and the racial nature of the incident) was admissible because it was relevant to motive, and that admitting the evidence regarding the 7-Eleven incident did not violate the First Amendment, nor did it violate the rule which generally prohibits the introduction of "other crimes evidence."

The court found that the sentences imposed for the crimes against Mc-Crae—assault with intent to maim, kidnapping, and committing a racially motivated crime—were not grossly disproportionate; it also found that the 10-year sentence for conspiracy to commit a racially motivated crime against Guillory was not grossly disproportionate.

Impact

The decision upheld Maryland's hate-crimes statutes and reinforced the ability of state prosecutors to introduce evidence of bias not directly linked to the crime in question.

PENNSYLVANIA V. DUANE BURLINGAME, TERRY ORNDORFF, AND CLYDE HARRIS
SUPREME COURT OF PENNSYLVANIA
672 A.2D 813 (1996)

Background

On August 30, 1994, Burlingame, Orndorff, and Harris were picketing in front of the Caterpillar heavy-equipment manufacturing plant in York, Pennsylvania, where Caterpillar and the United Auto Workers (UAW) were in the midst of a labor dispute. As workers who had crossed the picket lines were attempting to drive away from the plant at the end of their shift, the defendants allegedly approached the workers' cars, pointed fingers at the workers, and screamed insults, some of which included racial epithets. In addition, one of the defendants, Clyde E. Harris, allegedly spit on a car. The Court of Common Pleas of York County found that the defendants' actions constituted a violation of Pennsylvania Statute 2709(a)(3), which states that "a person commits the crime of harassment when, with intent to harass, annoy or alarm another person, he engages in a course of conduct or repeatedly commits acts which alarm or seriously annoy such other person and which serve no legitimate purpose." They were also charged with ethnic intimidation.

The court also found, however, that since appellees were parties to a labor dispute at the time they engaged in such conduct, the provisions of section 2709(e) required dismissal of the harassment charges. Subsection (e) of the statute was added by the Pennsylvania legislature in 1993 and reads:

"This section shall not apply to conduct by a party to a labor dispute . . . or to any constitutionally protected activity." The Commonwealth of Pennsylvania then appealed.

Legal Issues

The appellees argued that since the actions that gave rise to the harassment charges constituted conduct by a party to a labor dispute, the prosecution was barred by the provisions of section 2709(e), and that since ethnic intimidation cannot stand alone as a separate offense, that charge should also be dismissed.

Decision

On March 5, 1996, the Pennsylvania Supreme Court agreed with the defendants in this case. The opinion read, in part: ". . . the Commonwealth contends that the trial court erred in its application of section 2709(e). It argues that the language of section 2709(e) is ambiguous . . . However . . . when the words of a statute are clear and unambiguous, we must give effect to their plain meaning. Section 2709(e) provides, quite simply, that section 2709 of the Crimes Code, which defines the crime of harassment, does not apply to conduct by a party to a labor dispute as that term is defined by the Labor Anti-Injunction Act. Since it is beyond question that Appellees' conduct, however offensive, occurred during a labor dispute to which they were parties, it is shielded from prosecution under the harassment statute and the charges were properly dismissed."

Impact

The Pennsylvania case offers an example of a hate-crimes statute that cannot stand alone. The state supreme court found that an underlying criminal act, enforceable under ordinary statutes, must be committed before a hate crime can be charged and penalty enhancement be applied. In this case, however, the charges were dismissed, as the harassment occurred under circumstances that barred prosecution—therefore the hate-crimes charges also failed.

STATE OF ILLINOIS V. B.C. ET AL. (MINORS)
SUPREME COURT OF ILLINOIS
680 N.E. 2D 1355 (MAY 22, 1997)

Background

The state filed hate-crimes charges against the juvenile defendants, referred to as B.C. and T.C. in court documents, for allegedly committing disorderly conduct on October 14, 1994, by displaying "patently offensive depictions of violence toward African Americans. . . . The alleged depictions consisted of a hand drawing of an eerily smiling, hooded Ku Klux klansman who held an axe-like object from which drops of blood apparently fell. At the klansman's feet lay the prone body of a dark complexioned person. . ."

The defendants were accused of violating Section 12-7.1(a) of the state's criminal code. This hate-crimes statute borrowed from the Anti-Defamation League's model legislation and states, in part, that "A person commits a hate crime when, by reason of the actual or perceived race, color, creed, religion, ancestry, gender, sexual orientation, physical or mental disability, or national origin of another individual or group of individuals, he commits assault, battery, aggravated assault, misdemeanor or theft, criminal trespass to residence, misdemeanor criminal damage to property, criminal trespass to vehicle, criminal trespass to real property, mob action or disorderly conduct. . ." The phrase "actual or perceived" [race, color, and so on] was added to the law in 1994.

At the preliminary hearing, the parties stipulated that James Jeffries—a vice principal at the defendants' school (and listed as the victim on the criminal complaint)—was not an African American, nor did the defendants perceive him to be, but that other unnamed individuals who were African Americans were present at the time of the alleged offense. Also, such unnamed individuals were not identified in the petitions as victims. It was also stipulated that the allegedly patently offensive depictions of violence toward African Americans were confiscated from the respondents. The depictions were subsequently admitted without objection.

The circuit court dismissed the petitions for failure to state an offense, finding that the charges could not be sustained because Jeffries was not actually and was not perceived to be, by defendants, a member of the protected classifications, a necessary element of the offense of hate crime. The state appealed the dismissals. On review, the appellate court reasoned that if the victim of a hate crime was not, or at least thought to be, a member of the targeted group, under the statute, the word *perceived* within the provision would be superfluous. The appellate court affirmed the dismissal of the petitions because Jeffries was not, and was not perceived to be, African American.

The Illinois Supreme Court then heard the state's appeal of these decisions.

Legal Issues

The Illinois Supreme Court had to decide whether Section 12-7.1(a) of the state's Criminal Code requires that the victim of the offense be the individual whose actual or perceived race provided reason for the offense.

Alongside this issue was that of First Amendment protection for speech and opinion, in the form of the drawings in question, which the defendants held were constitutionally protected.

The state claimed that the hate-crime statute intends to focus on the accused's motive and conduct, and not on the status or the perceived status of any victim or victims. Further, according to the state, the provision includes no language that suggests that an accused's bias-motivated actions must be directed against even a particular victim in order for a hate crime to occur. The state claims that by inclusion of the phrase "actual or perceived," the legislature intended to focus not on the victim's status, but rather on the defendant's motivation.

The defendants maintained that a person cannot be a "victim" of a hate crime when the offender's improper bias in committing the underlying crime is not directed against that individual or the class to which he belongs. Thus, as applied to this case, James Jeffries cannot be the victim of a hate crime because the racially offensive materials were not directed against either him or his race.

Decision

On May 22, 1997, the court held that under Section 12-7.1(a), the victim of a bias-motivated crime does not have to actually belong to the protected group, either in fact or simply as perceived by the perpetrator. In their opinion, the justices stated that "the plain language of the hate crime statute states that the offense is committed when a person commits one of the underlying predicate offenses 'by reason of the actual or perceived race' . . . the statute includes no expression that the victim or complainant of the underlying offense must be that individual or of that group of individuals . . . In our view, the legislative history supports, instead, a generally more expansive meaning of the statute . . . the primary focus of the statute was intended to be directed towards the biased motivation of the perpetrator, rather than towards the status of the victim of the hate crime statute. . ."

A dissenting opinion held that the drawings in question, although offensive, fall "within that class of expression which the Supreme Court [in *R.A.V. v. St. Paul*] has declared 'government may not regulate based on hostility—or favoritism—towards the underlying message expressed' . . . The charge of disorderly conduct also does not pass constitutional scrutiny on the basis that the drawings depict or advocate violence."

Impact

The decision in this case broadened the state's powers to prosecute hate crimes, in that the protected status of the victims would now take second place to the motivations of the accused hate-crime offenders.

Hate Crimes

U.S. v. MACHADO
UNITED STATES DISTRICT COURT
SOUTHERN DISTRICT OF CALIFORNIA
SACR 96-142-AHS (1998)

Background

On Friday, September 20, 1996, 59 Asian-American students at the University of California, Irvine (UC Irvine) received identical e-mail messages, sent from an anonymous source, that read as follows:

Hey Stupid F——er:
    *As you can see in the name, I hate Asians, including you. If it weren't for asias at UCI, it would be a much more popular campus. You are responsible for ALL the crimes that occur on campus. YOU are responsible for the campus being all dirt. YOU ARE RESPONSIBLE. That's why I want you and your stupid a—— comrades to get the f—— out of UCI. If you don't I will hunt you down and kill your stupid a——. Do you hear me? I personally will make it my life career to find and kill everyone of you personally. OK??????
That's how determined I am.*
Get the f—— out.
Mother F—— (Asian Hater).

Several of the recipients reported the e-mail message to the UC Irvine Office of Academic Computing (OAC). An investigation of the e-mails showed that the sender had pulled up a list of all people then online at the time, and from that list selected 59 individuals based on their apparently Asian surnames. The user IDs were then entered into the "To:" field and sent to these users. The OAC immediately determined the identity of the sender: Richard Machado, a 19-year old student and naturalized U.S. citizen originally from El Salvador. Still at work in the computer lab at the time, Machado was asked to leave.

According to OAC's Computer and Network Policy, users may not "[use] computers or electronic mail to act abusively toward others or to provoke a violent reaction, such as stalking, acts of bigotry, threats of violence, or other hostile or intimidating 'fighting words.' Such words include those terms widely recognized to victimize or stigmatize individuals on the basis of race, ethnicity, religion, sex, sexual orientation, disability, and other protected characteristics."

The incident was reported to the campus police department, and campus police interviewed Machado on September 28. On meeting with a police officer, Machado admitted sending the e-mails out of frustration over the number of Asian-descended students on the UC Irvine campus (where the Asian-American population made up about half of the student body), over problems with his Asian roommate, and over his belief that Asian students were given preferential treatment.

Based on the suspected violation of the federal statute banning interference with federally protected activities (including attendance at a public educational institution), the Los Angeles FBI office began an investigation of the case on October 3. Machado was indicted by a federal grand jury but failed to respond to a summons to appear before a federal magistrate on November 25. A warrant was issued for his arrest, and Machado was finally apprehended on February 6, 1997, in Nogales, Arizona.

At his trial, which began on November 11, 1997, Machado pleaded not guilty to 10 counts of violation of Title 18, Section 245(b)2(A), Interference with Federally Protected Activities.

Legal Issues

The Machado case was a precedent-setting trial of hate crime committed on the Internet. Machado's defense team argued that his e-mail message was nothing more than a common online prank, a flame, in which the sender composes an inflammatory, obscenity-laced message with the intention of aggravating or intimidating the recipient. The defense also argued that the Internet, as a fairly new, open, and often anonymous means of communication, allows the airing of extreme opinions and that such speech, although unpleasant and sometimes racist in nature, should be protected by the First Amendment. The defense argued that the charges against Machado could have a chilling effect on free speech, as it is sometimes conducted on the Internet, and criminalizes thoughts rather than criminal actions. The defense also presented into evidence a questionnaire distributed to the recipients of Machado's e-mail, in which several answered that they had not felt directly threatened by the message, and that only 10 of the 59 recipients considered the threat serious enough to press charges against Machado.

The prosecution in the case argued that any threat against life that can reasonably be taken as serious by the recipient of an e-mail should be punishable just as such a threat would be if uttered in public or sent through the regular mail. The fact that the e-mail had been sent only to recipients with Asian surnames made it a case of a civil rights violation based on ethnicity. The prosecution also introduced evidence that Machado, using his roommate's computer, had previously used e-mail to send a threat to a campus newspaper.

Decision

The trial of Richard Machado began on November 4, 1997, in the U.S. District Court, Southern District of California. However, after three days of deliberations, the jury announced that it was deadlocked, 9 to 3, and could not reach a unanimous verdict. A mistrial was declared, but as Machado was considered a flight risk, he was denied bail and detained. A second trial began on January 27, 1998, in which Machado was charged with two counts of federal civil rights violations: sending the e-mail threats based on the ethnicity of the recipients and interfering with their federally protected right to attend a public educational institution. The jury in this case deliberated for a day before reaching a unanimous verdict of guilty on February 13, 1998. As Machado had already spent more than a year in prison, and the sentencing guidelines call for a prison term of a year for his conviction, he was released but fined $1,000, asked to attend racial tolerance counseling, banned from the UC Irvine campus, banned from the use of UC Irvine computers, and barred from any contact with the e-mail recipients.

Impact

The Machado decision was the first to set legal standards for content on the Internet. It followed the first Internet "hate crime" prosecution, in which violating federal civil rights statutes by e-mail put this communication medium on the same legal footing as regular mail or the telephone.

STATE OF WASHINGTON V. DAWSON
WASHINGTON COURT OF APPEALS
NO. 38411-2-I (1998)

Background

On the evening of November 3, 1995, at about 10 P.M., Corey Baker and Carolyn Crawford were leaving a college party in Bellingham, Washington. As they approached their vehicle, they encountered a group of whites standing in front of it. Baker asked the group if everything was okay. He looked around the front of the vehicle to see if there was a dent, and asked if the car parked in front of it had backed into it. Someone from the group said, "Yeah, there's a problem, n——r."

The group started walking toward Baker. Further racial slurs were directed at Baker. He backed up, put his hands in the air, and said there was no problem. Without seeing what happened, Baker heard and felt a blow from a 40-ounce beer bottle when it hit him in the face, fracturing his cheekbone. Baker ran. His companion, Crawford, ran after him. The group chased her, shouting racial epithets directed at her association with Baker. Other people from the college party responded to the situation and a fight ensued until the police arrived about 10 minutes later.

To police, Crawford pointed out individuals, later identified as Banner Dawson and Jason LaRue, as the instigators of the attack on Baker, and pointed to Dawson as the person who hit Baker with the bottle.

Legal Issues

The state charged Dawson with malicious harassment and a racially motivated assault. Before the trial began, the court, over Dawson's objection, granted the state's motion for an order directing the jail to shave Dawson's head so the state could inspect a tattoo on his scalp. A jury then convicted Dawson on both counts, and he appealed. Dawson contended that evidence of the tattoo was not material to the crimes charged and therefore should not have been admitted as evidence at his trial.

Decision

The Washington Court of Appeals affirmed the convictions for a racially motivated assault on January 26, 1998. The opinion stated, in part:

> *In a prosecution for malicious harassment, evidence of expressions or associations of the accused may not be introduced as substantive evidence at trial unless the evidence specifically relates to the crime charged. But in this case the State knew that Dawson had a tattoo on his scalp, and, having collected white supremacist materials in his possession, the State reasonably suspected that Dawson's tattoo might have been an expression of racist sentiments directed against African-Americans. If so, Dawson's tattoo would have specifically related to the crime charged because it would have tended to prove that Dawson had a racial motive in selecting Baker, an African-American, as a victim. The tattoo did not need to be directed personally at the victim, as Dawson argues, to be . . . admissible at trial. The tattoo may have been relevant to prove Dawson assaulted Baker because of his . . . perception of the victim's race.*

Impact

The *Washington v. Dawson* decision touched on the problem of evidence of motive, a sticking point in the prosecution of many hate-crimes cases. Assaults and other crimes are often accompanied by racial epithets, name-calling, and so forth, yet such speech does not necessarily prove that the defendant had a biased motive, or had selected his or her victim on the basis of race, religion, national origin, and so on. Such vagueness in the law is a common objection raised by those who generally oppose hate-crimes statutes, and the investigation of this case, in which a tattoo was used as evidence of biased motive, is sometimes cited in such objections.

MARTINEZ V. TEXAS
TEXAS COURT OF APPEALS
980 S.W. 2D 662 (1998)

Background

On the morning of June 20, 1994, Cindy Harris discovered her two-year old son, Johnny Vasquez, lying dead, face down on the top bunk of her children's bunk bed. The death, due to blunt abdominal trauma, was ruled a homicide by the Bexar County Assistant Medical Examiner, Dr. Jan Garavaglia.

Pablo Martinez was then indicted for capital murder under Texas Penal Code Section 19.03(a)(8) for the murder of a child under six years of age. At the criminal trial, the evidence showed that Martinez lived with Cindy Harris and her three children approximately three to five months prior to Johnny's death. Harris testified that Martinez expressed to her his dislike for Johnny because of the color of Johnny's skin, and that a dark birthmark over one eye was evidence that Johnny's father was African American.

Following the jury's verdict of guilty on the lesser offense of serious bodily injury to a child based on reckless conduct, the trial judge entered a finding that Martinez committed the offense because of bias or prejudice based on sex and race, and enhanced the punishment range to that of a second-degree felony, and so instructed the jury. The jury assessed punishment at the maximum penalty of 20 years' imprisonment and imposed a $10,000 fine.

Legal Issues

Martinez appealed his sentence, arguing that the evidence was insufficient to show that he intentionally selected Johnny as a victim because of a bias or prejudice, and that there was no evidence of a causal connection between his alleged bias and Johnny's fatal injury. In the appeal, the state argued that the record contained sufficient evidence to support the sentence enhancement under the statute.

In their published opinion, the appeals court judges quoted the trial judge as follows: "Well, the jury has found that the Defendant killed this child, caused the death of this child. This child is a male child. The evidence adduced by the Defense has shown relationships with female children not with male children. It's a male child that bared a birthmark and that the Defendant perceived as being of a dark race, or at least accused or called or classified that. So, in looking for a motive of why someone would torment a child for five months, eventually causing the death of that child in the fashion that we have heard in this Court, this Court is of the opinion that this Defendant selected this child in a biased and prejudiced fashion based both on sex and race."

Decision

The Texas Court of Appeals affirmed the trial judgment on July 22, 1998. According to the appeals court, the hate-crime punishment enhancement may be assessed when the assailant acted because of the victim's perceived race or color. Its opinion read, in part: "Although Johnny was not African-American, the State presented sufficient evidence through Cindy Harris' testimony from which a rational trier of fact could have found beyond a reasonable doubt that Martinez was biased against African-American people and that Martinez's pattern of abuse against Johnny was because he associated Johnny with the African-American race."

Further, the court held that the punishment enhancement may be based upon circumstantial evidence of the appellant's bias or prejudice motive, including previous racial epithets directed at the victim. "This evidence provides a sufficient basis from which the trial court could reasonably conclude that this bias or prejudice was the intentional motivation of the crime for which Martinez was convicted. . . . While the evidence does not directly show that Martinez acted out of any bias or prejudice at the time he caused the fatal injury to Johnny, such inference may be reasonably drawn from the proven pattern of abuse based on bias or prejudice."

Impact

The Martinez case extended culpability for a hate crime to those who, even if mistakenly, perceive their victims to be members of protected groups and who act on prejudice against such groups. The circumstantial evidence applied against the defendant would also make it easier to win a conviction on hate-crimes charges, even when the crime itself shows no direct evidence of prejudiced motive through the speech or actions of the defendant.

Tennessee v. Bakenhus
Tennessee Criminal Appeals Court
No. 01C01-9705-CC-00165 (1999)

Background

During the early morning hours of August 4, 1994, James L. Johnson and his family were awakened by a loud noise. Johnson told his wife to call 911, got a gun, and went to investigate. When he opened his front door, Johnson discovered his garage on fire and then noticed someone in a small white car drive by several times. Sometime after daylight, Johnson discovered melted siding and burned shutters. He found broken liquor bottles in the flowerbed and smelled gasoline or diesel fuel. Johnson found a hate letter in his mailbox and noticed eight or 10 small holes in his front gutter, which appeared to be caused by a shotgun blast.

This incident was followed by several more burglaries and arsons in the area. At one point, Robert Smith, a local newspaper photographer, received an anonymous phone call. The caller claimed that "A.F." was responsible for burning a house and that if the "n—— in the area didn't get out of the area, then he was going to kill them all."

Hate Crimes

Brian Beuscher had been introduced to the defendant, John Jason Bakenhus, in late July 1994 by a mutual friend, Charles Neblett. Beuscher recalled that the defendant, then 21 years old, was attempting to organize a group that would conduct acts of violence against African Americans and Hispanics in return for payment. Beuscher, age 16 at the time, signed an oath and joined the group. Five other members between the ages of 14 and 16 were also recruited by the defendant. Beuscher testified that he, Neblett, and the defendant prepared Molotov cocktails by filling liquor bottles with gasoline and inserting a cloth wick. They also had ski masks and gloves, a shotgun, and a note Beuscher had written at the direction of the defendant: "Dear Johnsons, A.F. wants you to leave our white community! You coons! Coon hunting season is open! A.F."

On August 4, the defendant was stopped in his vehicle, whereupon he consented to a search. Accelerants were discovered. Eventually, the defendant confessed. His statement led to the discovery of pawn tickets, a shotgun, number six and eight shells, and empty cans of spray paint. Police detectives took the defendant's briefcase from the garage of his father's house. It contained organization rules, regulations, oath, and a membership list. There were manuals on bomb making and war devices and a piece of paper listing types of grenades and explosives. Officers photographed a painting of a Nazi swastika on the wall of the defendant's bedroom. The defendant provided investigators with a small notebook containing hand drawings of a hooded Ku Klux Klan member lynching a man.

In his statements to Detective Clifton Smith, the defendant denied having animosity toward African Americans but acknowledged that he despised interracial marriages. Although he initially denied membership in an extremist organization, he inquired whether Detective Smith had found a note in a mailbox, whether anyone had called the newspaper, and whether any graffiti had been found on a roadway or building. Detective Smith reviewed the membership list, contacted and interviewed the members, and finally confronted the defendant, who then admitted his guilt.

Bakenhus was indicted for aggravated arson, two counts of arson, three counts of civil rights intimidation, aggravated burglary, theft of property over $500 and theft of property under $500. The jury returned guilty verdicts on all nine counts. The defendant was convicted for the same acts in federal court.

Legal Issues

In his appeal, the defendant argued, among other defenses, that the trial court erred by admitting a photograph of a swastika and a sketch of a Ku Klux Klan lynching.

Decision

The appeals court affirmed the criminal court decision on January 11, 1999, ruling that ". . .the photograph and sketch are valuable to prove the defendant's intent to intimidate his victims because of their race. While we concede that the exhibits may be offensive and crude, any prejudice is outweighed by their significant probative value as to the charged offense." The criminal trial verdict of guilty was affirmed.

Impact

This decision is one of many in state appeals courts that deal with the admissibility of racist signs, symbols, tattoos, and other accoutrements in proving a charge of bias motivation. State prosecutors in many cases have called such evidence forward in order to prove that a hate crime has taken place, especially when the state of mind of the defendant at the time of the crime cannot be shown through speech or action. In general, the courts have taken the position that such evidence can be taken into account when race is an issue in the crime, and when its probative value outweighs its prejudicial effect on the defendant's rights. If the purpose of such evidence is merely to undermine the character of the defendants, and it has no relevance to the defendant's mens rea (state of mind) at the time of the crime, then in general it is ruled inadmissible.

NEW JERSEY V. DOWELL ET AL.
NEW JERSEY SUPERIOR COURT
756 A.2D 1087 (2000)

Background

The Monmouth County Grand Jury indicted the defendants for kidnapping, conspiracy to commit same, aggravated assault and harassment by bias intimidation (New Jersey statutes 2C:12-1(e) and 2C:33-4(d)), terroristic threats, weapons offenses, and aggravated criminal sexual contact.

The victim, E.K. in court documents, was 23 years old at the time of the alleged assault. He was learning disabled, of low I.Q., exceptionally short in stature, deaf in one ear, and speech impaired. He had a pinhole defect in his heart. E.K. and some of the defendants attended special education classes together. Over a three-day period in January 1999, it was alleged that E.K. was kidnapped, forced to drink a mixture of iced tea and alcohol, and taped to a chair. He had his head and eyebrows shaved and was punched about his face and body, forced to drink urine, kiss the shoes of the defendants, lick a drink off the floor, and dress in women's clothing. He was beaten with beads and a curtain rod and had lit cigarettes put out on his chest, ashes flicked into his mouth, and a pillowcase placed over his head. Ultimately he was dumped into a deserted wooded area known as the "pit."

Legal Issues

According to New Jersey law, a defendant may be sentenced to an extended term of imprisonment if "the defendant in committing the crime acted with the purpose to intimidate an individual or group of individuals because of race, color, gender, handicap, religion, sexual orientation or ethnicity." When the New Jersey hate-crimes statutes were amended in 1997 to add gender and handicap as categories, the legislation did not define handicap or declare the legislature's intent.

Decision

In this case of first impression (meaning a statute or legal issue is being visited for the first time), the New Jersey Superior Court held on March 16, 2000, that the word *handicap* is not unconstitutionally vague both as applied or on its face. The superior court quoted the New Jersey Law Against Discrimination (Section 10:5-1), which defines handicap as "suffering from physical disability, infirmity, malformation or disfigurement which is caused by bodily injury, birth defect or illness, which shall include, but is not limited to, lack of physical coordination, blindness, or visual impediment, deafness or hearing impediment, speech impediment, any mental, psychological or neurological condition."

The court also held that a disability, disease, or defect must be of such a nature that a reasonable person in the position of the defendants would be on fair notice that their victim was handicapped: "Giving the state the benefit of the reasonable inferences of the evidence presented to the grand jury, E.K. falls within the definition of 'handicap' and the statutes in question are not vague facially or as applied to this case." The defendants' motion to dismiss the indictment was denied.

Impact

The decision in this case gave further impetus to hate-crimes prosecutions on behalf of the disabled, an important recent issue in the debate over hate-crimes law. The decision answered critics who maintain that the definition of *handicapped* or *disabled* is vague and open to a too-broad interpretation by police, prosecutors, and the courts.

CALIFORNIA V. CARR
CALIFORNIA COURT OF APPEAL
81 CAL. APP. 4TH 837 (2000)

Background

On the night of May 19, 1998, David Shostak, who is Jewish, was at his Huntington Beach, California, home with his wife Barbara, their 15-year-old son Jarod, and another son. David Shostak was just about to turn in when he noticed flames in his yard. When he looked outside, he saw a seven-foot cross burning on the side of his house. He sprinted to the cross, knocked it to the ground, and extinguished the flames with his garden hose.

An investigation into the matter led the police to Daniel Carr. A high school senior at the time, he had bragged to friends about burning a cross on "some Jew's lawn." He also responded with glee when shown a newspaper article about the incident. When the police searched his bedroom, they found Nazi paraphernalia and an American flag containing the initials S.W.P., which, according to an expert on racist ideology, stand for Supreme White Power.

Carr told police that on the night in question, he was drinking beer in a park with Derrick Yates and Dick Rutherford, who were friends of Jarod Shostak. At one point, he suggested that they burn a wooden cross he had built. Yates said they should burn it at Jarod's house, because the Shostaks were Jewish. Carr thought that was a good idea, so they retrieved the cross and, while Rutherford and Yates looked on, Carr placed it against the Shostak house and set it on fire. Carr told police he did it to show his "white power beliefs."

Legal Issues

Jarod Shostak invoked his Fifth Amendment privilege—the right not to incriminate oneself with sworn testimony—and refused to testify at the trial. However, the parties stipulated that one week prior to the incident, Jarod suggested to Yates and Rutherford that they should burn the cross at his house because "he was mad at his parents; he didn't like his curfew and other rules." California's Penal Code (§§ 11411, subd. (c)) prohibits only "unauthorized" cross burning. Thus the court had to determine whether Jarod Shotak had "authorized" the cross burning carried out by Carr, Yates, and Rutherford.

Decision

After the criminal trial, Carr was convicted for burning a cross on another person's property without authorization. On appeal, Carr contended the court and prosecutor impermissibly undermined his efforts to show the cross burning was authorized (by Jarod Shostak). He also faulted the court for disallowing the defense that he was intoxicated on the night of the incident. On June 20, 2000, the appeals court judges upheld the conviction, finding no merit in Carr's intoxication defense or in his argument that one person can authorize victimization of another.

Impact

The intoxication defense is often raised in criminal trials, but defendants have to prove either that intoxication was involuntary or that so removed their faculties of reason that they committed an act they would have had no sober intention of carrying out. In this case, the defendant's neo-Nazi views were well documented, as was his premeditation of the act of cross-burning. In California and other states, the intoxication defense is rarely raised in hate-crime cases, as the prosecution usually has no trouble drawing on police reports, witness statements, and other evidence to prove some form of bias motivation on the part of the accused.

KING V. TEXAS
TEXAS COURT OF APPEALS
NO. 73, 433 (2000)

Background

On June 7, 1998, police officers responded to a call to go to Huff Creek Road in the east Texas town of Jasper. In the road, in front of a church, they discovered the body of an African-American male missing the head, neck, and right arm. The remains of pants and underwear were gathered around the victim's ankles. About a mile and a half up the road, they discovered the head, neck, and arm by a culvert in a driveway.

A trail of smeared blood and drag marks led from the victim's torso to the detached upper portion of the victim's body and continued another mile and a half down Huff Creek Road and a dirt logging road. A wallet found on the logging road contained identification for James Byrd, Jr., a Jasper resident. Along the route, police also found Byrd's dentures, keys, shirt, undershirt, and watch. At the end of the logging road, the trail culminated in an area of matted-down grass, which appeared to be the scene of a fight.

At this site and along the logging road, the police discovered a cigarette lighter engraved with the words *Possum* and *KKK*, a nut driver wrench inscribed with the name *Berry*, three cigarette butts, a can of Fix-a-Flat, a compact disk, a woman's watch, a can of black spray paint, a pack of Marlboro Lights cigarettes, beer bottles, a button from Byrd's shirt, and Byrd's baseball cap.

Shawn Berry, Lawrence Russell Brewer, and John William King were arrested and charged with kidnapping and murder. At the time of their arrests, Texas did not have a hate-crimes statute. The state presented evidence linking all three men to Byrd's kidnapping and murder. DNA testing revealed that blood spatters underneath Berry's truck and on one of the truck's tires matched Byrd's DNA. In the bed of the truck, police noticed a rust stain in a chain pattern and detected blood matching Byrd's on a spare tire. Tire casts taken at the fight scene and in front of the church where Byrd's torso was found were consistent with those taken from the tires on the truck.

Shawn Berry shared an apartment with Brewer and King. Police and FBI agents searched the apartment and confiscated King's drawings and writings as well as clothing and shoes of each of the three roommates. DNA analysis revealed that the jeans and boots that Berry had been wearing on the night of the murder were stained with blood matching Byrd's DNA.

At the criminal trial, the state presented evidence of King's racial animosity, particularly toward African Americans. Several witnesses testified about how King refused to go to the home of an African American and would leave a party if an African American arrived. In prison, King was known as the "exalted cyclops" of the Confederate Knights of America (CKA), a white supremacist gang. Among the tattoos covering his body were a woodpecker in a Ku Klux Klansman's uniform making an obscene gesture; a patch incorporating "KKK," a swastika, and "Aryan Pride"; and a black man with a noose around his neck, hanging from a tree. King had on occasion displayed these tattoos to people and had been heard to remark, "See my little n——r hanging from a tree?"

A gang expert reviewed the writings that were seized from the apartment and testified that King used persuasive language to try to convince others to join in his racist beliefs. The writings revealed that King intended to start a chapter of the CKA in Jasper and was planning for "something big" to happen on July 4, 1998. The expert explained that to gain credibility, King would need to do something public. He testified that leaving Byrd's body in the street in front of a church—as opposed to hiding it in one of the many wooded areas around town—demonstrated that the crime was designed to strike terror in the community.

King was convicted of capital murder on February 25, 1999, and the trial judge sentenced him to death. In Texas, direct appeal in capital cases is automatic; on this appeal, King raised eight points of error.

Legal Issues

Evidence of the defendant's racial animosity was introduced as motive in the case, even though Texas had no hate-crimes statute at the time. Rather than combatting the introduction of such evidence, the defendant argued against the kidnapping conviction on technical grounds holding that "there was no evidence presented which would permit the jury to believe that prior to his being dragged to his death, the deceased was moved 'from one place to another.'" Although the defendant did not dispute that a fight occurred and that Byrd was chained to a truck and dragged to his death, he contended that this evidence failed to demonstrate that force was used to chain Byrd to the truck. He was guilty of "nothing more than a false imprisonment, in that the actor or actors would not let the victim go" and contended that no kidnapping occurred because Byrd "went along voluntarily." King's lawyers also suggested that no kidnapping occurred when Byrd was chained and dragged because he initially accepted a ride to his house in the pickup.

Decision

The court found that the act of chaining Byrd to the truck and dragging him for a mile and a half was, by itself, a kidnapping under the law, and that "dragging a chained man from a truck also constitutes the use of deadly force to restrain that person and prevent his liberation." The court found that DNA and other circumstantial evidence was sufficient for a jury to find beyond a reasonable doubt that the appellant was guilty of the criminal charges. In addition, according to the opinion, "the extensive evidence of appellant's hatred for African-Americans, including his graphic tattoos and drawings, is evidence that appellant had a motive to kill Byrd because of his race."

Impact

The James Byrd case became national news as the topic of hate crimes entered into the presidential election year of 2000. The lack of effective hate-crimes law in Texas became an important issue for opponents of George W. Bush, then Texas governor and a presidential candidate, who through the campaign voiced his opposition to such statutes. The killers of James Byrd, Bush maintained, would suffer the maximum penalty under the law—the death penalty—and for this reason he considered hate-crimes statutes an unnecessary complication and elaboration of criminal law. After extensive lobbying by groups favoring hate-crimes laws, however, and the generally negative publicity that came to Texas after the Byrd case, the Texas legislature passed a new hate-crimes statute in spring 2001.

U.S. V. NELSON
U.S. SECOND CIRCUIT COURT OF APPEALS
NOS. 98-1231 AND 98-1437 (2002)

Background

The Crown Heights disturbances in Brooklyn, New York, began on August 19, 1991, when two African-American children were struck by a station wagon driven by a Jewish man. An angry crowd soon gathered at the scene of the accident; members of the crowd began to attack the driver. An ambulance (readily identifiable as originating from a local Jewish hospital) arrived on the scene to aid the driver, then left after being warned off by police officers. Soon afterward, two New York City ambulances arrived to assist the children, who were both taken to the hospital, where one of them, Gavin Cato, later died.

Complaining about perceived preferential treatment for Jews, including the appearance of the Jewish ambulance at the scene, the crowd that had gathered at the scene of the accident grew unruly. An African-American man later identified as Charles Price roused his listeners to violence. Confrontations between blacks and Jews began taking place, a result of years of rising tensions between these two communities in the Brooklyn neighborhood. The riots resulted in a mob attack on a visiting Australian Hasidic Jew, Yankel Rosenbaum, who was beaten and then stabbed. Rosenbaum later died of his injuries.

On August 27, 1991, a 16-year-old African American, Lemrick Nelson, was charged with murdering Rosenbaum. He was tried in a state court and acquitted of the charge on October 29, 1992. The acquittal brought a public uproar, with many city and state officials charging that the jury had been biased in favor of the defendant. The FBI then undertook an investigation to determine if Nelson had violated a federal civil rights statute, Title 18, Section 245 (b)(2)(B) (Interference with Federally Protected Activities). The investigation resulted in the August 11, 1994, indictment of Nelson for the violation of Rosenbaum's civil rights. On August 7, 1996, a second indictment was handed down against Charles Price for violation of the same statute, and for aiding and abetting Nelson's violation of the statute. The indictment read, in part: "The defendants by force and threat of force did willfully injure, intimidate, and interfere with, and attempt to injure, intimidate and interfere with, Yankel Rosenbaum, an orthodox Jew, because of his religion and because he was enjoying facilities provided and administered by a subdivision of the State of New York, namely, the public streets provided and administered by the City of New York, and bodily injury to and the death of Yankel Rosenbaum did result."

Although the principle of double jeopardy would normally bar another trial for Nelson for the murder, the law allows prosecution of the same defendant on the same charge in federal court following the conclusion of the trial, based on the same evidence, in a state court. Price and Nelson were ultimately both found guilty of violating Title 18, Section 245, after four days of jury deliberations. Nelson was sentenced to 235 months in prison, Price to 260 months in prison.

Legal Issues

The evidence presented in the federal district court case showed that Price had encouraged Nelson (and others) to attack Rosenbaum, not only to avenge the death of Gavin Cato but also because Rosenbaum was Jewish (Rosenbaum was unrelated to the driver of the car that struck Cato). However, the empanelment of the jury was brought into question and became the basis for the appeal of the conviction in the Second Circuit Court of Appeals.

During the voir dire (pretrial examination) of potential jurors, the government used five out of nine peremptory challenges to strike African Americans from the jury pool. This represented 55 percent of the challenges allowed, even though African Americans represented 30 percent of the jury pool. In addition, a Jewish candidate for the jury (juror 108) admitted during the voir dire process that he had followed the first trial and was not sure he could be objective in the federal trial. Despite this admission, and although he was challenged for cause by the defense attorneys, the District Court judge, David Trager, insisted that this particular candidate be allowed to sit on the jury, stating during the proceedings that

> *I will not allow this case to go to the jury without 108 as being a member of that jury, and how that will be achieved I don't know. It may well be just by people falling out. It may well happen, in which event I propose never to make any findings on this issue, and if I can I would seal the whole discussion because I see it serving no one's interest. I am not sure I can get away with that. I don't know if the press will allow it, but I don't think it would serve the public's interest to have this discussion go on the record, and especially, if I don't make any findings and I hope that I will not have to make any findings.*

To reach an agreement and bring juror 108 onto the jury panel, Judge Trager agreed to accept an African-American candidate to the jury as well. Finally, when an African-American juror was excused from service due to illness, the court moved a white juror from the main panel to the alternate jury, and then filled the two open seats with alternate jurors selected out of order: one African-American and one Jewish candidate. Defense counsel as well as the defendants agreed to these decisions on the record.

In their arguments for overturning the district court conviction, however, the defendants argued that Section 245(b)(2)(B) is an unconstitutional law, because it reaches conduct that lies beyond congressional powers of regulation; that the evidence presented at the trial was insufficient to prove their biased intent under the same law; and that the extraordinary efforts made by the court to empanel a racially and religiously mixed jury was unconstitutional and should bring a reversal on appeal. Judge Trager was charged with mishandling the jury selection in order to obtain a panel prejudicial to the defendants. In his public statements following the trial, Trager stated that in his opinion the jury fairly represented New York's mixed religious and racial communities.

Decision

On January 7, 2002, the Second Circuit Court of Appeals reached a two-part decision. First, the court upheld the convictions of Price and Nelson under Section 245(b)(2)(B), which was found to be a constitutional law that fell within Congress's authority to enact statutes prohibiting acts of violence motivated by the victim's race or religion, under the Thirteenth Amendment's banning of slavery and the "badges and incidents of slavery." The court also found that Nelson and Price had acted because of their prejudice against Rosenbaum's religion, and that Rosenbaum's use of a public street at the time of the murder clearly and unambiguously falls within the meaning of "public facility" in the statute prohibiting bias-motivated interference with Rosenbaum's use of that facility.

The court also found, however, that Judge Trager's actions in the matter of jury selection had been improper; specifically, allowing juror 108 to sit on the jury despite his admitted lack of objectivity during the voir dire process. The court also found that the defendants' acceptance of juror 108 before the trial did not constitute a waiver of their rights to a proper jury selection. The case was remanded for a retrial.

Impact

The Crown Heights riots turned from a federal civil rights and hate-crimes case to a decision on the process of jury selection. In principle, the selection of jurors is a strictly defined procedure in which judges and attorneys strive to obtain a panel completely objective and unbiased, and in this way ensure a fair verdict in the case. Each side has a limited number of peremptory challenges, in which a juror can be barred from service for no particular cause. The Supreme Court has determined that using peremptory challenges to reject jurors based on their race or gender violates the Fourteenth Amendment, which guarantees equal protection of the laws. The Second Circuit found that Judge Trager erred in allowing an admittedly biased individual to sit on the jury, although his goal of seating a representative cross-section of the community might have been defensible. The problem remains of finding a truly neutral jury within communities that are politically, racially, or religiously homogenous, and therefore possibly biased for or against the defendant.

PEOPLE V. MAGIDSON ET AL. (2005)

Background

Gwen Araujo, formerly Edward Araujo, was a physically male transgender teenager who was living as a female in Newark, California. On the night of October 3, 2002, Araujo was assaulted at a party by several friends who had discovered that Araujo was male, although he was dressed as a female and had engaged in a physical relationship with his attackers. The attack continued for several hours until Araujo was dragged into a garage and strangled with a rope. The body was then transported to a remote area and dumped into a shallow grave.

Two weeks later one of the attackers, Jaron Nabors, confessed under police interrogation to participating in the attack and revealed the location of Araujo's body. In return for his cooperation, Nabors was charged with manslaughter, while Michael Magidson, Jason Cazares, and Jose Merel were charged with first-degree murder as a hate crime, with the state prosecutor seeking penalty enhancement under this charge.

Legal Issues

At the 2004 trial Magidson raised a "transgender panic" defense, claiming that the shock of discovering that the victim was biologically male justified a lesser charge of manslaughter. Under California law, a charge of manslaughter rather than murder is justified in cases where the perpetrator acts in the heat of passion and the killing is not premeditated.

There was conflicting testimony in the case, and the jury could not agree either on whether the murder was premeditated or who, exactly, had strangled Araujo. The deadlock on the charges against Magidson, Cazares, and Morel resulted in a mistrial.

A second trial was held in 2005. Magidson, Cazares, and Morel all testified, giving conflicting accounts of who took part in the beating, who tried to prevent the beating, who carried out the murder, and who directed the disposal of the body. In his closing argument, the attorney for Cazares pointed out that his client was the only one of the accused to render any kind of aid to Araujo during the assault, and who took part in the crime only in helping to bury the body. Magidson's attorney again raised the "transgender panic" defense. The prosecutor in summation called for murder convictions only for Magidson and Cazares.

Decision

On September 12, 2005, after a week of deliberation, the jury rejected the transgender panic defense and found Magidson and Cazares guilty of second-degree murder. The first-degree murder charges and hate-crime enhancement were thrown out. After several more days, a deadlock in Cazares' case was announced; the jury also rejected the hate-crime enhancement sought by the prosecutor. (Cazares later pled no contest to a charge of voluntary manslaughter.) Instead, members of the jury later stated that the victim held some responsibility for the incident by concealing his sexual identity from his attackers, even during and after engaging in a physical relationship with them.

Impact

This case effectively disallowed the "heat of passion" mitigation of a murder charge as it is claimed by defendants citing "transgender panic" or any other kind of "gay panic" defense. The shame or revulsion that an individual feels toward another because of some physical difference is based on preconceived biases toward that difference. Consequently, judges and juries cannot consider it as a part of a temporary, violence-inducing "heat of passion."

Cases Before the Supreme Court of Canada

The following landmark decision by the Supreme Court of Canada has set an important precedent for the prosecution of hate crimes in Canada. The *Keegstra* decision is cited by many critics of hate-crime legislation in the United States as an example of the way these laws can chill free expression. Some commentators warn that the decision leaves the Canadian law open to broad interpretation by authorities and raises the possibility of extending the law in Canada to ban certain forms of political debate and writing. In the United States, no cases have yet arrived that would bring analogous issues to the U.S. Supreme Court.

R. V. KEEGSTRA, 3 S.C.R. 697 (1990)

Background

This case was brought to the Supreme Court of Canada in 1990 six years after an Alberta high school teacher, James Keegstra, was arrested and charged under Section 281.2 (now 319(2)) of Canada's Criminal Code for promoting hatred against an "identifiable group"—in his case Jews—in his classroom. Keegstra held the Holocaust to be a false invention of the Jews, and regaled his students with virulently anti-Semitic opinions, on which the students were regularly tested. Keegstra moved in Alberta's Court of Queen's Bench to quash the charges as a violation of the Charter of Rights and Freedoms. The motion was denied, on the grounds that promoting hatred was demonstrably harmful to society and tended to promote violence. Keegstra was then tried and convicted. He appealed the verdict to the Court of Appeal, which accepted his arguments that the relevant sections of the Criminal Code violated the Charter, and that the infringement of freedom of expression was not justified under Section 1 of the Charter, which places "reasonable limits" on such expression.

This decision was then appealed to the Supreme Court of Canada, which had to decide whether the relevant statutes violated the principle of freedom of expression, enshrined in separate sections of the Canadian Charter of Rights and Freedoms.

Issues

This case revolved around the interpretation of several sections of the Charter of Rights and Freedoms, notably Section 2, which states:
Everyone has the following fundamental freedoms:

(a) freedom of conscience and religion;

(b) freedom of thought, belief, opinion and expression, including freedom of the press and other media of communication;
(c) freedom of peaceful assembly; and
(d) freedom of association.

While Keegstra's motion to drop the charges on the grounds of a violation of paragraph 2(b) of the Charter was denied, he still had a defense under Section 319(3)(a) of the Criminal Code, if he could prove the truth of his statements.

Decision

By a four-to-three vote delivered on December 13, 1990, the justices of Canada's Supreme Court found that section 319(2) of the Criminal Code violated the principle of freedom of expression as set out in Section 2(b) of the Charter. This section explicitly protects nonviolent expression; specifically hateful expression that is not communicated through violence or physical harm. Further, Section 319(2) could deter legitimate expression and the beneficial exchange of ideas; it may have no deterrent effect on hatemongers, who draw publicity for their views through criminal prosecutions and the attention of the media to their causes. However, the court's majority opinion also pointed out that such expression *could* be limited under Section 1 of the Charter, which states as follows:

The Canadian Charter of Rights and Freedoms guarantees the rights and freedoms set out in it subject only to such reasonable limits prescribed by law as can be demonstrably justified in a free and democratic society.

Thus the Charter allows "reasonable limits," and hateful expression was not necessarily protected, notably when it promotes violence or physical harm against an identifiable group. The opinion states that the intent of the Canadian Parliament in suppressing hate propaganda, to protect targeted groups from harm, and to reduce ethnic, racial, and religious tension throughout the country, promotes justifiable ends when limiting public expression, including the opinions stated by teachers in the classroom.

Impact

This landmark decision established that hate-speech laws were constitutional in Canada, although freedom of expression was still generally protected by the Charter of Rights and Freedoms. In contrast to the landmark *RAV v. St. Paul* decision by the U.S. Supreme Court, this decision has been interpreted as allowing Canadian prosecutors a fairly wide latitude in charging violations of hate-speech laws.

CHAPTER 3

CHRONOLOGY

This chronology presents historical background to the modern hate-crimes debate; significant hate-crime incidents of the past and present; important criminal cases, appeals, and Supreme Court decisions in cases related to hate crimes; and important federal legislation dating to 1866. By the reckoning of many historians of the era, this year marks the dawn of the modern civil rights struggle on the part of African-American organizations and of black leaders such as Martin Luther King, Jr., a struggle that ultimately resulted in the passage of new civil rights legislation and hate-crimes statutes.

1649

- The colony of Maryland, founded by Catholics, passes the Act of Toleration, extending religious freedom to all those who profess to believe in Jesus Christ and the Trinity. All others are subject to arrest, imprisonment, and execution.

1755

- Several thousand Acadians, or French-speaking Catholics, are driven away by the government of the British colony of Canada. They flee to other colonies in the Americas, from Massachusetts to the Spanish-controlled region around New Orleans, where they are known as Cajuns and where many join militias fighting against the British.

1762

- In the port of New Orleans, controlled by the kingdom of Spain, the Spanish governor orders all English, Protestants, and Jews to be driven out of the city.

1768

■ A wave of prejudice against Baptists sweeps through England's North American colonies and will continue for six years, a period known in American religious history as the Great Persecution. Baptists are assaulted; they are jailed for writing and distributing religious tracts; their homes and shops are burned; and they are driven from cities where the majority Anglican population despises them as political and spiritual troublemakers.

1776

■ Suspecting the loyalty of blacks to the American Revolution, the Commonwealth of Virginia forcibly relocates all black males over the age of 13 to the interior, well away from British forces along the seacoast.

1780

■ By the constitution of Massachusetts, all Christians are granted equal protection of the laws, but Catholics are required to repudiate the authority of the pope if they wish to hold public office.

1819

■ The first federal immigration statute is passed, regulating the number of passengers that can be transported on ships arriving from foreign ports.

1822

■ The first recorded arson of an African-American church takes place in South Carolina, the scene in the same year of a slave revolt led by Denmark Vesey.

1828

■ Abolitionist speaker Benjamin Lundy is attacked and beaten in the streets of Baltimore, Maryland.

1834

■ Anti-immigrant violence and mob battles between Protestants and Catholics, and between whites and blacks, flare in the eastern cities of the United States and continue for several years. In Philadelphia, a mob of several hundred whites attacks a crowd of African Americans, destroys homes in black neighborhoods, and burns down two churches.

Chronology

1835

- In Washington, D.C., abolitionist Reuben Campbell is nearly lynched by a proslavery mob, which then runs amok through the city's African-American neighborhoods. Black homes, shops, churches, and schools are burned.

1844

- A mob invades an Irish neighborhood of Philadelphia, killing the residents, looting homes, and burning several Catholic churches to the ground.

1863

- *June:* Riots erupt in New York City during a Union army conscription drive. Suspected of replacing white workers, blacks are hunted down, assaulted, burned, and lynched.

1866

- Congress passes the Civil Rights Act and the Freedmen's Bureau Act, granting equal rights to black citizens and freed slaves, and establishing the Freedmen's Bureau to provide education, health services, and job training to former slaves.
- A pro-Confederate organization known as the Ku Klux Klan is formed by Confederate veterans in Pulaski, Tennessee. Over the next several years, the Klan will spread to South Carolina, Florida, Mississippi, Georgia, Louisiana, and Alabama, its members raiding, killing, and torturing free blacks and attacking all symbols and institutions of Reconstruction imposed by the federal government on the defeated Confederacy.
- *April 30:* In Memphis, Tennessee, whites riot and kill 46 black citizens over three days of fighting.

1868

- *July 9:* The Fourteenth Amendment to the U.S. Constitution, holding that all blacks born or naturalized in the United States are citizens with the right of due process and equal protection of the law, is ratified.

1870

- *February 3:* The Fifteenth Amendment to the U.S. Constitution, holding that black citizens cannot be denied the vote on account of their race, is ratified.

Hate Crimes

1871

- During a wave of anti-immigrant violence, a Los Angeles mob attacks a Chinese neighborhood, lynching 22 residents.

1875

- By the Civil Rights Act passed by Congress in this year, discrimination against blacks is outlawed in public places such as theaters, hotels, and public conveyances.

1876

- New Hampshire becomes the last state to end the requirement that its governor and legislators be Protestants.

1881

- Eleven Italian Americans are randomly selected for arrest after the murder of the New Orleans police superintendent; after being found not guilty, they are lynched by a mob.

1882

- By the first of several "Exclusion Acts," immigration from China is suspended for a period of 10 years. In 1902, the Chinese Exclusion Act will be amended to become a permanent ban, not to be repealed until 1943.

1887

- By the Edmunds-Tucker Act, Congress disenfranchises Mormons, bars their church, and confiscates their property.

1896

- The Supreme Court decision in *Plessy v. Ferguson* upholds a Louisiana state law mandating "separate but equal" railroad accommodations for whites and blacks.

1906

- Accused of assaulting and killing a white bartender, 167 African-American soldiers posted near Brownsville, Texas, are dishonorably discharged from the U.S. Army.

Chronology

1909

- Mobs attack Greek Americans in the streets of Omaha, Nebraska, after rumors accuse a Greek man of killing a policeman.

1915

- After the 1913 murder of Mary Phagan, a young factory worker in Atlanta, Georgia, Leo Frank, the Jewish factory owner, is found guilty of the murder. After the governor commutes a death sentence passed on Frank, a mob kidnaps Frank from his prison cell and hangs him.

1919

- Race riots erupt in Chicago, Omaha, and across the Midwest and Northeast, pitting whites against blacks, immigrants, and suspected socialists and communists, resulting in hundreds of deaths and thousands of injuries.

1921

- By the Emergency Quota Act, total immigration from any European country into the United States is limited to 3 percent of the foreign-born population already in the country, as determined by the census of 1910.

1931

- *March 25:* In Paint Rock, Alabama, nine African-American men are arrested on assault and rape charges in what will become known as the Scottsboro case. Eight will be sentenced to death; in the next year the Supreme Court will reverse the convictions. Retrials and legal proceedings drag on until Alabama governor George Wallace officially pardons Clarence Norris, one of the original defendants, in 1976.

1939

- The SS *St. Louis*, a passenger steamship holding several hundred Jewish refugees from Nazi Germany, is turned away from the United States and forced back to Europe, where many passengers will be imprisoned and murdered by the Nazi regime.

1942

- During the "zoot suit riots" in Los Angeles, soldiers, police, and ordinary citizens attack Mexican-American and black citizens throughout the city.

Hate Crimes

1948

- By an executive order, President Harry Truman bars all segregation of African Americans in the U.S. military.

1954

- In the Supreme Court decision in *Brown v. Board of Education*, the Court strikes down the practice of "separate but equal" educational facilities for African Americans, beginning the era of school desegregation.

1955

- *May 7:* Reverend George Lee, a member of the National Association for the Advancement of Colored People (NAACP), is murdered in Belzoni, Mississippi.
- *August 28:* A 14-year-old African-American boy, Emmett Till, is kidnapped and murdered near Money, Mississippi, after allegedly whistling at a white woman. Men brought to trial for the murder are acquitted.
- *October 22:* During a spree of violence directed at the African-American community of Mayflower, Texas, a 16-year-old African American is killed and two others are wounded in a local café.

1956

- *January 30:* Rev. Martin Luther King's home in Montgomery, Alabama, is bombed.
- *February 3:* Rioting breaks out at the University of Alabama after a black woman, Autherine Lucy, attempts to attend classes. Lucy will be suspended and then expelled from the university.

1957

- *January 23:* A black truck driver, Willie Edwards, is kidnapped and forced to jump from a bridge over the Alabama River near Montgomery Alabama, by a group of Klansmen. The death is officially considered an accident until 1976, when one of the Klansmen confesses.

1958

- *August 24:* Two schools scheduled to be integrated in Deep Creek, North Carolina, are burned by an arsonist.
- *October 12:* A bomb explodes at an Atlanta, Georgia, synagogue known as the Temple, during a wave of bombings at southern synagogues, including those in Birmingham, Alabama; Miami, Florida; and Jacksonville, Florida.

Chronology

1959

- **April 25:** Accused of raping a white woman, black truck driver Mack Parker is taken from his jail cell and lynched by a mob in Poplarville, Mississippi.

1960

- **January:** A wave of vandalism against synagogues sweeps the nation, with incidents in New York, Chicago, Boston, and other cities.
- **January 28:** A Kansas City, Missouri, synagogue is bombed, an incident police later link to local neo-Nazi youths.
- **April 23:** A civil rights worker, William Moore, is murdered in Alabama, while marching alone from Tennessee to Mississippi.
- **August 27:** A riot erupts between blacks and Ku Klux Klan members in Jacksonville, Florida, resulting in dozens of injuries and more than 100 arrests.
- **November 15:** White and black citizens clash in New Orleans, Louisiana, over a period of three days.

1961

- **January 11:** A rowdy group of white students attack a desegregated dormitory at the University of Georgia in Athens over the admittance of an African-American woman.
- **May 14:** "Freedom Riders," demanding desegregated buses and other public facilities, are attacked and beaten by white mobs in Anniston and Birmingham, Alabama. Such attacks will continue through the spring and summer throughout the South.
- **September 25:** E. H. Hurst, a white state legislator, shoots and kills Herbert Lee, a black civil rights demonstrator, in Liberty, Mississippi.

1962

- **January 16:** Black churches are firebombed in Birmingham, Alabama.
- **April 9:** In Taylorsville, Mississippi, a white police officer shoots and kills Roman Ducksworth, a black soldier, after Ducksworth refuses to give up his seat on a segregated bus.
- **August 31:** White citizens open fire on the homes of black citizens in Lee County, Georgia, during a campaign to register black voters.

1963

- **June 12:** Black civil rights leader Medgar Evers is shot and killed in his driveway in Jackson, Mississippi. A Ku Klux Klan member, Byron De La

Beckwith, is later charged with the murder, but two hung juries bring about his release. In 1994, Beckwith will be tried and convicted for the murder and sentenced to life in prison.

- *August 10:* A black youth is killed by two whites outside a bar in Jersey City, New Jersey.
- *September 15:* The Sixteenth Street Baptist Church in Birmingham, Alabama, is bombed, resulting in the deaths of four black girls.
- *November 19:* A desegregated college dormitory is bombed in Tuscaloosa, Alabama.
- *December 22:* A fire breaks out at the Roanoke Baptist Church in Hot Springs, Arkansas.

1964

- *May 2:* Two black youths, Henry Dee and Charlie Moore, are kidnapped and murdered by members of the Ku Klux Klan in Meadville, Mississippi.
- *June 16:* Klan members attack black worshippers at the Mt. Zion Church in Philadelphia, Mississippi, and then destroy the church.
- *June 21:* Three civil rights workers, Michael Schwerner, James Chaney, and Andrew Goodman, are abducted and murdered by members of the Ku Klux Klan in Philadelphia, Mississippi.
- *July 11:* Members of the Ku Klux Klan attack a group of black soldiers in Colbert, Georgia, killing Lemuel Penn, a black officer.
- *September 7:* Herbert Oarsby, a black youth, is kidnapped and murdered in Pickens, Mississippi.

1965

- *March 9:* Three black ministers are beaten by a group of whites in Selma, Alabama, resulting in the death of Reverend James Reeb.
- *March 25:* A northern civil rights worker, Viola Liuzzo, is shot and killed by members of the Ku Klux Klan in Lowndesboro, Alabama. The case is solved by a white FBI informant and will bring the FBI into more active investigation and prosecution of bias crimes in the South.
- *August 20:* A priest is wounded and a white seminary student, Jonathan Daniels, is murdered by a member of the Klan in Haynesville, Alabama.

1966

- *January 3:* A black civil rights worker, Samuel Yonge, is murdered in Tuskegee, Alabama, by a white citizen who objects to Yonge's using a whites-only public restroom.
- *January 10:* Klan members bomb the home of Vernon Dahmer, a black civil rights activist, resulting in Dahmer's death.

Chronology

1968

- *January 20:* Black students stab and wound a white student at South High School in Philadelphia, resulting in a student riot and a dozen further injuries.
- *January–March:* Seventeen white-owned businesses are burned in a largely black area of Gainesville, Florida. The arson wave ends with the arrest of six suspects on March 13.
- *April 4:* African-American civil rights leader Martin Luther King is assassinated on the eve of a protest rally in Memphis, Tennessee. The killing brings a nationwide wave of rioting that leaves about 50 people dead.
- *April 19:* A group of eight black youths are assaulted by a white gang in Boston; one is stabbed to death.
- *April 22:* Two white soldiers are attacked and beaten by a group of black and Hispanic men in San Antonio, Texas. The incident is followed by a huge melee in which eight more people are injured.
- *August 4:* A white gunman opens fire from his home on a group of black pedestrians, sparking a wave of rioting and arson in York, Pennsylvania.
- *August 8:* A white youth is murdered in Woodside, New York. Six black men are charged in the crime, carried out in retaliation for the earlier beating of a black youth by a white truck driver.

1969

- The Anti-Defamation League of B'nai B'rith (ADL) is founded to combat anti-Semitic violence and prejudice. The ADL will become a leading organization in tracking hate groups and hate crimes and in the effort to enact new hate-crimes legislation.
- *March 31:* A white mob runs amok through a black neighborhood in Cairo, Illinois, sparking a night and day of random shootings, arson, and violence.
- *April 11:* White students are assaulted by a gang of black youths on the campus of the University of Florida in Gainesville.
- *April 25:* Snipers shoot and injure black youths in St. Louis, Missouri, bringing about two weeks of violence between white and black gangs roaming the city streets.
- *May 16:* Fighting erupts at Fenger High School in Chicago, Illinois, after a group of black youths commit random assaults against white students.

1970

- *April 25:* A wave of bombings and arson strikes Seattle, Washington, after the killing of a black man, Larry Ward, by the Seattle police.

- **June 21:** In Pittsburgh, Pennsylvania, a white sniper shoots and kills a black youth, Ernest Caldwell, by firing shots into Caldwell's house from the street. The murder sparks several days of rioting.
- **June 27:** As tensions between blacks and Jews rise in a Brooklyn, New York, neighborhood, a black girl is accidentally run down by a Jewish truck driver, sparking an assault on Hasidic Jews by a group of black men.
- **August 17:** One police officer is killed and seven others are wounded after a bomb goes off in an abandoned house in Omaha, Nebraska. Six Black Panthers are later charged with murder.
- **October 10:** A gang of Puerto Rican youths attack a synagogue during Yom Kippur services in Brooklyn, causing a brawl between Jews and Puerto Ricans in the street.

1971

- The Southern Poverty Law Center (SPLC) is founded in Montgomery, Alabama, by civil rights attorney Morris Dees. In 1980, the SPLC will establish the Klanwatch Project to gather information on the Klan and other hate groups and to combat hate crimes and bias-motivated violence through civil litigation.
- **May 26:** A white sniper shoots and kills a black student, Jo Etta Collier, shortly after her high school graduation ceremony in Drew, Mississippi.
- **August 30:** During a bitter public controversy over school desegregation and busing, 10 school buses are destroyed in Pontiac, Michigan. Robert Miles, a "grand dragon" of the Ku Klux Klan, will be charged and convicted of masterminding the arson.
- **September 9:** A white youth kills a black student, Willie Ray Collier, at a Lubbock, Texas, high school. Two days of rioting and arson follow the shooting.

1972

- **January 28:** Two white police officers, Gregory Foster and Rocco Laurie, are shot and killed by black militants in New York City.
- **December 31:** A black sniper, Mark Essex, opens fire on a group of police officers in New Orleans, Louisiana, killing one and wounding two. Essex escapes arrest and continues a one-man rampage on January 7, 1973.

1973

- The National Gay and Lesbian Task Force (NGLTF) is founded in Washington, D.C., to represent the interests of homosexuals. The NGLTF will create the Anti-Violence Project in 1982 to combat bias-motivated violence against gays and lesbians.

- *January 7:* In New Orleans, Mark Essex opens fire on white guests of a Howard Johnson motel. Seven people are killed before Essex is brought down by police. Essex was responsible for a sniping incident on December 31, 1972, when a white police cadet was killed, and for setting fire to two downtown warehouses on January 1, a deed that sparked a five-day downtown fire.
- *January 21:* Wesley Bad Heart Bull, a Native American, is murdered by a white man at a gas station in Buffalo Gap, South Dakota.
- *June 2:* A riot breaks out in Brooklyn after an African-American doctor is attacked by a group of Hasidic Jews.
- *October 2:* A white motorist, Evelyn Walker, is dragged from her car and burned to death by black youths in Boston, Massachusetts.
- *November 26:* A black minister, Reverend Edward Pace, is murdered at his home in Gadsden, Alabama, by a member of the Ku Klux Klan.
- *November 27:* Five white high school students are shot and wounded by a black sniper in Pontiac, Michigan.

1974

- *April 19:* A white store owner, Frank Carlson, is murdered by an African-American man in San Francisco. The killing is attributed to the Death Angels, a group of Black Muslim vigilantes blamed for nearly 100 murders in California.
- *November 30:* Five African-American fishermen are drowned near Pensacola, Florida, after their boat is sabotaged by a local white shop owner.

1975

- *July 28:* A black teenager, Obie Wynn, is shot and killed by a white bar owner in Detroit, Michigan. A race riot erupts after the bar owner's arrest, leading to the racially motivated murder of a white motorist, Marian Pyszko.
- *August 14:* A white motorist is dragged from his truck and beaten and stabbed by a group of Hispanic men, leading to a confrontation with police in which five people are injured.
- *September 14:* Richard Morales, a Hispanic prisoner, is shot and killed by the police chief of Castroville, Texas.

1976

- *June 15:* During a heavy thunderstorm in Boston, Massachusetts, white motorists are diverted through a black neighborhood, touching off confrontations and violence during which Phyllis Anderson, a white woman, is shot and killed by black youths.

- *September 8:* White youths rampage through Washington Square Park in New York City, killing one African-American victim and wounding 13 others.

1977

- *February 14:* A suspended worker linked to white supremacist groups, Fred Cowan, kills five people after a confrontation with a Jewish supervisor.
- *August 7:* An interracial couple, Alphonse Manning and Toni Schwenn, are murdered by a sniper in Madison, Wisconsin.
- *November 18:* Four African-American churches are firebombed in Wilkes County, Georgia.

1978

- California passes the first modern hate-crimes law, a penalty-enhancement measure that punishes murders motivated by bias against race, religion, color, or national origin.
- *August 4:* Paul Corbett, his wife, and his daughter are killed by a black racist group known as the Mau Mau in Barrington Hills, Illinois. The same group will be blamed for several similar murders in the Chicago area that take place during the year.

1979

- The Center for Democratic Renewal, formerly the National Anti-Klan Network, is established in Atlanta to monitor hate groups, particularly the Ku Klux Klan and its associated organizations, across the country.
- *June 4:* Loyal Bailey, a witness for the prosecution in a Ku Klux Klan trial in Birmingham, Alabama, is murdered by a member of the Klan.
- *July 22:* An African American, Harold McIver, is shot and killed in a restaurant by a sniper in Doraville, Georgia.
- *October 21:* An interracial couple, Jessie Taylor and Marion Bresette, are shot and killed in Oklahoma City.

1980

- The New York City Police Department establishes a task force to deal with a series of arsons and vandalism incidents at city synagogues. The task force will develop into the Bias Incident Investigation Unit, or Bias Unit, charged with investigating crimes for possible bias motivation and prosecution under hate-crimes statutes.

Chronology

- *January 20:* In Idabel, Oklahoma, a young African American is murdered near a whites-only club. The killing touches off riots and vandalism.
- *April 8:* Race riots erupt in Wrightsville, Georgia, during an anti-Klan demonstration conducted by African Americans.
- *May 3:* A white mob attacks and kills an African American, William Kelly, in the Charlestown neighborhood of Boston.
- *June 8:* A sniper kills two African Americans, Darrell Land and Dante Brown, in Cincinnati.
- *August 20:* White racist Joseph Franklin shoots and kills two African Americans, David Martin and Ted Fields.
- *September 24:* An African-American man, Joseph McCoy, is shot and killed in Niagara Falls, New York. The murder is linked to racial killings during the two previous days in Buffalo and is eventually attributed to Joe Christopher, dubbed the ".22-caliber killer."
- *November 8:* In Algiers, Louisiana, a white police officer, Gregory Neupert, is shot and killed while patrolling a housing project. While searching for the assailant, police officers kill four local African-American residents.

1981

- The Anti-Defamation League formulates a model statute for use by states seeking to pass hate-crimes laws. The statute proposes a penalty-enhancement scheme in which those found guilty of bias-motivated crimes would be given a longer jail term.
- *January 1:* A racist serial killer, Joe Christopher, stabs and wounds two African Americans, Larry Little and Calvin Crippen, in Buffalo, New York. The incident follows several similar attacks by Christopher in up-state New York.
- *March 21:* An African-American youth, Michael Donald, is kidnapped in Mobile, Alabama, driven to the next county, and hanged from a tree. Two members of the Ku Klux Klan will later be charged and convicted of murder.
- *December:* An African-American soldier, Lynn Jackson, appears to have been lynched in Walton County, Georgia, but the death is later ruled a suicide.

1982

- *March 13:* An African American, William Atkinson, is chased by a mob of white men before being hit and killed by a passing train in Boston.
- *June 19:* In Detroit, Michigan, a Chinese American named Vincent Chin is beaten to death by a father and a son who mistake him for a

Japanese, and who fear Japanese economic domination of the United States. The murderers are tried, found guilty, and sentenced to three years of probation.

1983

- **January 12:** In Memphis, Tennessee, members of a black cult abduct two white police officers and torture one of them to death. On the following day, a shootout results in the death of the cult's leader, Lindbergh Sanders.
- **July 28:** Seeking to destroy the records of Project Klanwatch to be used in a pending lawsuit, arsonists attack the headquarters of the Southern Poverty Law Center in Montgomery, Alabama.
- **September 1:** A sniper opens fire on Jewish students in New York City, killing a bystander named Lucille Rivera.

1984

- The National Institute Against Prejudice and Violence is founded in Baltimore. The organization's intent is to gather and disseminate information on interethnic violence and to inform victims of hate crimes of their remedies under the law.
- **March 15:** Rioting takes place in Miami, Florida, after a police officer is acquitted of the charge of murdering a black prisoner, Nevell Johnson.
- **June 18:** Alan Berg, a Jewish talk radio host, is murdered by members of the Order, a neo-Nazi group, in Denver, Colorado.
- **August 22:** In the case of *Massachusetts v. Poor and Tilton*, a state appeals court finds that racist comments are admissible as evidence if made in furtherance of a criminal act and may support a conviction on civil rights charges.
- **October 31:** Bombs explode at the Mapleton Park Hebrew Institute in Brooklyn, New York.

1985

- **March 21:** Congressional hearings begin on the Hate Crimes Statistics Act, which will be passed in 1990 and mandate collection of hate-crimes data by the Department of Justice.
- **April 15:** Members of the neo-Nazi Bruder Schweigen murder Jimmie Linegar, a Missouri state trooper, at Ridgedale, Missouri.
- **June 7:** Two African Americans, Walter Jones and Louis Wright, are murdered and their bodies left along a rural road near Panama City in the Florida Panhandle.

- *October 31:* An African-American woman, Joyce Sinclair, is raped and murdered by a member of the Ku Klux Klan in Robeson County, North Carolina.
- *November 20:* In Philadelphia, a mob of several hundred whites confronts a black family and forces them out of their home.
- *December 24:* David Rice, a Seattle white supremacist, murders a family of four, believing them to be Jews and Communists.

1986

- *March 16:* Fred Finch, a civil rights leader, and his wife are stabbed to death in their Dallas home.
- *April 29:* A one-man campaign against his black neighbors conducted by Carl Rosendahl, a Kansas City, Missouri, white supremacist, culminates in a bombing in the family's back yard.
- *September 29:* During a tense conflict between the white supremacist group Aryan Nations and their opponents in the Idaho town of Coeur d'Alene, a series of bombs explodes in the city center.
- *December 26:* In the Howard Beach neighborhood of Queens, New York, a black youth who is being chased by a white mob runs onto a highway and is struck and killed.

1987

- *November 11:* Jewish stores are vandalized in Chicago in imitation of and on the anniversary of Kristallnacht, when in 1938 Jewish-owned stores were burned and looted in Nazi Germany.
- *November 28:* In Wappingers Falls, New York, Tawana Brawley, a young African-American girl, is found beaten and tied up in garbage bags. Brawley claims that six white men had raped and beat her, but she will not identify the assailants and is ultimately accused of staging a hoax.

1988

- Congress passes 18 U.S.C. 247, providing federal jurisdiction in cases of religious vandalism in which the damages exceed $10,000.
- *March 26:* In Lumberton, North Carolina, Julian Pierce, a Native American, is murdered by two white gunmen during Pierce's campaign for county judge.
- *May 5:* David Price, a black teenager, is shot and killed by white assailants during a confrontation in Louisville, Kentucky.

- *August 17:* In the case of *New York v. Grupe*, a criminal court convicts a defendant on an enhanced misdemeanor charge for making bigoted comments during an assault.
- *November 13:* Mulugeta Seraw, an Ethiopian immigrant, is beaten to death by white skinheads on a Portland, Oregon, street. The murder will bring about a civil lawsuit by the Southern Poverty Law Center against the White Aryan Resistance.

1989

- *May 29:* In an Ohio state park, a white man named David Wyant utters threats and racial insults at African Americans who occupy a neighboring campsite. On the basis of this, he is later convicted of ethnic intimidation, but a challenge to the law, *Ohio v. Wyant*, reaches the Ohio Supreme Court in 1992.
- *June 24:* Max Kowalski, a Jewish resident of Brighton Beach, in Brooklyn, New York, is stabbed to death by a neighbor during an argument over the appearance of a swastika on Kowalski's apartment door.
- *August 23:* In Bensonhurst, Brooklyn, an African-American teenager, Yusuf Hawkins, is beaten and shot to death by a gang of white men.

1990

- *April 23:* President George H. W. Bush signs the Hate Crimes Statistics Act, mandating collection of statistics by the Department of Justice on crimes that "manifest prejudice based on race, religion, sexual orientation, or ethnicity."
- *June 20:* Congressional hearings begin on the Violence Against Women Act.
- *October 22:* The jury finds against White Aryan Resistance in the civil suit brought by the Southern Poverty Law Center over the death of Mulugeta Seraw in 1988, awarding more than $10 million to Seraw's family.

1991

- *January:* During and after the first Persian Gulf War, the ground phase of which ends in January, a sharp increase in hate-crime incidents against Arab Americans is reported. Anti-Arab hate crimes occur in Los Angeles, Cincinnati, Baltimore, New York, San Francisco, Detroit, and Tulsa.
- *August 19:* A riot breaks out in Crown Heights, a Brooklyn neighborhood, after a vehicle driven by a Jewish man strikes two African-

American children, one of whom—Gavin Cato—will die of his injuries. Roused to violence by Charles Price and others, 16-year-old Lemrick Nelson will fatally stab an Orthodox Jew, Yankel Rosenbaum. Price and Nelson will be tried and convicted in federal court with a violation of Title 18, Section 245, the federal civil rights statute, but the case will be remanded after an appeals court finds, in January 2002, that the judge in the federal trial improperly interfered with the jury selection.

1992

- *April 29:* Rioting erupts in Los Angeles after the acquittal of police accused of beating Rodney King, an African-American motorist, during a traffic stop. The riots will last for three days and result in more than 50 deaths.
- *June 22:* In the case of *R.A.V. v. St. Paul*, the U.S. Supreme Court overturns a St. Paul, Minnesota, city ordinance banning, among other symbols, burning crosses, a common method of ethnic intimidation.
- *August 26:* In the case of *Ohio v. Wyant*, the Ohio Supreme Court finds that the state's ethnic intimidation law violates the Ohio and U.S. constitutions, as the statute punishes protected forms of speech.

1993

- *June 11:* In the case of *Wisconsin v. Mitchell*, the U.S. Supreme Court upholds the sentence passed on defendant Todd Mitchell under Wisconsin's hate-crimes penalty-enhancement statute. The decision gives broad legal authority for penalty-enhancement laws, the primary statutory tool of hate-crimes prosecution.
- *July 1:* In the case of *Vermont v. Ladue*, the Vermont Supreme Court upholds a hate-crimes conviction for aggravated assault motivated by perception of the victim's sexual orientation.
- *October 2:* A group calling itself the Aryan Liberation Front claims responsibility for bombing the Japanese American Citizens League office in Sacramento, California.
- *November 2:* In the case of *Michigan v. Richards*, a state ethnic intimidation law is challenged on the grounds of vagueness, overbreadth, and its chilling effect on ordinary free speech; the Michigan Supreme Court upholds the statute.
- *December 23:* In Wyckoff, New Jersey, vandals steal a banner, erected by the New Jersey Chapter of American Atheists, celebrating the winter solstice. The incident will be investigated by the state police as a bias crime motivated by prejudice against atheists.

Hate Crimes

1994

- The Federal Violence Against Women Act of 1994 allows individuals to file federal lawsuits in cases of gender-based violence.
- The Violent Crime Control and Law Enforcement Act of 1994 is passed. By Section 280003, the law directs the U.S. Sentencing Commission to increase "offense levels" for hate crimes. Hate crime is defined as "a crime in which the defendant intentionally selects a victim, or in the case of a property crime, the property that is the object of the crime, because of the actual or perceived race, color, religion, national origin, ethnicity, gender, disability, or sexual orientation of any person." In this way, the federal government follows the examples of states that have already passed penalty-enhancement laws.
- *January 19:* In the case of *Iowa v. McKnight*, the Iowa Supreme Court upholds a conviction for "infringement of individual rights" and finds that a state hate-crimes statute does not violate a defendant's First Amendment rights.
- *February 10:* The Supreme Court of Florida, in *Dobbins v. Florida*, finds that the state hate-crimes law applies strictly to criminal conduct, and not opinion or speech, based on prejudice. Along with the Supreme Court decisions in *R.A.V. v. St. Paul* and in *Wisconsin v. Mitchell*, this decision helps to clarify the nature and enforceability of hate-crimes law.
- *May 26:* In the case of *New Jersey v. Vawter and Kearns*, the New Jersey Supreme Court finds that, although ordinary threats of violence may be punished, a statute prohibiting threats motivated by prejudice is unconstitutional, on the basis that the law discriminates against protected opinion.
- *July 21:* In *Ayers v. Maryland*, a Maryland statute prohibiting bias-motivated harassment is challenged but upheld by the Maryland Supreme Court, which also allows incidents not related to the crime to be introduced as evidence in order to show prejudiced motive.

1995

- *January 1:* The Bluff Road United Methodist Church in Columbia, South Carolina, is firebombed, the first of approximately 40 African-American churches to suffer arson attacks in the following 18 months. The Department of Justice will investigate 658 cases of suspicious fires and bombings from this date until August 18, 1998.
- *June 18:* Thanh Mai, a Vietnamese American, dies during an assault by three white men uttering racial epithets in an Alpine Township, Michigan, nightclub. One of the men, Michael Hallman, is charged and convicted of manslaughter, but prosecutors decline to bring hate-crimes charges.

Chronology

- **November 1:** An amendment of sentencing guidelines takes effect, announced by the U.S. Sentencing Commission. The amendment increases sentences for those found guilty of hate crimes.

1996

- **March 5:** In *Pennsylvania v. Burlingame et al.*, a charge of harassment is overturned on the grounds that the act took place among parties to a labor dispute, a situation which by state law shielded the defendants from the charges. Later hate-crimes statutes will include "membership in a labor union" as a protected status.
- **September 20:** Richard Machado, an undergraduate at the University of California, Irvine, circulates an e-mail to 59 Asian-American students in which he threatens to kill them. Machado becomes the first person prosecuted for hate crime committed via the Internet.

1997

- **February 10:** Lemrick Nelson and Charles Price are convicted of violating a federal civil rights statute (Title 18, Section 245) in the murder of Yankel Rosenbaum during the Crown Heights, Brooklyn, riot of August 19, 1991. Nelson will be sentenced to 235 months in prison, and Price to 260 months in prison. The convictions will later be overturned on appeal due to jury tampering by the judge.
- **February 23:** A police raid in southern Illinois uncovers a cache of bombs, weapons, and hand grenades and a plot by the neo-Nazi group New Order to bomb the Southern Poverty Law Center in Montgomery, Alabama, as well as the Simon Wiesenthal Center in New York.
- **April 26:** In Dallas, Donald Ray Anderson walks into the courtyard of the Baruch Ha Shem synagogue and fires a semiautomatic rifle into the air, then into the walls of the synagogue. He will be charged and convicted under state statutes of aggravated assault and deadly conduct, and then under the federal statute (Title 18, Section 247) prohibiting "damage to religious property and obstruction of the free exercise of religious beliefs."
- **April 27:** In Fort Lauderdale, Florida, Steven Goedersis is beaten to death for his alleged homosexuality.
- **June 7:** James Byrd, Jr., a 49-year-old African American, is chained to the back of a pickup truck and dragged to death in Jasper, Texas. On February 23, 1999, a jury convicts John William King of the murder and he is sentenced to death.
- **July 1:** Two African-American churches, the Tate Chapel African Methodist Episcopal Church and the St. Joseph Baptist Church, are vandalized and burned in Mobile, Alabama. The burnings prompt an investigation by the newly organized National Church Arson Task Force.

- *July 23:* In the case of *Montana v. Nye*, a hate-crimes conviction is upheld for the act of placing provocative bumper stickers on road signs, in mailboxes, and on private property.
- *October 6:* Matthew Shepard, a 21-year-old University of Wyoming student, is beaten, tied to a fencepost, tortured, and left for dead outside Laramie, Wyoming, by two men he met in a Laramie bar. He remains in a coma for six days before dying on October 12. On October 15, the U.S. House of Representatives passes a resolution condemning the murder.
- *November 3:* Alan Odom, Brandy Boone, and Kenneth Cumbie are found guilty of violating federal statutes in the arson and vandalism of the Tate and St. Joseph churches in Mobile, Alabama.

1998

- *January 26:* In the case of *Washington v. Dawson*, the Washington Court of Appeals allows the introduction of a tattoo as evidence to show that the defendant committed a racially motivated harassment and assault.
- *February 13:* Richard Machado is convicted of violating the federal statute prohibiting interference with "federally protected activities," (U.S. Code Title 18, Section 245(b)2(A)), in this case attendance at a public educational institution. Machado had been indicted for sending threatening e-mails to Asian-American students at the University of California, Irvine.
- *July 22:* In *Martinez v. Texas*, the Texas Court of Appeals upholds a hate-crimes conviction, finding that the defendant intentionally selected his victim, a two-year-old child, on the basis of the child's perceived race, even though the defendant was mistaken in his perception.

1999

- *January 20:* Two white and two black students at a Pontiac, Michigan, high school are suspended after a fight allegedly incited by racial slurs.
- *February 19:* Billy Jack Gaither is murdered with an axe and his body burned in Sylacauga, Alabama. Steven Mullins and Charles Butler, Jr., are charged with the crime and confess to plotting the crime after Gaither allegedly made a pass at them.
- *February 24:* In Fort Lauderdale, Florida, a skinhead shoots and kills Jody-Gaye Bailey, an African American, while Bailey is stopped at a red light accompanied by her white boyfriend.
- *March 1:* A homeless gay man is murdered and decapitated in Richmond, Virginia's James River Park. The severed head is left on a footbridge.

- *April 3:* Ashley Mance, a six-year-old black boy, is killed by a shot fired by Jessy J. Roten, who fired a semiautomatic weapon into Mance's home from an alley. Roten is charged with first-degree premeditated murder.
- *April 5:* Naoki Kamijima, a 48-year-old Japanese-American shop owner, is shot to death in Crystal Lake, Illinois, by a gunman who had been roaming the neighborhood and questioning store employees about their ethnic background.
- *May 16:* James Langenbach swerves his car into two young black bicyclists in Kenosha, Wisconsin. Langenbach is charged with attempted murder while armed with a dangerous weapon.
- *June/July 1999:* Three Sacramento, California–area synagogues are firebombed, causing $3 million in damage. Two brothers charged with the crime murder a gay couple several weeks later.
- *July 1:* James Tyler Williams murders Gary Matson and Winfield Scott Mowder, a gay couple, in Redding, California. Williams is charged and convicted of the crime, in addition to a firebombing of Sacramento-area synagogues.
- *July 4–6:* Benjamin Smith murders college basketball coach Ricky Byrdsong and later wounds six orthodox Jews in Chicago, then travels to Bloomington, Indiana, where he murders Won-Joon Yoon, a Korean American.
- *August 10:* Buford O. Furrow kills Joseph Ileto, a Filipino-American postal worker, and wounds five people at a Jewish community center in Los Angeles.
- *September 15:* Larry Ashbrook invades the Wedgwood Baptist Church in Fort Worth, Texas, and opens fire on the congregation, killing seven people and wounding seven others.
- *October 29:* Three men invade an Indianapolis, Indiana, apartment shared by two men they believed were homosexuals. They taunt and torture the men for 30 minutes, then set fire to the building. Later, they return to put the fire out.
- *October 31:* In Inverness, Florida, Richard Burzynski drives his car into a group of people dressed up for Halloween, shouting anti-gay epithets and killing 17-year-old Allison Decratel.

2000

- *January 28:* Two African girls are assaulted by three high-school students in a Boston subway car after being seen holding hands, a custom of their native country.
- *February 6:* A University of Arizona student is assaulted while sitting in a café in Tucson, Arizona. The attack inspires a campus rally against hate crimes that takes place a few days later.

- **March 1:** An African American goes on a shooting rampage in Wilkinsburg, Pennsylvania, killing three white men and wounding two others.
- **March 16:** In the case of *New Jersey v. Dowell et al.*, a New Jersey Superior Court upholds a conviction for harassment by bias intimidation, in the case of several defendants who kidnapped and assaulted a mentally and physically disabled person. The category of "handicapped" had been added to the New Jersey hate-crimes statute as a protected status in 1997.
- **April 28:** Richard Baumhammers, a 34-year-old lawyer, murders five people in and around Pittsburgh, including his Jewish neighbor, Anita Gordon; two Asian Americans at a Chinese restaurant; an African American at a karate school; and a grocery store owner from India.
- **May 17:** Thomas Blanton, Jr., and Bobby Frank Cherry are charged with the 1963 firebombing of the Sixteenth Street Baptist Church in Birmingham, Alabama.
- **June 20:** In the case of *California v. Carr*, a cross burning is defended on the grounds that it was authorized by a 15-year-old member of the victimized family (by the letter of California law, only unauthorized cross burnings are prohibited). An appeals court finds that such actions cannot legally be authorized.
- **June 26:** In the case of *Apprendi v. New Jersey*, a defendant argues that a finding of biased motive must be reached by a jury beyond a reasonable doubt, and an enhanced penalty (for biased motive) cannot be passed after the defendant enters a guilty plea (thus precluding a jury trial). The U.S. Supreme Court agrees, finding that the due process clause of the Fourteenth Amendment holds that any fact that increases the penalty for a crime beyond the statutory maximum must be submitted to a jury.
- **August 12:** A 50-year-old Laotian American, Somahn Thamavong, is beaten unconscious by two African-American teenagers in Baltimore. Although there was no apparent motive, the state claims to find evidence for a hate crimes charge.
- **October 8:** In the Bronx, a synagogue is firebombed; the attackers are the first to be charged under New York's new hate-crimes law, which went into effect the day of the attack.
- **October 13:** Two Arab Americans, Raussi Uthman and Ahed Shehadeh, break into the Temple Beth El in Syracuse, New York, and set fire to the building, causing about $1 million in damage.
- **October 18:** In *King v. Texas*, an appeal of convictions in the James Byrd, Jr., dragging murder, a Texas court rules that evidence of defendant's

hatred of African Americans, including tattoos and drawings found at the defendant's home, is sufficient to show biased motive.

2001

- *January 8:* David Lee Troutman shoots and kills an African-American man, Robert Spencer, at a grocery store in Lake County, Florida, a crime police concluded was racially motivated.
- *February 25:* In Anchorage, Alaska, three white teenagers are arrested after police seize a videotape showing a series of paintball-gun attacks on the city's Native Americans.
- *March 16:* Two Muslim men are attacked by two white men wielding baseball bats outside the Northern Nevada Muslim Community Center in Sparks, Nevada.
- *April 27:* Two Jewish men are attacked and beaten by a San Francisco attorney, Don Henning, who takes them for Palestinians.
- *May 25:* Two teenagers throw rocks, hurl antihomosexual epithets, and set the tents of gay campers on fire at Polihale State Park in Hawaii.
- *July 4:* Two white supremacists stab five African-American youths during a Fourth of July celebration in Waco, Texas.
- *July 14:* Richard Labbe murders Thung Phetakoune, a Laotian, in Newmarket, New Hampshire, while uttering threats and imprecations against Asian Americans. The state charges Labbe with a hate crime but changes the charge to manslaughter.
- *July 29:* Willie Houston is shot and killed after being mistaken for a homosexual in Nashville, Tennessee. The perpetrator, Lewis Davidson, is charged under a hate-crime statute that covers violence based on perceived sexual orientation.
- *September 13:* Two days after the terrorist attacks of September 11, 2001, a Sikh gas station owner, Balbir Singh Sodhi, is shot and killed in Mesa, Arizona. The assailant then drives to another gas station, where he fires shots at a Lebanese American. On the same day, a mosque is firebombed in Denton, Texas. Throughout the country, many more such reports of similar murders, assaults, firebombings, vandalism, and threats directed at Arab Americans and south Asians are recorded.
- *October 20:* A Tulsa doctor, Stanley Grogg, is charged with a hate-crime misdemeanor after assaulting an Afghani taxicab driver while touring downtown San Diego.
- *November 7:* A fight erupts at a Boston high school over head scarves worn by young Somali students, and police investigate the incident as a possible hate crime.

- *December 29:* Vandals break into the Islamic Foundation of Central Ohio, in Columbus, and cause about $500,000 in damages.

2002

- *January 7:* In *U.S. v. Nelson,* a case arising from the Crown Heights riots in Brooklyn, New York, a federal appeals court upholds a conviction of racially motivated violence but then remands the case on the basis that the judge improperly interfered with the selection of jurors in an effort to reach a racially balanced jury.
- *February 8:* The home of a lesbian couple is set ablaze in Missoula, Montana. One of the victims, Carla Grayson, is publicly known as a party to a lawsuit over the denial of same-sex benefits by her employer, the University of Montana.
- *April 8:* An Iranian man is attacked and beaten after offering assistance to a tow-truck driver on the Washington, D.C., Beltway in northern Virginia.
- *June 6:* A gang of men attack two gay men outside a bar in Riverside, California. One of the victims, Jeffery Owens, dies of his injuries.
- *August 10:* A 37-year-old Bangladeshi journalist, Mizanour Rahman, is murdered by a group of Hispanic Americans in Brooklyn. The police blame the murder on a case of mistaken identity in an ongoing confrontation between Hispanics and Bangladeshis in the neighborhood.
- *October 16:* Three men kill a 20-year-old white bystander who taunts the men during a melee outside a pool hall in North Phoenix, Arizona. Two of the suspects belong to the National Alliance, a neo-Nazi group; police suspect the motive for the murder was a difference of political opinion.
- *November 3:* At Morehouse College in Atlanta, student Gregory Love is attacked by a fellow student, Aaron Price, who believes Love is making homosexual advances. The first person to be charged with a hate crime under Georgia statutes, Price is acquitted when prosecutors fail to prove bias motive.

2003

- *January 19:* Four men go on a shooting spree in a largely African-American neighborhood in Portland, Oregon. Later in the month, a grand jury indicts the four suspects on ethnic intimidation charges.
- *January 24:* In Medford, Oregon, three National Guard members recently returned from peacekeeping duty in the Sinai Peninsula assault a motel owner whom they believe to be an Arab American.
- *January 31:* Anonymous hate letters are sent to African-American churches in Missouri and Kansas during preparations for the Martin Luther King, Jr., birthday observance.

- *February 3:* Vandals paint anti-Semitic graffiti and swastikas on the walls of Temple Beth El, a synagogue in Boca Raton, Florida, the second such incident since the beginning of the year.
- *April 5:* Two teenagers videotape their confrontation with a gay man on a New York City subway car and are arrested by the police. Anti-violence groups demand that the police classify the incident as a hate crime.
- *April 7:* In the case of *Virginia v. Black,* the Supreme Court rules 6 to 3 that cross burnings are not necessarily a form of First Amendment–protected speech and that the states can outlaw cross-burnings carried out with the intent to intimidate. The ruling upholds a Virginia law passed in 1952 and used to prosecute two separate cross-burnings (one done on private property with the owner's permission) in 1998.
- *April 19:* At the University of California Los Angeles Medical Center interfaith chapel, Muslim prayer rugs are defiled with pig's blood, and the FBI quickly opens an investigation into the incident as a hate crime.
- *May 19:* Avtar Singh, a 52-year-old Sikh who wears a turban and is a truck driver, is shot by two young white men, according to police, in Phoenix. Singh had parked his 18-wheeler and was waiting for his son to pick him up when the men yelled "Go back to where you belong!" and then opened fire.
- *June 25:* In New Bedford, Massachusetts, a 24-year-old pizza delivery driver, Saurabh Bhalerao, is robbed, beaten, and stuffed into the trunk of a car after he is mistaken for a Muslim.
- *August 26:* An arson fire destroys a small mosque at the Islamic Center, in Savannah, Georgia.
- *November 13:* An arsonist burns the Candles Museum, a small Holocaust museum in Terre Haute, Indiana. Before the attack the perpetrators spray-paint a greeting to Timothy McVeigh, the convicted bomber of the Murrah Federal Building in Oklahoma City, Oklahoma.

2004

- *October 11:* The House of Representatives strips out an expansion of federal hate crimes legislation written into a pending defense appropriations bill. The law would have added sexual orientation, gender, and disability as victim categories for bias crimes laws.
- *October 24:* The Georgia Supreme Court unanimously strikes down the state's hate-crime statute, characterizing it as unconstitutional. The decision was based on a 2002 assault conviction of two Atlanta men, who were given a two-year sentence enhancement for screaming racial epithets during the attack.

Hate Crimes

2005

- *January 15:* An Egyptian Coptic Christian family is murdered in Jersey City, New Jersey. The crime sparks unrest between Muslim and Christian communities in the city.
- *May 27:* The Hate Crimes Law of Colorado is expanded to include bias crimes against homosexuals and the disabled.
- *June 26:* The Illinois hate-crime law is expanded to include harassment and threats made via electronic communications, such as e-mail, instant messaging, and Internet links.

2006

- *February 1:* A gay bar in New Bedford, Massachusetts, is the scene of an assault with guns and machetes.
- *February:* A series of nine church burnings takes place in rural counties southwest of Birmingham, Alabama. Three college students confess to the arson, claiming it as a prank.
- *April 23:* David Ray Ritcheson, a Mexican American, is savagely beaten at a high school party in Spring, Texas. The crime attracts national attention; the victim is called to testify before members of the House of Representatives on the subject of anti-Hispanic hate crime, and legislators are inspired to write the David Ray Hate Crimes Prevention Act of 2007.
- *August:* Three nooses are found hanging from a tree on the campus of Jena High School in Jena, Louisiana. Three white students are suspended for their roles in the incident, which school authorities characterize as a prank.
- *October 29:* A Pakistani man is assaulted in Brooklyn by five Jewish teenagers, who shout "you f—— terrorist! Go back to your country!" just before the assault. The attackers are charged with gang assault and a hate crime.
- *December 15:* Cheryl Green, a 14-year-old African American, is shot and killed by a Hispanic gang in the Harbor Gateway neighborhood of Los Angeles. The killing raises accusations of "ethnic cleansing" by Hispanics against African Americans in the area.
- *December:* After months of rising racial tension in the town of Jena, Louisiana, fights break out between black students and white students they suspect of hanging nooses, a charged symbol of lynching, in August. Afterward six black students are charged with felony assault. The "Jena Six" case inspires protests nationwide and a march on Washington, D.C., led by civil rights groups.

Chronology

2007

- *January 7:* Nakia Ladelle Baker, a transgender female, is murdered in Nashville, Tennessee. Police initially classify the death as a suicide, but later rule it a homicide.
- *March 21:* Erica Keel, a transgender woman, is struck by a car in north Philadelphia and dies two days later. Witnesses claim Keel, a sex worker, got into the car, was quickly ejected, and was then deliberately run over four times. The medical examiner classifies the event as a hit-and-run accident.
- *April 2:* Three Arab Americans are assaulted in Allston, Massachusetts, after two men overhear them speaking Arabic in a restaurant. During the assault the attackers refer to the victims as "terrorists."
- *April 11:* A middle-school student in Lewiston, Maine, is charged with a hate crime after leaving a bag of ham steak on a lunch table where a group of Somali students customarily eat. As Muslims, the Somalis are proscribed from eating pork by religious tradition.
- *April 12:* Aaron Hall, a 35-year-old gay man, is beaten to death in Crothersville, Indiana, at the time one of five U.S. states without a hate-crime law.
- *May 3:* The expanded federal hate-crimes law, the Local Law Enforcement Hate Crimes Prevention Act of 2007 (H.R. 1592), is passed in the House of Representatives. The law expands federal hate-crime law to include sexual orientation, gender, gender identity, and disability. President George W. Bush promises to veto the law if it should arrive at his desk, characterizing it as unnecessary and unconstitutional.
- *June 4:* Kenneth Cummings, a flight attendant, is stabbed to death in Houston, Texas, by Terry Mangum, whom he met at a gay bar. Mangum cites his belief in God as motivation for the murder.
- *September 20:* More than 10,000 civil rights protestors gather in Jena, Louisiana, to demonstrate against what they regard as the unequal treatment of the "Jena Six."

2008

- *January 7:* A series of church arsons in Phenix City, Alabama, end with the arrest of two 21-year-old self-proclaimed Satanists, Geoffrey Parquette and James Clark.
- *January 20:* Brittany Williams, a black student at the University of Nebraska, is shot to death while sitting in her car at a Omaha, Nebraska, fast-food restaurant by a 19-year-old white man, Kyle J. Bormann. Bormann allegedly makes racial comments and is charged with murder.
- *January 24:* In Carrboro, North Carolina, two white students are arrested for ethnic intimidation after exchanging text messages containing threats against black students and then fighting with the students.

- *February 9:* Three members of the Christian Identity group spray-paint swastikas on a mosque in Columbia, Tennessee, and attempt to set the building on fire with Molotov cocktails. They are charged with arson of a religious building.
- *February 12:* Brandon McInerney, a 14-year-old student in Oxnard, California, is charged with a hate crime after shooting and killing an openly gay classmate at their school.
- *March 18:* In Brooklyn, an Arab American is charged with a hate crime after pulling a skullcap off the head of a rabbi and shouting "God is Great" in Arabic.
- *March 30:* In Orlando, four black men beat an elderly white woman and her two companions in a public park, allegedly for not paying a "fee" for being white. The accused are charged with a hate crime.
- *May 30:* Gary David Moss is charged with ethnic intimidation and reckless endangerment in Medford, Oregon, after allegedly burning a cross on the lawn of a mixed-race couple.
- *November 4:* Three men in Staten Island, New York, are arrested for "retaliatory" attacks on African Americans on the night of Barack Obama's election to the presidency.

2009

- *March 31:* Three current Columbia University professors and one former professor receive mail containing images of nooses and swastikas, and New York City police investigate the incident as a hate crime.

CHAPTER 4

BIOGRAPHICAL LISTING

Joseph Biden, six-term U.S. senator and vice president from Delaware who has been a prominent supporter of new federal hate-crime measures, particularly in the field of gender-based bias crimes. A native of Pennsylvania, he grew up in Delaware and graduated from the Syracuse College of Law in 1968. He was first elected to the Senate in 1972, at age 29, and has since won re-election five times. In the 1980s, he became chairman of the Senate Judiciary Committee. He helped to draft the Violent Crime Control and Law Enforcement Act of 1994 and the original Violence Against Women Act, which passed in the same year. Biden wrote and sponsored a second Violence Against Women Act in 1998, a comprehensive measure to address gender-based hate crimes with new federal statutes and federal money for policing, hot lines, and community organizations such as battered women's shelters. The second Violence Against Women Act was passed and signed into law in 2000 and reauthorized in 2005. Biden announced his candidacy for president in January 2007, but his campaign quickly folded after a poor showing in the Iowa Democratic caucuses in January 2008. He was selected by Democratic Party candidate Barack Obama as his running mate in August 2008. They won in the Novermber general election.

Sam Bowers, Imperial Wizard of the White Knights of the Ku Klux Klan, who played a prominent role in Klan activities in Mississippi during the 1960s civil rights struggle. The owner of a vending machine business in Laurel, Mississippi, Bowers founded the White Knights in 1963 in order to turn back the tide of civil rights protests then occurring in Mississippi and throughout the South. Within a few months, membership had risen to more than 10,000, with an especially large "klavern" (chapter) growing in Meridian, Mississippi, where young students were arriving to carry out a voter registration drive. Determined to stop them, Bowers ordered the murder of Michael Schwerner, a 24-year-old New Yorker who was employed by the Congress of Racial Equality (CORE). In 1966, Bowers also arranged the murder of Vernon Dahmer, a businessman whom Bowers believed too sympathetic to blacks. (Dahmer had allowed black voters to pay a $2 poll tax at his store in Hattiesburg, Mississippi, thereby encouraging them to vote.) Bowers was convicted of conspiracy in the Schwerner murder in 1967 and, in 1998, of the firebombing death of Vernon Dahmer, a conviction that brought him a life sentence. He died in prison in 2006.

Ricky Byrdsong, college basketball coach and corporate executive whose death at the hands of white supremacist Benjamin Smith became one of the nation's most notorious hate-crime murders. Byrdsong was born in Atlanta and graduated from Iowa State University in 1978. He served as a basketball coach at the University of Detroit, Mercy, and, in 1993, as head basketball coach at Northwestern University. He left this position in 1999, when he became vice president of community affairs for the Aon Corporation. On July 3, 1999, while talking with two of his children outside his home in suburban Chicago, Byrdsong was shot and killed by Benjamin Smith, who had just begun a rampage that would continue with shootings in Springfield, Decatur, and Urbana, Illinois, and end with Smith's suicide in Bloomington, Indiana.

Floyd Cochran, repentant racist and former Ku Klux Klan member from upstate New York. Cochran joined the Ku Klux Klan while still a youth in New York, then moved to the Pacific Northwest, home to many racist, neo-Nazi, and white separatist movements. Cochran became prominent in the Aryan Nations, a white supremacist organization that throughout the 1990s advocated acts of violence against African Americans and Jews. In 1992, Cochran turned against the group out of revulsion for its advocacy of violence against the disabled. He soon renounced the racism he had once avowed and became a prominent spokesman against the far right. Since that time he has toured the country denouncing Aryan Nations and the neo-Nazi movement.

John Conyers, Democratic representative from Michigan, credited by many with coining the term *hate crimes* and a prominent sponsor of federal hate-crimes legislation throughout his career as a legislator. Reelected in November 2006 with 87 percent of the vote in Michigan's Fourteenth Congressional District, Conyers is one of the founders of the Congressional Black Caucus. He wrote the legislation establishing the national Martin Luther King holiday in 1983 and was one of the authors of legislation raising the Environmental Protection Agency to cabinet-level status. Conyers sponsored the Violence Against Women Act in 1998 and wrote the Church Arson Prevention Act, two key federal hate-crime bills, and remains a strong advocate of the Hate Crimes Prevention Act, the latest hate-crime bill, which remained stalled and unpassed in 2008.

Abraham Cooper, rabbi and dean of the Simon Wiesenthal Center, which he helped to found in 1977. Since that time, Cooper has been active in combating anti-Semitic and other hate groups worldwide. He coordinates the Simon Wiesenthal Center's efforts to combat anti-Semitic and racist hate crimes and hate propaganda. He lectures around the world on the history, the manifestations, and the consequences of anti-Semitism. In particular, Cooper has actively combated Holocaust denial, the movement that denies the existence of the World War II genocide committed by Nazi Germany against the Jews and other groups.

Morris Dees, founder and chairman of the Southern Poverty Law Center. Born in 1936 in rural Alabama, Dees grew up in a family that held traditional white southern viewpoints regarding separation of the races and the civil rights movement. After graduating from the University of Alabama law school, however, he undertook several lawsuits against segregation in academia and in Alabama's public facilities. In 1971, he cofounded the Southern Poverty Law Center with Joseph Levin and Julian Bond. Since its founding, this organization has taken the lead in pro–civil rights legal action in the South and throughout the country. One of Dees's best-known battles was undertaken against the hate group White Aryan Resistance and its founder, Tom Metzger, who were effectively bankrupted by a civil action brought by Dees after the murder of an Ethiopian student by racist skinheads in Portland, Oregon. Dees was honored by the University of Alabama School of Law in 2006 with a new "Morris Dees Award," to recognize lawyers who have devoted their careers to public service.

David Duke, Louisiana politician closely associated with white supremacist organizations, particularly the Ku Klux Klan. Duke founded the White Student Alliance while a student at Louisiana State University. He graduated in 1974 with a degree in history and then formed the Louisiana Knights of the Ku Klux Klan, which he sought to turn into a more politically effective, media-savvy organization. In the same year, Duke became a national director of the Knights of the Ku Klux Klan. In 1975, he ran for the Louisiana senate but lost with one-third of the vote. In 1979, he ran again for the state senate from Metairie but lost again. In the same year, he was tried and convicted of incitement to riot after a Klan rally in New Orleans, after which he cut his ties to the Klan and formed the National Association for the Advancement of White People (NAAWP). During a campaign for president in 1988, Duke ran on the issues of affirmative action, civil rights, and immigration, and he remained a staunch opponent of hate-crimes legislation of any sort. His presidential bid failed with 47,000 votes, but Duke won a Louisiana House of Representatives seat in 1989. After a failed bid for Louisiana governor in 1991, Duke entered the Republican Party presidential primary in 1992, winning only 11 percent in his best state, Mississippi. In 2002, he was sentenced to 15 months in prison for filing a false tax return and mail fraud.

Abby Ferber, widely published scholar of the far right and hate groups, author of *Hate Crime in America: What Do We Know?* and *White Man Falling: Race, Gender, and White Supremacy.* Ferber is director of Women's Studies at the University of Colorado at Colorado Springs, and teaches on the subjects of race and gender. She conducts workshops on hate crime and the far right, and served as a panelist for the American Sociological Association's 1999 Press and Congressional Briefings on hate crime in the United States. She edited *Home Grown Hate: Gender and Organized Racism,* published in 2004.

David Goldman, founder of Hatewatch, a prominent World Wide Web site dedicated to researching and exposing far-right organizations, particularly those employing the Internet. The group originated with a web page entitled "A Guide to Hate Groups on the Internet," which Goldman originally created simply as an exercise in web page design. The site earned several accolades, and in March 1996, Goldman launched Hatewatch as an outgrowth of his work investigating far-right organizations on the Internet. Since that time he has often appeared in national and international print and broadcast media as a specialist on the topic and Hatewatch has become a part of the Southern Poverty Law Center web site.

Matthew Hale, prominent white supremacist and head of the racist organization known as the World Church of the Creator, based in East Peoria, Illinois. In 1996, Hale took over the moribund organization, which stands for the advancement of the white race and had been founded in 1973 by a Florida state legislator and Ukrainian immigrant named Ben Klassen. Assuming the title of Pontifex Maximus, Hale moved the group to East Peoria, headquarters of the Caterpillar Corporation and a town hit hard by labor strife and unemployment. Hale made the World Church of the Creator one of the most prominent racist organizations to appear on the Internet, a medium that attracted most of its new members. But his application for a law license was turned down in the early summer of 1999, on the grounds that Hale's beliefs and character made him unfit for a law license. Hale's very public campaign for an Illinois law license gained him national media notoriety, and his rejection may have inspired one of his more dedicated members, Benjamin Smith, to carry out a shooting rampage through Illinois and Indiana on the July 4 weekend of that year. In 2003, Hale was arrested for conspiracy to murder a federal judge, Joan Lefkow, who had presided over Hale's trial for trademark infringement with the use of the name "Church of the Creator." In 2005 he was sentenced to a 40-year prison term.

Gregory Herek, prominent author and academic researcher on the subject of antihomosexual violence and prejudice. Holding a doctorate in social psychology from the University of California, Davis, Herek currently is a psychology professor at the same institution. He has become an internationally recognized expert on the subject of antigay violence, having published a number of articles and books on the topic since 1992, when he edited a seminal volume on the topic entitled *Hate Crimes: Confronting Violence Against Lesbians and Gay Men.* In 1997, Herek participated in the White House Conference on Hate Crimes; at this time he also participated actively in the debate over the admittance of homosexuals into the armed forces. Herek has also achieved prominence in the field of AIDS-related prejudice.

James Jacobs, author and leading opponent of hate-crimes legislation. As the director of the Center for Research in Crime and Justice at the New York University School of Law, Jacobs lectures and writes actively on the constitutional problems and social dangers of laws that treat prejudice as a basis for criminal prosecution. With Kimberly Potter, Jacobs coauthored *Hate Crimes: Criminal Law and Identity Politics,* an effective and eloquent summary of the position against hate-crime laws.

Valerie Jenness, sociology professor at the University of California, Irvine and a leading author on hate crimes, gender politics, and law. She has written two well-regarded books on the subject, *Making Hate a Crime: From Social Movement to Law Enforcement Practice* and *Hate Crimes: New Social Movements and the Politics of Violence.*

Brian Levin, attorney practicing in the area of civil rights and discrimination and director of the Center for the Study of Hate and Extremism at California State University. A graduate of the Stanford Law School and a former New York City policeman, Levin has served as a director of the Klanwatch center in Montgomery, Alabama, and of the Center for the Study of Ethnic and Racial Violence in Newport Beach, California. Levin authored an amicus curiae brief in the landmark Supreme Court test of hate crime law, *Wisconsin v. Mitchell.*

Jack Levin, specialist in the study of prejudice and hate crimes. Levin is director of the Brudnick Center on Conflict and Violence at Northeastern University in Boston. He has written more than 150 articles and more than 30 books, including *Hate Crimes: The Rising Tide of Bigotry and Bloodshed,* one of the most widely circulated publications in the hate-crimes debate. Levin also authored *Why We Hate* (2004) and *The Violence of Hate* (2007).

Karen Narasaki, executive director of the Asian American Justice Center (AAJC). A graduate of Yale University and the University of California at Los Angeles School of Law, she was the Washington, D.C., representative for the Japanese American Citizens League before joining AAJC. She is a prominent spokesperson on the matter of anti-Asian hate violence. In the wake of the terrorist attacks of September 11, 2001, Narasaki focused on anti-immigrant prejudice and violence through executive positions with the Leadership Conference on Civil Rights and the Coalition for Comprehensive Immigration Reform.

William L. Pierce, a leader in the American neo-Nazi movement, mainly as the author of the book *The Turner Diaries.* A prominent member of George Lincoln Rockwell's American Nazi Party, Pierce was a fanatical anti-Semite and a determined foe of the federal government, which he saw as dominated by Jewish interests. Leader of his own neo-Nazi organization known as the National Alliance, and the founder of the anti-Semitic Cosmotheist Church, Pierce wrote *The Turner Diaries* in 1978 under the pseudonym of Andrew Macdonald. The book describes a neo-Nazi underground group that mounts a coup against the U.S. government and eventually comes to dominate world government. *The Turner Diaries* in turn inspired Robert Matthews, founder of The Order, a group that carried out threats and violence against individuals as well as government institutions. Pierce died in 2002.

William Rehnquist, former chief justice of the U.S. Supreme Court who oversaw the Court's two important decisions regarding hate crimes laws. Rehnquist was born in Milwaukee in 1924. He served in the U.S. Army Air Corps during World War II, then graduated first in his class from Stanford University law school in 1952. He worked as a clerk to Supreme Court justice Robert Jackson; through the 1960s he remained a staunch political conservative, generally opposed to school integration and other new civil rights measures on the grounds that the Constitution decrees a limited role for the federal government. Rehnquist was appointed to the Supreme Court in 1971, becoming a standard-bearer for states' rights and conservative positions on racial discrimination and equal opportunity cases. He was appointed chief justice in 1986. Writing in support of the Court's 1993 decision in *Wisconsin v. Mitchell,* Rehnquist stated that "the First Amendment . . . does not prohibit the evidentiary use of speech to establish the elements of a crime or to prove motive or intent." With this decision, the Rehnquist court determined that the penalty-enhancement hate-crimes laws enacted by Wisconsin and other states should not be struck down on First Amendment grounds. Rehnquist retired from the Court in 2005 and died in the same year.

Michael Schwerner, civil rights worker whose murder in 1964 touched off a widespread public outcry for enhanced federal civil rights measures, a direct precursor to modern hate-crimes legislation. Aged 24 at the time, Schwerner was a New York City native who was hired as a field worker by the Congress of Racial Equality (CORE). He worked in Meridian, Mississippi, to organize a community center and to carry out voter registration among African Americans. On June 21, while driving with James Chaney and Andrew Goodman in rural Neshoba County, Schwerner was pulled over by Sheriff's Deputy Cecil Price, who then turned over the three men to Ku Klux Klan members. Determined to make an example of Schwerner and to discourage any other northern civil rights workers who might be inclined to work in Mississippi, Klan leader Sam Bowers ordered a summary execution, and Schwerner, Chaney, and Goodman were murdered the same night. Media coverage of the crime inspired the FBI to take a direct role in the case, the first time J. Edgar Hoover's FBI made a concerted effort to solve a civil rights case.

Benjamin Smith, a white supremacist who carried out a series of bias-motivated shootings over the weekend of July 4, 1999. A 21-year-old college student at the University of Indiana, Smith had since June 1998 been a committed member of the World Church of the Creator, a white supremacist group based in East Peoria, Illinois. Well known on the Indiana campus for his racist views, he left the university in spring 1999 and moved to Chicago, where he was arrested in suburban Wilmette in April for distributing anti-Semitic literature. On July 3, armed with two loaded pistols and driving a blue Ford Taurus, Smith began his shooting spree in Rogers Park, an orthodox Jewish neighborhood of northwest Chicago, then proceeded to the predominantly Jewish suburb of Skokie, where he killed former Northwestern University head basketball coach Ricky Byrdsong. That afternoon, Smith continued the rampage in Springfield, Decatur, and Urbana. On the next day, Smith shot and killed a Korean student in Bloomington, Indiana, then committed suicide when confronted by police. In all, two people were killed and eight wounded in what became one of the nation's most notorious hate-crime sprees.

Kenneth Stern, attorney, member of the American Jewish Committee, and leading spokesman on the topic of anti-Semitic prejudice, Holocaust denial, and anti-Semitic violence. Stern's 1993 book *Holocaust Denial* was one of the first works to describe in detail the methods and philosophies of those who hold the opinion that the Holocaust never took place and is nothing more than cleverly orchestrated propaganda. Stern participated in the 1997 White House Conference on Hate Crimes as a presenter. In 2000 he successfully defended author Deborah Lipstadt and Penguin Books against a charge of libel brought by historian David Irving, a prominent Holocaust denier.

Lu-In Wang, legal expert on the topic of hate crimes law and the author in 1994 of *Hate Crimes Law*, a groundbreaking textbook on the subject that is updated annually. An associate dean and law professor at the University of Pittsburgh School of Law, Wang has expanded her legal research into a multidisciplinary approach to racism and discrimination, investigating the social and psychological factors that lead to the commission of hate crimes. Her articles have appeared in a variety of law and academic journals; her 2006 book, *Discrimination by Default: How Racism Becomes Routine*, explores the effect of common assumptions and stereotypes on racial prejudice and disparities.

CHAPTER 5

GLOSSARY

advocacy Defending or supporting a cause, legal position, group, philosophy, individual, etc.

aggravated assault An attack against an individual for the purpose of inflicting serious injury, often with the use of a weapon or other means likely to produce death or severe harm.

anti-Semitism Prejudice against Jews and the Jewish religion.

assault A verbal or physical attack by one individual against another, or simply a threat to carry out the same.

bias A negative opinion held against a group or individual on the basis of race, color, religion, national origin, etc. The generally recognized forms of bias, for the purpose of legislation and criminal prosecution, are racial bias, ethnic bias, religious bias, sexual orientation bias, and disability bias.

bias indicators Facts or circumstances surrounding a criminal act that suggest the act was perpetrated on the basis of prejudice against the victim's race, color, religion, national origin, etc.

bias motive Prejudice or hatred against a group or individual (based on race, color, religion, national origin, etc.) that plays a role in the commission of a crime carried out against that group or individual.

bipartisan Characterized by support across the two major political groups or viewpoints, generally Democrat/Republican and liberal/conservative.

chilling effect The consequence of limiting or inhibiting free speech caused by a proposed law or court verdict.

complaint A written accusation of a criminal act, filed by a prosecuting attorney in order to initiate legal action against an individual.

discrimination Prejudicial treatment of an individual based on the individual's membership in a group, whether it be religious, ethnic, socioeconomic, cultural, or nationality.

fighting words Speech that deliberately provokes violent or criminal acts, held by legal precedent not to be protected by the free-speech provisions of the First Amendment.

Glossary

freestanding statute   A hate-crimes law that creates and defines an entirely new category of criminal act, such as ethnic intimidation, related to the biased motivation of the perpetrator.

hate crime   An act of violence, trespassing, intimidation, and/or vandalism perpetrated against a person or group on the basis of prejudice or hatred towards the actual or perceived race, color, religion, national origin, gender, disability, or sexual orientation of the victim.

hate speech   Spoken words or printed text that is motivated by bias, prejudice, or hatred against a group or individual based on that group or individual's actual or perceived race, color, religion, national origin, etc.

homicide   The killing of one person by another.

institutional violence   Criminal acts such as arson, trespassing, or vandalism carried out against property such as churches, synagogues, cemeteries, schools, and/or monuments.

juvenile   A person not yet of adult age and, by general legal definition, between 10 and 16 years old.

Ku Klux Klan (KKK)   An organization founded in Pulaski, Tennessee, after the Civil War for the purpose of protecting and furthering southern traditions such as the separation of the races.

libel   A malicious or false statement made in written form against an individual group.

lynching   The killing of an individual outside of the legal system for suspected criminal acts, or on the basis of the individual's race, group affiliation, or other characteristic.

mens rea   Mental state, or intent; in law, mens rea usually denotes the motivation of someone accused of a crime. Most hate crime law requires prosecutors and juries to decide on the state of mind of the accused, in terms of bias towards a group or individual based on certain identified characteristics, such as race, religion, national origin, etc.

misogyny   The aversion to the opposite sex, most often used to denote sexism by men against women (the aversion of women to men is known more specifically as misandry).

model statute   A legislative act, such as a criminal statute, composed to serve as a template to be adopted by lawmaking bodies and adapted to local problems and concerns.

neo-Nazi   An individual who subscribes to the beliefs and practices of Adolf Hitler and Nazi Germany.

nolo contendere   A plea entered by an individual on trial in which the accused does not admit guilt but agrees to a sentence or punishment commensurate with the crime.

nongovernmental organization (NGO)   A group formed to address specific issues or concerns, such as racial prejudice, outside the apparatus of public agencies.

nonresponding agency A law enforcement agency that does not comply with requirements to make a hate-crimes report to either federal or state agencies authorized to collect such data.

overall crime rate A number expressing the total number of crimes as a percentage of the overall population figure.

"panic" defense An argument offered to justify or seek lesser punishment for violent action taken against another person upon learning that person's sexual orientation ("gay panic") or gender identity ("transgender panic").

participating agencies (reporting agencies) Law enforcement agencies that comply with requirements to carry out a hate-crimes report covering their jurisdictions.

penalty enhancement An increase in a convicted criminal's sentence, sometimes based on the finding that the crime was motivated by prejudice or bias against the victim's race, color, religion, national origin, etc.

post-traumatic stress disorder A physical reaction to a traumatic event, such as a witnessed death or a violent encounter, that manifests as anxiety, depression, insomnia, and/or flashbacks.

prejudice Opinions or views of an individual or group, usually negative, based on misperceptions of or bias against the group.

prevalence The number of certain crimes, such as hate-crime assaults, that take place in a reporting jurisdiction.

primary prevention An effort to prevent future social problems and criminal acts through education, public programs, etc.

property crimes Generally defined as burglary, theft, arson, and/or vandalism, crimes that directly harm material objects rather than human victims.

protected status A legal categorization of members of a certain group, such as African Americans, who thereby enjoy the protection of the law against discrimination and bias-motivated actions.

punitive damages Monetary award granted via a civil trial to the victim of an illegal act.

qualitative data Information gathered from interviews and questions, generally not statistically based or scientifically analyzed.

quantitative data Information and/or data collected through a strictly defined method, in which those questioned are given carefully structured responses from which to choose.

racial profiling The selection of members of a certain ethnic group for closer scrutiny by police or other authority figures.

racialism Claims or views about natural differences in ability or intelligence between members of an ethnic group or nationality.

racism The doctrine that certain ethnic groups are as a rule inferior or superior to others based on perceived characteristics among members of that group.

reverse racism   Racism or discrimination directed against the members of a majority ethnic, religious, or socioeconomic group or nationality.

robbery   The commission of theft through the use of intimidation, threats, or bodily harm.

secondary prevention   An attempt to head off such problems as violence, bigotry, and hate crimes among a population considered at risk for such problems.

sentencing guidelines   Uniform penalties set down by a state or federal law for the commission of certain crimes.

sexism   The view that holds one sex to be superior to the other, either in intellectual or physical capacity.

skinheads   A group characterized by shaven heads, which in some (but not all) cases stands as an emblem of certain beliefs, such as racism or white supremacy.

slander   A malicious or false characterization or accusation made against an individual or group, legally defined as an oral (not written) statement.

synagogue   A Jewish house of worship, ritual, and prayer.

tertiary prevention   An attempt to resolve a threat or problem once it has begun to take place.

Uniform Crime Reports (UCR)   Annual statistical surveys on the incidence of crime that are gathered and published by the FBI.

violent crimes   Generally defined as murder, forcible rape, robbery, assault, and/or aggravated assault.

white supremacist   Someone who believes that white (European-descended) people should hold a dominant place over people of other ethnicities, such as black or Asian.

zero report   A report of an agency, such as a police department or prosecutor's office, that indicates that no hate crimes have been committed within a particular jurisdiction during a stated time period.

PART II

GUIDE TO FURTHER RESEARCH

CHAPTER 6

HOW TO RESEARCH HATE CRIMES

The researcher of hate crimes and hate-crime law is faced with a very diverse, unfocused, and often opinionated field of source material, including books, newspaper and magazine articles, court cases, legal tracts, web sites, and printed and electronic sources offering conflicting statistics. Although the heyday of hate-crimes legislation took place in the early 1990s, and the topic has subsided as a focus of public interest in more recent years, a new federal statute on hate crimes—the Local Law Enforcement Hate Crimes Prevention Act—was reintroduced in the House of Representatives in 2007. A highly partisan debate over amending or writing new hate-crimes law on the federal level will likely continue.

The student should at all times be aware of the two fundamentally opposed positions on the issue of hate-crimes law: the stand of those, generally but not always identified as political conservatives, who see such laws as an unconstitutional abridgement of free speech and opinion, and the position of those, generally identified as political liberals, who view hate crimes as worthy of more severe punishment by reason of the greater threat they pose to the community at large, and as a redress of historical discrimination. In most cases, those who take a stand one way or another on the subject continue to use these positions as the basis of their argument.

TIPS FOR RESEARCHING HATE CRIMES

- **Define the topic and the question at issue:** The researcher should develop a very specific issue or question before proceeding into the thicket of research materials and before proceeding to original work. The subject of hate crimes and hate-crimes law gives rise to a variety of secondary subjects: the proper role of the federal government in making criminal

147

law; the history of racism and discrimination; procedures of the modern criminal justice system; the origins and ongoing effect of civil rights legislation; courtroom procedure; the victims' rights movement; the rise of hate groups; the socioeconomic condition of certain minority groups; the role of the media, the Internet, and talk radio; the influence of advocacy groups, and so on. The researcher will soon note that many articles and books on hate crimes suffer from a lack of focus and float interminably from one of these topics to the next, greatly weakening whatever original point the author wished to make.

- **Develop a grounding in the recent history of hate crimes law:** The researcher should first and foremost get a handle on the legislative background, most importantly the federal statutes that have been proposed and written since the Hate Crimes Statistics Act of 1990 (the Hate Crimes Sentencing Act, the Violence Against Women Act, the Church Arsons Prevention Act, and the proposed Hate Crimes Prevention Act). A good source for this review is the web document "Hate Crimes Laws," produced by the Anti-Defamation League and available at http://www.adl.org/99hatecrime/intro.asp. Without a basic knowledge of these laws, the available texts on hate crimes, and especially legal scholarship, can become confusing, as specialized authors in the field tend to assume this knowledge on the part of their readers. Researchers can also help themselves by reviewing a few good texts on the history of the civil rights struggle of the 1950s and 1960s, which turned out to be a precursor to the hate-crimes debates of the 1980s and 1990s.

- **Beware of statistics:** Authors on hate crimes make free use of statistics gleaned from a variety of sources, quite often unattributed, and the researcher will soon note the numbers changing and conflicting. In fact, there are several different ways of counting hate crimes, and law enforcement agencies use their own guidelines when police have to make the decision whether to designate a criminal act as bias motivated. The most important difference to keep in mind is the occurrence of hate crimes actually prosecuted by law enforcement and hate incidents reported by victims, which do not always signify a police investigation or a public prosecutor's case. Advocacy sites with hot lines available to the public, for example, will often publish the total number of reports and contacts as hate incidents. The most widely quoted statistical set on hate crimes remains the Hate Crimes section of the FBI's Uniform Crime Reports (UCR), although the UCR is also open to doubt and interpretation. The 2006 table is available at http://www.fbi.gov/ucr/hc2006/openpage.htm.

- **Know the source:** When delving into the World Wide Web and the Internet, the researcher should be aware of the political stand taken by the source he or she is using. Favoring or opposing hate-crimes law is an all-or-nothing proposition to most of these sources, and the articles, statistics, even photographs and graphics selected are put to use to support the favored stand. To strengthen their impact on the public, web sources will often dress themselves in a deceptive cloak of neutrality, down to the name the organization has selected for itself. As much as possible, the researcher should investigate the background of authors, the history of organizations, the political viewpoint of periodicals and, in some cases, of book publishers.

BIBLIOGRAPHIC RESOURCES

The researcher of hate crimes should begin with public or university libraries. (Bookstores will have a limited number of titles on hand on this very specific topic, although any book in print can usually be ordered.) A good academic library is the most useful research source of all, as the library will hold not only books and periodicals but also a variety of bibliographic resources such as catalogues, indexes, and bibliographies that can point the student in a very specific direction.

INTERNET RESEARCH

The Internet is a global network of computer servers that share TCP/IP, a common protocol that allows the servers to communicate with each other. Most universities, public libraries, and government agencies have a presence on the Internet as well as a direct connection to it, either through their own servers or through an Internet service provider (ISP).

A variety of activities have been carried out on the Internet since its inception and early growth in the 1960s and 1970s. Chat rooms allow users to instantly communicate with each other; forums allow users to post and reply to opinions, news, and general information; webcams broadcast live video and sound; voice-over IP is gradually replacing landline telephone systems; shared workplaces allow one user to see and manipulate data on a computer thousands of miles distant; web logs or "blogs" allow their creators to maintain daily commentary on their research, activities, or field of interest. The video-sharing web site YouTube is used to access free streaming videos, originally designed for amateur videographers. The universal acceptance of this site has made it a useful research tool for anyone looking into breaking news, stories, criminal trials, police investigations, and the like.

By FTP (file transfer protocol), large files can be downloaded from remote sites. By far the largest and most active system present on the Internet is the World Wide Web.

Hate Crimes

The World Wide Web is made up of millions of pages and sites, all sharing a common programming language known as hypertext markup language (HTML). The language was created to provide direct electronic links to other sites, by far the Web's most valuable feature. Through the Web, federal agencies such as the Department of Justice, federal and state courts, nongovernmental public-interest agencies, private corporations, and so on can be accessed and investigated to some extent by a researcher seeking information that may be difficult to find in traditional print media such as books, magazines, and reports.

Searching the Internet through the World Wide Web can be quite helpful or quite frustrating. A query for "hate crimes" on Google, a relatively comprehensive Internet search engine, on November 9, 2007, returned a grand total of 1,650,000 results. A thorough researcher might have the time to open and examine a few hundred web sites of interest to the topic at hand. The researcher must bring a critical eye to the content of these sites, as the creations of the World Wide Web range in quality from vital and comprehensive to useless, but there are several useful criteria when looking at a web page. Consider the author or organization that has created the web page. Points of view can be either expressed or hidden by proper names and acronyms. Researchers always must carefully examine any material presented for bias. The most important consideration is the relative expertise held by members of the group in the subject they purport to describe and analyze.

Generally, authoritative web sites will carry plentiful links to other sites (of varying viewpoints); the links will operate properly (demonstrating that the URLs in use are still valid). A wider range of resources given—books, articles, reports, other web pages, and so on—marks the site as broadly useful rather than narrowly focused. Within the documents on the site, reference notes should be provided, with or without Internet links, and these sources should be easily verified.

Good web sites are updated frequently (the Last Updated date is frequently visible). Contact information will be provided: name, physical address or post office box number, phone number, e-mail address. Sponsorship of the site should be given, whether by governmental or nongovernmental organizations, academic institutions, or corporations. Advertising should be kept to a minimum.

Although a subjective consideration, the appearance and overall design of the web page is also a clue to validity. Links within the site should be logical and intuitive. Graphics should serve a useful function, rather than being presented as an end in themselves. A good design reflects careful programming, which in turn signifies a large investment in time and money by the individual or organization that created the page. Proper spelling, punctuation, grammar, and paragraph formatting also reveal that the page creator has taken pains to present information in a manner that is easy to understand.

How to Research Hate Crimes

Viewing World Wide Web pages requires a software program known as a browser. On instructions from the user, the browser reads the computer code stored on web pages and presents it as text, graphics, photographs, and so on. The most commonly used browsers are Firefox, Safari, and Internet Explorer.

WEB SITES OF INTEREST

Hate Crimes Research Network
  URL: http://www.hatecrime.net
  A site based at Portland State University that is designed to provide a pool of information on academic research being done on the topic of hate crimes. With useful pages giving bibliographies, journal articles, links to hate crime-related web sites, and names and addresses of researchers.
"Hate in America: What Do We Know?"
  URL: http://www.publiceye.org/hate/Hate99ASA.htm
  Ten essays on the history and prevalence of hate crimes and hate groups collected from a press conference sponsored by the American Sociological Association on August 6, 1999. Includes "What Are the Aggregate Patterns of Hate Crime in the O.S.," a breakdown of hate crimes according to race, ethnicity/national origin/religion, sexual orientation, disability, and multiple bias, as distilled from the FBI's Uniform Crime Reporting (UCR) program.
Lambda GLBT Community Services
  URL: http://www.qrd.org/www/orgs/avproject/main.htm
  Title: "Hate Crimes and Homophobia," a section with official statements, crime reports, FBI statistics, and research on antigay hate crime.
Matthew Shepard
  URL: http://www.mattshepard.org
  Dedicated to Matthew Shepard, a gay college student who was beaten to death outside Laramie, Wyoming.
National Criminal Justice Reference Service
  URL: http://www.ncjrs.org/hate_crimes/hate_crimes.html
  A site operated by the crime information service of the U.S. Department of Justice, giving summaries of hate-crimes statistics, information on grants and funding, Justice Department programs, legislation, links to hate-crimes websites as well as relevant Department of Justice sites, and a large database of useful article abstracts.
Stop Hate Crimes, University of California at Davis Psychology Department
  URL: http://psychology.ucdavis.edu/rainbow/html/hate_crimes.html
  Information, articles, and links to current news and articles on hate crimes. Links to books and articles on the subject by Dr. Gregory Herek.

SEARCH ENGINES

Search engines require the user to enter a word or phrase that will return links to hopefully pertinent and useful sites. Surrounding a phrase with quotation marks assures that only the specific phrase—not its components—will be used by the search engine. Entering "hate crimes," as mentioned above, however, returns more sites than the user could ever hope to visit. Therefore, the search has to be further narrowed by adding words—places, dates, people, court cases, and so on. To accomplish this, the user enters modifying phrases after the word AND (capital letters), thus instructing the search engine to return all sites that include both phrases. For instance:

"Hate crimes" AND "federal statutes"
"hate crimes" AND "FBI statistics"
"Clinton Administration" AND "Hate Crime laws"

Seeking the web page of a certain organization can be accomplished by specifying "Home page" after the name of the organization.

"Anti-Defamation League" AND "home page"

Anyone using search engines on the Internet should be aware that prominent listings can be purchased by web page creators, and that organizations that operate search engines can feature (or filter out) certain sites according to their own criteria. Following are some of the most useful search engines now operating on the World Wide Web.

AllTheWeb.com or FAST Search (http://www.alltheweb.com) One of the largest indexes on the World Wide Web, with large multimedia and mobile/wireless web indexes first created in 1999.

Alta Vista (http://www.altavista.com) One of the original crawler search engines, Alta Vista allows users to build very specific searches with the Advanced Query mode. A Refine feature helps the researcher narrow the search and the user can translate text to or from several foreign languages.

AOL Search (http://search.aol.com) For America Online members, allowing them to search the web as well as providing "priority content" that can only be accessed through an AOL subscription.

Ask.com (http://www.ask.com) A search engine in which the user employs natural language to get responses to very specific requests. The response comes in the form of a list of sites that provide relevant information on a subject phrase recognized by the engine.

Google (http://www.google.com) A vast searchable database of web pages has made Google one of the most useful Internet search engines in existence. The Advanced Search feature allows users to specify language, file format, date of the web pages, domains, and placement of the phrase searched for on the page. Users can also browse recent news stories on the topic. The user can have foreign language pages translated and also set the maximum number of results.

HotBot (http://www.hotbot.com) A site that draws on results from other sites, including Ask.com, MSN, and lyGO.com (a search site that returns images of relevant web pages). This engine is now run by Lycos, a company that maintains another search engine under its own name.

Lycos (http://www.lycos.com) Lycos started out as a crawler service and then was transformed into a directory, in which users search through indexes created by web programmers.

Open Directory (http://dmoz.org) A search engine launched in 1998 and maintained by volunteers, whose catalogues and directories are made freely available to other sites such as Google, Lycos, and HotBot.

Yahoo! (http://www.yahoo.com) The oldest and most popular web search engine, Yahoo! draws on a team of editors who constantly update and streamline its directories. Although drawing on a smaller database than Google, Yahoo! provides users with an organized subject index, somewhat more useful than simply searching keywords, and provides users the alternative of seeing results provided by Google.

Legal Search Engines

There are two important search engines devoted to the subject of law, court cases, statutes, and the like: FindLaw (http://www.findlaw.com) and Wash-Law WEB (http://www.washlaw.edu). The two major legal databases in current use are Westlaw and LexisNexis, both of which are expanding with a variety of nonlegal resources. Loislaw, a division of Aspen Publishers, Inc., has created another subscription website for electronic legal research.

Westlaw and LexisNexis are fee-based subscription services that allow users to search a constantly updated collection of state and federal statutes, cases, regulations, public records, corporate information, and international law databases. The LexisNexis database is located at http://www.lexis.com; Westlaw resides at http://www.westlaw.com. A researcher may be able to access these databases through a subscription held by a public, academic, or law library.

Westlaw

Westlaw (www.westlaw.com) is a product of West Group, a company formed by the merger of West Publishing and Thomson Legal Publishing. This membership site, which is available in most academic libraries, organizes a wide variety of information under the heading of each state.

For the state of Florida, for example, Westlaw offers the following (among many more databases) that may be useful for those researching hate crimes:

FL-CS: Florida Cases. Documents from the appellate courts of Florida, including decisions and orders published in the *Southern Reporter*. This database includes "quick opinions," which are made available online before they appear in print.

FL-CS-ALL: Cases from state courts, federal district courts within Florida, and the Eleventh Circuit (federal appeals).

FL-AG: Florida Attorney General Opinions. This section includes opinion letters released by the Florida Attorney General's office. As in the Florida Administrative Code, this section can be searched by several different criteria.

FL-ST-ANN: Florida Statutes—Annotated. Court rules and statutes, including the complete set of updated and revised statutes and the Florida constitution. Also includes state court rules and federal district and bankruptcy court rules as they appear in West Publishing's *Florida Rules of Court*.

FL-LEGIS: Florida Legislative Service—Current. Documents (chapters or resolutions) passed by the state legislature, not including special acts or general acts of local application.

FL-BILLTXT: Florida—Bill Tracking—Full Text. This database contains the full text (including all available amended versions) of all legislative initiatives, including pending and recently passed bills, beginning with the most recent legislative session.

WSB-FL: Westlaw State Bulletins—Florida. Documents prepared by the West Group that summarize recent legal developments, such as recent important court decisions, in Florida law.

FLCJ-CS. Florida Criminal Justice Cases—A case law database dealing exclusively with criminal justice cases.

FLNP. Florida Papers. Contents of the *Miami Herald, Orlando Sentinel, Palm Beach Post, St. Petersburg Times, Fort Lauderdale Sun Sentinel*, and other papers from 1988 or 1989 to the present.

COURT CASES

Federal and state courts are the final arbiter of hate-crimes laws, as it is within these venues that the constitutionality of these statutes are finally decided. Court decisions are indexed according to a standard format, in which the title represents *Plaintiff v. Defendant*, or *Appellant v. Appellee*, then gives the volume number of the reporting publication, the starting page of the case, the venue (federal or state court), and finally the year.

A sample would be the case of *R.A.V. v. City of St. Paul, Minnesota*, 505 U.S. 377 (1992). The case can be found in the 505th volume of the *Supreme Court Reporter* (the publication is simply designated as "U.S."), starting on page 377 (the case was decided in 1992).

Many state supreme courts and appeals courts publish their full decisions online, and nearly all provide an index to the printed reporting source. There are also several useful private online sources of case law, used by legal scholars and researchers who can now avoid the laborious task of searching the volumes owned by law libraries. These online sources include the Legal Information Institute, which publishes all Supreme Court decisions since 1990, plus more than 600 "historic decisions" at http://supct.law.cornell.edu/supct.

THOMAS

The once-frustrating and time-consuming process of tracking current and recent legislative action by the U.S. Congress has been considerably eased by the creation of THOMAS, a World Wide Web site (at http://thomas.loc.gov) devoted to federal legislative information. THOMAS has the *Congressional Record* and the full text of legislation available from 1989 to the present. In addition, the THOMAS page known as *Congressional Documents and Debates 1774–1873* offers a record of congressional proceedings from the legislature's first century.

The About THOMAS page has the following links to be used by researchers: Bills, Resolutions; Activity in Congress; Congressional Record; Schedules, Calendars; Committee Information; Presidential Nominations; Treaties; Government Resources; For Teachers; Help and Contact. The searcher must specify the Congress by number (congressional sessions last two years and are consecutively numbered; the 2008–2009 session is thus known as the 109th Congress). By default, the links go to the Congress currently in session. The Search Bill Text link can return bills pending in the current Congress. Users may also browse bills by sponsor

The Bill Text link can be searched by two different criteria: Word/Phrase or Bill Number. Entering the bill number will return the current and all past versions of the bill in question. Using a Word/Phrase search will return all the bills relating to that subject.

Bill Summary and Status presents related information: how the bill originated, who is sponsoring it, its status in committee, amendments attached to it, scheduled votes, and so on, prepared by an organization known as the Congressional Research Service. In Bill Summary and Status, the researcher has several ways to search: Word/Phrase, Subject Term, Bill/Amendment Number, Stage in Legislative Process, Date of Introduction, Sponsor/Cosponsor, and Committee. This link will not allow the researcher to read the full text of the bill, however; that is the work performed by the

Bill Text search. The Bill Summary and Status information includes the following:

Titles
Bill Status (with links to the online *Congressional Record* and information on votes)
Committees
Related House Committee Documents
Amendments
Related Bill Details
Subjects (CRS index terms)
Cosponsors
CRS Summary

Researchers looking for legislative texts and documents prior to 1989 and that are not available on the THOMAS site must locate a Federal Depository Library. There are approximately 1,350 of them in the United States and U.S. possessions, and at least one in each congressional district; a list can be accessed and searched at http://www.gpo.gov/su_docs/locators/findlibs/index.html.

ONLINE BOOK CATALOGS

Retail book catalogs available online include Barnesandnoble.com (or bn.com) and Amazon.com. These sites can prove quite useful to the researcher, as they give not only title and publication information but, in many cases, selected reviews by readers and critics as well as text extracts and tables of contents. Tracking down out-of-print books is also possible, as the sites offer links to associated sites that specialize in out-of-print and hard to find books.

The most comprehensive library online catalog is that of the Library of Congress, available at http://lcweb.loc.gov. This site offers useful guides and indexes for researchers, links to other library catalogs, access to foreign collections, interlibrary loan services, and a special section on law research.

Yahoo! also offers a library listing at http://dir.yahoo.com/Reference/Libraries. Most usefully for the hate-crimes researcher, this page includes links to law libraries and government document collections. Most public libraries offer their catalogs online as well, free for research, and their books can often be ordered for borrowing through the interlibrary loan system.

The catalogs can usually be searched by author, title, subject category, or keyword. Entering the words "hate crime" (with quotation marks) will return all titles or (sometimes) book descriptions with that exact phrase included. For a comprehensive search, the researcher is better advised to use a subject heading. Relevant subject headings for the topic include:

- hate crimes
- hate speech
- prejudice
- racism
- legislation
- bias
- bias crimes

ONLINE DATABASES

There are many useful online information databases, which can often be accessed free at subscribing public or university libraries. These databases offer indexes of books, periodicals, audiovisual materials, dissertations, government documents, law cases, online federal and state statutes, and the like, as well as indexes to reference works such as bibliographies, encyclopedias, and dictionaries (which in many cases can be accessed online as well through a direct link provided by the database). Among the most comprehensive are InfoTrac and Wilson SelectPlus. The LexisNexis database is an immense online research tool, grouped into topical and state-specific libraries and subdivided into files that may be searched by keyword, author, title, date, and subject. The researcher may browse or search databases specific to a single state, as in Westlaw. Many newspapers and magazines also offer online databases and indexes through their own Web sites.

In many cases, the database will also offer a full-text version or a one-paragraph abstract of a book or article, giving the researcher a clear idea of the subject covered within the work and the author's approach to the topic and point of view. For the hate crimes researcher, material from the late 1980s and early 1990s will generally cover the first period of hate-crimes legislation, when the debate over the constitutionality of hate crimes was running hot; the late 1990s and the years 2000–07 will bring materials related to the further refinement of hate-crime laws to cover protected statuses of gender, sexual orientation, and disability. Older works can be useful when researching civil rights legislation, the legal precursor to modern hate-crimes law, or the general subjects of racism, prejudice, and bigotry.

GOVERNMENT AGENCIES AND STATISTICS

One of the most useful web sites to any researcher of crime and the criminal justice system is the Bureau of Justice Statistics page at http://www.ojp.usdoj.gov/bjs. This site publishes statistics on crime, crime victims, criminal offenders, law enforcement (federal, state, local, and campus), courts and sentencing, corrections (probation, jails, and capital punishment), and the federal justice system.

The traditional federal crime report consisted of a tally of offenses and arrests for certain types of crimes, published in the FBI's annual Uniform Crime Report (UCR). This system is being updated and improved by the National Incident-Based Reporting System (NIBRS), an FBI program that collects more details on more categories of crime, including concurrent offenses, weapons, injury, location, property loss and characteristics of the victims, offenders and arrestees. As of December 2003 (the most recent information available), more than 5,271 agencies in 23 states were submitting NIBRS data. The NIBRS also captures a wide range of information on hate crimes, and the Bureau of Justice Statistics published these findings in *Hate Crimes Reported in NIBRS, 1997–1999* (publication number NCJ 186765), available through the site.

Another important publication is the *Sourcebook of Criminal Justice Statistics*, available online at http://www.albany.edu/sourcebook. This reference collects information from more than 100 sources into more than 1,000 tables, most recently from the year 2005. The tables include "Bias-Motivated (Hate) Crimes Known to Police, by Offense, United States," "Bias Motivations in Hate Crimes Known to Police, United States, 2005," and "Race of Suspected Offender in Bias-Motivated (Hate) Crimes Known to Police, By Type of Bias Motivation, United States, 2005."

CHAPTER 7

━━━━━━━━━━━

ANNOTATED BIBLIOGRAPHY

The following chapter represents a sample of available printed, audiovisual, and online materials dealing with hate crimes. The material is broken down into the following general categories:

General Works on Racism, Prejudice, and Bigotry
Modern Racist and Hate Groups
History of Hate Violence
Legal and Constitutional Aspects of Hate-Crime Legislation
Criminology, Law Enforcement, and Research
Anti-Homosexual Bias Crime

These categories are further divided into books, periodicals, reports, Internet documents, and videos, where applicable. Most of the articles and books selected are for the general reader, although there is a good sampling of academic scholarship on the psychology of prejudice and hate-crimes perpetrators as well as legal papers on the constitutionality and historical precedents of modern hate-crimes law. Many of the articles listed are also available online from subscription databases such as InfoTrac and Lexis-Nexis and on the web sites operated by the periodicals themselves, which can often be accessed free of charge or via databases provided by public or university libraries.

GENERAL WORKS ON RACISM, PREJUDICE, AND BIGOTRY

BOOKS

Allport, Gordon. *The Nature of Prejudice.* Menlo Park, Calif.: Addison Wesley, 1979. The author, a pioneering psychologist in the field of religious belief and prejudice, offers a long and detailed exploration of the sources of bigotry and discrimination within the human personality, and why such characteristics often erupt into violence. A seminal publication, the book was adopted as a handbook by the civil rights leaders of the 1960s.

Babacan, Hurriyet, and Narayan Gopalkrishnan, eds. *Racisms in the New World Order: Realities of Cultures, Colours and Identity.* Newcastle upon Tyne, UK: Cambridge Scholars Publishing, 2007. The editors and authors in the collection of essays identify "modern" forms of racism and the related phenomena of ageism and sexism, placing the question in the context of ongoing political events such as the "War on Terror." Gopalkrishnan describes the official and unofficial uses of media in "Neo-Liberalism and Infeartainment: What Does a State Do?", and several essays examine the problem of racism in Australia.

Better, Shirley Jean. *Institutional Racism: A Primer on Theory and Strategies for Social Change.* 2nd ed. Lanham, Md.: Rowman & Littlefield, 2008. The author explores the phenomenon of institutionalized racism, which is perpetuated by social groups and organizations in order to protect their interests. The book offers suggestions, for individuals and groups, on overcoming discriminatory policies and attitudes.

Bonilla-Silva, Eduardo. *Racism Without Racists: Color-Blind Racism and the Persistence of Racial Inequality in the United States.* Lanham, Md.: Rowman & Littlefield, 2006. Through interviews and data analysis, the author develops a theory of contemporary racial ideology, which he labels "color-blind racism," and which in his view arises from the application of liberal ideas to racial matters. This "soft racism" is apparent in situations where the idea of race is supposedly banished as a basis of evaluating one's ability—a scenario the author himself experienced as an arrival in American academia from his native Puerto Rico.

Brown, Michael K., et al. *Whitewashing Race: The Myth of a Color-Blind Society.* Berkeley, Calif.: University of California Press, 2005. The authors, coming from various academic fields, point out the persistence of racial inequality in a nation supposedly offering opportunity for all. They note the recent fashion of declaring racism a thing of the past and poverty the result of individual failings.

Dray, Philip. *At the Hands of Persons Unknown: The Lynching of Black America.* New York: Random House, 2002. A study of the history of lynching of African Americans, finding that lynching was far from rare. The author maintains that lynching was an important element of systematic discrimination against African Americans, particularly in the South, and was used purposefully as a weapon of terror with widespread sanction in the greater community. The author also documents the gradual end of lynching in the mid-20th century as black servicemen returned home from World War II to set an example of racial pride, patriotism, and heroism, and as dedicated individuals and organizations pressured state and federal legislatures to take more effective action against violations of civil rights.

Annotated Bibliography

Feagin, Joe R. *Racist America: Roots, Current Realities, and Future Reparations.* New York: Routledge, 2000. Despite any advances made during and as a result of the civil rights era, the author finds racism still permeating American society, present in the actions and attitudes of every person in the country and influencing basic decisions such as where to live and what to wear.

Ferber, Abby L. *White Man Falling: Race, Gender and White Supremacy.* Lanham, Md.: Rowman & Littlefield, 1998. The author, the director of Women's Studies at the University of Colorado at Colorado Springs, is a widely recognized expert on far right political movements and organized hate groups. She offers a history of the concept of race and background on the white supremacist movement in the United States, and reaches the conclusion that gender issues—particularly the reassertion of their traditional power and authority by men—lie at the heart of contemporary racism.

Frederickson, George M. *Racism: A Short History.* Princeton, N.J.: Princeton University Press, 2002. The author finds the origins of modern racism in medieval Europe's treatment of Jews, whose refusal to convert to Christianity was considered a basic character flaw, and in the Enlightenment's more scientific classification of nationalities. This racism reached the level of official policy in the 19th century, when nations put in place strict immigration policies to keep their own populations racially "pure," but was finally discredited among the mainstream by the actions of Nazi Germany in the Holocaust.

Hall, Patricia Wong, and Victor M. Hwang. *Anti-Asian Violence in North America: Asian American and Asian Canadian Reflections on Hate, Healing, and Resistance.* Walnut Creek, Calif.: AltaMira, 2001. A wide spectrum of Asian-American and Asian-Canadian contributors—attorneys, students, businesspeople, and activists—discuss the impact of bias crime and racism on themselves and on their communities. The writers cover racism and hate crimes as well as other aspects of the race problem, including Internet-based racism, police bigotry, economic and legal barriers, and immigration issues. They also offer possible solutions and strategies to assist victims, prosecute offenders, and combat ingrained prejudice.

Hemphill, Paul. *The Ballad of Little River: A Tale of Race and Restless Youth in the Rural South.* New York: Free Press, 2000. The author investigates a series of violent crimes, which may or may not have been motivated by race prejudice, and the burning of a black church by five white youths in the poor, isolated hamlet of Little River, Alabama, offering as he does so an in-depth look at race relations in the rural South.

Hier, Sean P., and B. Singh Bolaria. *Race and Racism in 21st Century Canada: Continuity, Complexity, and Change.* Peterborough, Ontario, Canada: Broadview Press, 2007. A collection of 16 scholarly articles on racial minorities within Canada, which are growing as a percentage of the population and giving rise to a debate over legal, social, political, and economic cooperation and competition in a country with some of the strictest hate-speech laws in the world.

Johnson, Sandra E. *Standing on Holy Ground: A Triumph Over Hate Crime in the Deep South.* Columbia, S.C.: University of South Carolina Press, 2005. The author describes the struggles of a white activist who involved herself in the rebuilding of a vandalized South Carolina church during the 1980s. The book covers not only this local case but also gives a general account of the wave of arson that struck at black churches through the 1980s and 1990s, the activities of a renascent Ku Klux Klan, and the lingering effects of racial prejudice on law enforcement in the South.

Kennedy, Randall. *Nigger: The Strange Career of a Troublesome Word.* New York: Vintage, 2003. A Harvard law professor traces the history of a racial slur that originated as a neutral noun in the 17th century and evolved into an insult employed in books, songs, movies, politics, law courts, and everyday speech. The author covers the debate over removing the word from dictionaries, banning it in classroom studies, and the "historical right" of blacks to use it, showing that the word has become a powerful symbolic reminder of the entire history of race relations in the United States.

Kotlowitz, Alex. *The Other Side of the River: A Story of Two Towns, A Death, and America's Dilemma.* New York: Doubleday, 1998. The story of a black teenager's death in the St. Joseph River, an event that was either an accident or a bias-motivated murder and that polarized the two communities of Benton Harbor and St. Joseph, Michigan.

Levin, Jack. *The Violence of Hate: Confronting Racism, Anti-Semitism, and Other Forms of Bigotry.* 2nd ed. Boston: Allyn & Bacon, 2007. The author analyzes the psychological makeup of racists and bigots and explores the various social factors, including what he terms "the tacit approval of ordinary, even decent people" that bring about hate crimes. The book includes an appendix of antihate Web sites.

Levin, Jack, and Jack McDevitt. *Hate Crimes: The Rising Tide of Bigotry and Bloodshed.* New York: Plenum Press, 1993. The authors discuss the growth of hate crimes in the 1980s and early 1990s and argue that stereotypes that appear in the popular media contribute to such crimes. They advocate special bias-crime units within police departments and rehabilitation programs for "thrill-seeking" hate-crimes perpetrators.

Levin, Jack, and Gordana Rabrenovic. *Why We Hate.* Amherst, N.Y.: Prometheus Books, 2004. The authors grapple with the question of why human beings express hatred, often through violence and intimidation, toward unfamiliar or foreign individuals. The book analyzes both localized and global/national prejudice based on race, religion, or nationality, and searches for origins of that prejudice in emotions and basic human psychology.

Annotated Bibliography

Macedo, Donaldo, and Panayota Gounari, eds. *The Globalization of Racism.* Boulder, Colo.: Paradigm Publishers, 2005. This collection of 15 essays treats the subject of racism in various locales and strives to find the underlying cause in political ideology (as it is used in Europe, Africa, and the United States) and in the "unleashing" of economic globalization.

Massey, Douglas. *Categorically Unequal: The American Stratification System.* New York: Russell Sage Foundation, 2007. The author looks at the inequalities that seem inherent in American society, while also covering the technological and economic problems facing other nations in an era of globalization. The problem, he concludes, arises from natural human tendencies to categorize people depending on their race, social status, and gender. The result, an ever-widening gap between the wealthy and poor, is magnified by the physical separation of ethnic groups and social classes and in some instances leads to bias crimes and violence.

McClintock, Michael, and Judith Sunderland. *Antisemitism in Europe: Challenging Official Indifference.* New York: Human Rights First, 2004. The book surveys recent anti-Semitic incidents in Europe and gives a comprehensive overview of the laws regarding bias crimes, underlining inadequate and unequal enforcement across the continent.

Memmi, Albert. *Racism.* Minneapolis: University of Minnesota Press, 2000. The author gives a thorough historical and psychological analysis of racism, which he regards as a social pathology that takes many different forms but arises from the same source: the drive to empower one group of people at the expense of another.

Min, Pyong Gap, ed. *Encyclopedia of Racism in the United States.* 3 vols. Westport, Conn.: Greenwood Press, 2005. A collection of 447 entries, written by 32 contributors, on theories of race, everyday discrimination, American nativism, and specific legal topics such as affirmative action and coverage of important Supreme Court decisions. The third volume reproduces 26 original documents useful to the researcher.

Minow, Martha. *Breaking the Cycles of Hatred: Memory, Law and Repair.* Princeton, N.J.: Princeton University Press, 2002. A book of essays and lectures exploring cycles of violence, in which one act brings about another, setting off a self-perpetuating cycle of vengeance that can occur among families, ethnic groups, and nations. Minow explores innovative legal and political solutions to this phenomenon, arguing, for example, that civil rather than criminal actions against hate groups and bias crimes will prove most effective in preventing such incidents.

Moore, John Hartwell, ed. *Encyclopedia of Race and Racism.* New York: Macmillan, 2007. A three-volume reference work of about 400 entries, written by 350 contributors, defining and describing the concept of race and the phenomenon of racism, in the United States and around the world. The set includes a filmography, photographs, and maps; each article is followed by a short bibliography.

Moore, Wendy Leo. *Reproducing Racism: White Space, Elite Law Schools, and Racial Inequality.* Lanham, Md.: Rowman & Littlefield, 2008. The author describes racist currents running through top U.S. law schools, which host various forms of discrimination in their faculty and student selection, courses, and institutional outlook. The clubby nature of elite schools, in the author's opinion, keeps the door largely closed for minorities and also affects the outlook of politicians and community leaders who have graduated from these institutions.

Morrison, Melanie, and Todd G. Morrison, eds. *The Psychology of Modern Prejudice.* New York: Nova Science Publishers, 2008. This collection of scholarly essays explores modern prejudice and the stance that discrimination is a historical issue, rather than a problem with current relevance, because stigmatized groups now have all the rights they need. Individuals with highly developed modern prejudices defend the status quo, believing that these groups make unfair demands and receive public attention disproportionate to their numbers. The essays in this collection explore the manifestations of these subtle negative attitudes toward groups such as gays, lesbians, and African Americans.

Neiwart, David. *Death on the Fourth of July: The Story of a Killing, a Trial, and Hate Crime in America.* Basingstoke, Hampshire, U.K.: Palgrave Macmillan, 2005. The author describes a racially charged incident in Ocean Shores, Washington, that took place on July 4, 2000, and resulted in the trial of an Asian American—the putative hate-crime victim—on charges of manslaughter. The author covers the effect of racial prejudice in small communities and uses the incident as a platform for a more general discussion of hate-crime laws and how they work.

Nelson, Todd D. *The Psychology of Prejudice.* 2nd ed. Boston: Allyn & Bacon, 2006. This textbook introduces the birth of research into stereotypes and examines the major theories of prejudice and stereotyping in use today. The focus of this book is on empirical studies, but the presentation is designed to get readers to think about what causes, maintains, and reduces prejudice, and to formulate personal opinions about issues such as ageism, sexism, and racism.

Pred, Allen. *The Past Is Not Dead: Facts, Fictions, and Enduring Racial Stereotypes.* Minneapolis: University of Minnesota Press, 2004. The author examines racial stereotyping in literature and letters from centuries past.

Rattansi, Ali. *Racism: A Very Short Introduction.* Oxford: Oxford University Press, 2007. The author attempts to disentangle the phenomenon of racism from the modern political, economic, and social theories surrounding it and to make a scientific study, based on genetics, of how it has evolved and manifested in nearly every human society. A key question discussed is the persistence of racism in the contemporary world despite the scientific discrediting of the notion of "race."

Russell, Diana E. H., and Roberta A. Harmes, eds. *Femicide in Global Perspective.* New York: Teachers College Press, 2001. A series of articles by the editors and others defining and discussing "femicide" (the murder of women) and recounting the incidence of hate crimes against women in Africa, Asia, and North America.

Salaita, Steven George. *Anti-Arab Racism in the USA: Where It Comes From and What It Means for Politics Today.* London: Pluto Press, 2006. Blending personal narrative, theory, and pointed argument, Salaita (who is himself Arab American) explores anti-Arab racism in America. He asserts that this deep-rooted racism infuses Americans of all political stripes and describes how it affects U.S. laws and culture.

Singular, Stephen. *The Uncivil War: The Rise of Hate, Violence, and Terrorism in America.* Beverly Hills, Calif.: New Millennium Press, 2001. The author draws on prominent incidents of violence, such as the Columbine school shootings in Colorado and the assassination of radio talk-show host Alan Berg, to argue that the United States is suffering an upsurge in hate violence, and that such actions have moved from the fringes of society into mainstream institutions such as schools, churches, and media outlets.

Sowell, Thomas. *Ethnic America: A History.* New York: Basic Books, 1981. The author describes in depth the history and culture of nationalities that have arrived as major immigrant groups in the United States, concentrating on how these foreign cultures eventually blended into the melting pot. The book provides a valuable background for anyone studying the history of immigration and the often-violent story of ethnic rivalries and economic competition in the New World.

Steinberg, Stephen. *Race Relations: A Critique.* Stanford, Calif.: Stanford Social Sciences, 2007. In this essay, the author examines the modern view of race relations and the language used in analyzing racism, developed by the dominant "white" culture, and declares them outmoded tools that no longer serve their purpose. He criticizes the modern infrastructure of foundations, academia, and politics as promoting, rather than abating, discriminatory conditions, and he advocates a new view of the problem based on the outlook of the minorities whom it directly affects.

Sternberg, Robert J., and Karin Sternberg. *The Nature of Hate.* New York: Cambridge University Press, 2008. The authors analyze the hate impulse, exploring its origin in human psychology and its propagation through fear and ignorance. Hatred of those distant and different manifests itself in various forms, not only in single hate crimes but also in mass movements dedicated to violence and in terrorism and genocide sponsored by governments.

Tautz, Birgit, ed. *Colors 1800/1900/2000: Signs of Ethnic Difference.* New York: Rodopi, 2004. In this volume of essays, scholars discuss racism in German history, from the 18th century to the present, using historical, literary, and anthropological approaches. Several essays reveal that philosophies of blood, color, and race have persisted to present-day German society, legal codes, and writing.

Temple-Raston, Dina. *A Death in Texas: A Story of Race, Murder, and a Small Town's Struggle for Redemption.* New York: Henry Holt, 2002. A book describing the 1998 dragging murder of an African American, James Byrd, Jr., by three white men in the East Texas community of Jasper. The author ponders the nature of small-town racism and describes the effect that the brutal crime and the subsequent nationwide attention and media publicity had on the community.

Trepagnier, Barbara. *Silent Racism: How Well-Meaning White People Perpetuate the Racial Divide.* Boulder, Colo.: Paradigm Publishers, 2007. Defining silent racism as racism by people who regard themselves as not racist, Trepagnier argues that all individuals harbor some racist thoughts and feelings, and she supports her position with interview transcripts of whites who classify themselves as nonracists. She urges well-meaning white people who see themselves as not racist to raise their awareness of race in order to improve race relations in the United States.

Upchurch, Thomas Adam. *Legislating Racism: The Billion Dollar Congress and the Birth of Jim Crow.* Lexington, Ky.: University Press of Kentucky, 2004. The writer covers the transition from post–Civil War Reconstruction to the Jim Crow era, when amended state constitutions deprived African Americans of their rights as voters and citizens. The book takes the Republican Party to task for abandoning its core value of humanitarianism and for making itself the party of pork-barrel spending and big business. In the author's view, this trend laid the foundation for the following century of social conflict and legalized, institutionalized discrimination against African Americans and other ethnic minorities.

Waller, James. *Prejudice Across America.* Jackson, Miss.: University Press of Mississippi, 2000. A professor and students from Whitworth College in Spokane, Washington, carry out a three-week long cross-country trek, visiting several cities in an attempt to find and understand the phenomenon of race prejudice.

Welch, Michael. *Scapegoats of September 11th: Hate Crimes & State Crimes in the War on Terror.* Critical Issues in Crime and Society series. Piscataway, N.J.: Rutgers University Press, 2006. The author describes the many changes in American society wrought by the terrorist attacks of September 11, 2001, including a wave of anti-Arab violence and security measures that in the author's view are discriminatory and ineffective. A criminology professor at Rutgers University, Welch studies the scapegoating of Muslims through bias crimes in the United States and abroad.

Welsh, John. *After Multiculturalism: The Politics of Race and the Dialects of Liberty.* Lanham, Md.: Lexington Books, 2008. The author argues that the contemporary idea of multiculturalism has obscured and confused racial matters and has done nothing to counter racist attitudes and institutions. Instead, he favors a libertarian approach to a "postethnic" future as expounded in the works of Ayn Rand and others.

PERIODICALS

Akomolafe, Femi. "Blame Everything Bad on Immigrants." *New African,* vol. 474, June 2008, p. 88. A story on the wave of anti-immigrant and racist sentiment present in the Netherlands, expressed in political figures such as Geert Wilders, a member of the Dutch parliament, and others who seek to end the country's constitutional ban on discrimination.

Anonymous. "Faking the Hate: Faked Hate Crimes on College Campuses." *US News and World Report,* vol. 128, no. 22, June 5, 2000. Discusses hoax hate crimes and the possible motivation of perpetrators in proving the pervasiveness of racism and sexism on campus.

Anonymous. Untitled. *America,* vol. 184, no. 19, June 4–11, 2001, p. 3. This editorial characterizes hate crimes as "an affront to the national conscience." The editorial discusses hate crimes against Asian Americans in the wake of recent immigration; the reaction of law enforcement to hate-crime complaints on the part of Asian Americans, and the prevention of hate crimes through education.

Begley, Sharon. "Racism Isn't Hard-Wired." *Newsweek,* vol. 151, no. 9, March 2, 2008, pp. 26–27. The author explores the extent to which racism can be overcome with respect to voting behavior.

Burnette Davis, Alice J. "Simply Because We Are Black; The Message of the Illinois Shooting: Race Matters." *Sojourners,* September/October 1999, pp. 10–11. In the wake of Benjamin Smith's racially inspired killings in Illinois and Indiana in July 1999, the writer contends that African Americans are strangers, "others," in their own land; and that because of this otherness, African Americans are brought together in ways that nonblacks do not understand.

Burns, Robert E. "Hate Makes Waste." *U.S. Catholic,* March 1999, p. 2. The writer contends that society must bear some responsibility for instilling in individuals the type of loathing witnessed in hate crimes, and that the murder of Matthew Shepard, a 21-year-old college student from Wyoming, and the death of a Texas man at the hands of a group of white racists, should prompt an examination of society in general.

Bush, Janet. "The White Country: Is Our Multicultural Society a Myth?" *New Statesman*, August 28, 2006, p. 28. The author covers the subject of racism and segregation in rural England, where the population is overwhelmingly English and Caucasian. Long-held biases and ignorance manifest themselves when laborers from Asia and eastern Europe show up, although conflicts are not as immediate, or violent, as they often are in London and other cities. The basic problem is one of unfamiliarity and changing social conditions, naturally resisted by people with long family ties in isolated locales.

Cochrane, Kira. "Truths We Must Face Up To." *New Statesman*, November 12, 2007, p. 22. The author describes several violent crimes against disabled persons and speculates on a growing tendency to mark those who appear physically different for poor treatment.

Craig, Kellina M. "Retaliation, Fear, or Rage: An Investigation of African American and White Reactions to Racist Hate Crimes." *Journal of Interpersonal Violence*, vol. 14, no. 2, June 1999, pp. 138–51. The author describes and analyzes an experiment in the varying responses to hate crimes viewed by white and African-American subjects. The experiment is designed to study the question of whether hate crimes are more harmful by provoking more emotional and violent reactions among those who witness or hear about them—an important justification for hate-crime laws among supporters.

DeAngelis, Tori. "Understanding and Preventing Hate Crime." *Monitor on Psychology*, vol. 32, no. 10, November 2001. In the wake of the September 11, 2001, terrorist attacks and the subsequent random violence committed against Arab Americans, the author describes efforts of researchers to understand hate crimes and their perpetrators, as well as the phenomenon of ethnic stereotyping, and why some people "turn their ethnic discomfort into drastic action."

Echeverria, Beth-Hatt, and Ji-Yeon Jo. "Understanding the 'New' Racism Through an Urban Charter School." *Educational Foundations*, vol. 19, no. 1, Winter/Spring 2005, p. 51. An article that finds "white" privileges enduring at urban charter schools, a sign of a white backlash against racial "preferences" and a reaction to the changing demographics in U.S. cities and the country at large. White liberal rhetoric, which has adopted the themes of multiculturalism and diversity, masks an attempt to further stratify white social classes and separate the races on the basis of a self-defined intellectual privilege, in turn absolving whites, in the author's opinion, of confronting institutional racism.

Erbe, Bonnie. "Racism in the Presidential Race." *U.S. News and World Report*, May 14, 2008. Available online. URL: http://www.usnews.com/blogs/erbe/2008/5/14/racism-in-the-presidential-race.html. Accessed on August 14, 2008. The author describes strong currents of racism encountered by Barack Obama's campaign workers during the primary season of early 2008. Above and beyond opposition to Obama's political views is the fear of African Americans in positions of power, particularly the presidency.

Fiske, Susan T. "What We Know Now About Bias and Intergroup Conflict, the Problem of the Century." *Current Directions in Psychological Science*, vol. 11, no. 4, August 2002, pp. 123–28. An overview of psychological studies of prejudice, which is found to be a subtle condition in most individuals, but in extreme cases arises from economic and cultural conflict. The author finds that education and economic opportunity relieve both degrees of prejudice.

Gillborn, David. "Rethinking White Supremacy." *Ethnicities*, vol. 6, no. 3, 2006, pp. 318–340. Defining white supremacy as a condition in which subjects regard the interests of whites as "normal," the article analyzes two contrasting episodes in the United Kingdom: the London bombings of July 2005 and the education system's process of conducting national education assessments. The author argues that in both cases, white interests mobilized structural and cultural forces to defend white power at the expense of the racialized "other."

Glascock, Jason. "The Jasper Dragging Death: Crisis Communication and the Community Newspaper." *Communication Studies*, vol. 55, 2004, pp. 29–47. An article describing the murder of James Byrd, a notorious East Texas hate crime that brought national attention and fierce debate over the presence of organized hate groups in the surrounding county. Black residents describe incidents of discrimination and generally belie the assertion of local law enforcement that racism is strictly a historical problem.

Green, Donald P., Laurence H. McFalls, and Jennifer K. Smith. "Hate Crime: An Emergent Research Agenda." *Annual Review of Sociology*, vol. 27, 2001, pp. 479–504. A study of the literature of hate crimes and a data collection by researchers attempting to measure and spot trends in hate crimes. The authors advocate more systematic and consistent methods of collecting data and new research on the link between economic, social, and political trends to ethnic conflict.

Horowitz, Craig. "The New Anti-Semitism." *New York*, vol. 26, no. 2, January 11, 1993, pp. 20–28. The author describes a rash of hate crimes in New York City that culminated in the Crown Heights riots, as well as identifying new and more virulent forms of anti-Semitism that he believes find wide acceptance through dissemination in the popular media.

Isaac, Jeffrey C. "Responding to Hate: Bloomington United." *Dissent*, Winter 2000, pp. 9–11. The writer describes his community's response to anti-Semitic and racist literature being circulated in the college town of Bloomington, Indiana.

Kaplan, Jeffrey. "Islamophobia in America?: September 11 and Islamophobic Hate Crime." *Terrorism and Political Violence*, vol. 18, no. 1, March 2006, pp. 1–33. After the terrorist attacks of September 11, 2001, a rise in anti-Muslim and anti-Arab hate crime occurred in the United States, lasting approximately nine weeks before the number of such crimes fell sharply. The author attributes the sudden drop to intervention by the president and by law enforcement, grassroots outreach by community and public-interest groups to Muslims, and the disappearing consensus on the proper course of action to be taken by the government and military against the terrorist threat. The author compares the post–September 11 period to other crisis periods, including the start of World War II and the Red Scare of the 1950s.

Lacey, James. "Hate-Crime Statistics Distort Truth of American Tolerance." *Insight on the News*, January 7, 2003, p. 50. The author cites an FBI statistic showing a 1,500 percent increase in crimes against Arabs and Muslims in the wake of the terrorist attacks of September 11, 2001, but also points out that with some perspective the United States proves itself to be a remarkably tolerant nation. Hate-crime statistics, in his view, are "politically stacked" and arbitrary, and require law-enforcement to make subjective decisions on the motive and intent of criminals.

Lemke, Tim. "NASCAR Riled by Show Seeking Anti-Muslim Bias." *The Washington Times*, April 6, 2006, p. A01. Controversy erupts over an attempt by *Dateline*, a network television news journal, to record treatment of Muslims by racing fans. Investigating opinion polls that show a large percentage of people holding strongly anti-Muslim bias, the show planned to place Arab-Americans at NASCAR events, as well as other public sporting events, and film any incidents of bias or discrimination. A NASCAR official protests the idea as "creating news as opposed to reporting the news."

Lovato, Roberto. "Juan Crow in Georgia." *The Nation*, vol. 286, no. 20, May 26, 2008. The author describes Georgia's system of discriminatory institutions and customs, collectively tagged "Juan Crow," directed against illegal Latino immigrants.

MacGinty, Roger. "Hate Crimes in Deeply Divided Societies: The Case of Northern Ireland." *New Political Science*, vol. 22, no. 1, March 2000, pp. 49–60. The author demonstrates the ways in which hate crime is "masked" or submerged in societies in conflict, using the example of Northern Ireland and its divided Protestant and Catholic populations. In such societies, paramilitary groups may mask hate crimes with political justification; in addition, the populations at odds may be physically segregated, lessening the opportunity for bias crimes.

Mandel, Daniel. "Crying Wolf: Is America a Dangerous Place for Its Muslim Citizens?" *National Review*, vol. 58, no. 4, March 13, 2006, p. 24. The article cites the perception that anti-Muslim violence increased after the attacks of September 11, 2001, and finds that many reports of arson, assault, and other bias-motivated incidents were exaggerated or false. In addition, the author maintains that Muslim stereotypes found in such media as Hollywood films have no basis in prejudice but rather belong to the long tradition of stock characters and situations employed by American moviemakers.

Medoff, Marshall H. "Allocation of Time and Hateful Behavior: A Theoretical and Positive Analysis of Hate and Hate Crimes." *The American Journal of Economics and Sociology*, October 1999, pp. 959–973. A rational-choice economic approach to analyze hateful behavior, predicting that hateful activity decreases with increases in (i) the market wage rate, (ii) the value of time, (iii) age, and (iv) law enforcement activity. The theory is tested on U.S. state hate-crime data, and the results provide convincing support for the model.

"The New Bigotry: A Primer." *Esquire*, June 2008, p. 116. In this collection of short articles and graphics, the magazine covers the phenomenon of 21st century racism, pointing out that although bigotry has largely gone out of style, it is still present in diverse and subtle ways. The features include opinion polls, interviews, FBI statistics, and sidebars on "Cracking the Racial Code," "A Recent History of Outrageous Behavior," and other related topics.

Obama, Barack. "A More Perfect Union." *Vital Speeches of the Day*, vol. 24, no. 5, May 2008, p. 194. A speech given by candidate Obama in Pennsylvania on March 18, 2008, on the subject of divisive attitudes on race.

Peirce, Gareth. "Was It Like This for the Irish?" *London Review of Books*, vol. 30, no. 7, April 10, 2008, p. 3. Available online. URL: http://www.lrb.co.uk/v30/n07/peir01_.html. The author compares the experiences of modern Muslims and historical Irish in Britain. Both groups faced economic discrimination and outright racial hostility, which the author details, and were subject to a harsh system of arrests, indefinite detainment, and summary trials.

Pruzan, Adam. "What Is a Hate Crime?" *The American Enterprise*, January/February 2000, p. 10. The author believes that coverage in the *New York Times* of a gun attack at the North Valley Jewish Community Center in Los Angeles, California, and of the murder of seven people at a Baptist church in Fort Worth, Texas, was indicative of a remarkable resurgence in "genteel prejudice." The author points out that the California incident received more prominent coverage than the Fort Worth incident, and that the former was labeled a hate crime but the latter was not.

Quarmby, Katharine. "Disability: Vicious New Hate Crime." *New Statesman*, September 10, 2007, p. 18. The author recounts several incidents of murder, torture, and violent crime perpetrated against the disabled in England.

Quist-Adade, Charles. "What Is 'Race' and What Is 'Racism'?" *New African*, April 2006, p. 46. In a three-part series, the author gives a history of racial prejudice. In the conclusion the author claims that openly racist attitudes and actions have been replaced by insidious, unconscious habits of mind. In this more subtle racism, individuals accentuate differences and repress shared characteristics, ultimately curtailing empathy for members of other ethnic groups.

Remba, Gidon. "Anti-Semitism: New or Old?" *The Nation*, vol. 278, no. 14, April 12, 2004, p. 2. This opinion piece discusses the theory of a "new" anti-Semitism, based on anti-Zionism, directed at Jews as representatives of the nation of Israel and its various military and political policies. The author claims that anti-Zionism belongs to the tradition of bias based on economic and political competition between Jews and Gentiles, and that the change in motivation does not mitigate the severity or wrongfulness of anti-Semitic prejudice.

Rolo, Mark Anthony. "Damage Control at Dartmouth: Anti–American Indian Incidents at the Ivy League College Create Unease for Native Students." *Diverse Issues in Higher Education*, vol. 23, no. 23, December 28, 2006, p. 17. A short article on racist activity at the Ivy League school, including the distribution of offensive T-shirts, a confrontation at the performance of a drum circle, and the use of "Fighting Sioux" as a nickname by a visiting hockey team. Taken together, the incidents cause unease among Dartmouth's large Native American community and inspire an antihate rally, as well as accusations by conservative members that an overreaction is occurring.

Steyn, Mark. "Vandals in the Churchyard." *The American Spectator*, vol. 33, number 4, May 2000, pp. 52–54. The author believes that hate crimes against religions, including Christianity and Catholicism, are seldom reported, and describes attacks on a dozen Brooklyn Catholic churches and an Episcopal church. The author asserts that false reports of church burnings were exploited by a news media interested in playing up racial hatred, while the recent and genuine attacks only demonstrate antireligious hatred, in which the media take little interest.

Taylor, Rebecca. "Vandalism Victims Feel Targeted over Faith." *The Register-Guard* (Eugene, Oregon), December 22, 2007, p. A1. A newspaper article describing the vandalism of a nativity scene, in which the figures of Jesus were replaced with severed pigs' heads. Police in Eugene, Oregon, investigate the incident as a possible bias crime, which would carry longer sentences for anyone convicted.

United Nations Human Rights Council. "Incompatibility Between Democracy and Racism," in *Report of the Human Rights Council*, p. 13. Geneva: UNHRC, 2006 (2nd session). This resolution documents the UN Human Rights Council's arguments for rejecting racism and xenophobia as rationales for political platforms, legislation, and organization in UN member states.

Wallis, Jim. "America's Original Sin: The Legacy of White Racism." *Cross Currents*, Summer 2007, p. 197. Despite the legal and economic gains made by African Americans over the years, the author claims, racism remains a persistent phenomenon and for many minority ethnic groups the situation is getting worse, not better.

Wolfe, Kathi. "Bashing the Disabled: The New Hate Crime." *The Progressive*, November 1995, pp. 24–27. An analysis of the hostility and the hate crimes being perpetrated against the disabled. The author writes that according to disability-community leaders, the backlash against the disabled is being fueled by resentment of the Americans with Disabilities Act (1990).

Yaqoob, Salma, Gareth Peirce, and Ambalavaner Sivanandan. "Racism, Liberty and the War on Terror: Linking the Struggles." *Race and Class*, vol. 48, no. 4, 2007, pp. 93–96. This document records the two keynote speeches, the closing speech, and excerpts from the proceedings of the conference "Racism, Liberty and the War on Terror." Hosted by the Institute of Race Relations in London in September 2006, the conference considered the future of multiculturalism and the impact of the "war on terror," both in the United Kingdom and internationally.

REPORTS

"1998–2000 Report on Hate Crimes and Discrimination Against Arab-Americans." Washington, D.C.: American-Arab Anti-Discrimination Committee, 2001. In the main, this 77-page report covers discrimination against Arab Americans in education and in employment as well as defamation, hostile public opinion, and media bias. The first section, Legal Issues, details hate crimes committed against Arab Americans.

Beirich, Heidi. "Of Race and Rockets: Space Pioneer Funds Racist Foundation." Southern Poverty Law Center. Available online: URL: http://www.splcenter.org/intel/intelreport/article.jsp?aid=912. Posted in summer 2008. An Intelligence Report on Walter Kistler, a rocket scientist who has given significant amounts to the Pioneer Fund, a foundation supporting "race scientists" and anti-immigrant groups that is on the SPLC's list of hate groups. The report details the origins of the Pioneer Fund in the 1930s and Kistler's staunch defense of the organization's research in the field of "human differences."

WEB DOCUMENTS

Alterman, Eric, and George Zornick. "Think Again: Hatred for Sale." Center for American Progress. Available online. URL: http://www.americanprogress.

org/issues/2008/06/hatred_sale.html. Posted on June 4, 2008. The authors describe a rising tide of anti-immigrant opinion in the print and broadcast media, where in their opinion pundits and reporters are distorting statistics and sensationalizing crime stories in order to rouse public opinion and draw larger audiences. The report refutes many of the economic claims against immigrants and says that the escalating anti-immigrant resentment is strengthening hate groups.

Anti-Defamation League. "2006 Audit of Anti-Semitic Incidents." Available online. URL: http://www.adl.org/main_Anti_Semitism_Domestic/Audit_2006.htm. Downloaded on November 17, 2007. A survey of anti-Semitic violence and incidents, published annually since 1979, and currently including a count of harassment, vandalism, anti-Semitism in the schools, harassment by hate groups, anti-Jewish incidents on campus, a regional breakdown, charts and graphs, and a summary of federal law and initiatives dealing with anti-Semitic hate crime. The audit represents a primary resource for those monitoring trends in anti-Semitism in the United States.

———. "American Attitudes Towards Jews in America: An Anti-Defamation League Survey." Available online. URL: http://www.adl.org/Anti_semitism/poll_2007/Anti-Semitism%20Poll%202007.pdf. Downloaded on August 22, 2008. A graphic presentation created from a national telephone survey of 2,000 respondents in October 2007. It finds anti-Semitic propensities holding stable among the population, that more men than women tend to hold anti-Semitic views, that Hispanics born outside the United States tend to hold more anti-Semitic views than those born within the country, that African Americans have a higher propensity to anti-Semitism, and that education level is the most accurate indicator of anti-Semitic views.

———. "Extremists Declare 'Open Season' on Immigrants: Hispanics Target of Incitement and Violence." Available online. URL: http://www.adl.org/main_Extremism/immigration_extremists.htm. Posted on May 23, 2006. Coverage of anti-immigrant organizing and violence on the part of far-right and white supremacist groups, including a description of several major incidents and details of the activities of far-right leaders, radio hosts, and writers.

———. "A Parents Guide to Hate on the Internet." Available online. URL: http://adl.org/issue_education/parents_guide_hate_net.asp. Downloaded on June 22, 2008. This report describes the various ways young Internet users can be confronted with racism and antireligious bigotry online and offers strategies for parents dealing with the phenomenon.

CivilRights.org. "Cause for Concern: Hate Crimes in America, 2004 Update." Available online. URL: http://www.civilrights.org/publications/reports/cause_for_concern_2004/. Issued by the prominent advocacy group for hate-crime legislation, this comprehensive report on hate crime and hate groups includes information on hate on the Internet, recommendations, a bibliography, and several appendices detailing current statistics from the FBI.

Fienberg, Howard. "America the Tolerant." Tech Central Station. Available online. URL: http://www.hfienberg.com/clips/hate.htm. Posted on October 21, 2002. The author believes that despite the occurrence of anti-Arab and anti-Muslim bias crimes in the wake of the September 11, 2001, terrorist attacks, America remains by and large a country tolerant of differences. The author describes a report of the council on American Islamic Relations, a nonprofit organization, which accounted for 1,516 incidents of anti-Arab bias and violence after September 11, 2001, including denial of religious accommodation, harassment, discrimination, bias, threat, assault, and several murders. Many of these incidents, according to the author, can be discounted as either not bias-related, as ambiguous, or as concerning a lack of religious accommodation rather than outright discrimination.

Hutchinson, Earl Ofari. "Made in America? Sniper Killings and Home-Grown Terrorism." Pacific News Service. Available online. URL: http://news.pacificnews.org/news/view_article.html?article_id=1cb6d39d313c8c4eab0975787924cd5a. Posted on October 16, 2002. The author uses the Washington, D.C.–area sniper killings of 2002 to describe the daily terror felt by members of ethnic and religious minorities when faced with bias-motivated violence at the hands of racists and skinheads. Police and local officials are reluctant to profile or monitor those who are prone to hate violence, and the federal laxity on gun laws allows "home-grown" killers to terrorize entire metropolitan areas.

Martin, Roland S. "Don't Sanitize Helms' Racist Past." CNN.com. Available online. URL: http://www.cnn.com/2008/POLITICS/07/09/roland.martin/index.html#cnnSTCText. Posted on July 2, 2008. The author reviews the life of Senator Jesse Helms of North Carolina, widely known as a champion of conservative values but also a man who displayed overt racism in his personal dealings and his political career.

Shah, Anup. "Racism." Global Issues. Available online. URL: http://www.globalissues.org/article/165/racism. Last updated on December 20, 2004. An article describing racism as it is occurring in the United States and abroad. Coverage is broken down into major global regions, and has sections on immigration, the Internet, globalization, neo-Nazism, and the 2001 UN World Conference on Racism.

U.S. Department of Education. "Preventing Youth Hate Crime." Available online. URL: http://www.ed.gov.publ/HateCrime/start.html. Downloaded on November 17, 2007. A brochure prepared to assist schools in confronting and eliminating bias-motivated harassment, violence, and intimidation. The document reviews the applicable federal laws; gives examples of effective school- and community-based programs; and includes classroom activities, useful organizations, and a bibliography.

———. "Protecting Students from Harassment and Hate Crime: A Guide for Schools." Available online. URL: http://www.ed.gov/offices/OCR/ archives/Harassment/harassment.pdf. Downloaded on November 17, 2007. A publication prepared for use by public schools, giving the DOE's approach to the hate-crime issue and guidance on writing and implementing policies on bias-motivated incidents. The document includes formal complaint/grievance procedures, suggestions on developing a written antiharassment policy, samples of school policies, reference materials, sources of technical assistance, and a bibliography.

VIDEOS

Anti-Semitism on the College Campus. Anti-Defamation League, 1993. An examination of anti-Semitic incidents on campus and the reaction against such events on the part of students and educators.

Brotherhood of Hate. First Run/Icarus Films, 2000. Directed by Pamela Yates. A video describing the Kehoe family of Coleville, Washington, and Chevie Kehoe, a white supremacist who aspired to build a whites-only settlement in the Pacific Northwest. During a nationwide rampage of theft and murder, Kehoe committed a triple homicide outside of rural Russellville, Arkansas. The video follows the investigation of the murder and the trail followed by Deputy Sheriff Aaron Duvall across the country to an isolated pocket of virulent anti-Semitism and racial prejudice.

Crimes of Hate. Anti-Defamation League, 1998. A documentary overview of the phenomenon of hate crimes, divided into segments on racism, anti-Semitism, and gay bashing, and the methods used to combat them by law enforcement and other public officials.

Learning to Hate. Anti-Defamation League, 1997. This video describes the origins of bigotry in childhood experiences within the family as well as the surrounding cultural environment, which sometimes breeds mistrust and fear of outsiders and those who look, sound, and act different. The film compares and contrasts anti-Semitic and antigay discrimination in several locales.

Natives: Immigrant Bashing on the Border. Filmmakers Library, 1993. A documentary covering white/Hispanic conflict and American xenophobia along California's Mexican border, and the problems of illegal immigration and undocumented aliens. Shot in black and white, the film follows the activities of groups organized to combat illegal aliens and draws a sharp contrast between support of liberty and the often antidemocratic values espoused for illegal aliens.

Not in Our Town. The Working Group, 1995. A documentary shot in Billings, Montana, during a wave of violence directed against Jews, blacks, and Native Americans, and the efforts of local citizens to combat the hate-crime wave. A follow-up video, *Not in Our Town II*, was produced in 1996, revisiting Billings to examine the effects of the earlier conflicts and to survey reaction against bias-motivated violence in other communities.

Who Killed Vincent Chin? Filmakers Library, 1990. A study of the killing of a young Chinese American and the anti-Asian prejudice that inspired this hate crime.

MODERN RACIST AND HATE GROUPS

BOOKS

Alibrandi, Tom, and Bill Wassmuth. *Hate Is My Neighbor.* Boise: University of Idaho Press, 2002. A book describing the often violent combat between the white supremacist group Aryan Nations and its opponents in the Coeur d'Alene region of northern Idaho.

Barkun, Michael. *Religion and the Racist Right: The Origins of the Christian Identity Movement.* Chapel Hill: University of North Carolina Press, 1994. A political science professor at Syracuse University, Barkun examines the roots and beliefs of the Christian Identity movement, an anti-Semitic, white supremacist ideology that holds that whites are the descendants of the biblical Israelites, that Jews are the descendants of Satan, and that the world is about to experience an apocalyptic battle between Aryans and Jews.

Blee, Kathleen M. *Inside Organized Racism: Women in the Hate Movement.* Berkeley: University of California Press, 2002. The author interviews women in skinhead, Ku Klux Klan, neo-Nazi, Christian Identity, and anti-Semitic groups to discover their backgrounds and motivations. Through these interviews and brief life histories, the book reveals certain common threads running through female members of American hate groups and then offers five suggestions for confronting and dealing with their point of view.

Boaz, Claire Kreger. *White Supremacy Groups.* At Issue series. San Diego, Calif.: Greenhaven Press, 2003. A collection of short essays, interviews, and opinion pieces for the student/researcher, covering white supremacist groups, "white power" music, women in the movement, lone-wolf terrorists, racist video games and Internet sites, and advocacy on the part of movement leaders, including Matthew Hale and Bishop Alma White.

Dinnerstein, Leonard. *Anti-Semitism in America.* New York: Oxford University Press, 1994. A scholarly history of American anti-Semitism, from the colonial era to the late 20th century. The author relates the most virulent periods of anti-Semitism to times of economic or social stress, particularly wartime, and traces the history—in some cases back to medieval Europe—of various conspiracy theories surrounding the Jews.

Dobratz, Betty A., and Stephanie L. Shanks-Meile. *The White Separatist Movement in the United States: White Power, White Pride*. Baltimore, Md.: Johns Hopkins University Press, 2000. Through interviewing more than 100 members of white separatist groups, and doing extensive field research on the phenomenon, the authors explore the nature of white power groups and white separatism in an attempt to set aside the preconception that the members of such groups come from a single stratum of American society.

Ferber, Abby. *Home-Grown Hate: Gender and Organized Racism*. New York: Routledge, 2004. Essays by researchers and academics on various gender-related topics: women in racist groups, the "politics of reproduction," the ideal of motherhood in white supremacist thinking, white nativist environmental movements, and the role of women in preventing and changing racist attitudes and affiliations among men.

Gerstenfeld, Phyllis B. *Hate Crimes: Causes, Controls, and Controversies*. Thousand Oaks, Calif.: Sage Publications, 2003. The author of this college-level textbook gives a general overview of the hate-crimes phenomenon, delving into the causes of prejudice, the nature of extremist groups, first-person accounts of hate crimes, profiles of perpetrators and victims, and developments in the law.

Kaplan, Jeffrey, ed. *Encyclopedia of White Power: A Sourcebook on the Radical Racist Right*. Walnut Creek, Calif.: Altamira Press, 2000. Within more than 100 entries, contributors aspire to an unbiased and comprehensive description of racist groups and movements in Europe and the United States, breaking them down into eight major categories. Many of the contributors are former members of these organizations, and the book includes quotations of primary source documents, cross-references, and useful bibliographies.

Kinsella, Warren. *Web of Hate: Inside Canada's Far-Right Network*. Toronto: HarperCollins, 2001. A detailed account, written for the general public, of the white-power and neo-Nazi movement in Canada and of the little-known alliance of white-supremacist groups in Canada and the United States.

Martinez, Thomas, with John Guinther. *Brotherhood of Murder*. New York: McGraw-Hill, 1988. An insider's close look at his own background as a racist and his association with the Order, a violent white supremacist group. After changing his ways, the author helped the FBI track Robert Matthews, the leader of the Order, who was betrayed by other members and killed in a fiery shootout with the authorities.

Annotated Bibliography

Oppenheimer, Martin. *The Hate Handbook: Oppressors, Victims, and Fighters.* Lanham, Md.: Lexington Books, 2005. Using recent examples of terrorism, police brutality, war crimes, and genocide, the author attempts to explain the origins of extremist views and groups, and explains how hate groups gain members and influence through the use of persuasive propaganda and historical example. The book also offers remedies for the problem of extremist recruitment and violence.

Phillips, John W. *Sign of the Cross: The Prosecutor's True Story of a Landmark Trial Against the Klan.* Louisville, Ky.: Westminster John Knox Press, 2000. Prosecutor Phillips recounts a long struggle conducted by his office and law enforcement against activities of the Ku Klux Klan in southern California.

Ramsland, Katharine, et al. *Into the Devil's Den: How an FBI Informant Got Inside the Aryan Nations and a Special Agent Got Him Out Alive.* New York: Ballantine Books, 2008. This book recounts the adventures of Dave Hall, a drug dealer turned FBI informant who infiltrated the extreme-right Aryan Nations group. Hall's acting ability and sheer physical presence served him well in the ranks of the group, and he eventually won a position of trust. The attempt to assume an entirely foreign identity, and the repulsive acts he is asked to carry out, strain his sanity to the breaking point before he eventually leaves the group.

Ridgeway, James. *Blood in the Face: The Ku Klux Klan, Aryan Nations, Nazi Skinheads, and the Rise of a New White Culture.* New York: Thunder's Mouth Press, 1995. A study of the rise of white supremacist movements and groups, updated to include the Oklahoma City bombing and the militia movement of the mid-1990s.

Roberts, Kelly, and Michael Reid. *White Supremacy: Behind the Eyes of Hate.* Victoria, B.C.: Trafford Publishing, 2004. The author infiltrates a branch of the neo-Nazi Aryan Nations in rural Pennsylvania and is promptly appointed chief of security. He begins networking with members of the extreme right in an attempt to gather information about white supremacy groups nationwide.

Ryan, Nick. *Into a World of Hate: A Journey Among the Extreme Right.* New York: Routledge, 2004. The author delves into the extreme right, encountering members and leaders of groups ranging from the Worldwide Church of the Creator to Combat 18 to the Reform Party.

Schlatter, Evelyn A. *Aryan Cowboys: White Supremacists and the Search for a New Frontier, 1970–2000.* Austin, Tex.: University of Texas Press, 2006. The author claims that white supremacist groups are not necessarily operating on the fringes of society, particularly in the American west. The Aryan Nations and other groups are employing the old frontier ideals of self-reliance, freedom, and escape to develop a movement to make the western states into a new white homeland.

Swain, Carol M. *The New White Nationalism in America: Its Challenge to Integration.* Cambridge: Cambridge University Press, 2002. The author covers the rise of white nationalism and the many grievances of those who promote it: crime, inner city blight, reverse discrimination, multiculturalism, affirmative action, and demographic change within the United States.

Weller, Worth H., and Brad Thompson. *Under the Hood: Unmasking the Modern Ku Klux Klan.* North Manchester, Ind.: DeWitt Books, 1998. A journalist's account of the rise of the American Knights of the Ku Klux Klan, an organization that flourished in Indiana in the late 1990s.

Williams, Mary E. *Hate Groups: Opposing Viewpoints.* Opposing Viewpoints series. San Diego, Calif.: Greenhaven Press, 2004. Essays from academics and journalists on the pros and cons of criminalizing hate violence; whether hate crimes are rising significantly or are exaggerated; on the effect of nationalism, capitalism, and rhetoric on bigoted attitudes; and on the legal rights of "white-power" groups and the creators of Internet sites.

Young, Mitchell, ed. *White Supremacy Groups.* Detroit: Greenhaven Press, 2008. Essays on white supremacy, by authors advocating separate white communities, nationalist groups as a buffer against immigrants, Europe's white-power and nationalist groups, and the role of women in white supremacist groups.

PERIODICALS

Blazak, Randy. "White Boys to Terrorist Men: Target Recruitment of Nazi Skinheads." *American Behavioral Scientist.* vol. 44, no. 6, 2001, pp. 982–1,000. The article states that hate group activity is increasing in the United States, even though the rate of hate crimes may be on the decline, and describes the increased recruitment of skinheads among disaffected juveniles through hate group web sites.

Furin, Terrance L. "Confronting a Neo-Nazi Hate Group: A Superintendent Finds Teachable Moments for a Community in Crisis through Creation of a Public Pedagogy." *School Administrator,* vol. 64, no. 10, November 2007, p. 32. A school administrator in suburban Philadelphia confronts the appearance of a neo-Nazi group on campus, as students find flyers celebrating Heinrich Himmler, head of the SS in Nazi Germany. The article details the methods used to ease tensions over the incident and neutralize recruiting efforts by the group at his school.

Gerstenfeld, Phyllis B., Diane R. Grant, and Chau-Pu Chiang. "Hate Online: A Content Analysis of Extremist Internet Sites." *Analyses of Social Issues and Public Policy,* vol. 3, no. 1, December 2003, pp. 29–44. The authors analyze 157 extremist web sites, created by groups as well as unaffiliated individuals, and find that the Internet has become a powerful medium for the dissemination of extremist views and for the purposes of recruitment and coordination, both within the United States and internationally.

Green, D. P., and A. Rich. "White Supremacist Activity and Crossburnings in North Carolina." *Journal of Quantitative Criminology*, vol. 14, no. 3, September 1998, pp. 263–282. The author examines cross burning in North Carolina, questioning whether it increases in areas where white supremacist organizations such as the Christian Knights of the Ku Klux Klan have held rallies or demonstrations. The data, taken from Klanwatch and North Carolinians Against Racial and Religious Violence, covered cross burnings and white supremacist activities in 100 North Carolina counties annually from 1987 through 1993. It was found that none of the suspected cross burners had apparent ties to white supremacist groups. The author concludes that such white supremacist rallies encourage fellow travelers to engage in this form of racial intimidation.

Jasper, William F. "The Rise of the Citizen Militias." *The New American*, February 6, 1995, pp. 4–29. The author defends militias and their members, maintaining that such organizations do not promote violence or racism but instead are an understandable response to an increasingly oppressive federal government.

Keller, Amy. "Hate in the Sunshine State: Florida Trails Only California in the Number of Organized Hate Groups." *Florida Trend*, vol. 49, no. 6, September 2006, p. 80. A probation officer discovers that one of his charges has joined the National Alliance and has come under investigation by the FBI and state law enforcement. The article uncovers a rise in neo-Nazi groups and active recruitment throughout the state.

Langer, Elinor. "The American Neo-Nazi Movement Today." *The Nation*, July 16/23, 1990, pp. 82–108. At the time of writing, this article provided a thorough and detailed description of the neo-Nazi movement, giving names and backgrounds of the leaders and their recent activities.

Loggins, K., and S. Thomas. "Menace Returns: Mark of the Beast." *Southern Exposure*, vol. 8, no. 2, summer 1980, pp. 2–6. The authors describe the resurgent Ku Klux Klan of the late 1970s, when Klan membership and Klan-related violence rose sharply after a long period of dormancy. A new and more media-savvy version of the Klan was led by leaders expert at generating publicity and manipulating the media in promoting the Klan as a family-oriented, civil rights organization committed to justice for whites.

Phillips, Amanda. "Skinheads in America." *Law Enforcement Technology*, vol. 34, no. 10, October 2007, p. 64. The author provides tips for law enforcement on how to deal with skinhead and neo-Nazi groups and hate crimes.

The article suggests open communication with the media and the community, the use of public meetings to lessen tensions, coordinating clean-up efforts, protecting the privacy of victims, and providing support services and victim advocates.

Shively, Michael, and Carrie F. Mulford. "Hate Crime in America: The Debate Continues." *NIJ Journal*, no. 257, June 2007, pp. 8–13. A summary of the status of the hate-crime debate today, provided by the National Institute of Justice, which is the research arm of the U.S. Department of Justice. The authors note that legislators, law enforcement officials, prosecutors, and the American public continue to grapple with fundamental questions about hate crime: what it is, how widespread it is, and how criminal justice with respect to hate crimes should be handled.

Turpin-Petrosian, Carolyn. "Hateful Sirens . . . Who Hears Their Song? An Examination of Student Attitudes Toward Hate Groups and Affiliation Potential." *Journal of Social Issues*, vol. 58, no. 2, Summer 2002, pp. 281–301. From a survey of high school and university students, the author explores why young people affiliate themselves with hate groups, finding that although individuals are responsible for the majority of hate crimes, organized hate groups play an important part by attracting disaffected students and giving them a sense of belonging and an outlet for personal frustrations.

REPORTS

"Final Report." Sacramento, Calif.: California Governor's Advisory Panel on Hate Groups, 2000. A report on the activities of California hate groups during the 1990s, giving findings and recommendations in the areas of existing legislation, law enforcement, education, Internet activity, and the actions of public interest and community groups.

"Hate Violence and White Supremacy: A Decade Review, 1980–1990." Montgomery, Ala.: Southern Poverty Law Center, 1999. A nationwide overview of racial violence committed during the 1980s by white supremacist groups.

"Intelligence Report." Montgomery, Ala.: Southern Poverty Law Center. This quarterly report covers the subject of hate crimes, hate groups, and the activities of racist and white power groups such as the Ku Klux Klan, as monitored by the organization known as Klanwatch.

Simon Wiesenthal Center. "Online Terror + Hate: The First Decade." Available online. URL: http://www.wiesenthal.com/site/apps/s/link.asp?c =fwLYKnN8LzH&b=4145951. Downloaded on August 22, 2008. A 2008 report describing the next generation of high-technology neo-Nazi and far-right groups that are using Facebook, YouTube, web logs, games, and other emerging e-media to publish, recruit, and advocate for separation of the races. With little in the way of legal or physical barriers, the Internet provides a fruitful ground for such groups to publicize themselves around the world. The report counts more than 8,000 sites that "promote hate and terrorism or display extremist or discriminatory postings."

VIDEOS

Downs, Hugh, and Meredith Vieira. *The Hate Conspiracy: The Rise and Fall of the Order.* Princeton, N.J.: Films for the Humanities & Sciences, 2000. A documentary on the rise of the Order, a white supremacist group held responsible for the killing of a radio talk-show host and for a murderous attack on a Jewish day-care center.

Evil Among Us: Hate in America. Princeton, N.J.: Films for the Humanities & Sciences, 2003. A three-part series presenting key figures and events in the development of America's right-wing extremist groups since the 1980s. The first installment, "Open Warfare," describes far-right groups who have been inspired by events such as the Oklahoma City bombing, the Ruby Ridge shootout in Idaho, and the confrontation with David Koresh at Waco, and it examines the major figures of the far-right, including Richard Butler, leader of the Aryan Nations. The second, "Trail of Terror," focuses on the founding and growth of extremist groups including the Ku Klux Klan, Aryan Nations, Posse Comitatus, the Covenant, and a group known as the Sword and Arm of the Lord. The third installment, "The Lone Gunman," focuses on the elusive solo assassins and criminals who, in many cases, are inspired by focused bigotry and the exhortations of far right and extremist groups. The video includes interviews with federal agents responsible for tracking and capturing bias-crime outlaws.

Kurtis, Bill. *The Hate Network.* New York: A&E Home Video, 2000. A video documenting the transformation of hate into a well-organized social and political force in the late 20th century, through the use of modern means of communication and propaganda.

Mogull, Lisa, et al. *The New Skinheads.* New York: A&E Home Video, 2002. A history of the skinheads, from their rise in England during the 1980s among a subculture of juvenile delinquents and petty criminals to a much larger and more dangerous movement of members who have effectively blended into society and become less visible but more sophisticated.

20th Century with Mike Wallace: Hate Across America. New York: History Channel Video, 2002. A documentary on hate crimes in the United States, starting with the murder of three civil rights workers by the Ku Klux Klan in 1964. The video explains how these crimes spread outside of the South as hate groups became more sophisticated in their methods of recruitment and their means of disruption, and moved their focus from individuals to the federal government.

Valensise, Daria. *Raised on Hate.* New York: A&E Home Video, 2001. A video describing the murder of the Mueller family in Arkansas by Chevie O'Brien Kehoe, a model student whose father was a white supremacist, and whose views inspired the son to his actions.

WEB SITES

Civilrights.org. URL: http:www.civilrights.org/issues/hate. A comprehensive site covering news and issues surrounding the topic of hate crimes. It includes fact sheets, reports, legislative updates, an event calendar, press releases, and opinion pieces. It also provides links to articles, videos, and other material from public government and law enforcement sources as well as the commercial media.

The Hate Directory. URL: http://www.bcpl.net/~rfrankli/hatedir.htm. Compiled by Raymond Franklin and updated on July 15, 2007, the web site includes a listing of Internet sites of individuals and groups that, in the opinion of the author, advocate violence to others based upon race, religion, ethnicity, gender, or sexual orientation. The organizations are listed with their name, URL, and category devised by the author, including Holocaust Revisionism, Anti-Gay, Anti-Semitic, Racist Games, Racist Friendly Web Hosting Services, and so on.

National Coalition of Anti-Violence Programs. URL: http://www.ncavp.org. Formed in 1995, this group represents more than 20 local gay and bisexual agencies, focusing in particular on antiviolence programs throughout the United States and providing contact information for each of the programs. The member agencies focus on domestic violence as well as antigay bias violence. The site includes a report entitled "Anti-Lesbian, Gay, Bisexual and Transgender Violence in 2006."

Stop the Hate. URL: http://www.stop-the-hate.org. Provides resources and links to hate-crime and hate-group-related sites, including neo-Nazi and nationalist hate groups, the Ku Klux Klan, religion-based hate groups, and militia groups. There is also a comprehensive listing of anti-hate resources and support.

HISTORY OF HATE VIOLENCE

BOOKS

Allen, James, ed. *Without Sanctuary: Lynching Photography in America.* Santa Fe, N.M.: Twin Palms Publishers, 2000. A collection of nearly 100 lynching photographs, some collected from family albums and some published as souvenir photos. The album was linked with an exhibition that traveled to various cities in the year 2000. The photos reveal the casual brutality with which the act of lynching was carried out and the carnival-like atmosphere that often accompanied it.

Chalmers, David. *Hooded Americanism: The History of the Ku Klux Klan.* Durham, N.C.: Duke University Press, 1987. A comprehensive and detailed history of the Klan from its inception through its expansion in the early decades of the 20th century and its more recent incarnations. Making full use of newspaper and other contemporary accounts, the author details how the Klan moved outside of its regional home in the South to other sections of the country. It also describes the legislative reaction against the Klan in the form of antimask and antilynching laws, precursors to modern hate-crime statutes targeting bias crimes and racial violence.

Dixon, Thomas. *The Flaming Sword.* Lexington, Ky.: University Press of Kentucky, 2005. Dixon was a best-selling writer known for his racist and Klan novels; this was his last book, first published in 1939. The author's intent was to present a record of race conflict in the United States in the 20th century, using a plot centered on a defeat of the United States by an alliance of communists and African Americans. The novel includes an introduction and notes provided by the author to explain his ideas and offers many insights into a mainstream outlook of earlier times that would be considered unacceptably bigoted in the 21st century.

Ferrell, Claudine L. *Nightmare and Dream: Anti-Lynching in Congress, 1917–1922.* New York: Garland, 1986. A scholarly study of congressional debate and federal measures taken to combat lynching in the turbulent years following World War I.

Hirsch, James S. *Riot and Remembrance: America's Worst Race Riot and Its History.* Mariner Books, 2003. A well-researched chronicle of the Tulsa riots of 1921, which began with a confrontation between an elevator operator and a delivery boy and escalated into a battle that devastated the city and left hundreds of African-American residents of the city's prosperous Greenwood neighborhood dead or injured. The book follows the effects on the city and survivors that continue to the present day.

Lutz, Chris. *They Don't All Wear Sheets: A Chronology of Racist and Far Right Violence, 1980–1986.* Atlanta, Ga.: Center for Democratic Renewal, 1987. A short, straightforward, and selective listing of bias incidents through the early 1980s, divided first among states and then chronologically.

Madison, James H. *A Lynching in the Heartland: Race and Memory in America.* London: Palgrave Macmillan, 2003. The author focuses on the hanging of two black men in Marion, Indiana, in 1930, the source of a world-famous photograph that is reproduced on the book's cover. The incident occurred when three black teenagers were accused of killing a white man and raping a white woman. Two of the accused were dragged from their cells and hanged, while the third was spared by the crowd, eventually pardoned for a conviction by the state governor, and awarded the keys to the city of Marion in 1993.

Moore, Jack B. *Skinheads Shaved for Battle: A Cultural History of American Skinheads.* Bowling Green, Ohio: Bowling Green State University Popular Press, 1993. An exploration of the skinhead phenomenon as it arose among the working class in Great Britain and as it was exported to the United States during the 1970s and 1980s, when it was diverted into a neo-Nazi and racist subculture.

Nelson, Jack. *Terror in the Night: The Klan's Campaign Against the Jews.* Jackson: University of Mississippi Press, 1996. An account of a Klan assault against several small Jewish communities in Mississippi during the 1960s, undertaken in reprisal for Jewish support of civil rights workers and overshadowed by the turmoil over desegregation then taking place in the Deep South.

Newton, Michael, and Judy Ann Newton. *Racial and Religious Violence in America: A Chronology.* New York: Garland, 1991. A comprehensive 728-page timeline of more than 8,000 hate crimes and bias-related incidents in the United States, dating from the European discovery of the New World in the 16th century. The book is particularly useful for scholars of the civil rights era of the 1950s and 1960s, as it covers not only hate crimes but also hundreds of lesser-known incidents of riot and mayhem that manifested the racial malaise of the time.

Newton, Michael, and Judy Newton, eds. *Ku Klux Klan: An Encyclopedia.* New York: Garland, 1991. A reference work of some 8,000 entries on the Ku Klux Klan. The author includes both pro- and anti-Klan organizations, victims and opponents of the Klan, and entries for states and nations that have Klan groups and Klan-related activities. The work spans the Klan's prehistory in the American colonial era and continues up to the current Klan organization and its various subgroups and activities.

Perry, Barbara. *Hate and Bias Crime: A Reader.* New York: Routledge, 2003. An anthology of writings on hate crimes and hate groups, including perspectives on the effects of the September 11, 2001, attacks in the United States and the global rise in terrorism.

———. *Silent Victims: Hate Crimes Against Native Americans.* Tucson, Ariz.: University of Arizona Press, 2008. The author, a professor of criminology at the University of Ontario, conducts extensive research in the West and Midwest to survey the incidence of bias crimes against Native Americans, and she finds the problem to be poorly covered in the media as well as academic studies of hate crime. The book usefully delves into the history of frontier settlement and military conflict, underlining the lasting effects of ignorance and fear on the part of the dominant culture.

Annotated Bibliography

Roy, Patricia, *The Oriental Question: Consolidating a White Man's Province, 1914–1941.* Vancouver and Toronto: UBC Press, 2003. The second of three volumes in which the author undertakes a history of anti-Asian racism in the far-western Canadian province of British Columbia, relying heavily on primary source documents and especially newspapers. The first volume, *A White Man's Province: British Columbia Politicians and Chinese and Japanese Immigrants, 1858–1914,* covered the period up to World War I, while this volume ends just before Canada forcefully relocated Japanese Canadians at the outbreak of World War II in the Pacific. The third volume ends with important changes in the Canadian immigration law in 1967.

Ruiz, J. *Black Hood of the Ku Klux Klan.* Bethesda, Md.: Austin and Winfield, 1998. This book chronicles the 1922 murder of two white men by the Ku Klux Klan. Klan violence against whites, particularly respected members of their communities, was virtually unknown until 1922. In the summer of that year, two white men in Morehouse Parish, Louisiana, were kidnapped by the Klan, tortured and murdered. Autopsies of the bodies revealed they had been extensively mutilated. The book presents a detailed examination of the investigation that followed the murders and develops a picture of the Klan's grip on the South of the time, a society muted by fear and intimidation. The book includes a historical profile of northeastern Louisiana; an introduction to the Ku Klux Klan; a description of the social setting and other events in the South in the summer and fall of 1922; the search and subsequent discovery of the two bodies; the open hearing and its aftermath; and an account of the present-day Klan in Louisiana.

Swinney, Everette. *Suppressing the Ku Klux Klan: The Enforcement of the Reconstruction Amendments, 1870–1877.* New York: Garland, 1987. A book describing the original civil rights laws written to combat Klan violence in the wake of the Civil War, and often cited by scholars of modern hate-crimes lawmaking and litigation.

Till-Mobley, Mamie. *Death of Innocence: The Story of the Hate Crime That Changed America.* New York: One World/Ballantine, 2004. The mother of Emmett Till writes about the murder of her son in 1955 in Mississippi, a crime that shocked the nation and played an important role in the modern civil rights movement. Till-Mobley offers Emmett Till's background and character, showing how his upbringing in Chicago left him dangerously unprepared for expected behavior in the Deep South.

PERIODICALS

Carrigan, William D. "The Lynching of Persons of Mexican Origin or Descent in the United States, 1848 to 1928." *Journal of Social History*, vol.

37, no. 2, Winter 2003, p. 411. Relying on archival and primary-source research, the author finds at least 597 instances of Mexicans being lynched in the United States between 1848 and 1928, and he attempts to describe and explain this little-known aspect of racial conflict in American history. Economic competition, diplomatic tensions, and the legacy of western expansion all contributed, while ethnic Mexicans sought to defend themselves by forming mutual defense organizations and appealing to the Mexican government.

Kelley, Robin. "Remembering Scottsboro." *Colorlines Magazine*, vol. 6, no. 3, Fall 2003, p. 32. An article describing a series of linoleum cuts created in the 1930s to commemorate the trial of the Scottsboro Boys, nine black men who were falsely accused and sentenced to death for allegedly raping two white women on a train.

McMahan, Karol Nelson. "Fighting for Freedom in the Mississippi Sun." *Newsweek*, July 25, 2005, p. 21. The author recounts her summer in 1964 Mississippi, when she worked as a "Freedom Teacher" alongside the Freedom Riders. These white northerners, most of them college students, were attempting to bring voting rights to black citizens and serve as a trip wire for federal intervention should any police or mob violence break out.

Petrosino, Carolyn. "Connecting the Past to the Future: Hate Crime in America." *Journal of Contemporary Criminal Justice*, vol. 15, no. 1, February 1999, pp. 22–47. The author explores bias crimes from the earliest colonial period through the 19th century, arguing that racism and hate crimes have been endemic to the United States, that hate crimes will increase in number and severity in the future, and that the problem may lessen with increased exposure in the media and in political debate.

Reardon, Patrick. "We Have to Face Our History: Some Unflinching New Books Tackle America's Ugly Racial Past." *Black History Bulletin*, vol. 65, no. 3, July–December 2002, p. 17. The author reviews several books dealing with Jim Crow laws, race riots, lynching, and other historical aspects of bigotry and race violence. The appearance of the books, discussions with the author, and coverage of various public forums on the subject hold out hope that an ongoing reconciliation between the races is taking place in contemporary society.

Satzewich, Vic. "Racism in Canada: Change and Continuity." *Canadian Dimension*, vol. 38, no. 1, January/Feburary 2004, p. 20. The author reviews the history of race relations in Canada, pointing out that Europeans made up the vast majority of Canadian immigrants and citizens (apart from Native Americans) and that several factors in recent times have contributed to changes in the racial situation and the prevailing attitudes.

Seeber, Michael. "Racism Breeds Ignorance: How Bigotry Holds Us Back." *Psychology Today*, vol. 34, no. 5, September/October, 2001, p. 28. A brief article on a study by Richard Petty, who attempted to determine the cognitive disadvantages suffered by people who hold prejudicial views and believe in racial stereotypes. The test showed that those tending to hold stereotypes scored lower on math problems.

Smith, Kevin D. "From Socialism to Racism: The Politics of Class and Identity in Postwar Milwaukee." *Michigan Historical Review*, vol. 29, no. 1, Spring 2003, p. 71. The author describes a watershed mayoral election of 1956 in Milwaukee in which incumbent Frank Zeidler, a member of the Socialist party, was accused of inviting southern blacks to the city in order to take advantage of public housing and welfare benefits. The rumor campaign was denounced in the national press and held up as an example of northern racism. Zeidler won the election but racial tensions continued to simmer in the city, where the events became a harbinger of the "identity" politics that emerged full-blown on a national scale during the 1960s.

Webb, Clive. "The Ku Klux Klan." *Modern History Review*, vol. 13, no. 4, April 2002, p. 22. A detailed review of the history of the Ku Klux Klan, from its origins in the South during Reconstruction, to its revival in the early 20th century, the height of its popularity in the 1920s, and its splintering in the current era into several rival and poorly coordinated subgroups.

Weisenburger, Steven. "The Columbians, Inc.: A Chapter of Racial Hatred from the Post–World War II South." *Journal of Southern History*, vol. 69, no. 4, November 2003, p. 821. An extensive article on an Atlanta group that committed several terrifying acts of intimidation against the city's African-American community in the late 1940s. The "Columbians," a legally chartered nonprofit corporation, opposed the movement of African Americans into a previously white neighborhood and advocated the expulsion of blacks and Jews from the city and the state. The author draws connections between this group, which adopted brown shirts and Nazi regalia and had imitators across the country, and the founding of white racist groups, largely inspired by the Nazis, in later years.

LEGAL AND CONSTITUTIONAL ASPECTS OF HATE-CRIME LEGISLATION

BOOKS

Bell, Derrick A. *Race, Racism, and American Law*. 5th ed. New York: Aspen Publishers, 2006. The originator of critical race theory prepared this extensive casebook and study of race and the American legal system for use by law professors and students. The fifth edition includes updated sections on education, the Supreme Court decision on cross-burning and the

First Amendment, interracial relationships, racial profiling, voting rights, the Patriot Act, and employment discrimination.

Connors, Paul G., ed. Current Controversies series. Detroit, Mich.: Greenhaven Press, 2007. An updated pro/con book on hate crimes in North America and Europe, speech codes, Indian logos for sports teams, antihomosexual bias crime, anti-Muslim violence, and the need for hate crime laws. Several authors present the case for either exaggeration of the issue on the part of advocacy groups or the discriminatory effect of hate-crime laws.

Cortese, Anthony. *Opposing Hate Speech.* Westport, Conn.: Praeger Publishers, 2005. The author attempts to strike a balance between speech codes and the principle of freedom of speech and expression, striving toward a definition of "hate speech." Reasoning that there are degrees of severity, just as in any other action that is defined as a crime, he argues that there is some legal justification for speech codes, although constitutional First Amendment principles stand against most forms of prosecution and restriction.

Jacobs, James, and Kimberly Potter. *Hate Crimes: Criminal Law & Identity Politics.* New York: Oxford University Press, 1998. A New York law professor argues against hate-crime legislation, suggesting that as written, hate-crimes laws violate the First Amendment protection of free speech.

Jenness, Valerie. *Making Hate a Crime: From Social Movement to Law Enforcement.* New York: Russell Sage Foundation, 2001. The author focuses on the concept of hate crime and how this relatively new legal category, a redefining of violence motivated by innate human prejudices, has emerged in the United States over the past two decades. The author speculates on the origins of this category in social movements, in modern political debate, and in the American system of lawmaking and the criminal justice system.

Katznelson, Ira. *When Affirmative Action Was White: An Untold History of Racial Inequality in Twentieth-Century America.* New York: W. W. Norton, 2006. The author contends that laws designed to heal discrimination have instead exacerbated the problem. He traces the origins of affirmative action programs to the New Deal–era legislation designed to pull the United States and its workers out of the Depression. Southern lawmakers deliberately denied many economic benefits to those working as domestics and farmhands—work traditionally done by minorities. The administration of benefits, such as the GI Bill, through local governments also resulted in economic inequalities between black and white. These measures eventually brought about the affirmative action policies of the 1960s, which have resulted in a political backlash.

Annotated Bibliography

Lewis, Anthony. *Freedom for the Thought That We Hate: A Biography of the First Amendment.* New York: Basic Books, 2007. The author examines the ramifications of the First Amendment of the U.S. Constitution and its doctrine of "freedom of expression." Explaining that there has always been very limited legal sanction for repressing speech, the author considers the advisability of new restrictions on speech that is intended to incite terrorism and hate crime.

Perry, Barbara. *In the Name of Hate: Understanding Hate Crimes.* New York: Routledge, 2001. The author creates a comprehensive theory of hate crimes, supports an expansion of the definition of hate crimes in the law, and argues that the hate-crime phenomenon is the result of a long history of racism within the United States.

Waldrep, Christopher. *Racial Violence on Trial: A Handbook with Cases, Laws, and Documents.* On Trial series. Santa Barbara, Calif.: ABC-CLIO, 2001. A useful reference book detailing prominent bias-motivated crimes and the trials associated with them, offering transcripts and other primary-source documents associated with the cases, alphabetical listings of important laws, concepts, and individuals, a chronology, and an annotated bibliography.

Wang, Lu-In. *Hate Crimes Law.* Deerfield, Ill.: Clark Boardman Callaghan (annual). A reference book and legal treatise detailing federal and state hate-crimes laws, updated annually by a nationally recognized expert on the subject.

Williams, Robert A. *Like a Loaded Weapon: The Rehnquist Court, Indian Rights, and the Legal History of Racism in America.* Minneapolis: University of Minnesota Press, 2005. The author describes how the Supreme Court supported discriminatory federal policy toward Native Americans in the 19th century and how this approach was upheld by the modern "Rehnquist court" (1986–2005). The book offers a strategy for Indian legal rights based on the *Brown v. Board of Education* decision of 1954, which ended segregation of African Americans in the public schools.

Winters, Robert. *What Is a Hate Crime?* At Issue series. Detroit, Mich.: Greenhaven Press, 2007. An anthology of essays examining the definition of hate crimes. Several of the essays address the issue of antigay bias crimes and homophobia.

PERIODICALS

Bantley, Kathleen. "Judicial Activism and Progressive Legislation: A Step Towards Decreasing Hate Attacks." *Albany Law Review,* vol. 71, no. 2, 2008, pp. 545–564. The author introduces and analyzes the history of institutionalized "heterosexism" and antigay violence in the United States, and she notes the effect of new laws that allow civil marriage for homosexuals: Antigay hate crimes have fallen in states that struck down restrictions on gay marriage.

Butler, Amir. "Lessons in Legislation." *Index on Censorship*, vol. 35, no. 1, January 2006, p. 183. An article condemning laws against incitement to religious hatred in Australia. It advocates the public confrontation of extremism, and the full and legal public disclosure of extremist views, as a way to curb harmful speech.

Byers, Bryan, and Benjamin Crider. "Hate Crimes Against the Amish: A Qualitative Analysis of Bias Motivation Using Routine Activities Theory." *Deviant Behavior*, vol. 23, no. 2, March/April 2002, pp. 115–148. The article uses the narratives of eight hate-crime perpetrators to examine hate crimes committed against Amish citizens and the particular bias motivations involved in such incidents.

Byers, Bryan D., and Richard A. Zeller. "Official Hate Crime Statistics: An Examination of the 'Epidemic Hypothesis.'" *Journal of Crime & Justice*, vol. 24, no. 2, 2001, pp. 73–85. A study that examines the "epidemic hypothesis" with regard to hate crime. The author draws on data from the Uniform Crime Reports, which show a relatively steady frequency of hate crimes reported by police departments to the FBI. The author suggests that any changes from year to year may result from variations in reporting and/or measurement practices, and that the rhetoric over the hate-crime problem is not supported by statistical evidence.

Chilton, Bradley S., Gail Caputo, James Woods, and Holly Walpole. "Hate Beyond a Reasonable Doubt: Hate Crime Sentencing After *Apprendi v. N.J.*" *Corrections Compendium*, vol. 26, no. 8, August 2001, pp. 1–3, 20–21. This article presents an analysis of the Supreme Court decision in *Apprendi v. N. J.*, focusing on the implications of this decision for hate-crime legislation and for law enforcement, courts, sentencing, and corrections. The author finds that the decision will reduce the processing of hate crimes and the number of sentencing enhancements, and decrease the number of inmates and state and federal funding that flows from inmate counts. The article also predicts that thousands of appeals will be filed under the *Apprendi* doctrine in hate-crime cases.

Chorba, Christopher. "The Danger of Federalizing Hate Crimes: Congressional Misconceptions and the Unintended Consequences of the Hate Crimes Prevention Act." *Virginia Law Review*, vol. 87, no. 2, 2001, pp. 319–379. The author believes that the incidence of hate crimes is being distorted by faulty statistics, that hate-crimes laws may do more harm than good (citing the higher incidence of interracial violence committed by minority groups), and that hate crimes should not involve the federal government and federal laws.

Cockburn, Alexander. "Hate Crimes Follies." *The Nation*, May 21, 2001, p. 10. The writer discusses why he believes that hate-crimes laws are both pointless and dangerous and contends that the promotion of hate-crimes legislation wastes time that should be spent on urgent issues, including the cases of innocent people on death row.

Dunbar, Edward. "Defending the Indefensible: A Critique and Analysis of Psycholegal Defense Arguments of Hate Crime Perpetrators." *Journal of Contemporary Criminal Justice*, vol. 15, no. 1, February 1999, pp. 64–77. An article concerning the strategies used by defense attorneys when handling hate-crimes cases. The author considers the validity of these strategies according to current research in psychology and behavioral science, and in more general terms how such research is used in the courtroom.

Eidsmoe, John. "Is Telling Lawyer Jokes a Hate Crime? The Hate Crimes Prevention Act of 2007 Is Dangerous, Not Only on Its Own Terms But Because of Its Role in the Culture Wars That Will Shape America for Generations to Come." *The New American*, April 2, 2007, p. 22. The author analyzes the latest version of federal hate-crimes law, which criminalizes violence against persons because of their sexual orientation, and speculates on the extremes to which hate-crime laws might go. He points out that behavior once condemned in the Bible is now the basis for legal protections, and in this development he sees a danger of ever-worsening moral decline and social chaos.

Ford, Glyn. "In the Wake of Xenophobia: The New Racism in Europe." *UN Chronicle*, September 2007, p. 22. A story that describes the re-emergence of fascism in 1980s Europe, buoyed by conflict over immigration, the opening of eastern Europe after the fall of communism, and sensational crime stories in the media. More recently, far-right parties have turned to anti-Islamic activities and "fascist light," a form of right-wing populism, and have moved nationalism and xenophobia into the political mainstream.

Gellman, Susan. "Brother, You Can't Go to Jail for What You're Thinking: Motives, Effects, and Hate Crime Laws." *Criminal Justice Ethics*, vol. 11, no. 2, Summer/Fall 1992, pp. 24–29. The article considers First Amendment challenges to the ADL model hate-crimes statute and laws written according to the model. The author claims that the model statute addresses a serious problem in a way that infringes not only upon speech, but upon freedom of thought, and concludes that an "effects-based statute" serves the state's interest in punishing the special harms of bias crimes and ensures maximum protection of speech, thought, and belief.

———. "Sticks and Stones Can Put You in Jail, But Can Words Increase Your Sentence? Constitutional and Policy Dilemmas of Ethnic Intimidation Laws." *UCLA Law Review*, December 1991, pp. 333–396. A seminal and widely influential article on hate-crimes law, written after the passage of the Hate Crimes Statistics Act but before the major Supreme Court decisions regarding the constitutionality of the new laws. The author argues vigorously on constitutional grounds against creating a new class of criminal act.

Gellman, Susan B., and Frederick M. Lawrence. "Agreeing to Agree: A Proponent and Opponent of Hate Crime Laws Reach for Agreement." *Harvard Journal on Legislation*, vol. 41, 2004, pp. 421–448. In this essay, two legal scholars with long histories on opposite sides of the debate over bias-crime legislation (Gellman against, Lawrence for) identify their points of difference with respect to both First Amendment protections and punishment for the specific harm inflicted by hate crime. They then identify substantial areas of agreement in their legal reasoning and conclude with a proposed model statute designed to punish special harms while protecting freedom of thought.

Grattet, Ryken, and Valerie Jenness. "The Criminalization of Hate: A Comparison of Structural and Political Influence on the Passage of 'Bias-Crime' Legislation in the United States." *Sociological Perspectives*, vol. 39, no. 1, 1996, pp. 129–154. Using a complete statistical analysis of hate-crimes statutes as they stood at the time of writing, this article analyzes the political and social motivation of such legislation and analyzes the reasons for the criminalization of hate as it progressed in the mid-1990s.

Greenspan, Edward L. "Should Hate Speech Be a Crime?" *Queen's Quarterly*, Spring 2004, p. 73. The author reports on the hate-crime trials of Canadian defendants Ernst Zundel and James Keegstra. Zundel was accused of distributing anti-Semitic literature; Keegstra was charged with promoting hatred against Jews. Though only Keegstra was convicted, ultimately Zundel was deemed a national security threat and deported to Germany. The article points out that the distinction between speech and action is disappearing in Canada when it comes to the prosecution of hate crimes.

Guenif-Souilamas, Nacira. "The Other French Exception: Virtuous Racism and the War of the Sexes in Postcolonial France." *French Politics, Culture and Society*, vol. 24, no. 3, 2006, p. 23. The author explains that a "virtuous racism" is emerging in modern France, making scapegoats of Islamic immigrants and attempting to impose a uniformity of dress, speech, politics, and culture on new arrivals from the country's former colonies. The phenomenon is clearly marked in attitudes toward gender roles and appearance.

"Hate Crimes: Federal Prosecution of Bias-Motivated Incidents." *Congressional Digest*, vol. 86, no. 6, June 2007, p. 161. This short article, and several others accompanying it in this issue of the *Congressional Digest*, explain the issues and debate surrounding the Local Law Enforcement Hate Crimes Prevention Act, which was the subject of hearings and came to a vote in the House of Representatives in spring 2007.

"Hate Crimes: Should They Carry Enhanced Penalties?" *ABA Journal*, May 1993, pp. 44–45. A point-counterpoint piece by two noted commentators. In "Yes: Discriminatory Crimes," Nadine Strossen, an attorney and the president of the American Civil Liberties Union, argues that expression can be used as circumstantial evidence, as the Constitution does not bar the use of words to prove criminal intent; also that lawmakers have every justification to treat discriminatory criminal acts more severely than other criminal acts. In "No: Equality Among Victims," political commentator Nat Hentoff argues against hate-crimes law as an abridgement of First Amendment rights and as a precursor to the policing of thought and opinion by the state.

Hentoff, Nat. "Prosecuting Hate Crimes: Laws Are Tailor-Made for Personal Bias." *Washington Times*, May 28, 2007, p. A19. The author opines that hate crime laws, specifically the proposed Local Law Enforcement Hate Crimes Prevention Act, unfairly establish an unconstitutional, two-tier justice system that will grant the federal government greater power to define the limits of thought, speech, and expression.

Hernandez, Greg. "Bittersweet Justice: In the Wake of the Gwen Araujo Trial, Activists Are Grimly Aware of How Difficult It Is to Obtain a First-Degree Murder Conviction When the Victim Is Transgender." *The Advocate*, November 22, 2005, p. 35. An article reviewing two well-publicized murders and trials in the San Francisco area, in which the accused cited "transgender panic" as a defense for murder.

"House Rebuffs Claims of Religious Right in Hate-Crimes Vote." *Church & State*, June 2007, p. 20. An editorial describing the extreme rhetoric employed by both sides in the debate over the Local Law Enforcement Hate Crimes Prevention Act of 2007, also known as the Matthew Shepard Act, the updated federal hate-crimes law that passed the House of Representatives in May 2007.

Hussey, Andrew. "Lyons: City of Outsiders; Beneath the Civilized, Bourgeois Exterior of the 'Gateway to the South' Lie the Sharpest Racial and Social Divisions in France." *New Statesman*, April 9, 2007, p. 31. Like many cities in France, the placid, middle-class town of Lyons hides a variety of virulent small-town prejudices. The city is balkanized into several ethnic neighborhoods, and intolerance and discrimination touch many of the city's Arab immigrants, who feel completely shut out of the city's social and economic mainstream.

Hudson, Anthony. "Law and a Sort of Order." *Index on Censorship*, vol. 35, no. 1, January 2006, p. 160. The author reviews the Racial and Religious Hatred Bill and the struggle over the proposed law between the British government and members of Parliament. The author alleges that changes in social attitudes and perception govern the degree of tolerance toward speech as expressed in a nation's laws.

Hate Crimes

Jacobs, James B. "Should Hate Be a Crime?" *The Public Interest*, vol. 113, Fall 1993, pp. 3–14. The author argues that the notion of hate crimes is an artificial, politically motivated, and unnecessary legal construct that suffers from vagueness, from illogical and inconsistent application by prosecutors and the courts, and unconstitutionality. He also contends that writing new criminal law is not the proper means to combat social problems such as prejudice against ethnic and religious minorities.

Jasket, Kristen. "Racists, Skinheads and Gay-Bashers Beware: Congress Joins the Battle Against Hate Crimes by Proposing the Hate Crimes Prevention Act of 1999." *Seton Hall Legislative Journal*, vol. 24, no. 2, 2000, pp. 509–540. The author believes that the rising rate of hate crimes warrants the inclusion of bias against sexual orientation in hate-crimes statutes, and that a more comprehensive federal law is needed to close loopholes in the existing law and supplement inadequate or nonexistent state hate-crimes laws.

Jenness, Valerie. "Managing Differences and Making Legislation: Social Movements and the Racialization, Sexualization, and Gendering of Federal Hate Crime Law in the U.S." *Social Problems*, vol. 46, no. 4, 1999, pp. 548–571. A study of the various federal hate-crimes laws passed in the 1990s and the origins of such legislation in the activities of nongovernmental organizations and interest groups.

———. "Social Movement Growth, Domain Expansion, and Framing Processes: The Gay/Lesbian Movement and Violence Against Gays and Lesbians as a Social Problem." *Social Problems*, vol. 42, 1995, p. 145. The author reiterates an important thesis of her books on the subject of hate crimes: that hate-crimes law originates with new social movements imitative of the Civil Rights movement of the 1950s and 1960s, and that the phenomenon of "domain expansion" tends to bring about new statutes that extend protection to newly defined minority groups.

Jenness, Valerie, and Ryken Grattet. "Examining the Boundaries of Hate Crime Law: Disabilities and the 'Dilemma of Difference.'" *Journal of Criminal Law and Criminology*, vol. 91, no. 3, Spring 2001, pp. 653–697. The authors argue against new hate-crimes law to protect those with disabilities, on the grounds that creating such a protected group tends to reinforce society's negative stereotypes about such a group, making the disabled more vulnerable to discrimination.

Jost, Kenneth. "Hate Crimes: Are Longer Sentences for Hate Crimes Constitutional?" *CQ Researcher*, January 8, 1993, pp. 1–24. The writer offers an overview and analysis of the *R.A.V. v. St. Paul* decision reached by the Supreme Court in 1992, and a useful general discussion of the history of hate-crimes legislation.

Koenig, Thomas H., and Michael L. Rustad. "'Hate Torts' to Fight Hate Crimes: Punishing the Organizational Roots of Evil." *American Behavioral*

Scientist, vol. 51, no. 2, October 2007, p. 302. The article illustrates the use of "hate tort" law to defend clients against intimidation and bias violence. In the absence of effective criminal penalties, the practice seeks redress by bankrupting organizations that preach and practice racial violence.

Lawrence, Frederick M. "Enforcing Bias Crime Laws Without Bias: Evaluating the Disproportionate Enforcement Critique." *Journal of Law and Contemporary Problems*, vol. 66, no. 3, 2003, pp. 49–70. The disproportionate-enforcement critique is a standard argument of those who challenge the effectiveness, legality, or need for bias-crime laws; it asserts that bias-crime laws will disproportionately be used against minority defendants and will otherwise cause disproportionate harm to minority groups. This essay examines the disproportionate-enforcement critique and rejects it, concluding that it is largely based on a misunderstanding of the goal of bias-crime laws.

Levin, Brian. "Bias Crimes: A Theoretical and Practical Overview." *Stanford Law and Policy Review*, vol. 4, 1992–93, pp. 165–181. The author gives a general overview of the nature of bias crimes, stating that bias crimes are more likely than other crimes to involve physical assault and they tend to be more severe than other assaults. In addition, gay men seem to be the group most often targeted for violent assault, while Jews tend to report bias crimes more often than other victimized groups. The author believes that the unprovoked nature of these attacks and the likelihood of further victimization intensifies the psychological damage inflicted by hate crimes. The article recommends improved data collection; coordination between police, prosecutors, private agencies, and other government officials; and bias crime training.

———. "From Slavery to Hate Crime Laws: The Emergence of Race and Status-Based Protection in American Criminal Law." *Journal of Social Issues*, vol. 58, no. 2, Summer 2002, pp. 227–245. The author takes a historical perspective on modern hate-crime law, tracing the new statutes back to the remedies for slavery that underlay the post–Civil War civil rights amendments and federal laws. Historic cases, laws, and constitutional changes describe the gradual evolution of modern hate-crime law.

Liebmann, George. "Clinton's Police State." *American Enterprise*, vol. 11, number 4, June 2000, p. 12. The Clinton administration, according to the author, promoted a sort of liberal police state through the creeping federalization of criminal law. The author believes that new hate-crimes laws would mean more of the same. "The result of all this would mean that the degree of punishment for a crime would rest not on how evil the crime is, but on the religion, race, or sexual practices of the victim or the politics of the perpetrator."

McAllister, J. F. O. "Drawing a Fine Line: In the Age of Cultural Rage, Democracies Are Under Fire to Decide When Free Speech Is Hate

Speech." *Time International (Europe Edition)*, vol. 167, no. 8, p. 22. Reviewing the strong reaction in Europe to cartoons in a Danish periodical lampooning Muslims and Mohammed, the author reviews censorship laws across the continent, which vary significantly from one country to the next depending on that country's historical experience. Publicly posting images of Hitler, for example, can bring a punishment of up to three years in jail in Germany; France bans Islamic head scarves as an illegal public expression of religious faith; and countries where the Catholic Church has traditionally been strong can punish expressions of blasphemy or satirical treatment of religion.

McKay-Panos, Linda. "Hate Crimes in Canada: Special Report on What You Say Can Hurt You." *LawNow*, vol. 28, no. 4, 2004, p. 29. A review of the hate-speech laws enacted as part of the Criminal Code in Canada, and the balance struck between the principle of freedom of expression and legitimate restrictions on speech intended to harm others or incite violence. The author notes that hate-speech codes arose in response to a rise in racist activities in the country in the 1950s and 1960s.

McPhail, Beverly. "Gender-Bias Hate Crimes: A Review." *Trauma, Violence & Abuse: A Review Journal*, vol. 3, no. 2, April 2002, pp. 125–143. The article reviews the debate over including gender as a status category in hate-crimes law, giving arguments both for and against. The author cautions against the inclusion of an entire gender as a protected status, as it may simply overgeneralize the hate-crime category as it applies to true minority groups, making it nothing more than a symbolic gesture.

———. "Hating Hate: Policy Implications of Hate Crime Legislation." *Social Service Review*, vol. 74, no. 4, 2000, pp. 635–653. The author describes the current state of hate-crimes law and policy from a social worker's perspective, controversies surrounding and unintended consequences of the new laws, and the debate between those who see in hate-crimes law the further balkanization of America and those who see the laws as necessary to promote social harmony.

Newport, Frank. "Public Favors Expansion of Hate Crime Law to Include Sexual Orientation." *The Gallup Poll Tuesday Briefing*, May 2007, p. 66. Poll results on the opinion of the general public on the topic of hate crimes and the extension of hate-crime laws to include sexual orientation.

Pfeiffer, Laura. "To Enhance or Not to Enhance: Civil Penalty Enhancement for Parents of Juvenile Hate Crime Offenders." *Valparaiso Law Review*, vol. 41, no. 4, Summer 2007, p. 1,685–1,737. The author covers the complex topic of extending penalties for discriminatory violence to parents, who under this doctrine would be held responsible for actions by their offspring that may escape serious penalties.

Phillips, Scott, and Ryken Grattet. "Judicial Rhetoric, Meaning-Making, and the Institutionalization of Hate Crime Law." *Law & Society Review*, vol. 34, 2000, pp. 567–606. This article examines the transformation of the concept of hate crime into a concrete legal construct that has, over time, been accepted as legitimate. The authors track changes in judicial rhetoric in 38 appeals court opinions that examined the constitutionality of hate crimes from 1984 through 1999. They conclude that the meaning of hate crime had become richer in expression than the words found in the statutes themselves, while the domain of hate crime gradually came to include broader ranges of behavior. The authors demonstrate how lawmakers and the court system tend to fix a legal definition of a term by developing a standard interpretation of that term.

Pollitt, Katha. "Hate Crimes Legislation." *The Nation*, November 29, 1999, p. 10. The author describes the debate over whether hate-crimes laws favor some victims over others, and contends that hate-crimes legislation deals with a class of motives rather than people on the grounds that bias crime perpetrators try to intimidate an entire community.

Potok, Mark. "Ten Years After Federal Officials Began Compiling National Hate Crime Statistics, the Numbers Don't Add Up." *Southern Poverty Law Center's Intelligence Report*, no. 104, Winter 2001, pp. 6–15. An article focusing on the problems of compiling hate crime statistics. The author believes that the national effort to document hate-motivated crime is inadequate, pointing out how the reporting system is riddled with errors and outright falsification of data. The author believes that while the published hate crime totals have been running at some 8,000 cases a year, the real figure is probably closer to 50,000. In some jurisdictions, the article claims, opposition or indifference towards data-collection has compromised the effort and has discouraged already reluctant victims from coming forward.

Ray, Larry, and David Smith. "Racist Offenders and the Politics of 'Hate Crime.'" *Law and College*, vol. 12, no. 3, December 2001, pp. 203–221. The authors examine the political trends and climate that have given rise to the emergence of hate crime as a new category of public controversy and of criminal conduct in the United States and the United Kingdom. The author uses data from the English city of Manchester to examine trends in hate crimes, describing hate-crime laws as a result of the increasingly legalized self-management of a complex modern society. "Hate crimes have thus acquired powerful rhetorical focus for mobilization of victim and identity politics," he states.

Redish, Martin H. "Freedom of Thought as Freedom of Expression: Hate Crime Sentencing Enhancement and First Amendment Theory." *Criminal Justice Ethics*, vol. 11, no. 2, Winter/Spring 2002, pp. 29–42. This article examines "free speech theory," claiming that, whether viewed as a catalyst or as a fundamental element, protection of freedom of thought is essential to the free speech right. In addition, penalty-enhancement laws punish the holding of political or social attitudes that the government deems offensive or unacceptable. The author believes that these laws are a serious threat to the values of free expression.

Rushdy, Ashraf H. A. "Reflections on Jasper: Resisting History." *The Humanist*, March/April 2000, pp. 24–28. The author contends that politicians have not taken the opportunity to improve hate-crimes legislation following the conviction of the killers of James Byrd, Jr., of Jasper, Texas. The need to strengthen federal hate-crimes legislation is discussed, and the historical precedent of responding to violent crime with calls for laws with harsher penalties is examined.

Shaw, Millicent. "Hate Crime Legislation and the Inclusion of Gender: A Possible Option for Battered Women." *Domestic Violence Report*, vol. 6, no. 5, June–July 2001, pp. 65–78. The author presents an analysis of hate crime legislation that focuses on the inclusion of gender as an option for battered women. The article finds that including gender has not resulted in an overwhelming number of gender-based crimes reported as an extension of domestic violence and rape cases. The analysis concludes that the majority of rape, domestic violence, and stalking cases will not become hate-crime cases, but that having the statute available for certain gender-bias cases will aid prosecutors in their decisions.

Simons, Kenneth W. "Equality, Bias Crimes, and Just Deserts." *Journal of Criminal Law and Criminology*, vol. 91, no. 1, Fall 2000, pp. 237–267. An article on victims' rights and criminal justice theory in which the author analyzes legislation regarding hate crimes and discusses "retributivist focus," which measures the culpability of the offender and the wrongdoing the offender commits. The analysis concludes that retributivist theory can justify higher sanctions for bias crimes and can do so more easily than can the principle of fair protection.

Sullivan, Andrew. "What's So Bad About Hate?" *New York Times Magazine*, September 26, 1999, pp. 50–57. The author argues that laws prescribing special punishments in hate-crimes cases make little sense. Hatred, he argues, is a very vague concept—"far less nuanced an idea than prejudice, or bigotry, or bias, or anger, or even mere aversion to others." And if hate instead is restricted to "a very specific idea or belief, or set of beliefs, with a very specific object or group of objects," then the antihate war will "almost certainly" be unconstitutional.

Tatchell, Peter. "The Reggae Lyrics of Hate." *New Statesman*, September 29, 2003, p. 16. This article describes antigay lyrics in popular reggae tunes and queries the sale of the material in major British music outlets such as HMV and Virgin. The article notes that under English law, incitement to the commission of a crime or violence is a prosecutable offense, whether or not that incitement actually leads to a criminal incident.

Annotated Bibliography

Ward, Jon. "Bush Vows to Veto Hate-Crime Expansion for Gays." *Washington Times*, August 7, 2007, p. A03. Through a spokesman, the president gives his objection to the updated federal hate-crimes law, threatening to veto the measure even if it is attached to a defense authorization bill.

Weinstein, James. "First Amendment Challenges to Hate Crime Legislation: Where's the Speech?" *Criminal Justice Ethics*, vol. 11, no. 2, Summer/Fall 1992, pp. 6–20. The author reviews Susan Gellman's 1991 article in which she claimed that hate crime legislation violated the First Amendment. This paper challenges the claim that such laws are invalid on their face—that is, regardless of the circumstances in which they are applied, a statute that enhances the punishment for racially motivated crimes violates the First Amendment. The author believes that an attack on the constitutionality of hate-crime legislation undermines the validity of all antidiscrimination laws.

"Why Hate Crimes Differ." *The Register-Guard* (Eugene, Oregon), October 2, 2007, p. A8. An editorial praising the support for a new hate-crimes law provided by Senator Gordon Smith (R-Oregon), who had introduced the bill in the Senate each of the previous five previous years. The article quotes Smith on his reasons for sponsorship of the bill, lately in cooperation with Senator Ted Kennedy (D-Mass.), including the severely violent nature of hate crimes and their intent to intimidate entire groups of people.

Young, Cathy. "Gender War Crimes." *Reason*, January 1999, pp. 55–57. Discussion of the radical feminist theory of gender violence, a theory incorporated within the Violence Against Women Act (VAWA), which allows federal civil rights suits for violent crimes "motivated by gender." The writer reveals that the application of the VAWA is, however, limited by the fact that it provides only for monetary damages. By contrast, the passage of the federal Hate Crimes Prevention Act would allow federal criminal prosecutions for sexual assault or domestic violence.

WEB DOCUMENTS

Anti-Defamation League. "ADL Hails Passage of Bill Mandating Enhanced Hate Crime Reporting on College Campuses." Available online. URL: http://adl.org/PresRele/Education_01/5345_01.htm. Posted on August 14, 2008. This short press release covers the passage of the Higher Education Opportunity Act, a new federal law signed by President Bush in August 2008, that in part mandates improved hate-crime data reporting and collection on college campuses.

Ortiz, Jon. "Details About Clery Disclosure." *The State Hornet*. Available online. URL: http://media.www.statehornet.com/media/storage/paper1146/

news/2002/10/16/News/Details.About.Clery.Disclosure-2421099.shtml. Posted on October 21, 2002. The author gives details on the Clery Act, which requires colleges to report crime statistics including incidents of hate crimes, which are defined as crimes motivated by a victim's race, gender, religion, sexual orientation, ethnicity, or disability.

REPORTS

American Prosecutors Research Institute (APRI). "A Local Prosecutor's Guide for Responding to Hate Crimes." 2000. The APRI is the research arm of the National District Attorneys Association (NDAA). This resource guide was originally created for use by local district attorneys and lists agencies and organizations specializing in hate crimes, case management methods for prosecutors, and prevention measures. Model procedures used by district attorneys in the prosecution of hate crimes are given, as well as a list of individuals who are currently prosecuting hate crimes.

Center for Democratic Renewal. *When Hate Groups Come to Town: A Handbook of Model Community Responses.* 1992. A handbook for local law enforcement and citizens in dealing with outside hate groups, such as the Ku Klux Klan, that gather for meetings or parades and tend to incite violence and division in the community.

Shively, Michael. "Study of Literature and Legislation on Hate Crime in America, Final Report." Rockville, Md.: ABT Associates, Inc., U.S. Department of Justice, National Institute of Justice, 2005. This 147-page report reviews hundreds of documents and web sites, summarizes hate-crimes literature and legislation, and identifies current hate-crime issues, evidence of effective practices and innovative responses, and gaps in the law and research on hate crime. The report includes extensive figures; a 435-item bibliography; and appended material on resource organizations, bias-crimes statutes and related provisions, Wisconsin's penalty enhancement statute, and the text of the Anti-Defamation League Model.

Smith, Alison M. "Constitutional Limits on Hate Crime Legislation." Washington, D.C.: Congressional Research Service, 2008. This report, prepared by the public policy research arm of Congress, outlines the constitutional constraints on legislation concerning hate crimes as of February 20, 2008. The Congressional Research Service (CRS) is under the umbrella of the Library of Congress and works exclusively for members of Congress, their committees, and their staffs. Individuals can obtain CRS reports from a member of Congress or from one of the many free clearinghouses of these documents on the Internet.

Annotated Bibliography

MAJOR CONGRESSIONAL HEARINGS

U.S. House of Representatives Judiciary Committee. 1993. *Crimes of Violence Motivated by Gender.* Superintendent of Documents #Y4. J89/1:103/51.

———. *Hate Crimes Prevention Act of 1997: Hearing Before the Committee on the Judiciary, House of Representatives, One Hundred Fifth Congress.* Washington, D.C.: Government Printing Office, 2000. From hearings held July 22, 1998. Available online. URL: http://www.access.gpo.gov/su_docs/.

———. *Implementation of the Church Arson Prevention Act of 1996: Hearings, March 19, 1997.* Superintendent of Documents #Y4.J89/1:105/4. Hearings convened during a period of concern on arson and bombings of African-American churches. The testimony includes the implementation of the Church Arson Prevention Act, covering the role of federal and local law enforcement agencies in preventing church arson.

U.S. House of Representatives Judiciary Committee, Subcommittee on Crime and Criminal Justice. *Bias Crimes: Hearings, May 11, 1992.* Superintendent of Documents #Y4.J89/1:102/80. Hearings on hate crimes in general, including witnesses from gay rights, Asian-American, Jewish, women's rights, and African-American organizations, as well as the FBI. The agenda also included witnesses and testimony on the Hate Crimes Sentencing Act of 1992.

———. *Hate Crimes Sentencing Enhancement Act of 1992: Hearing, July 29, 1992.* Superintendent of Documents #Y4:J89/1:102/64. Hearings on proposed legislation that would provide for enhanced penalties when defendants were found to have committed a bias-motivated crime.

U.S. House of Representatives Judiciary Committee, Subcommittee on Crime, Terrorism, and Homeland Security. *Local Law Enforcement Hate Crimes Prevention Act of 2007.* Government Printing Office, Serial No. 110-71. Available online. URL: http://judiciary.house.gov. A hearing held on April 17, 2007, on the updated hate-crimes bill, H.R. 1592, which included new provisions against hate crimes perpetrated against homosexuals and the disabled.

U.S. Senate Foreign Relations Committee, Subcommittee on European Affairs. *Anti-Semitism in Europe.* Government Printing Office, Serial No. 95-528. Available online. URL: http://frwebgate.access.gpo.gov/cgi-bin/getdoc.cgi?dbname=108_senate_hearings&docid=f:95528.wais. A Senate hearing on April 8, 2004, in which witnesses from B'nai B'rith, Human Rights First, and the Anti-Defamation League describe a rising tide of anti-Semitic incidents in Europe.

U.S. Senate Judiciary Committee. *Combating Hate Crimes: Promoting a Responsive and Responsible Role for the Federal Government. United States Senate,*

One Hundred Sixth Congress. Washington, D.C.: Government Printing Office, 2000. From hearings held May 11, 1999. Available online. URL: http://www.access.gpo.gov/su_docs/.

———. *Combating Violence Against Women: Hearing, May 15, 1996.* Superintendent of Documents #Y4.J89/2:S.Hrg 104-842. Hearing on the incidence of gender-based violence against women and implementation of the Violence Against Women Act of 1994.

———. *Hate Crime on the Internet: Hearing Before the Committee on the Judiciary, United States Senate, One Hundred Sixth Congress.* Washington, D.C.: Government Printing Office, 2001. From hearings held September 14, 1999. Available online. URL: http://www.access.gpo.gov/su_docs/. The hearing report is further subtitled Ramifications of Internet Technology on Today's Children, Focusing on the Prevalence of Internet Hate, and Recommendations of How to Shield Children From the Negative Impact of Violent Media.

CRIMINOLOGY, LAW ENFORCEMENT, AND RESEARCH

BOOKS

Bell, Jeannine. *Policing Hatred: Law Enforcement, Civil Rights, and Hate Crime.* Critical America series. New York: New York University Press, 2004. The author studies hate crimes from the perspective of those charged with enforcing the law. The book studies the impact on police officers, who often have to make difficult judgments of motivation and intent when assessing an incident as a hate crime. The author finds that the handling of a case, suspects, and witnesses often varies with the ethnic background of the people involved.

Best, Joel. *Random Violence: How We Talk About New Crimes and New Victims.* Berkeley: University of California Press, 1999. The creation and treatment of what the author terms "new crimes" such as wilding (rampaging through a neighborhood), freeway violence, and hate crimes, in American society; the development of a "victim industry"; and how institutions such as government and the media manufacture new social problems to further their own interests.

Cunningham, David. *There's Something Happening Here: The New Left, The Klan, and FBI Counterintelligence.* Berkeley: University of California Press, 2004. Examining previously classified FBI documents, the author describes the long campaign of the FBI against groups on the left and on the right, including the Klan and other hate groups, finding in the FBI's undercover operations a mission to stamp out political dissent and any opinions tending toward disorder and defiance of the federal government.

Ferber, Abby L., Ryken Grattet, and Valerie Jenness. *Hate Crime in America: What Do We Know?* Washington, D.C.: American Sociological Association, 2000. A brief volume providing expert testimony on several areas of research and data on hate crimes, including summaries of recent legislation, and a useful list of experts working in the field.

Flint, Colin. *Spaces of Hate: Geographies of Discrimination and Intolerance in the U.S.A.* London: Routledge, 2004. A book that examines the role of location and geography on the nature and occurrence of hate crimes, and the founding and operations of hate groups. The authors describe the differences between rural and urban hate crimes and the characteristics of locations that tend to foster hate crimes.

Gerstenfeld, Phyllis B., and Diana Ruth Grant, eds. *Crimes of Hate: Selected Readings.* Thousand Oaks, Calif.: Sage Publications, Inc., 2004. This collection of scholarly articles from the fields of criminology, psychology, political science, and sociology examines the field of hate-crimes law, incorporating discussion questions and resource lists.

Quarles, Chester L. and Paula L. Ratliff. *Crime Prevention for Houses of Worship.* Alexandria, Va.: American Society for Industrial Security, 2001. A handbook for houses of worship of all faiths, aiming to prevent vandalism, arson, and other bias-motivated crimes against property and against congregation members.

Ronczkowski, Michael R. *Terrorism and Organized Hate Crime: Intelligence Gathering, Analysis and Investigations,* Second Edition. London: CRC, 2006. The second edition of a useful guide for professionals—investigators, law enforcement agents, and government analysts—who are combating organized hate and terrorist groups, giving insights into the motivations and methods of these groups and how they are taking advantage of modern communications and transportation systems. The book was updated to include religious extremist groups, in the United States and in foreign countries.

Turnbull, Linda S., and Elaine Hallisey Hendrix, eds. *Atlas of Crime: Mapping the Criminal Landscape.* Phoenix, Ariz.: Oryx Press, 2000. In the chapter entitled Hate Crime, author Damon Camp charts the occurrence of hate crimes and hate groups across the country, concluding that hate groups are more prevalent east of and along the Mississippi and on the Pacific Coast. In addition, the majority of hate-crime activity is associated with right-wing extremists and white supremacist groups, which are tied to survivalism, paramilitarism, neo-Nazism, and Holocaust revisionism. The chapter also reviews hate crime legislation in the states, dividing criminal laws into institutionalized violence and intimidation/harassment.

Hate Crimes

PERIODICALS

Adams, David M. "Punishing Hate and Achieving Equality." *Criminal Justice Ethics*, vol. 24, no. 1, January 2005, p. 19. The author argues that hate crimes should not count as a distinctive category of wrongdoing, as the quality and intensity of prejudice in violent crime varies from one criminal to the next, and that penalty enhancement statutes that punish hate crimes are legally flawed.

Aynesworth, Hugh. "Killer Says He Wasn't There for '98 Dragging: Appeal Claims Hate Crime Was Drug-Related." *Washington Times*, August 21, 2006, p. A03. One of the accused in the 1998 James Byrd dragging case claims he was not present at the time of the murder, and that rather than a hate crime the murder resulted from a drug deal gone bad. The accused also names two men who were never charged with actually committing the murder.

Balboni, Jennifer, and Jack McDevitt. "Hate Crime Reporting: Understanding Police Officer Perceptions, Departmental Protocol, and the Role of the Victim: Is There Such a Thing as a 'Love' Crime?" *Justice Research and Policy*, vol. 3, no. 1, Spring 2001, pp. 1–27. The authors discuss the impact on hate-crime reporting of various factors: lack of infrastructure to support accurate reporting, lack of training, disincentives to police officers to accurately report, and hesitation on the part of victims to involve the police. The authors draw on a sample of data taken from police departments across the nation as well as interviews with law enforcement officials and government and private-sector professionals involved with the issue.

Craig, Kellina. "Examining Hate-Motivated Aggression: A Review of the Social Psychological Literature on Hate Crimes as a Distinct Form of Aggression." *Aggression and Violent Behavior*, vol. 7, no. 1, January–February 2002, pp. 85–101. This article reviews the literature on hate crimes in social psychology and other related fields. The author attempts to identify factors common to the various types of hate crimes to clarify the nature of hate-motivated crimes, their prevalence, and causes. The paper also discusses membership in organized hate groups, religious values, psychopathology and deviancy, the authoritarian personality and right-wing authoritarianism, and the decision to join a hate group.

Deirmenjian, John M. "Hate Crimes on the Internet." *Journal of Forensic Sciences*, vol. 45, no. 5, 2000, pp. 1,020–1,022. Offering six case studies in electronic hate crime, the author describes the effort to investigate and prosecute such acts, the difficulties of combatting hate crime in the anonymous and borderless world of the Internet, and the intervention efforts against hate groups and hate sites on both local and national levels.

Dharmapala, Dhammik. "Penalty Enhancement for Hate Crimes: An Economic Analysis." *American Journal of Psychiatry*, vol. 160, May 2003, pp. 979–989. The writer offers an analysis that shows that bias crimes have a more harmful social effect, economically speaking, than non-bias crimes, even when the physical harm to the victim is identical.

Edwards, Jim. "Statistics Don't Bear Out Feared Wave of Bias Cases Against Muslims, Arabs." *New Jersey Law Journal*, vol. 168, no. 11, June 10, 2002, p. 1. The author investigates complaints of bias incidents and racial profiling against Arab Americans after the September 11, 2001, terrorist attacks, claiming that although there was a rise in such incidents, the increase was not serious or "statistically significant."

Geller, Joshua. S. "A Dangerous Mix: Mandatory Sentence Enhancements and the Use of Motive." *Fordham Urban Law Journal*, vol. 32, no. 3, 2005, p. 623. The author describes a case in which a 15-year sentence for assault is doubled simply on the basis of a few antihomosexual epithets uttered by the defendant. He questions the imposition of hate-crime penalty enhancements, which must be decided by a jury asked to analyze the psyche of the criminal, at the time of the crime, beyond a reasonable doubt.

Grattet, Ryan. "Making the Most of General Orders." *The Police Chief*, vol. 71, no. 2, p. 63. The author reviews the implementation of standing instructions to police officers on dealing with hate-crime incidents.

Haider-Markel, Donald P. "Implementing Controversial Policy: Results from a National Survey of Law Enforcement Department Activity on Hate Crime." *Justice Research and Policy*, vol. 3, no. 1, Spring 2001, pp 29–61. This research report explores the implementation of hate crime policy by police departments, emphasizing policies and procedures related to antihomosexual bias crimes. The author sampled 250 of the nation's largest cities and concludes the support of police leaders and officers, the presence of state hate crime policies, police resources, and public opinion all shaped the effectiveness of local efforts to deal with hate crimes.

———. "Perception and Misperception in Urban Criminal Justice Policy: The Case of Hate Crime." *Urban Affairs Review*, vol. 39, no. 4, 2004, pp. 491–512. This article deals with differences in perception of the hate-crime issue depending on organizational and community context. The main contrast in perception is drawn between community and interest-group leaders and law enforcement personnel.

Heilman, Dan. "Hate Crimes in Minnesota Are Difficult to Track." *Minnesota Lawyer*. May 21, 2007. The author describes gray areas of the Minnesota hate-crimes law, which provides only for penalty enhancements if bias is found to be a motivating factor—a determination that can be made at any stage of the case, from the first investigation to sentencing.

Extrapolating from various statistics, the author concludes that a hate crime has only a one in 500 chance of being successfully prosecuted as such.

Horne, Brian. "Kriss Killed in 'Appalling Act of Sheer Inhumanity'; Defenceless Schoolboy Died after Horrific Race-Hate Crime, QC Tells Jury." *Daily Mail* (London, England), November 3, 2006, p. 5. A story describing the trial of three men accused of the kidnapping, torture, and murder of a 15-year-old in Glasgow, Scotland. Three accused men were deported from Pakistan in order to stand trial for the murder.

Hudson, Audrey. "Koran Abuse Draws Hate-Crime Charge; Former Student Said to Have Left Books in Toilets." *Washington Times*, July 31, 2007, p. A03. A Ukrainian student at Pace University is accused of a hate crime for taking copies of the Koran and leaving them in toilets. The charge was criminal mischief as a hate crime.

Hurd, Heidi M., and Michael S. Moore. "Punishing Hatred and Prejudice." *Stanford Law Review*, vol. 56, no. 5, 2004, p. 1,081. The authors provide a detailed history of hate-crime law and analyze 10 years of scholarly writings on the subject, finding in the extensive literature little more justification or "acceptable doctrinal framework" for such law, no matter what basis or thesis is used by proponents.

Isaacs, Tracy. "Domestic Violence and Hate Crimes: Acknowledging Two Levels of Responsibility." *Criminal Justice Ethics*, vol. 20, no. 2, Summer/ Fall 2001, pp. 31–43. The author believes that counseling should be mandatory in cases of hate-crime conviction, with the goal of erasing negative stereotypes and misconceptions about minorities among hate-crime perpetrators.

Jenness, Valerie, and Ryken Grattet. "The Law-In-Between: The Effects of Organizational Perviousness on the Policing of Hate Crime." *Social Problems*, vol. 52, no. 3, August 2005, pp. 337–359. This article examines the effect of certain environmental conditions—including the rate of local violent crime and the availability of resources—on the treatment of hate crimes and enforcement of hate-crime laws by law enforcement agencies.

King, Ryan D. "Conservatism, Institutionalism, and the Social Control of Intergroup Conflict." *The American Journal of Sociology*, vol. 113, no. 5, March 2008, p. 1,351. The author's research shows that the number of hate-crime prosecutions varies with social attitudes in the surrounding communities, and that jurisdictions where conservatism and religious fundamentalism prevail tend to have fewer such prosecutions.

Kolker, Robert. "When Is a Hate Crime Not a Hate Crime?" *New York*, vol. 40, no. 40, November 12, 2007, p. 30. The article describes a Brooklyn murder prosecuted as an antigay hate crime and defended on the grounds that the perpetrator of the crime was also gay.

Lieberman, Joel D., Jamie Arndt, Jennifer Personius, and Alison Cook. "Vicarious Annihilation: The Effects of Mortality Salience on Perceptions of Hate Crimes." *Law and Human Behavior,* vol. 25, no. 6, December 2001, pp. 547–566. The article describes terror management theory, which maintains that intolerance toward those who are different stems from personal vulnerability and fear of mortality. The paper reports on research that explored this theory by examining perceptions of hate crimes among 140 undergraduate students at the University of Nevada. The author suggests that the solution to intolerance lies in education to supplant deeply rooted prejudices.

Lynch, Michael F. "Responding to Hate Crime and Bias-Motivated Incidents on Campuses." *Campus Law Enforcement Journal,* vol. 31, no. 3, May/June 2001, pp. 23–25. The author reviews the diverse cultural landscape of college campuses, which often brings about bias-motivated incidents as well as exacerbated racial and ethnic tensions. The article reviews the proactive role of campus law enforcement in dealing with hate crimes emphasizing standard operating procedure, training and education, and the use of conciliation on the part of law enforcement. The author also discusses the role of college administrations in formulating hate-crime policies, in agreements with victim-support agencies, and in cooperation with local police departments.

Lyons, Christopher J. "Individual Perceptions and the Social Construction of Hate Crimes: A Factorial Survey." *The Social Science Journal,* vol. 45, no. 1, March 2008, pp. 107–131. The author compares and contrasts how people perceive hate crimes and how hate-crime legislation is written and passed by lawmakers.

———. "Stigma or Sympathy? Attributions of Fault to Hate Crime Victims and Offenders." *Social Psychology Quarterly,* vol. 69, no. 1, March 2006, pp. 39–59. The author studies the influence of social status on the view of hate crime victims and offenders. The status of race, gender, and sexual orientation all have certain tendencies in the treatment of the crime by law enforcement and the courts as well as the popular view. The results of the study tend to show that gay victims garner less sympathy and are held more accountable for their actions.

Marcus-Newhall, Amy, and Laura Palucki Blake, with Julia Baumann. "Perceptions of Hate Crime Perpetrators and Victims as Influenced by Race, Political Orientation, and Peer Group." *American Behavioral Scientist,* vol. 46, no. 1, January 2002, pp. 108–135. The authors present three studies of the influence of bias factors—race of victim, race of perpetrator, and political orientation—on the decisions made by mock jurors in hate-crimes cases. The results generally revealed that guilty verdicts and higher sentences were reached when the victim was African American and the perpetrator white.

209

Martin, Susan E. "Police and the Production of Hate Crimes: Continuity and Change in One Jurisdiction." *Police Quarterly*, vol. 2, no. 4, 1999, pp. 417–437. A study of hate crimes from 1987 through 1996 in Baltimore County, Maryland, and the actions of the Baltimore police in reporting, community outreach, training, and investigation of hate crimes. The author describes the ambiguities in the system of reporting hate crimes, showing that it may lead to distortion and uncertainty in statistics reported by local police departments.

Mason, Gail. "Hate Crime and the Image of the Stranger." *British Journal of Criminology*, vol. 45, no. 6, March 7, 2005, pp. 837–859. The authors examine the relationship between victim and perpetrator in racist and homophobic attacks, based on records compiled by London's Metropolitan Police Service.

Medoff, Marshall H. "Allocation of Time and Hateful Behavior: A Theoretic and Positive Analysis of Time and Hate Crime." *Journal of Economics and Sociology*, vol. 58, no. 4, October 1999, pp. 959–973. A statistical analysis of hate-crime data for 1995, this article concludes that hate crimes were positively related to the unemployment rate, the percentage of population between 15 and 19 years old, the extent of a state's liberal ideology, and educational levels. Hate crimes were negatively related to wage rates, while law enforcement efforts, religious belief, urbanization, low occupational status, and downward social mobility did not have a statistically significant impact.

Messner, Steven F., Suzanne McHugh, and Richard B. Felson. "Distinctive Characteristics of Assaults Motivated by Bias." *Criminology*, vol. 42, no. 3, August 2004, pp. 585–618. Examining statistics on hate crimes from 11 U.S. states, the authors find evidence suggesting that hate-crime perpetrators are more likely to use drugs or alcohol, are more likely to seriously injure the victim, and that the risk of becoming a victim of a bias crime is similar for blacks and other minorities.

Miller, Alexandra J. "Student Perceptions of Hate Crimes." *American Journal of Criminal Justice*, vol. 25, no. 2, Spring 2001, pp. 293–305. The author studies undergraduate criminal justice majors and non–criminal justice majors, using the hypothesis that criminal justice majors would have a better understanding of hate crimes and be more likely to identify incidents as such. This hypothesis was proven wrong. While criminal justice majors tended to be older and more likely male, both groups had similar portions of whites and blacks. It was also found that females and non–criminal justice majors are more likely to disagree over all types of hate crimes, while criminal justice majors were less likely to identify sexual minorities, females, or Jews as victims. According to the author, the findings demonstrate the need for separate courses within the criminal justice curriculum to address the issues of gender and multiculturalism.

Annotated Bibliography

Nolan, James J., Yoshio Akiyama, and Samuel Bernahu. "The Hate Crimes Statistics Act of 1990: Developing a Method for Measuring the Occurrence of Hate Violence." *American Behavioral Scientist*, vol. 46, no. 1, January 2002, pp. 136–153. The authors describe the FBI's hate-crime data-collection program, which was developed as an adjunct to its annual Uniform Crime Reports. The article examines trends in local law enforcement participation in the program, as well as trends in hate crimes revealed by the more comprehensive collection of data on the local level.

Parks, Carlton, and Kamilah M. Woodson. "Anxiety Symptoms Among Sexually Abused Ethnic Minority Male Survivors of Racially Motivated Hate Crimes: An Exploratory Study." *Family Violence & Sexual Assault Bulletin*, vol. 18, no. 2, Summer 2002, pp. 13–19. A study documenting the psychological impact of forced sexual activity within the context of racially motivated hate crimes. The study sample was composed of 187 men of color (47 percent African American, 21 percent Latino, 18 percent Asian American/Pacific Islander, 8 percent American Indian, and 6 percent biracial/multiracial). Eighteen of the men reported having a history of male sexual assault during racially motivated hate crimes. Compared with men who did not report having a sexual assault history, these men were more likely to have involvement with both male and female survivors of child sexual abuse and sexual assault. The authors discuss the implications of these findings for future research.

Quigley, Bill. "Racial Discrimination and the Legal System: The Recent Lessons of Louisiana." *UN Chronicle*, September 2007, p. 56. The author reviews the Jena Six case in Louisiana. Pointing out that the judge, jury, local police, school officials, and nearly all other authority figures in the town are white, the author asserts that racial discrimination is still widespread in the U.S. legal system.

Rubenstein, William B. "The Real Story of U.S. Hate Crime Statistics: An Empirical Analysis." *Tulane Law Review*, vol. 78, 2004, pp. 1,213–1,246. Also available online. URL: http://www.law.ucla.edu/williamsinstitute/publications/HateCrimes.pdf. The author argues that raw hate-crime statistics have been rather misleading, and he draws a distinction between "neutral" categories of victim and more specific "subgroups," including blacks, Jewish people, and gays, which he finds have reported by far the highest number of hate crimes. He analyzes the per-capita incidence of hate crimes among these groups and finds that gay victims are more likely to report personal assaults as opposed to attacks on property. The article also examines the incidence of anti-Muslim and anti-Arab hate crimes.

Saucier, D. A., J. M. Hockett, and A. S. Wallenberg. "The Impact of Racial Slurs and Racism on the Perceptions and Punishment of Violent Crime."

Journal of Interpersonal Violence, vol. 23, no. 5, 2008, pp. 685–701. This article reports on a study that used vignettes of violent crimes, varying races for the perpetrators and victims, severity of assault, and presence or absence of racial slurs by the perpetrators. The researchers' goal was to see how these variables would affect subjects' perception of the crimes as "hate crimes," sentencing recommendations, and tendency to blame victims. Results showed that each variable influenced how participants perceived and punished violent crime.

Savelsberg, Joachim, and Ryan D. King. "Institutionalizing Collective Memories of Hate: Law and Law Enforcement in Germany and the United States." *American Journal of Sociology*, vol. 111, 2005, pp. 579–616. The author contrasts the effect of hate-crimes laws and enforcement of collective memories in the United States and Germany, finding that Americans focus on individual victimization, outside of historical context, and Germans focus on the Holocaust. These characteristics have far-ranging results on the political debate surrounding hate-crime law in the two countries and on the institutions set up to deal with the problem.

Seper, Jerry. "3 Hispanics Sentenced to Life in Killing of Blacks." *Washington Times*, November 22, 2006, p. A03. Article covering the random murder of two black men by Hispanic gang members in Los Angeles. The crime was the culmination of a "reign of terror" in the Highland Park neighborhood, which saw rising violence between its African-American and Hispanic communities.

———. "Most Hate Crimes Spurred by Racial Bias, FBI Says: Report Finds 6 Percent Drop in Incidents Nationwide in '05." *Washington Times*, October 1, 2006, p. A06. This article reviews the hate-crime statistics contained within the FBI's Uniform Crime Reports for 2005. The FBI report details the motivation of hate crimes, finding that more than half were motivated by racial bias, a slight increase over 2004. The overall number of hate crimes dropped, however, by 6 percent. The most common crimes listed were intimidation, simple assault, and aggravated assault.

Stohr, Mary, Salvador Vasquez, and Shandell Kleppinger. "It Is Not Paranoia If People Really Are Out to Get You: The Nature and the Extent of Hate Crime Victimization in Idaho." *Journal of Ethnicity in Criminal Justice*, vol. 4, no. ½, 2006, pp. 65–91. This article reports data (in seven tables and 75 references) that was collected in a survey of randomly selected Idaho households: 4,000 households in 2000 and 4,250 in 2001. The results indicated that members of racial and ethnic minorities were almost three times as likely to feel vulnerable to a hate crime as whites. The authors urge policymakers to use this study as a starting point for conducting a thorough investigation of the incidence of hate crime at the state level.

Annotated Bibliography

"Teen Accused of Hate Crime Strikes a Deal." *Daily Herald* (Arlington Heights, Illinois), June 21, 2007, p. 5. This short article describes the case of an Illinois high schooler accused of a hate crime under state law for distributing antigay fliers. The accused strikes a plea bargain and is convicted of disorderly conduct and resisting a police officer. The article illustrates the tension between hate-crime statutes and First Amendment rights.

Umemoto, Karen, and C. Kimi Mikami. "Profile of Race-Bias Hate Crime in Los Angeles County." *Western Criminology Review*, vol. 2, no. 2, 2000, pp. 1–34. The authors study hate crimes based on racial bias in Los Angeles County, based on law enforcement statistics collected fom 1994–97. The article maps 1,837 reported bias incidents and locates areas where hate crimes occur in relatively high density; in addition, the authors conducted interviews and undertook archival research. Their results suggest that hate crimes committed in cluster locations more often involve perpetrators who are members of gangs. A related finding was the strong indication of race-bias hate crime among minority-based gangs in which the motive was hatred toward the victim's ethnicity and not the defense of territorial boundaries against other gangs.

Washington, Adrienne. "Noose Is No Prank, and Not to Be Tolerated." *Washington Times*, September 11, 2007, p. B02. The author describes a noose-hanging incident at the University of Maryland. The incident may have been linked to fund-raising efforts for the Jena Six at nearby Howard University, where students rallied in support of six African-American teenagers charged with attempted murder in a small Louisiana town.

White, Rob, and Santina Perrone. "Racism, Ethnicity and Hate Crime." *Communal/Plural: Journal of Transnational & Cross-Cultural Studies*, vol. 9, no. 2, 2001, pp. 161–181. The authors explore street fights involving ethnic-minority youth in Melbourne, Australia, attempting to show how marginalization could serve to fuel racist political attacks on such groups. Two main types of group conflict are addressed: street fights and school fights. The author finds that while racism was implicated in street violence, the main variable was that of power, and that fights among groups of relatively powerless sections of the community were less a matter of hate crime than of social dislocation. In addition, street violence tended to reinforce the stereotypes and social divisions which racial and hate crime feeds.

WEB DOCUMENTS

American Civil Liberties Union. "Sanctioned Bias: Racial Profiling Since 9/11." New York: ACLU, 2004. This 18-page report compares public statements and actions of U.S. government authorities in the wake of the terrorist attacks of September 11, 2001, and concludes that ethnic profiling of Arab Americans became official government policy. The authors state that profiling of any kind is not only at odds with core American values, but also counterproductive, and they recommend alternatives.

Anti-Defamation League. "ADL Hails Passage of Bill Mandating Enhanced Hate Crime Reporting on College Campuses." Available online. URL: http://adl.org/PresRele/Education_01/5345_01.htm. Posted on August 14, 2008. Short press release on the passage of the Higher Education Opportunity Act, a new federal law signed by President Bush in August 2008, that in part mandates improved hate-crime data reporting and collection on college campuses.

Bune, Karen N. "Law Enforcement Must Take Lead on Hate Crimes." *The Police Chief,* vol. 71, no. 4, April 2004. Available online. URL: http://police chiefmagazine.org/magazine/index.cfm?fuseaction=display_arch&article_id=270&issue_id=42004. An article detailing the leadership steps that law enforcement executives must take in preventing hate crimes and prosecuting the offenders.

California Department of Justice. "Hate Crime in California, 2006." Available online. URL: http://ag.ca.gov/cjsc/publications/hatecrimes/hc06/preface06.pdf. Posted on July 6, 2007. Comprehensive report on hate crimes in the state, broken down by offense category, bias motivation, prosecutorial and trend data, location, victim, and so on, in simple and direct graphic-and-text format.

Canadian Centre for Justice Statistics. "Hate Crime in Canada: An Overview of Issues and Data Sources." Available online. URL: http://hate monitor.csusb.edu/other_countries_laws/HateCrime-English.pdf. Posted in January 2001. A comprehensive report on the history of hate crime in Canada, on data collection issues and police procedures, results from surveys, and a comparison with hate-crime data collection efforts in the United States.

Federal Bureau of Investigation. "Hate Crime Data Collection Guidelines: Uniform Crime Reporting." Available online. URL: http://www.fbi.gov/ucr/hatecrime.pdf. Last updated in October 1999. The FBI published this set of guidelines for the use of local law enforcement agencies attempting to comply with the Hate Crimes Statistics Act of 1990 and provide hate-crimes data to the bureau for its annual Uniform Crime Reports. The guidelines include the criteria to be applied to hate crimes (such as how to determine bias motivation), example forms for submitting hate-crime data to the UCR program as well as the National Incident-Based Reporting System (NIBRS), the text of the Hate Crimes Statistics Act, and "offense definitions."

————. "Hate Crime Statistics, 2006." Available online. URL: http://www. fbi.gov.ucr/hatecrime.pdf. Downloaded on November 17, 2007. An annual survey of hate crimes throughout the United States, giving a detailed breakdown by type of bias motivation, race of offenders and victims, and type of incident. This report is the outcome of the original Hate Crimes Statistics Act and has become the standard source for journalists, criminologists, and academics for national hate-crimes statistics and trends.

Grattet, Ryken. "Hate Crimes: Better Data or Increasing Frequency?" Population Reference Bureau. Available online. URL: http://www.pro. org/Articles/2000/HateCrimesBetterDataorIncreasingFequency.aspx. Posted in July 2000. The author gives a summary of hate-crime data collection efforts, analyzing the numbers through 1998 and revealing that "some of the best information comes from local rather than national sources." From this information, several researchers have pointed out the importance of "territorial defense as a key underlying factor in the commission of hate crime." The author includes a short bibliography of academic articles on hate crime.

Greenhouse, Linda. "Justices Seek Federal Guidance on Sentencing." *New York Times.* Available online. URL: http://query.nytimes.com/gst/fullpage.html?res=9905EEDE163CF931A15753C1A9649C8B63. Posted on October 21, 2002. Article detailing the fallout of the Supreme Court's *Apprendi v. New Jersey* decision, which held that evidence used to increase a sentence beyond the statutory maximum must be subject to a jury verdict. The finding of biased motivation that brings a hate-crimes penalty enhancement, for example, must be proven to a jury and cannot be left up to a judge during the sentencing phase. The Supreme Court asks for guidance from the federal government on the question of whether penalty enhancement based on prior offenses, which had been the single exception to this rule, is out of place in the jury-based sentencing procedure established by *Apprendi v. New Jersey.*

Holthouse, David, and Mark Potok. "The Year in Hate: Active U.S. Hate Groups Rise to 888 in 2007." Southern Poverty Law Center. Available online. URL: http://www.splcenter.org/intel/intelreport/article.jsp?aid=886. Downloaded on July 14, 2008. This annual Intelligence Report from the Southern Poverty Law Center provides a brief roundup of hate crime statistics and a snapshot of current activities of active hate groups.

Justice Research and Statistics Association. "Hate Crime Reporting: Understanding Police Officer Perceptions, Department Protocol, and the Role of the Victim." Available online. URL: htt;://www.jrasinfo.org/pubs/journal/past_issues/Spring2001/balboni_etal.html. Accessed on November 22, 2007. A paper exploring the problems in reporting hate crime—including the "disincentives to accurately report" among the police and hesitation of the victims—and how these problems affect published statistics. Using surveys of police officers and interviews with advocacy and human rights professionals, the report makes suggestions for improvements in police/community relations and in department infrastructure.

Los Angeles County Human Relations Commission. "July 2003–June 2005 Annual Report." Available online. URL: http://humanrelations.co.la.ca. us/news/activities.htm. Downloaded on August 22, 2008. A summary of hate-crime reports, political activities, corporate and school initiatives, anti-discrimination efforts, city and police projects, and hate-crime services in Los Angeles County. The report notes an increase in hate crimes in the county and a record number of incidents involving Middle Eastern ethnic groups in the wake of the September 11, 2001, terrorist attacks.

Matier, Phillip, and Andrew Ross. "Long, Strange Journey of Hate-Crime Case." SF Gate: home of the *San Francisco Chronicle.* Available online. URL: http://www.sfgate.com/cgi-bin/article.cgi?f=/c/a/2002/10/07/BA223469. DTL. Posted on October 7, 2002. The curious case of John Henning III, a respected San Francisco lawyer who was accused of bias-motivated assault after a fistfight with two Hasidic Jews outside the city's Schneerson Synagogue. The Anti-Defamation League labeled the incident an "act of terror," but Henning benefited from a plea bargain in which the hate-crime charge was dropped and the charges reduced to misdemeanors. The deal was labeled a political payoff by critics of the San Francisco district attorney's office, which is considered one of the most zealous in the country in prosecuting hate crimes.

National Asian American Pacific Legal Consortium. "2002 Audit of Violence Against Asian Pacific Americans, Tenth Annual Report." Available online. URL: http://www.advancingequality.org/files/2002_Audit.pdf. A compendium of statistics of hate crimes against Americans of Asian and Pacific Islander origin, gathered from law-enforcement agencies in all 50 U.S. states and the District of Columbia that were participating in the FBI's Uniform Crime Report program.

Richardson, Valerie. "Wichita to Revisit Brutal Slayings as Testimony Begins." *Washington Times.* Available online. URL: http://www.frontpagemag.com/ Articles/Read.aspx?GUID=61EB61FA-AEEF-4F24-8711-2E47E9004B68. Posted on October 7, 2002. A story covering the multiple-murder charges against Reginald and Jonathan Carr, who were accused of kidnapping, rape, robbery, and five murders in connection with a rampage that took place in Wichita, Kansas, in December 2000. The crime brought controversy over hate-crime legislation, as the perpetrators were black and the victims were white. Opponents of hate-crimes law pointed out that media coverage of the killing was almost nonexistent and that the Carrs were not charged under any civil rights or bias-crime statutes.

Stotzer, Rebecca. "Comparison of Hate Crime Rates Across Protected and Unprotected Groups." The Williams Institute, UCLA School of Law.

Annotated Bibliography

Available online. URL: http:/www.law.ucla.edu/williamsinstitute/publications/Comparison%20of%20Hate%20Crime%20Formatted.pdf. Posted in June 2007. A report designed to highlight issues surrounding the expansion of federal hate-crime law to cover new protected categories of sexual orientation and gender identity. The author compares hate-crime rates between those groups already covered by the law and those that have yet to be afforded protection.

Tennessee Bureau of Investigation. "2007 Hate Crime Report." Available online. URL: http://www.tbi.state.tn.us/Info%20Systems%20Div/TIBRS_unit/Publications/2007%20Hate%20Crime%20in%20Tennessee%20.pdf. The TBI's annual report finds a total increase of 27.5 percent in hate-crime incidents over 2006, with the greatest increase in the category of disability bias. The report is useful to the researcher in explaining how hate crimes are broken down and the different methods by which hate-crime incidents are reported by local law enforcement.

Tomsen, Stephen. "Hate Crimes and Masculinity: New Crimes, New Responses and Some Familiar Patterns." Australian Institute of Criminology. Available online. URL: http://www.aic.gov.au/conferences/outlook4/Tomsen.html. Last updated November 14, 2003. A paper presented at a crime symposium held in Canberra, Australia, this document examines research in antihomosexual and race-related crime committed by working class and socially disadvantaged males. Using his own study of antihomosexual murders in New South Wales, the author argues that prejudice toward racial and sexual minorities is linked to the attainment of masculine identity. The author believes that *hate crime* has become an overly simplistic term that misses the true motivation. He advocates antipoverty and family support measures, schooling for the disadvantaged, or employment/diversion programs for young men.

U.S. Department of Justice, Civil Rights Division. "Civil Rights Division National Origin Working Group Initiative to Combat the Post-9/11 Discriminatory Backlash." Available online. URL: http://ww.usdoj.gov/crt/nordwg.html. Posted on July 30, 2002. In the wake of the September 11, 2001, terrorist attacks, the United States experienced a rise in bias incidents directed against Muslims and Arabs. This document describes the federal initiative undertaken against this backlash, updates current activities by the Civil Rights Division, describes the procedure for filing a complaint of discrimination, and provides links to statements from government offices as well as to information from federal agencies on civil rights and the available response to discrimination.

U.S. Department of Justice, Community Relations Service. "Hate Crimes: The Violence of Intolerance." Available online. URL: http://www.usdoj.gov/crs/pubs/hatecrm.pdf. Posted on December 2001. This paper describes the local projects of the Community Relations Service in defusing racial tensions and dealing with racial incidents and details its various practices in preventing such occurrences from escalating into civil disturbances. These practices include model ordinances for local government, the building of coalitions among community groups, dealing with local media, investigating and reporting hate crimes, establishing task forces and training programs, and offering appropriate assistance to victims, witnesses, and offenders.

Wessler, Stephen, and Margaret Moss. "Hate Crimes on Campus: The Problem and Efforts to Confront It." Bureau of Justice Assistance, Office of Justice Programs, U.S. Department of Justice. Available online. URL: http://www.ncjrs.gov/pdffiles1/bja/187249.pdf. Posted in October 2001. The director and associate director of the Center for the Prevention of Hate Violence in Portland, Maine, describe prejudice, hate crimes, and bias incidents in campus settings. The authors note that even statistics based on a small number of reporting schools indicate that hate crimes on campus were a significant problem. Hate crimes occurred relatively infrequently on most campuses, but bias incidents (acts of prejudice not accompanied by crimes) were far more common. Students consistently reported the widespread use of degrading language and slurs by other students directed toward people of color, women, homosexuals, Jews, and others who belong to groups that have traditionally been the target of bias, prejudice, and violence. The book offers strategies to counter hate crimes and implement prevention programs.

Wolf Harlow, Caroline. "Bureau of Justice Statistics Special Report: Hate Crime Reported by Victims and Police." Bureau of Justice Statistics, Office of Justice Programs, U.S. Department of Justice. Available online. URL: http://www.ojp.usdoj.gov/bjs/pub/pdf/hcrvp.pdf. Posted in November 2005. Text-and-graphics comparison of the hate crimes with comparable crimes that were determined not to be bias-motivated, drawn from the National Criminal Victimization Survey and Uniform Crime Reporting data from July 2000 through December 2003. Among conditions that distinguish hate crimes from other crimes, according to the analysis, are that hate crimes occur in public spaces and are more likely to be violent than other crimes. Most victims perceive race as the principal reason for the hate crime. The author estimates that only 44 percent of hate crimes are ever reported.

CURRICULUM AND TRAINING MATERIALS

Hoffheimer Bettman, Ellen, and Lorraine Tiven. "Building Community and Combating Hate: Lessons for the Middle School Classroom." Partners Against Hate. Available online. URL: http://www.partnersagainst-hate.org/educators/middle_school_lesson_plans.pdf. Posted in March

2004. Ten lessons for middle school educators to help young people come to terms with their fears after the attacks of September 11, 2001. The lessons explore four themes: conflict resolution, escalation of violence, the historic consequences of bias and scapegoating, and the rights and responsibilities of people living in a democracy. Partners Against Hate, the producer of this online book, is a collaboration of the Anti-Defamation League and the Leadership Conference on Civil Rights Education, funded by both the U.S. Department of Justice and the U.S. Department of Education.

Malloy, Stephanie. *Reviving Hope in the Face of Hate: A Guide for Countering Juvenile Hate Crime.* Newton, Mass.: National Center for Hate Crime Prevention, Education Development Center, Inc., 2000. A guide written for educators and juvenile justice professionals, offering a range of strategies for dealing with juvenile hate-crime offenders. Included are general background and current trends on the hate-crime issue, offender motivations, hate-crime diversion programs, and a description of nine innovative model programs.

McLaughlin, Karen A., Stephanie M. Malloy, Kelly J. Brilliant, and Cynthia Lang. *Responding to Hate Crime: A Multidisciplinary Curriculum for Law Enforcement and Victim Assistance Professionals.* Newton, Mass.: National Center for Hate Crime Prevention, Education Development Center, Inc., 2000. Available online. URL: http://www.ojp.usdoj.gov/ovc/publications/infores/responding/files/ncj182290.pdf. Accessed on November 22, 2007. An updated and condensed version of the *National Bias Crimes Training Manual,* this is a course on responding to hate crime. Included are suggested actions to investigate and respond to hate crimes, victim assistance, reproducible materials such as handouts and transparencies, and background notes for training law enforcement professionals in this field.

Southern Poverty Law Center. "Online Hate-Crime Training Course." Available online. URL: http://www.splcenter.org/pdf/static/hctraining_fall07.pdf. Accessed on November 22, 2007. This page provides a link to an Introduction to Hate and Bias Crimes course offered by the SPLC in conjunction with Auburn University, Montgomery, and the Federal Law Enforcement Training Center. The tuition course encompasses 12–15 hours of online work, including participation in live chat sessions.

U.S. Department of Justice. "Hate Crime Training: Core Curriculum for Patrol Officers, Detectives and Command Officers." Available online. URL: http://www.usdoj.gov/crs/pubs/hct.pdf. Accessed on November 22, 2007. A model curriculum, 280 pages in length, with instruction on law enforcement procedures and practices, victim assistance programs, and community relations for the use of patrol officers, detectives, and policy-level officers.

Wiley-Cordone, Jennifer. *Preventing Hate Crime Through Community Action.* Newton, Mass.: National Center for Hate Crime Prevention, Education Development Center, Inc., 2000. The author presents strategies for communities dealing with the occurrence or threat of hate crimes. Written for juvenile justice, education, law enforcement, and social service professionals, the guide offers examples of successful hate-crime prevention strategies, and gives tips on victim assistance, coalition building, and media relations.

ANTIHOMOSEXUAL BIAS CRIME

BOOKS

Deschamps, Benedicte, Michel Prum, and Marie-Claude Barbier, eds. *Racial, Ethnic, and Homophobic Violence: Killing in the Name of Otherness.* New York: Routledge Cavendish, 2007. A collection that examines how racism and homophobia produce violence. Essays by writers in several Western countries consider the political groups responsible for outbursts of hatred, their modes of operation, and the institutional aspects of hate crime.

Levin, Jack, and Jack McDevitt. *Hate Crimes Revisited: America's War on Those Who Are Different.* New York: Basic Books, 2002. An update by two of the country's leading experts on hate crimes of their classic book on the same topic (*Hate Crime: The Rising Tide of Bigotry and Bloodshed,* 1993). The authors explore the causes and characteristics of such acts of hatred and their consequences for society as a whole.

Loffreda, Beth. *Losing Matt Shepard: Life and Politics in the Aftermath of Anti-Gay Murder.* New York: Columbia University Press, 2000. A University of Wyoming professor describes the society of Laramie, Wyoming, the experience of homosexuals in the state, the impact of the Matthew Shepard murder on the community, the trial of those charged with the crime, the consequences for proposed hate-crime legislation, and the role of religious organizations in supporting and opposing homosexuals.

Sloan, Lacey M., and Nora S. Gustavsson, eds. *Violence and Social Injustice Against Lesbian, Gay, and Bisexual People.* New York: Haworth Press, 1998. Not a book on hate crimes per se, this volume explores pervasive, everyday discriminatory acts and attitudes against homosexuals. The editors suggest that complacency and apathy contribute to a general social milieu in which truly violent acts, including the most famous incidents covered and analyzed in the national media, can take place.

Swigonski, Mary E., Robin S. Mama, and Kelly Ward, eds. *From Hate Crimes to Human Rights: A Tribute to Matthew Shepard.* New York: Harrington Park Press, 2001. Twelve essays on antihomosexual prejudice and violence. Published simultaneously as *Journal of Gay & Lesbian Social Services*, vol. 3, nos. 1/2, 2001.

PERIODICALS

Anderson, George M. "People Are Getting Hurt." *Commonweal*, February 23, 1993, p. 16. A description of an increase in gay-bashing and intimidation, caused, the author maintains, by increased visibility of gays in public and the debate over ballot initiatives and legislation concerning civil rights for homosexuals.

Christensen, Jen. "Scotty's Last Moments: The Murder of a Gay Teen—Allegedly at the Hands of His Best Friends—Has Rattled a Small Alabama Town." *The Advocate*, September 28, 2004, p. 30. An 18-year-old is brutally murdered by a group of people in Pine Grove, Alabama. The perpetrators include one of the victim's childhood friends; the severity of the wounds lead investigators and the local district attorney to characterize the murder as an antigay hate crime.

DeLeon, Virginia. "Profanity Keeps Play Off LC Stage," *Spokesman-Review*. Available online. URL: http://www.spokesmanreview.com/news-story.asp ?date=101602&ID=s1235579&cat=section.spokane. Accessed August 22, 2008. At the Lewis and Clark High School in Spokane, Washington, controversy swirls around the performance of "The Laramie Project," which is canceled by school administrators objecting to the play's use of profanity. The teacher in charge of the production believes that the importance of the message delivered by the play, based on the murder of Matthew Shepard, outweighs any objection to strong or offensive language, which students have heard before.

Henneman, Todd. "Murder in Detroit." *The Advocate*, April 10, 2007, p. 18. The murder of a 72-year-old homosexual man in Detroit, the author asserts, manifests a trend toward bias crime in the city. In the opinion of many, Mayor Kwame Kilpatrick is fostering an atmosphere of intolerance that has contributed to the city's high crime and murder rates. The author argues that the situation shows the need for adding antigay crimes to the legal definition of hate crime in new federal legislation.

Herek, G. M. "Hate Crimes Against Lesbians and Gay Men: Issues for Research and Policy." *American Psychologist*, vol. 44, 1989, pp. 948–955. In an analysis of trends in antigay hate crimes, the author maintains that most antigay hate crimes are not reported, that there have been no comprehensive surveys of the problem, and that antigay hate crimes have become a serious national problem.

———. "Hate Crimes and Stigma-Related Experiences Among Sexual Minority Adults in the United States: Prevalence Estimates from a National Probability Sample." *Journal of Interpersonal Violence*, vol. 3, no. 28, April

2008. Using survey responses (collected via the Internet) from a U.S. national probability sample of gay, lesbian, and bisexual adults, this article estimates the rates at which these groups are targeted for various types of crime based on their sexual orientation. According to respondents' reports, around one in five had suffered a personal or property crime based on their sexual orientation; about half had experienced verbal harassment; and more than one in 10 reported employment or housing discrimination. Gay men were significantly more likely than lesbians or bisexuals to experience violence and property crimes. Employment and housing discrimination were significantly more likely among gay men and lesbians than among bisexual men and women.

Kibelstis, Teresa Eileen. "Preventing Violence Against Gay Men and Lesbians: Should Enhanced Penalties at Sentencing Extend to Bias Crime Based on Victims' Sexual Orientation?" *Notre Dame Journal of Law, Ethics, and Public Policy*, vol. 9, no. 1, 1995, pp. 309–343. The author provides statistics and background data on crimes against homosexuals and analyzes the legal problems and debate over including homosexual bias within hate-crimes legislation.

Kim, Richard. "The Truth About Hate Crimes Laws." *The Nation*, July 12, 1999, p. 20. Although national lesbian and gay groups are pursuing hate-crimes laws with single-minded zeal, the author believes there is nothing to suggest that such laws actually put a stop to hate crimes. The author also points out that antiviolence programs that are focused on community organizing, outreach, and education are struggling with few resources.

Lisotta, Christopher. "Killed in Broad Daylight: Sacramento Has Long Been Considered a Tolerant City, but a Gay Man's Violent Death Has Exposed the Wide Divide Between LGBT Residents and the Area's Slavic Evangelical Christians." *The Advocate*, December 4, 2007, p. 28. A report on the murder of a gay man by Russian-speaking men at a Sacramento-area state park. The article offers as background to the event increasing antigay rhetoric and actions among churches serving recent immigrants from the former Soviet Union.

Locke, Michelle. "Slaying of Teen May Be Hate Crime." Associated Press, October 19, 2002. Available online at http://www.sltrib.com/10192002/nation_w/8670.htm. This online report gives an account of a murder in the San Francisco suburb of Newark, California, in which a 17-year-old boy dressed as a girl was beaten to death and buried in a shallow grave. Police were investigating the murder as a hate crime. The crime took place during a controversy over the performance of "The Laramie Project," a play based on the killing of Matthew Shepard, at Newark Memorial High School.

"New Mexico's Mecca in Turmoil." *The Advocate*, April 12, 2005, p. 16. A short news article on an incident of antigay hate crime in Santa Fe, a city with a high percentage of gay couples and generally known for its tolerance.

Ocamb, Karen. "West Hollywood Survivor: Trev Broudy, Whose September Bashing Infuriated a Gay Neighborhood, Speaks for the First Time About His Recovery, His Anger, and His Future." *The Advocate*, March 4, 2003, p. 20. An assault in West Hollywood, in which a homosexual is attacked with a baseball bat, is not classified as a hate crime by the attorney general, raising an outcry. Instead, three suspects are charged with aggravated mayhem and assault with a deadly weapon. The author reports the details of the attack and interviews the victim.

Peters, Jeff. "When Fear Turns to Hate and Hate to Violence: The Persecution of Gays Is Increasing." *Human Rights*, vol. 18, no. 1, February 1996, pp. 22–30. Using statistics and victim accounts, the author contends that antigay violence is on the rise and offers a survey of federal and state legislature designed to stem the tide.

Quist, Ryan M., and Douglas M. Wiegand. "Attributions of Hate: The Media's Causal Attributions of a Homophobic Murder." *American Behavioral Scientist*, vol. 46, 20.1, January 2002, pp. 93–107. An analysis of the different attributions given to the murder of Matthew Shepard by media sources of different political orientation. The authors find that conservative sources tended to downplay situational factors, such as the political climate; tended to disfavor the entire concept of "hate crime"; and tended toward describing homosexuality as a controllable condition—something of a provocation on Shepard's part.

"Spurred to Action: Laramie Wyo. Police Officer D. O'Malley Becomes Advocate for Hate Crimes Legislation After Murder of M. Shepard." *People Weekly*, vol. 54, no. 25, December 11, 2000, pp. 99–102. An account of a police officer involved in the investigation of the Matthew Shepard case. After the case closed, Officer O'Malley lobbied vigorously for the addition of sexual orientation and gender as categories of protected status within federal hate-crimes law.

Winer, Anthony S. "Hate Crimes, Homosexuals, and the Constitution." *Harvard Civil Rights/Civil Liberties Law Review*, Summer 1994, pp. 387–438. An essay on the incidence of bias crimes against homosexuals and a legal brief in support of including homosexual bias under hate-crimes statutes.

REPORTS

Amnesty International. *Crimes of Hate, Conspiracy of Silence: Torture and Ill-Treatment Based on Sexual Identity*. New York: Amnesty International USA, 2001. Available online. URL: http://www.amnesty.org/library/index/engact400162001. Accessed on November 22, 2007. A report on the torture and abuse of gay, lesbian, bisexual, and transgender individuals, on legal and economic discrimination directed at homosexuals, and the efforts of Amnesty International to address and solve these issues around the world.

National Coalition of Anti-Violence Programs. "Anti-Lesbian, Gay, Bisexual and Transgender Violence in 2007." Available online. URL: http://www. ncavp.org/common/document_files/Reports/2007HVReportFINAL.pdf. Accessed on August 22, 2008. An annual report based on data collected from more than 35 organizations affiliated with the coalition. It found that violence against gay, lesbian, bisexual, and transgender individuals decreased in New York City and Colorado but increased in San Francisco, Pennsylvania, Minnesota, Michigan, Kansas City, and Los Angeles in 2007.

Statistics Canada: Canada's National Statistical Agency. "Study: Hate Motivated Crime, 2006." Available online. URL: http://www.statcan.ca/Daily/ English/080609/d080609a.htm. Posted on June 9, 2008. This analysis of national data from Canadian police services, which covered 87 percent of Canada's population for 2006, finds that while only one in 10 hate crimes in Canada was motivated by sexual orientation, more than half of such crimes were violent.

VIDEOS

Boys Don't Cry. Searchlight Pictures, 1999. A feature film, starring Hilary Swank, that dramatizes the true story of Brandon Teena, a transgender man (originally named Teena Brandon) living in Nebraska who is raped and murdered by her erstwhile friends when her secret comes out.

The Brandon Teena Story. New Video, 1999. Produced and directed by Susan Muska and Greta Olafsdottir. A documentary on the case of Teena Brandon (Brandon Teena), a woman living as a man who was raped and murdered in rural Falls City, Nebraska, in 1993.

Investigative Reports: Anti-Gay Hate Crime. A & E Home Video, 1999. Originally broadcast on July 6, 1999, this documentary hosted by Bill Kurtis details antigay hate crimes, including the beating death of Matthew Shepard and the lesser-known murder of Alan Walker of Arkansas. The film also investigates right-wing and fundamentalist religious groups that encourage or support antigay discrimination.

Licensed to Kill. New Video Group, 2005. This Sundance Award–winning documentary by filmmaker Arthur Dong was originally released in 1997, before the murder of Matthew Shepard made national headlines. The film presents Dong's face-to-face cellblock interviews with convicted murderers of gay men, highlighting their backgrounds and their attitudes toward gays before and after their crimes.

Not in Our Town, Northern California: When Hate Happens Here. Oakland, Calif.: Working Group/KQED-TV, 2005. In the manner of its 1995 predecessor (which covered the activities of hate groups in Billings, Montana), this documentary follows five communities in the northern California region over the course of five years. Each is the site of deadly hate violence—motivated variously by racism, anti-Semitism, and gender or sexual orientation—that community members must respond to and recover from.

Pink Triangles: A Study of Prejudice Against Lesbians and Gay Men. Cambridge Documentary Films, 1982. A study of antihomosexual prejudice and more generally the origins of bigotry and discrimination as suffered by other minority groups throughout history.

CHAPTER 8

ORGANIZATIONS AND AGENCIES

This chapter presents a list of organizations directly or indirectly concerned with hate-crimes-related law, monitoring, data collection, lobbying, education, and prevention. The list is broken down into four sections:

- federal government organizations
- academic organizations
- national advocacy organizations, and
- state and local advocacy organizations.

The URL address, which allows a researcher to locate the organization's World Wide Web site, is provided where available. As web addresses frequently change, and as these organizations may change their names and their missions, the researcher should consult a good search engine for up-to-date information.

FEDERAL GOVERNMENT ORGANIZATIONS

Bureau of Justice Assistance (BJA)
URL: http://www.ojp.usdoj.gov/BJA/
E-mail: askbja@usdoj.gov
Phone: (202) 616-6500
Fax: (202) 305-1367
810 Seventh Street, NW
Fourth Floor
Washington, DC 20531
The Bureau of Justice Assistance is a component of the Office of Justice Programs, U.S. Department of Justice, which also includes the Bureau of Justice Statistics, the National Institute of Justice, the Office of Juvenile Justice and Delinquency Prevention, and the Office for Victims of Crime. According to its public mission statement, BJA's mandate is "to provide leadership and assistance in support of local criminal justice strategies to achieve safe communities. . . . To

achieve these goals, BJA programs emphasize enhanced coordination and cooperation of federal, state, and local efforts." Under a grant provided by the BJA, the National Criminal Justice Association prepared *A Policymaker's Guide to Hate Crimes*, a report on federal, state, and local response to hate-crime incidents, on hate-crime cases, and on the methods used by local law enforcement in investigating and prosecuting hate crimes. The BJA has also funded training curricula for local law enforcement and offers several monographs online, including *Addressing Hate Crimes: Six Initiatives that Are Enhancing the Efforts of Criminal Justice Practitioners* and *Hate Crimes on Campus: The Problem and Efforts to Confront It.* For the use of law enforcement, the BJA has produced *Roll Call Video: Responding to Hate Crimes; Responding to Hate Crimes: A Police Officer's Guide to Investigation and Prevention;* and *Resource Guide for Prosecutors.*

Bureau of Justice Statistics
URL: http://www.ojp.
  usdocj.gov/bjs/
E-mail: askbjs@ojp.usdoj.gov
Phone: (800) 732-3277
633 Indiana Avenue, NW
  #1142
Washington, DC 20531
This site offers a comprehensive collection of crime statistics reported to the Justice Department, including hate crimes reported to the FBI's National Incident-Based Reporting System (NIBRS). Several online publications give in-

depth information on hate-crime trends. These include *Hate Crimes Reported by Victims and Police*, dating to November 2005, which provides information on the number of hate crimes reported to the National Crime Victimization Survey (NCVS) and their characteristics: the motivations for hate crime as perceived by victims; the types of crimes victims thought were hate-related; reasons for reporting or not reporting hate crimes to police; police response to victim's notification of a crime; the time and place at which hate crimes occurred; and offenders' gender, race, age, relationship to the victim, use of weapons, and gang membership. The Bureau of Justice Statistics has also made an important grant to researchers at the Center for Criminal Justice Policy Research at Northeastern University in Boston, who carried out a survey of hate-crime collection methods nationwide and made recommendations for sustaining participation by local reporting agencies.

Community Relations Service
  (CRS)
URL: http://www.usdoj.gov/crs/
Phone: (202) 305-2935
Fax: (202) 305-3009
600 E Street, NW
Suite 6000
Washington, DC 20530
The Community Relations Service is a federal agency charged with mediating intergroup disputes. The CRS employs a staff of trainers and mediators whose job it is to

resolve conflicts and prevent violence when racial tensions begin to occur. When a community is asked to host a Klan rally, or a march by another group likely to cause some kind of public disorder or racial tension, CRS personnel are often called in to provide assistance. The CRS was established by Title X of the Civil Rights Act of 1964. In the wake of the terrorist attacks of September 11, 2001, the CRS has hosted awareness programs and protocol seminars for security personnel to foster cultural understanding of Arab, Muslim, and Sikh immigrants and train the attendees in defusing threatening public confrontations. The CRS has developed a national hate-crimes response training curriculum that trains police and community leaders in the prevention of and response to hate-crimes incidents.

Federal Bureau of Investigation (FBI)
URL: http://www.fbi.gov
Phone: (202) 324-3691
935 Pennsylvania Avenue, NW
Washington, DC 20535-0001

Uniform Crime Reporting Section
Phone: (202) 324-5015
409 Seventh Street, NW
Suite 4
Washington, DC 20004
The FBI and its 12,492 special agents are charged with investigation of violations of federal law, including federal hate-crimes statutes. FBI headquarters in Washington,

D.C., provides program direction and support services to 56 field offices, approximately 400 satellite offices known as resident agencies, four specialized field installations, and 60 offices known as "Legal Attaches." Under the Hate Crimes Statistics Act, the FBI is charged with training local law enforcement in the investigation of hate crimes and the collection of hate-crime statistics. The agency publishes *Training Guide for Hate Crime Data Collection* as well as *Hate Crime Data Collection Guidelines*, which are regularly updated. The annual Uniform Crime Report (UCR), a national snapshot of crime broken down by category and location, is a useful reference tool for researchers, scholars, and the public. The UCR currently includes comprehensive statistics on the occurrence of hate crimes, state by state, county by county.

Office for Victims of Crime (OVC)
URL: http://www.ojp.usdoj.gov/ovc
Phone: (202) 307-5983
810 Seventh Street, NW
Washington, DC 20531
The Office for Victims of Crime was established by the 1984 Victims of Crime Act (VOCA) to oversee diverse programs that benefit victims of crime. OVC provides substantial funding to state victim assistance and compensation programs. The agency created a training program, *Bias Crimes: National Bias Crime Training for Law Enforcement and*

Victim Assistance Professionals, designed to educate criminal justice and allied professionals regarding the rights and needs of crime victims. Also available online is *Hate and Bias Crime*, from the National Victim Assistance Academy, which examines hate and bias crimes as well as new developments in the field of victim assistance.

Office of Community Oriented Policing Services (COPS)
URL: http://www.cops.
usdoj.gov/
E-mail: egov.issues@usdoj.gov
Phone: (202) 514-2058
Fax: (202) 616-8594
1100 Vermont Avenue, NW
Washington, DC 20530
This office is dedicated to community policing practices, in which law enforcement personnel take a more active and public role in the communities they serve. The COPS office provided funding for the Hate Crime Summit held in June 1998 by the International Association of Chiefs of Police as well as funding for bias-crime prevention initiatives under a grant program known as the Problem-Solving Partnership.

Office of Juvenile Justice and Delinquency Prevention (OJJDP)
URL: http://ojjdp.ncjrs.org/
E-mail: Askjj@ncjrs.org
Phone: (202) 307-5911
Fax: (202) 307-2093
810 Seventh Street, NW
Washington, DC 20531

The Office of Juvenile Justice and Delinquency Prevention is a bureau of the federal Department of Justice. In 1992, the OJJDP was charged with conducting a national assessment of the motives and characteristics of youths who commit hate crimes. Begun in 1993, the survey was completed in July 1996 as the *Report to Congress on Juvenile Hate Crime*. The agency publishes an annual school safety report, which in 2000 focused on student discipline and included data on harassment and hate crime among students. The OJJDP also has developed a curriculum called Healing the Hate for the purpose of the prevention of hate crimes by juveniles.

U.S. Commission on Civil Rights (USCCR)
URL: http://www.usccr.gov
Phone: (202) 376-7700
624 Ninth Street, NW
Washington, DC 20425
The U.S. Commission on Civil Rights is an "independent, bipartisan, fact-finding agency" of the executive branch established under the Civil Rights Act of 1957. The commission investigates complaints of discrimination against eligible voters, collects information relating to discrimination or a denial of equal protection of the laws, and issues public service announcements to discourage discrimination or denial of equal protection of the laws. In the wake of the September 11, 2001, terrorist attacks against the United States, the USCCR set up a hot line (800-552-6843) for reporting hate

crimes against Muslims and Arab Americans.

U.S. Department of Education (DOE)
URL: http://www.ed.gov
Phone: (800) 872-5327
400 Maryland Avenue, SW
Washington, DC 20202

Through the 1990s, this federal cabinet-level department has played an increasingly active role in hate-crimes prevention and hate-crimes initiatives. In 1992, Congress incorporated antiprejudice initiatives into the Elementary and Secondary Education Act (ESEA), legislation that provides federal funding for public schools. By its Title IV, the ESEA created a hate-crimes prevention initiative that promoted teacher training and the development of curricula specifically designed to combat hate crimes. The Ed.Gov web site offers an extensive list of publications related to hate crimes in the schools and on campus.

U.S. Department of Justice
URL: http://www.usdoj.gov
E-mail: ASKDOJ@doj.gov
Phone: (202) 514-2000
950 Pennsylvania Avenue
Washington, DC 20530-0001

The stated mission of the U.S. Department of Justice, the federal agency charged with enforcing federal laws, is "to enforce the law and defend the interest of the United States according to the law, to provide Federal leadership in preventing and controlling crime, to seek just punishment for those guilty of unlawful behavior, to administer and enforce the Nation's immigration laws fairly and effectively, and to ensure fair and impartial administration of justice for all Americans." The Department of Justice includes the Civil Rights Division, the Community Relations Service, the Office of Juvenile Justice and Delinquency Prevention, and the Office for Victims of Crime.

U.S. House of Representatives Judiciary Committee
URL: http://www.judiciary.
house.gov
E-mail: judiciary@mail.
house.gov
Phone: (202) 225-3951
2138 Rayburn Office Building
Washington, DC 20515

The committee debates and considers new federal legislation. Hearings held before the committee bring important hate-crimes issues to the media forefront, allowing the public a glimpse of academic, legal, and law enforcement experts and a consideration of the issues and opinion on proposals for new hate-crimes law.

U.S. Senate Judiciary Committee
URL: http://www.senate.gov/
~judiciary
E-mail: webmaster@
judiciary.senate.gov
Phone: (202) 224-5225
Dirksen Office Building

Room SD-224
Washington, DC 20510-6275
The committee debates proposed new federal laws. This website and the parallel site belonging to the House Judiciary Committee allow users to track the status of pending legislation.

ACADEMIC ORGANIZATIONS

Gonzaga University Institute for Action Against Hate
URL: http://gonzaga.edu/againsthate
E-mail: againsthate@gonzaga.edu
Phone: (509) 323-3665
502 East Boone Avenue
Spokane, WA 99258
This organization was founded in 1997 at this Jesuit university to combat hate crimes on campuses and in communities, with a special focus on the Northwest region. The stated goal of the institute is to "focus multi-disciplinary academic resources on the causes and effects of hate as well as potential strategies for combating hate." The institute develops courses and course materials, and it recently mounted a traveling exhibition, *Fighting the Fires of Hate: America and the Nazi Book Burnings.*

Northeastern University Brudnick Center on Violence and Conflict
URL: http://www.violence.neu.edu
E-mail: brudnick@neu.com
Phone: (617) 373-4987
Fax: (617) 373-8646
567 Holmes Hall
Boston, MA 02115
The Brudnick Center seeks solutions to problems of hostility and hatred based on group differences. The center involves faculty from a range of disciplines and initiates research projects and educational endeavors in the area of intergroup tensions and violence in the schools, state-sponsored terrorism, hate crimes, international conflict and warfare, hate speech on campus, skinhead activity, religious persecution, organized hate groups, and so on.

NATIONAL ADVOCACY ORGANIZATIONS

American-Arab Anti-Discrimination Committee (ADC)
URL: http://www.adc.org
Phone: (202) 244-2990
Fax: (202) 244-3196

4201 Connecticut Avenue, NW
Suite 500
Washington, DC 20008
Founded by Senator James Abourezk in 1980, the ADC, according to its Mission Statement, "is a

civil rights organization committed to defending the rights of people of Arab descent and promoting their rich cultural heritage." The ADC claims to be nonsectarian and nonpartisan and offers advocacy in cases of defamation, legal action in cases of discrimination, and counseling in matters of immigration. The ADC has published a series of reports on anti-Arab hate crimes and has organized departments of legal services, media and publications, educational programs, and a research institute.

American Civil Liberties Union (ACLU)
URL: http://www.aclu.org
E-mail: aclu@aclu.org
Phone: (212) 549-2500
Fax: (212) 549-2646
125 Broad Street
18th Floor
New York, NY 10004-2400

This organization was founded in 1920 to advocate constitutional freedoms and civil liberties under attack in the wake of World War I. ACLU attorneys appear in court and in state and federal legislatures to, as the organization states, "defend and preserve the individual rights and liberties guaranteed . . . by the Constitution and laws of the United States." The ACLU has filed briefs and appeared as counsel in several important hate-crimes cases on behalf of defendants whose First Amendment free-speech rights it sees threatened by hate-crimes laws and prosecutions. It also involves itself in cases concerning the death penalty, police procedures, religious liberty, prisons, national security, and gay rights.

American Jewish Committee (AJC)
URL: http://www.ajc.org
Phone: (212) 751-4000
Fax: (212) 891-1450
P.O. Box 705
New York, NY 10150

An organization seeking to safeguard the welfare and security of Jews around the world, with chapters in several dozen U.S. cities. Although principally concerned with Middle East problems and policy and ties between American Jews and Israel, the AJC also tracks anti-Semitic hate crimes and offers several publications and reports on the subject, including "Using the Internet to Fight Hate in the Real World."

American Psychological Association (APA)
URL: http://www.apa.org
Phone: (800) 374-2721
Fax: (202) 336-6063
750 First Street, NE
Washington, DC 20002-4242

An organization of academic and clinical psychologists, actively involved in the matter of hate crimes through research and publications and by providing assistance to individuals suffering prejudice and hate-motivated violence. The APA also organizes law enforcement training focusing on understanding the causes and effects of hate-related criminal behavior.

Organizations and Agencies

Anti-Defamation League (ADL)
URL: http://www.adl.org
E-mail: contactus@adl.org
Phone: (212) 885-7700
605 Third Avenue
New York, NY 10158-3560

ADL Government Affairs
URL: http://www.adl.org
E-mail: natlgov@adl.org
Phone: (202) 452-8320
1100 Connecticut Avenue, NW
Suite 1020
Washington, DC 20036
Founded in 1913 to fight discrimination in schools and workplaces against Jews, the Anti-Defamation League now advocates more generally against hate crimes, having written a model hate-crimes statute in 1981 that has been adopted by many state legislatures and local governments. The ADL has also produced an anti-hate-crime training video, a handbook of existing hate-crime policies and procedures at various police departments, and a training program in discrimination and bias-motivated behavior for law enforcement. The organization operates 26 regional offices in the United States. ADL tracks American extremists and hate groups, monitoring hate on the Internet and maintaining the frequently updated online encyclopedia *Extremism in America: A Guide.*

Arab American Institute (AAI)
URL: http://www.aaiusa.org
Phone: (202) 429-9210
Fax: (202) 429-9214
1600 K Street

Suite 601
Washington, DC 20006
The Arab American Institute was cofounded in 1985 to serve as a national organization for Americans of Arab descent. The AAI lobbies Congress on behalf of Arab Americans and has been most recently concerned with an anti-Arab backlash inspired by the September 11, 2001, terrorist attacks on the United States.

Asian American Justice Center
URL: http://www.
  advancingequality.org
Phone: (202) 296-2300
Fax: (202) 296-2318
1140 Connecticut Avenue, NW
Suite 1200
Washington, DC 20006
The Asian American Justice Center is dedicated to preserving the civil rights of citizens of Asian-Pacific descent. In cooperation with similar organizations across the country, it conducts regular surveys of anti-Asian violence in the United States.

**Asian American Legal Defense
  and Education Fund
  (AALDEF)**
URL: http://www.aaldef.org
Phone: (212) 966-5932
Fax: (212) 966-4303
99 Hudson Street
12th Floor
New York, NY 10013
The AALDEF was founded in 1974 to protect and promote the civil rights of Asian Americans through litigation, legal advocacy, and community education. In the wake of

the September, 11, 2001, attacks, the AALDEF is, according to its website, "providing legal representation to victims of racial/religious violence, police violence, racial profiling, immigration detainment and other forms of discrimination."

Asian Law Caucus (ALC)
URL: http://www.
   asianlawcaucus.org
Phone: (415) 896-1701
Fax: (415) 896-1702
939 Market Street
Suite 201
San Francisco, CA 94103
This organization describes its mission as follows: "To promote, advance and represent the legal and civil rights of the Asian and Pacific Islander communities." To this end, the organization integrates legal services, education programs, community organizing, and advocacy. The specific program areas include anti-Asian violence.

Asian Pacific American Legal
   Center (APALC)
URL: http://apalc,org
Phone: (213) 977-7500
Fax: (213) 977-7595
1145 Wilshire Boulevard
2nd Floor
Los Angeles, CA 90017
This organization works with the city of Los Angeles and the Los Angeles Police Department to improve responses to and prevention of hate crimes against Asian Americans. APALC also participates in the Hate Violence Monitoring program

of the LAPD, which streamlines the tracking of hate violence and trains officers in the investigation of hate violence cases.

Association of State Uniform
   Crime Reporting Programs
URL: http://www.asucrp.net
E-mail: statistics@asucrp.org
Phone: (517) 322-1424
Fax: (517) 322-5385
7150 Harris Drive
Lansing, MI 48913-0001
This organization includes participants of the National Uniform Crime Reporting Program (UCR) and the National Incident Based Reporting System (NIBRS) on the state, regional, and national levels. The introduction of NIBRS in member states provides additional data to define levels and types of violent and property crime and address current criminal justice issues, including hate crimes.

Center for Democratic Renewal
   (CDR)
URL: http://www.thecdr.org
Phone: (404) 221-0025
Fax: (404) 221-0045
P.O. Box 50469
Atlanta, GA 30302-0469
An information-gathering organization, the CDR bills itself as a "community-based coalition fighting hate-group activity." The organization serves as a clearinghouse for information on the white supremacist movement. It conducts research and provides training for law enforcement, schools, churches, and community organizations. The CDR has

produced more than 40 publications, including the resource manual *When Hate Groups Come to Town*, to assist communities experiencing hate-motivated violence or intimidation.

Center for Women Policy Studies
URL: http://www.centerwomen policy.org
Phone: (202) 872-1770
Fax: (202) 296-8962
1776 Massachusetts Avenue, NW
Suite 450
Washington, DC 20036
Founded in 1972 as the nation's first feminist policy research organization, the Center for Women Policy Studies provides reports and information resources for academics, community leaders, advocates, and policy makers. The group supports the inclusion of gender bias as a criterion for hate-crimes law and has made violence against women a key area of interest; in 2001, the center published an updated report, "Violence Against Women as Bias-Motivated Hate Crime: Defining the Issues."

Educators for Social Responsibility
URL: http://www.esrnational.org
E-mail: educators@ esrnational.org
Phone: (800) 370-2515
Fax: (617) 864-5164
23 Garden Street
Cambridge, MA 02138
Educators for Social Responsibility states its mission as "to make

teaching social responsibility a core practice in education so that young people develop the convictions and skills needed to shape a safe, sustainable, democratic, and just world." To that end, the group offers a variety of curriculum materials, including lesson plans focused on the issue of race discrimination and bias crimes, as well as training materials for educators dealing with the issue of racism, intergroup conflict, and hate violence.

Gay, Lesbian and Straight Education Network (GLSEN)
URL: http://www.glsen.org
Phone: (212) 727-0135
Fax: (212) 727-0254
90 Broad Street
Second Floor
New York, NY 10004
This organization was formed to combat discrimination and antigay violence against students and school personnel. Its mission statement includes the following: "GLSEN believes that the key to ending antigay prejudice and hate-motivated violence is education. And it's for this reason that GLSEN brings together students, educators, families and other community members—of any sexual orientation or gender identity/expression—to reform America's educational system." Volunteers from the organization participate in a national network of chapters and work with local schools, teachers, administrators, and librarians; a public policy department works with public officials at local, state, and federal levels.

Ministries in the Midst of Hate and Violence
Hate Crime Data Collection Project
URL: http://gbgm-umc.org/programs/antihate/
United Methodist Church
475 Riverside Drive
Room 1502
New York, NY 10115-0050
Believing that hate crimes are underreported to the authorities and the media, this organization collects clippings and information on hate crimes from volunteers through its web site. The site states that "this project will help us understand the current situation, accumulate data nationwide, do trend analysis, report on the findings and initiate a dialogue based upon empirical data to address underlying causes." The site offers articles collected under "Spiritual Resources," "Responding to Hate and Violence," "Church and Synagogue Arsons," and other news and views related to hate crimes and bias incidents.

Human Rights Campaign (HRC)
URL: http://www.hrc.org
Phone: (202) 628-4160
Fax: (202) 347-5323
1640 Rhode Island Avenue, NW
Washington, DC 20036
The HRC is an advocacy organization for gay and transgender issues. Its HRC Action Center works to pass the Hate Crimes Prevention Act, the pending federal hate-crimes legislation that would bring up to date the 34-year-old hate-crimes law by adding real or perceived gender,

sexual orientation, and disability to categories currently covered.

International Association of Chiefs of Police
URL: http://www.theiacp.org
Phone: (703) 836-6767
Fax: (703) 836-4543
515 North Washington Street
Alexandria, VA 22314
The International Association of Chiefs of Police is the world's oldest and largest nonprofit membership organization of police executives. The organization's web site includes links, resources, and publications dedicated to the subject of hate-crimes investigation and reporting.

Japanese American Citizens League
URL: http://www.jacl.org
E-mail: jacl@jacl.org
Phone: (415) 921-5225
P.O. Box 7144
San Francisco, CA 94120-7144
The Japanese American Citizens League was founded in 1929 to address issues of discrimination against persons of Japanese ancestry residing in the United States. The current organization, which includes 113 chapters and five regional offices, states that its mission is "protecting the rights of all segments of the Asian Pacific American community." The organization provides scholarships and grants and advocates for legislation concerning Asian Americans. It has created an active hate-crimes program that includes the produc-

tion of anti-hate-crime brochures, community outreach programs, and digital hate conferences focusing on hate groups on the Internet.

Justice Research and Statistics Association (JRSA)
Phone: (202) 842-9330
Fax: (202) 842-9329
777 North Capitol Street, NW
Suite 801
Washington, DC 20002
A national nonprofit organization that provides statistics and analysis on criminal justice issues for use by state and federal agencies. The organization also provides training in records management, data analysis, and forecasting, as well as reports on the latest research on criminal justice issues being conducted by local, state, and federal agencies. JRSA has published several papers on the hate-crime data collection efforts mandated by the Hate Crimes Statistics Act of 1990.

Lawyers' Committee for Civil Rights Under Law
URL: http://www.
lawyerscomm.org
Phone: (202) 662-8600
Fax: (202) 783-0857
1401 New York Avenue, NW
Suite 400
Washington, DC 20005
The nonprofit Lawyers' Committee for Civil Rights Under Law was formed in 1963 at the request of President John F. Kennedy to involve the private bar in providing legal services to address racial discrimination. The organization's mis-

sion statement reads in part, "Given our nation's history of racial discrimination, de jure segregation, and the de facto inequities that persist, the Lawyers' Committee's primary focus is to represent the interest of African Americans in particular, other racial and ethnic minorities, and other victims of discrimination, where doing so can help to secure justice for all racial and ethnic minorities." The organization provides a hate crimes page linked to a number of useful press and informational releases, speeches, and a hate crimes resource list at http://www.lawyerscomm.org/publicpolicy/hatecrimeresourcelist.html.

Leadership Conference on Civil Rights (LCCR)
URL: http://www.civilrights.org/lccr
Phone: (202) 466-3311
Fax: (202) 466-3435
1629 K Street, NW
10th Floor
Washington, DC 20006
The Leadership Conference on Civil Rights was founded during the era of new civil rights legislation of the 1960s and today describes itself as "the nerve-center for the struggle against discrimination in all its forms." Beginning with 30 civil rights and labor groups, the LCCR has grown to more than 185 national organizations, representing ethnic minorities, women, children, labor unions, individuals with disabilities, older Americans, major religious groups, gays and lesbians, and civil liberties and human rights

groups. The LCCR states as one of its primary goals "a strong and effective federal policy against hate crimes."

The Matthew Shepard Foundation
URL: http://www.matthew shepard.org
Phone: (307) 237-6167
Fax: (307) 237-6156
301 Thelma, #512
Casper, WY 82601
The Matthew Shepard Foundation was founded to memorialize its namesake, the victim of a widely reported antigay murder in Wyoming. On its web site, the foundation states that its mission is to "replace hate with understanding, compassion, and acceptance." The foundation has organized educational programs and speaking tours, and lobbied for passage of a new federal hate-crimes law, which would include antigay hate crimes.

National Association for the Advancement of Colored People (NAACP)
URL: http://www.naacp.org
Phone: (877) 622-2798
4805 Mount Hope Drive
Baltimore, MD 21215
Since its founding in 1909, the National Association for the Advancement of Colored People has grown to 2,200 chapters and claims more than 500,000 members. The NAACP represents the country's original civil rights organization, founded to protect and preserve legal rights of African-American cit-

izens. The NAACP actively lobbies on behalf of new hate-crimes bills.

National Center for Victims of Crime
URL: http://www.ncvc.org
Phone: (202) 467-8700
Fax: (202) 467-8701
2000 M Street, NW
Suite 480
Washington, DC 20036
A nonprofit organization founded in 1985 and dedicated to services and programs for crime victims, including training and technical assistance to victim service organizations, attorneys, and other individuals and groups associated with the criminal justice system. The organization offers hate-crimes information and links at http://www.ncvc.org/9-11/hate_crimes.htm.

National Conference for Community and Justice (NCCJ)
URL: http://www.nccj.org
E-mail: nationaloffice@nccj.org
Phone: (212) 545-1300
Fax: (212) 545-8053
475 Park Avenue South
19th Floor
New York, NY 10016
Founded in 1927 as the National Conference of Christians and Jews, this group combats racial and religious bigotry through educational programs, campaigns and special events, policy research, and legal advocacy. The group also offers a range of publications and annual reports on the topics of intergroup relations and bias.

Organizations and Agencies

National District Attorneys
  Association
American Prosecutors Research
  Institute (APRI)
URL: http://www.ndaa.org
Phone: (703) 549-9222
Fax: (703) 836-3195
99 Canal Center Plaza
Suite 510
Alexandria, VA 22314
Information and resources for local
prosecutors, including the report
"A Local Prosecutor's Guide for
Responding to Hate Crimes." The
organization also holds conferences,
including a national training semi-
nar for hate-crimes prosecutors,
investigators, and victim/witness
advocates, which took place in June
2000 at the National Advocacy Center in Columbia, South Carolina.

National Gay and Lesbian Task
  Force (NGLTF)
URL: http://www.thetaskforce.
  org
Phone: (202) 332-6483
Fax (202) 332-0207
5455 Wilshire Boulevard
Suite 1505
Los Angeles, CA 90036
Founded in 1973, the NGLTF is a
national advocacy organization dedicated to promoting civil rights for
homosexuals. The NGLTF is active
in promoting new hate-crimes legislation at the state and federal level
that targets antihomosexual prejudice and recognizes homosexuals as a
protected group. The Anti-Violence
Project of the NGLTF promotes
an appropriate official response to
antigay violence, strives to improve

the treatment of lesbians and gay
men by the criminal justice system,
and assists communities combatting prejudice and bias-motivated
violence. The organization also
publishes annual reports on antigay
violence and harassment.

National Organization for
  Women (NOW)
URL: http://www.now.org
Legal Momentum: Advancing
  Women's Rights
URL: http://legalmomentum.
  org
Phone: (202) 628-8669
Fax: (202) 785-8576
1100 H Street, NW
3rd Floor
Washington, DC 20005
NOW was founded in 1966 to combat discrimination against and promote full equal rights for women.
The organization supports the effort to make antigender prejudice
a component of hate-crimes laws.
The NOW web site features several
articles and news on the current hate
crimes debate. Legal Momentum:
Advancing Women's Rights works
within the justice system and among
the members of Congress to further
the parent organization's mission.

National Organization of Black
  Law Enforcement Executives
URL: http://www.noblenational.
  org
Phone: (703) 658-1529
Fax: (703) 658-9479
4609-F Pinecrest Office Park
  Drive
Alexandria, VA 22312

This organization provides training for law enforcement executives in the matter of bias violence, conducts research on law enforcement practices and policies, and works with victim assistance organizations.

Not in Our Town
URL: http://www.pbs.org/niot
E-mail: hometeam@kvcr.pbs.org
Phone: (510) 268-9675
P.O. Box 70232
Oakland, CA 94612
According to its web site, this organization "promotes public dialogue and provides a model for community response to hate crimes and other associated problems." The web site offers educational resources such as classroom discussion guides that cover hate crimes and community response handbooks, which allow local civic leaders to formulate a response to hate groups.

Partners Against Hate
URL: http://www.
   partnersagainsthate.org
E-mail: webmaster@
   partnersagainsthate.org
Phone: (202) 452-8310
Fax: (202) 296-2371
1100 Connecticut Avenue, NW
Suite 1020
Washington, DC 20036
Partners Against Hate is a joint effort of the Anti-Defamation League, the Leadership Conference Education Fund, and the Center for the Prevention of Hate Violence. This collaboration implements programs of outreach, public education, and training to prevent and reduce ju-

venile hate crimes. The organization's web site offers a useful and very thorough hate-crimes database with updated statistics and related information on bias crimes, including a state-by-state breakdown of hate-crimes laws and hate-crime incidents.

People for the American Way
URL: http://www.pfaw.org
E-mail: pfaw@pfaw.org
Phone: (202) 467-4999
Fax: (202) 293-2672
2000 M Street, NW
Suite 400
Washington, DC 20036
An organization that takes part in current debates over constitutional issues, religious freedom, judicial appointments, civil liberties and civil rights and is generally supportive of new hate-crimes laws.

PFLAG (Parents and Friends of Lesbians and Gays)
URL: http://www.pflag.org
E-mail: info@pflag.org
Phone: (202) 467-8180
Fax: (202) 467-8194
1726 M Street, NW
Suite 400
Washington, DC 20036
PFLAG is a national nonprofit organization of parents, families, and friends of lesbian, gay, bisexual, and transgendered persons. The organization states part of its mission as "education, to enlighten an ill-informed public; and advocacy, to end discrimination and to secure equal civil rights." The Web site's hate-crimes information page, with

links, press releases, events, and legislative information and updates, is located at http://www.pflag.org/education/hatecrimes.html.

Police Executive Research Forum (PERF)
URL: http://www.policeforum.org
Phone: (202) 466-7820
Fax: (202) 466-7826
1120 Connecticut Avenue, NW
Suite 930
Washington, DC 20036

An organization of police executives dedicated to improving police services, PERF supports and promotes hate-crime law and assists local law enforcement in the reporting of hate crime. The organization has been advocating hate-crime data collection since 1987, when it became one of the first national police associations to endorse the Hate Crimes Statistics Act. PERF offers a "cultural differences" training curriculum for law enforcement officials.

Political Research Associates
URL: http://www.publiceye.org/pra
Phone: (617) 666-5300
Fax: (617) 666-6622
1310 Broadway
Suite 201
Somerville, MA 02144

"An independent, nonprofit research center, based on progressive values, that serves as a national resource for information on antidemocratic, authoritarian and other oppressive movements and trends."

The organization's web site, the Public Eye, carries articles, links, and resources on the consequences of the September 11, 2001, terrorist attacks on the United States, including in particular bias crimes against Arab Americans. The site also offers printed resources, activist resource kits, online resources (including *Public Eye Magazine*), and links to books, articles, reports and research studies.

Prejudice Institute
URL: http://www.prejudiceinstitute.org
E-mail: prejinst@aol.com
Phone: (410) 243-6987
2743 Maryland Avenue
Baltimore, MD 21218

The Prejudice Institute is a nonprofit, nonpartisan research organization, the successor to the National Institute Against Prejudice and Violence. The work of the institute is organized around several projects, including studies of the social and psychological effects of victimization; the nature of violent attitudes and behavior; the nature of prejudice, conflict, and ethnoviolence as they are played out in college campus and workplace settings; and the role of the news media in communicating prejudice.

Public Good Project
URL: http://www.com/publicgood.org
Phone: (360) 734-6642
P.O. Box 28547
Bellingham, WA 98228

Public Good advertises itself as "a research and education network illuminating conflicts where democratic values are being challenged." The organization began as a 1993 investigation into political extremism in Whatcom County, Washington. It has since become a network of contributors who find and upload primary source documents on political extremism, the militia movement, white supremacists, and hate groups. The indices to the available documents are located at http://www.publicgood.org/reports.

The Rainbow/PUSH Coalition (RPC)
URL: http://www.
 rainbowpush.org
Phone: (773) 373-3366
Fax: (773) 373-3571
930 East 50th Street
Chicago, IL 60615-2702
The Rainbow/PUSH Coalition is a multi-issue organization founded by Rev. Jesse L. Jackson, Sr., with headquarters in Chicago. The organization was created through the merger of Jackson's Operation PUSH, founded in 1971, and the National Rainbow Coalition. The RPC advertises its mission as "uniting people of diverse ethnic, religious, economic and political backgrounds to make America's promise of 'liberty and justice for all' a reality." The RPC has lobbying bodies at the state and federal levels and has long been a strong advocate of tougher hate-crimes laws.

Recovering Racists Network (RRN)
URL: http://www.sumner
 mckenzie.com
E-mail: info@rrnet.org
Phone: (415) 577-8331
517 Tamalpais Drive
Mill Valley, CA 94941
The Recovering Racists Network is a project founded by John McKenzie. The organization holds workshops on overcoming racism, publishes books and pamphlets on intolerance and prejudice, and works actively on conflict resolution and hate-crimes related issues on a local level.

Simon Wiesenthal Center
URL: http://www.
 wiesenthal.com
E-mail: information@
 wiesenthal.net
Phone: (800) 900-9036
Fax: (310) 553-4521
1399 South Roxbury Drive
Los Angeles, CA 90035
Established in 1977, the Simon Wiesenthal Center is an international Jewish human rights organization. The center concerns itself with the issues of racism, anti-Semitism, and terrorism. The center closely interacts with a variety of public and private agencies, meeting with elected officials, U.S. and foreign governments, diplomats, and heads of state. The Task Force Against Hate is an educational initiative, while the National Institute Against Hate Crimes trains law enforcement personnel and prosecutors. Other

issues that the center deals with include the prosecution of Nazi war criminals; Holocaust and tolerance education; Middle East affairs; and extremist groups, neo-Nazism, and hate on the Internet.

Security on Campus, Inc.
URL: http://www.
  securityoncampus.org
Phone: (888) 251-7959
Fax: (610) 768-0646
133 Ivy Lane
Suite 200
King of Prussia, PA 19406
This nonprofit organization is dedicated to reporting and fighting crime on university campuses. The web site provides links to statistics collected by the FBI (Uniform Crime Reports) and the Department of Education. By the Crime Awareness and Campus Security Act of 1990, colleges and universities must disclose annual information about campus crime and security policies. The act was championed by the originators of this web site, Howard and Connie Clery, after their daughter Jeanne was murdered at Lehigh University in 1986 (the act was renamed in memory of Jeanne Clery in 1998 and is now known as the Clery Act). Campus Crime Statistics, which include the subcategory of hate crimes, are reported to the Department of Education and published on the World Wide Web at http://www.campussafety.org/crimestats/doe2001.pdf. The hatecrimes statistics are also summarized at the Security on Campus site.

Southern Christian Leadership Conference (SCLC)
URL: http://www.sclcnational.org
Phone: (404) 522-1420
Fax: (404) 527-4333
320 Auburn Avenue, NE
Atlanta, GA 30303
The SCLC was founded by Dr. Martin Luther King, Jr., and others, and became the leading organization in the Civil Rights movement of the 1950s and 1960s. King and the SCLC adopted nonviolent tactics and spearheaded a mass political movement against prejudice, lynchings, Jim Crow policies, and institutionalized racism, particularly in the South. The SCLC survived King's assassination in 1968, and currently takes part in legislative and judicial actions concerning prejudice, hate crimes, and racism; publishes a magazine; and offers informational resources at http://www.sclcmagazine.com/index.htm.

Southern Poverty Law Center (SPLC)
URL: http://www.splcenter.org
Tolerance.org, A Project of the Southern Poverty Law Center
URL: http://www.tolerance.org
Phone: (334) 956-8200
Fax: (334) 956-8481
400 Washington Avenue
Box 548
Montgomery, AL 36104
The Southern Poverty Law Center began as a small civil rights law firm in 1971 and has remained a nonprofit organization that combats racism through litigation and

243

educational projects. Founders Morris Dees and Joe Levin have successfully prosecuted several hate groups through civil lawsuits, and they track hate groups and their activities throughout the country. Most recently, the center has become internationally known for its success in developing novel legal strategies to shut down extremist activity and to help victims of hate crimes win monetary damages against groups such as the Ku Klux Klan. The SPLC project known as Klanwatch monitors hate crimes and hate groups throughout the nation, publishing *The Intelligence Report*, a bimonthly review of hate crimes and activities of white supremacist groups. Klanwatch also provides training for law enforcement and seminars on white supremacist groups for community organizations.

STATE AND LOCAL ADVOCACY ORGANIZATIONS

CALIFORNIA

Asian Pacific American Legal Center of Southern California
URL: http://apalc.org
Phone: (213) 977-7500
Fax: (213) 977-7595
1145 Wilshire Boulevard
2nd Floor
Los Angeles, CA 90017
Established in 1983, this group provides legal services and education programs geared to Southern California's Asian-American community. Attorneys working on behalf of this program are involved in immigration, education, and interethnic relations and take part in prominent race-violence and hate-crimes cases such as the murder of Joseph Ileto in 1999.

ILLINOIS

Chicago Lawyers' Committee for Civil Rights Under Law, Inc.

Project to Combat Bias Violence
URL: http://www.clccrul.org
E-Mail: info@clccrul.org
Phone: (312) 630-9744
Fax: (312) 630-9749
100 North LaSalle Street
Suite 600
Chicago, IL 60602-2403
A public interest legal consortium of Chicago's leading law firms, the Chicago Lawyers Committee for Civil Rights Under Law, Inc., claims 48 member firms, whose attorneys log 15,000 hours of pro bono legal services on civil rights cases and issues each year. The Project to Combat Bias Violence provides representation for people targeted for crime because of race, religion, ethnic origin, sexual orientation, disability, and gender. The project promotes improvements in hate-crimes legislation and law enforcement and also

provides hate-crimes educational programs.

New York City Gay and Lesbian Anti-Violence Project
URL: http://www.avp.org
E-mail: webmaster@avp.org
Phone: (212) 714-1141
240 West 35th Street
Suite 200
New York, NY 10001

The project provides free and confidential services, including counseling, legal advocacy, referrals, and information to victims of bias-motivated violence. The group's web site mission statement also states that "by documenting violence motivated by hate against the lesbian, gay, transgender, bisexual and HIV-positive communities . . . the Project works to change public attitudes that tolerate, insulate or instigate hate-motivated violence, and to promote public policies designed to deter such violence."

INTERNATIONAL ADVOCACY ORGANIZATIONS

CivilRights.org
URL: http://www.CivilRights.org
Phone: (202) 466-3311
Leadership Conference on Civil Rights
1629 K Street, NW
10th Floor
Washington, DC 20006
This organization is an Internet-based civil rights network, linking users to a wide variety of groups and publications working in the area of civil rights, immigration, labor, voting rights, criminal justice, education, and poverty/welfare issues. A section on hate crimes offers reports, resources, and news updates on hate crimes and hate crimes law.

Searchlight magazine
URL: http://www.
  searchlightmagazine.com

Phone: 020 7681 8660
Fax: 020 7681 8650
P.O. Box 1576
Ilford IG5 0NG
United Kingdom
Founded in London in 1962 in a response to a resurgence of neo-Nazi activities, *Searchlight* bills itself as an "international anti-fascist magazine." The monthly magazine documents hate crimes around the world, while the organization also serves as an information clearinghouse for academics, schools, journalists, and investigators. According to the organization's home page, "Any organisation with a genuine interest in fighting racism or fascism can come to Searchlight for information about racist organisations and individuals and for advice on how to deal with the problem."

PART III

APPENDIXES

APPENDIX A

IDENTIFYING A HATE CRIME IN NEW YORK

Since the 1980s, New York City has played a prominent role in the issue of hate crime. Bias-motivated violence in the 1980s gave strong impetus to the first state and federal hate-crime laws, and New York was the first city to establish a separate police unit dealing specifically with bias crimes. The city's various interest groups and communities remain closely attuned to the presence and prosecution of such crimes, and the issue of whether or not a crime should be identified as a hate crime often sparks heated debate.

Following are the official guidelines used by the New York City Police Department Bias Unit for identifying a hate crime.

CRITERIA

1. The motivation of the perpetrator.
2. The absence of any motive.
3. The perception of the victim.
4. The display of offensive symbols, words, or acts.
5. The date and time of occurrence (corresponding to a holiday of significance, i.e, Hanukkah, Martin Luther King Day, Chinese New Year, etc.).
6. A common-sense review of the circumstances surrounding the incident (considering the totality of the circumstances).
   A. The group involved in the attack.
   B. The manner and means of the attack.
   C. Any similar incidents in the same area or against the same victim.
7. What statements, if any, were made by the perpetrator.

Hate Crimes

QUESTIONS TO BE ASKED

1. Is the victim the only member or one of a few members of the targeted group in the neighborhood?
2. Are the victim and perpetrator from different racial, religious, ethnic, or sexual orientation groups?
3. Has the victim recently moved to the area?
4. If multiple incidents have occurred in a short time period, are all the victims of the same group?
5. Has the victim been involved in a recent public activity that would make him/her a target?
6. What was the modus operandi? Is it similar to other documented incidents?
7. Has the victim been the subject of past incidents of a similar nature?
8. Has there been recent news coverage of events of a similar nature?
9. Is there an ongoing neighborhood problem that may have spurred the event?
10. Could the act be related to some neighborhood conflict involving area juveniles?
11. Was any hate literature distributed by or found in the possession of the perpetrator?
12. Did the incident occur, in whole or in part, because of a racial, religious, ethnic, or sexual orientation difference between the victim and the perpetrator, or did it occur for other reasons?
13. Are the perpetrators juveniles or adults, and if juveniles, do they understand the meaning (to the community at large and to the victim) of the symbols used?
14. Were the real intentions of the responsible person motivated in whole or in part by bias against the victim's race, religion, ethnicity, or sexual orientation, or was the motivation based on [something] other than bias, for example: a childish prank, unrelated vandalism, etc.?

Note: If after applying the criteria listed and asking the appropriate questions, substantial doubt exists as to whether or not the incident is bias motivated or not, the incident should be classified as bias motivated for investigative and statistical purposes.

Source: Jacobs & Potter: *Hate Crime: Criminal Law and Identity Politics,* pp. 97–98.

APPENDIX B

STATE STATUTES GOVERNING HATE CRIMES, 2005

The following (edited) table of state hate-crimes statutes was compiled by Charlene Austin and Paul S. Wallace for the Congressional Research Service (CRS), and was published on September 21, 2005. CRS is a division of the Library of Congress that conducts policy research for Congress, which members of Congress use to inform their positions on legislative issues. For the most current information, the researcher should search the statute books of individual U.S. states, many of which are available complete and free of charge online from public agencies or via subscription from the Lexis database (http://www.lexis.com). Charts and maps giving state-by-state comparisons of current hate-crimes law (without the statute numbers or specific language) are available from the Anti-Defamation League (http://www.adl.org/learn/hate_crimes_laws/map_ frameset.html).

ALABAMA

PENALTY ENHANCEMENT

Ala. Code §13A-5-13 imposes additional penalties for hate crimes "where it is shown that a perpetrator committing the underlying offense was motivated by the victim's actual or perceived race, color, religion, national origin, ethnicity, or physical or mental disability."

INSTITUTIONAL VANDALISM

Ala. Code §13A-11-12 (1994)—desecration of "venerated objects" includes places of worship.

ALASKA

PENALTY ENHANCEMENT

Alaska Stat. § 12.55.155(c)(22)—Aggravating factors considered by the court include the selection of a victim "because of that person's race, sex, color, creed, physical or mental disability, ancestry, or national origin."

INSTITUTIONAL VANDALISM

Alaska Stat. § 34.50.020(2002)—Penalizes the destruction of real or personal property by minors which belong to a religious or charitable organization.

ARIZONA

PENALTY ENHANCEMENT

Ariz. Rev. Stat. Ann. §13-702[C][14]—Identifies as an aggravating sentencing factor that the defendant committed an offense out of malice toward the victim's real or perceived identification with a group listed in §41-1750[A][3].

INSTITUTIONAL VANDALISM

Arizona Stat. § 13-1604(2001)—A person commits aggravated criminal damage by intentionally or recklessly damaging, defacing, or tampering with the property of another without the express permission of the owner.

DATA COLLECTION

Ariz. Rev. Stat. Ann. §41-1750[A][3]—The Arizona Highway Patrol is responsible for the centralized collection of data relating to crimes manifesting a malice on the basis of race, color, religion, national origin, sexual orientation, gender, or disability.

ARKANSAS

INSTITUTIONAL VANDALISM

Ark. Code Ann. § 5-71-215(3)—Covers damage of "any place of worship, cemetery, or burial monument."

Ark. Code Ann. § 5-71-207(8)—Disorderly conduct includes damage of a "patriotic or religious symbol that is an object of respect by the public or a substantial segment thereof."

Ark. Code. Ann. §5-38-301(a)(5)—Outlaws burning churches.

Appendix B

CALIFORNIA

PENALTY ENHANCEMENT

Cal. Penal Code § 422.75—" . . . [A] person who commits a felony that is a hate crime or attempts to commit a felony that is a hate crime, shall receive an additional term of one, two, or three years in the state prison, at the court's discretion."

Cal. Penal Code § 422.76—Commission of a felony because of specified belief or characteristics of the victim shall be considered a circumstance in aggravation of the crime in imposing a term under subdivision (b) of Section 1170.

Cal. Penal Code § 628.1—"Hate crime" means an act or attempted act against the person or property of another individual or institution which in any way manifest evidence of hostility toward the victim because of his or her actual or perceived race, or sexual orientation. This includes, but is not limited to, threatening telephone calls, hate mail, physical assault, vandalism, cross-burning, destruction of religious symbols, or firebombings.

Cal. Penal Code § 666.7—"The term "sentence enhancement" means an additional term of imprisonment in the state prison added to the base term for the underlying offense. A sentence enhancement is imposed because of the nature of the offense at the time the offense was committed or because the defendant suffered a qualifying prior conviction before committing the current offense."

Cal. Penal Code § 422.7—Additional punishment for hate crime committed for purpose of intimidating or interfering with constitutional rights of another.

Cal. Penal. Code § 1170.75—Treats as an aggravating factor that the crime of conviction was motivated by malice towards the victim's race, color, religion, nationality, country of origin, ancestry, disability, gender, or sexual orientation.

INSTITUTIONAL VANDALISM

Cal. Penal Code § 594.3—Criminalizes vandalism of places of worship and interference with religious worship and if shown to have been committed by reason of the race, color, religion, or national origin of another individual or group of individuals and to have been committed for the purpose of intimidating and deterring persons from freely exercising their religious beliefs, is guilty of a felony punishable by imprisonment in the state prison.

Cal. Penal Code § 11413—Outlaws burning churches or other places of worship.

DATA COLLECTION

Cal. Penal Code § 628.1—Mandates development of a standard reporting form for hate crimes for use by all school districts and county offices of education.

LAW ENFORCEMENT TRAINING

Cal. Penal Code § 13519.6—Covers hate-crimes training for peace officers.

COLORADO

PENALTY ENHANCEMENT

Colo. Rev. Stat. § 18-9-121—It is the right of every person, regardless of race, color, ancestry, religion, or national origin, to be secure and protected from fear, intimidation, harassment, and physical harm caused by the activities of individuals and groups.

CONNECTICUT

PENALTY ENHANCEMENT

Conn. Gen. Stat. Ann. § 53a-181j to 53-181l—Covers intimidation based on bigotry or bias in the first degree as a class C felony.

INSTITUTIONAL VANDALISM

Conn. Gen. Stat. Ann. § 46a-58—Covers deprivation of rights, desecration of property, and cross-burning.

DELAWARE

PENALTY ENHANCEMENT

11 Del. Code Ann. § 1304—Imposes additional penalties for hate crimes where it is shown that a perpetrator committing the underlying offense was motivated by the "victim's race, religion, color, disability, sexual orientation, national origin or ancestry."

INSTITUTIONAL VANDALISM

11 Del. C. § 1331 (2005)—"A person is guilty of desecration if the person intentionally defaces, damages, pollutes or otherwise physically mistreats any public monument or structure, any place of worship, the national flag

or any other object of veneration by the public or a substantial segment thereof, in a public place and in a way in which the actor knows will outrage the sensibilities of persons likely to observe or discover the actions."

DISTRICT OF COLUMBIA

PENALTY ENHANCEMENT

D.C. Code § 22-3701—Covers definitions of "bias-related crime" and designated act.

D.C. Code § 22-3703—"A person charged with and found guilty of a bias-related crime shall be fined not more than 1½ times the maximum fine authorized for the designed act and imprisoned for not more than 1½ times the maximum term authorized for the designed act."

D.C. Code § 22-3704—Imposes additional penalties for hate crimes where it is shown that a perpetrator committing the underlying offense was motivated by the "victim's actual or perceived race, color, religion, national origin, sex, age, marital status, personal appearance, sexual orientation, family responsibilities, physical handicap, matriculation, or political affiliation."

D.C. Code § 22-4004—The perpetrator's "designated act shall have a civil cause of action in a court of competent jurisdiction for appropriate relief."

INSTITUTIONAL VANDALISM

D.C. Code § 22-3312.02—Covers defacing or burning cross or religious symbol and display of certain emblems.

DATA COLLECTION

D.C. Code § 22-3702—"The Metropolitan Police force shall afford each crime victim the opportunity to submit with the complaint a written statement that contains information to support a claim that the designated act constitutes a bias-related crime."

FLORIDA

PENALTY ENHANCEMENT

Fla. Stat. Ann. § 775.085—Covers general penalties of crimes motivated by the "victim's race, color, ancestry, ethnicity, religion, sexual orientation, national origin, mental or physical disability, or advanced age of the victim."

Fla. Stat. § 775.0845—Covers general penalties for wearing mask while committing offense.

INSTITUTIONAL VANDALISM

Fla. Stat. § 806.13—Criminalizes damages to places of worship and real or personal property belonging to another. Section also includes penalties for minors.

DATA COLLECTION

Fla. Stat. § 877.19—"The Florida Department of Law Enforcement shall collect and disseminate data on incidents of criminal acts that evidence prejudice based on race, religion, ethnicity, color, ancestry, sexual orientation, or national origin."

GEORGIA

PENALTY ENHANCEMENT

Ga. Code §§ 17-10-17 to 17-10-19—Authorizes penalty enhancements for crimes committed because of bias or prejudice.

INSTITUTIONAL VANDALISM

Ga. Code § 16-7-26—Vandalism to a place of worship.

HAWAII

PENALTY ENHANCEMENT

Hawaii Rev. Stat. § 706-662—"Criteria for extended terms of imprisonment when (6)(b) the defendant intentionally selected a victim, or in the case of a property crime, the property that was the object of a crime, because of hostility toward the actual or perceived race, religion, disability, ethnicity, national origin, gender identity or expression, or sexual orientation of any person."

INSTITUTIONAL VANDALISM

Hawaii Rev. Stat. § 711-1107—"A person commits the offense of desecration if the person intentionally desecrates: (a)Any public monument or structure; or (b)A place of worship or burial; (c) In a public place the national flag or any other object of veneration by a substantial segment of the public."

Appendix B

Data Collection

Hawaii Rev. Stat. § 846-51—"Covers definitions of hate crime reporting."

Hawaii Rev. Stat. § 846-52—"The department of the attorney general shall be responsible for the collection, storage, dissemination, and analysis of all hate crime data from all agencies that have primary investigative, action, or program responsibility for adult or juvenile offenses. . . ."

Hawaii Rev. Stat.§ 846-53—"Agencies that have investigative, detention, custodial, adjudicative, or program responsibility for adult or juvenile offenses shall cooperate with the attorney general in establishing the hate crime reporting system."

Hawaii Rev. Stat. § 846-54—"The attorney shall summarize and analyze reports of hate crimes data that are received, and shall compile and transmit an annual report of hate crime data to the governor, the judiciary, the department of public safety, and the legislature."

IDAHO

Penalty Enhancement

Idaho Code § 18-7092—"It shall be unlawful for any person, maliciously and with the specific intent to intimidate or harass another person because of that person's race, color, religion, ancestry, or national origin."

Institutional Vandalism

Idaho Code § 18-7902—Malicious harassment prohibited which includes injury to person or property of another because of that person's race, color, religion, ancestry, or national origin.

Data Collection

Idaho Code § 67-2915—Provides for statistical reporting of malicious harassment crimes.

ILLINOIS

Penalty Enhancement

720 Ill. Comp. Laws Ann. § 5/12-7.1—Outlaws hate crimes (violent crimes committed because of animus towards victim's actual or perceived race,

color, creed, religion, ancestry, gender, sexual orientation, physical or mental disability, or national origin).

730 Ill. Comp. Laws Ann. § 5/5-5-3.2—Lists the aggravating factors that may be considered by the court, including the selection of a victim because of the victim's actual or perceived race, color, creed, religion, ancestry, gender, sexual orientation, physical or mental disability, or national origin.

INSTITUTIONAL VANDALISM

720 Ill. Comp. Laws Ann. § 5/21-1.2—Criminalizes damage to places of worship, schools, educational facilities or community centers committed because of or by reason of the race, color, creed, religion, or national origin of another.

DATA COLLECTION

20 Ill. Comp. Laws Ann. § 2605/55a31—Provides for the collection and dissemination of hate-crimes data.

LAW ENFORCEMENT TRAINING

20 Ill. Comp. Laws Ann. § 2605/55a31—Mandates training for state police officers in identifying, responding to, and reporting hate crimes.

INDIANA

INSTITUTIONAL VANDALISM

Ind. Code Ann. § 35-43-1-2(b)—Outlaws property damage to places of worship, schools or community centers.

DATA COLLECTION

Ind. Code Ann.§ 10-13-3-38—"A law enforcement agency shall collect information concerning bias crimes."

Ind. Code Ann.§ 10-13-3-1(b—"Bias crime" means an offense in which the person who commits the offense knowingly or intentionally damaged or otherwise affected property because of the color, creed, disability, national origin, race, religion, or sexual orientation of the owner or occupant of the affected property.

IOWA

PENALTY ENHANCEMENT

Iowa Code Ann. § 708.2C, 712.7, 716.6A, 716.8—Outlaws hate crime as defined in §729A.2 (crimes committed because of the victim's race, color, religion, ancestry, national origin, political affiliation, sex, sexual orientation, age, or disability).

INSTITUTIONAL VANDALISM

Iowa Code Ann. § 716.6A—Increases the penalty for institutional vandalism one degree higher than the underlying offense which is also a hate crime as defined in § 729A.2.

DATA COLLECTION

Iowa Code Ann. § 692.15(7)—Mandates reporting of hate crimes.

LAW ENFORCEMENT TRAINING

Iowa Code Ann. § 729A.4—Covers sensitivity training for law enforcement personnel.

KANSAS

PENALTY ENHANCEMENT

Kan. Stat. Ann. § 21-4716(c)(2)(C)—Establishes as an aggravating sentencing factor a crime that was motivated by the victim's race, color, religion, ethnicity, national origin, or sexual orientation.

INSTITUTIONAL VANDALISM

Kan. Stat. Ann. § 21-4111—Covers institutional vandalism and desecration of religious institutions.

KENTUCKY

PENALTY ENHANCEMENT

Ky. Rev. Stat. § 532.031—"A person may be found by the sentencing judge to have committed an offense specified below as a result of a hate crime if the person intentionally because of race, color, religion sexual orientation, or national origin of another individual or group of individuals . . ."

Ky. Rev. Stat. § 346.055—Victim of hate crime deemed victim of criminally injurious conduct.

INSTITUTIONAL VANDALISM

Ky. Rev. Stat. § 525.113—"A person is guilty of institutional vandalism when he, because of race, color, religion, sexual orientation, or national origin of another individual or group of individuals, knowingly vandalizes, defaces, damages, or desecrates objects . . ."

Ky. Rev. Stat. § 525.110—Covers desecration of venerated objects in the second degree.

DATA COLLECTION

Ky. Rev. Stat. § 17.1523—"Uniform offense report to provide for indication of bias-related crime."

LAW ENFORCEMENT TRAINING

Ky. Rev. Stat. § 15.331—Covers basic law enforcement training to include training on bias-related crime.

LOUISIANA

Penalty Enhancement Yes La. Rev. Stat. §14:107.2—"It shall be unlawful for any person to select the victim of the following offenses against person and property because of actual or perceived race, age, gender, religion, color, creed, disability, sexual orientation, national origin, or ancestry . . ."

INSTITUTIONAL VANDALISM

La. Rev. Stat.§14.225—Criminalizes knowingly vandalizing, defacing, or otherwise damaging places used for religious worship, schools, or community centers.

Data Collection Yes La. Rev. Stat. 15:1204.2B(4)—Mandates the reporting of data regarding crimes directed against individuals or groups, or their property, by reason of their actual or perceived race, age, gender, religion, color, creed, disability, sexual orientation, national origin, or ancestry.

Appendix B

LAW ENFORCEMENT TRAINING

La. Rev. Stat.§ 40:2403—Covers Council on Peace Officer Standards and Training.

MAINE

PENALTY ENHANCEMENT

17 Me. Rev. Stat. § 1151—Covers general sentencing provisions for crimes motivated because of the victim's "race, color, religion, sex, ancestry, national origin, physical or mental disability or sexual orientation of that person or of the owner or occupant of that property."

17 Me. Rev. Stat. § 2931, 2932—Outlaws interference with the exercise or enjoyment of civil rights.

INSTITUTIONAL VANDALISM

17 Me. Rev. Stat.§ 507—Covers desecration and defacement of places of worship.

DATA COLLECTION

25 Me. Rev. Stat. § 1544—Provides for reporting on crimes that manifest evidence of prejudice based on race, religion, disability, sexual orientation, or ethnicity.

MARYLAND

PENALTY ENHANCEMENT

Md. Crim. Code Ann. § 10-305—Covers specific penalties associated with hate crimes.

Md. Crim. Code Ann. § 10-306—"Prosecution of a person under this subtitle does not preclude prosecution and imposition of penalties for another crime in addition to the penalties imposed under this subtitle."

INSTITUTIONAL VANDALISM

Md. Crim. Code Ann. § 10-301—Covers damaging property of religious entity.

Md. Crim. Code Ann. § 10-302—"A person may not, by force or threat of force, obstruct or attempt to obstruct another in the free exercise of that person's religious beliefs."

Md. Crim. Code Ann. § 10-303—Covers "harassment; destruction of property because of another's race, color, religious beliefs, or national origin..."

Md. Crim. Code Ann. § 10-304—Covers damage to associated building.

DATA COLLECTION

Md. Crim. Code Ann. 88B, § 9(b)—Mandates the collection and analysis of information relating to incidents directed against an individual or group because of the individual's or group's race, religion, ethnicity, or sexual orientation.

MASSACHUSETTS

PENALTY ENHANCEMENT

Mass. Gen. Laws Ann. ch. 265, § 37—Outlaws interference with the exercise or enjoyment of civil rights.

Mass. Gen. Laws Ann. ch. 265, § 39—Covers intimidation because of race, color, religion or national origin; assault or battery; damage to property; fines; imprisonment; diversity awareness program.

INSTITUTIONAL VANDALISM

Mass. Gen. Laws Ann. ch. A266 § 126A—Criminalizes defacement of real or personal property.

Mass. Gen. Laws Ann. ch. 266 § 127—Criminalizes anyone who destroys or injures the personal property, dwelling house, or building of another.

DATA COLLECTION

Mass. Gen. Laws Ann. ch. 22C § 33—Provides for the promulgation of regulation relative to the collection of hate crime data.

Mass. Gen. Laws Ann. ch.22C § 34—Provides for the summary and analysis of hate crime data and the publication of annual reports.

LAW ENFORCEMENT TRAINING

Mass. Gen. Laws Ann. ch. 6, § 116B—"The municipal police training committee shall provide instruction for police officers in identifying, responding to and reporting all incidents of hate crime. . . ."

MICHIGAN

PENALTY ENHANCEMENT

Mich. Comp. Laws. Ann. § 750.147b—Outlaws ethnic intimidation on the basis of race, color, religion, gender, or national origin.

DATA COLLECTION

Mich. Comp. Laws. Ann. § 28.257a—Requires that ethnic intimidation offenses be reported to the central record repository.

MINNESOTA

PENALTY ENHANCEMENT

Minn. Stat. Ann. § 609.2231[subd.4], 609.5595[subd. 1a], 609.749[subd. 3(a)]—Covers assault, property damage, and harassment motivated by victim's or another's actual or perceived race, color, religion, sex, sexual orientation, disability, age, or national origin.

Minn. Stat. Ann. ch. 244 App. [II][2][b][11]—Establishes an aggravating sentencing factor for offenses motivated by the animus noted above.

INSTITUTIONAL VANDALISM

Minn. Stat. Ann. § 609.595—Covers damage to property.

DATA COLLECTION

Minn. Stat. Ann. § 626.5531—Covers reporting of crimes motivated by bias.

LAW ENFORCEMENT TRAINING

Minn. Stat. Ann. § 626.8451—Covers training in identifying and responding to certain crimes.

MISSISSIPPI

PENALTY ENHANCEMENT

Miss. Code Ann. § 99-19-307—Imposes additional penalties for hate crimes "in the event it is found beyond a reasonable doubt that the offense was committed by reason of the actual or perceived race, color, ancestry, ethnicity, religion, national origin or gender of the victim."

Miss. Code Ann. § 99-19-305—Covers sentencing proceedings; required findings for enhanced penalty.

Miss. Code Ann. § 99-19-301—Covers penalties subject to enhancement.

INSTITUTIONAL VANDALISM

Miss. Code Ann. § 97-17-39—Describes penalties for injuring, destroying, or defacing certain public buildings, schools or churches, or property thereof.

MISSOURI

PENALTY ENHANCEMENT

Mo. Ann. Stat. § 557.035—Provides enhanced penalties for motivational factors in certain crimes . . . "which the state believes to be knowingly motivated because of race, color, religion, national origin, sex, sexual orientation or disability of the victim or victims."

INSTITUTIONAL VANDALISM

Mo. Ann. Stat. §574.085—Criminalizes vandalism or damages to places used for religious worship or other religious purpose, schools, community centers, and any personal property contained therein.

MONTANA

PENALTY ENHANCEMENT

Mont. Code Ann. § 45-5-222—Sentence enhancement for offenses committed because of victim's race, creed, religion, color, national origin, or involvement in civil rights or human rights activities.

INSTITUTIONAL VANDALISM

Mont. Code. Ann. § 45-5-221—Criminalizes damages to another's property motivated by race, creed, religion, color, national origin, or involvement in civil rights or human rights activities.

NEBRASKA

PENALTY ENHANCEMENT

Neb. Rev. Stat. § 28-111—Imposes additional penalties for "any person who commits one or more of the following criminal offenses against a person or a person's property because of the person's race, color, religion, ancestry, national origin, gender, sexual orientation, age, or disability. . . ."

Neb. Rev. Stat. § 28-113—A victim of hate crime "may bring a civil action for equitable relief, general and special damages, reasonable attorney's fees, and costs."

DATA COLLECTION

Neb. Rev. Stat. § 28-114—Provides for the establishment of a central repository for the collection and analysis of information regarding criminal offenses committed against a person because of the person's race, color, religion, ancestry, national origin, gender, sexual orientation, age, or disability.

NEVADA

PENALTY ENHANCEMENT

Nev. Rev. Stat. § 207.185—Penalty for commission of certain unlawful acts by reason of actual or perceived race, color, religion, national origin, physical or mental disability or sexual orientation of another person or group of persons.

Nev. Rev. Stat. § 193.1675—Additional penalty: commission of crime because of certain actual or perceived characteristics of victim.

Nev. Rev. Stat. § 41.690—"Cause of action for damages resulting from criminal violation if perpetrator was motivated by certain characteristics of victim."

INSTITUTIONAL VANDALISM

Nev. Rev. Stat. § 206.125—Damage of property used for religious or educational purposes, for burial or memorializing dead or as community center; damage of property contained therein.

NEW HAMPSHIRE

PENALTY ENHANCEMENT

N. H. Rev. Stat. Ann. § 651:6—Imposes extended term of imprisonment where a perpetrator was "substantially motivated to commit the crime because of hostility towards the victim's religion, race, creed, sexual orientation, national origin or sex."

NEW JERSEY

PENALTY ENHANCEMENT

N. J. Stat. Ann. § 2C:44-3—Provides that a court may enhance penalties for crimes committed with a purpose to intimidate an individual or group because of race, color, gender, handicap, religion, sexual orientation, or ethnicity.

N. J. Stat. Ann. § 2C:16–1—Outlaws bias intimidation on the basis of the victim's race, color, religion, gender, handicap, sexual orientation, or ethnicity.

INSTITUTIONAL VANDALISM

N. J. Stat. Ann. § 2C:33-11—Criminalizes purposeful defacement or damage to any private premises or property primarily used for religious, educational, residual, memorial, charitable, or cemetery purposes, by placing a symbol or object that exposes another to threat of violence.

DATA COLLECTION

N. J. Stat. Ann. § 52:9DD-9—Covers efforts to promote prejudice reduction and prevent and deter crimes based upon the victim's race, color, religion, national origin, sexual orientation, ethnicity, gender, or physical, mental or cognitive ability.

LAW ENFORCEMENT TRAINING

N. J. Stat. Ann. § 52:9DD-9—Covers development of cultural diversity training for law enforcement personnel.

NEW MEXICO

PENALTY ENHANCEMENT

N.M. Stat. Ann. § 31-18B-1—This act 31-18B-1 to 31-18B-5 NMSA 1978 may be cited as the "Hate Crimes Act." Will allow a year of prison to be added to each felony charge proved by the prosecutors.

INSTITUTIONAL VANDALISM

N.M. Stat. Ann. § 30-15-4—Criminalizes desecration of a church.

DATA COLLECTION

N.M. Stat. Ann. § 31-18B-4—Shall provide the FBI with data concerning a crime motivated by hate in accordance with guidelines established pursuant to the Federal Hate Crime Statistics Act.

LAW ENFORCEMENT TRAINING

N.M. Stat. Ann. § 31-18B-5—Provides for law enforcement training concerning the detection, investigation, and reporting of a crime motivated by hate.

NEW YORK

PENALTY ENHANCEMENT

N.Y. Penal § 485.10—When a person commits a hate crime, the penalty shall be deemed to be one category higher than the specified offense the defendant committed, or one category higher than the offense level applicable to the defendant's conviction for an attempt or conspiracy to commit a specified offense.

N.Y. Penal § 240.30, 240.31—Outlaws aggravating harassment on the basis of the victim's real or perceived race, color, national origin, ancestry, gender, religion, religious practices, age, disability, or sexual orientation.

NORTH CAROLINA

PENALTY ENHANCEMENT

N.C. Gen. Stat. § 14-3—Enhances punishment for offenses committed because of victim's race, color, religion, nationality, or country of origin.

INSTITUTIONAL VANDALISM

N.C. Gen. Stat. § 14-49—Covers willful and malicious damage to buildings of worship by use of explosive.

N.C. Gen. Stat. § 14-144—Covers damage to buildings of worship by another means than burning or attempt to burn.

N.C. Gen. Stat. § 14-62.2—Covers church burning.

NORTH DAKOTA

PENALTY ENHANCEMENT

N.D. Cent. Code, § 12.1-14-04—"A person is guilty of a class B misdemeanor if, whether or not acting under color of law, he, by force, or threat of force or by economic coercion, intentionally 1. injures, intimidates, or interferes with another because of his sex, race, color, religion, or national origin..."

OHIO

PENALTY ENHANCEMENT

Ohio Rev. Stat. Ann. § 2927.12—Enhances penalty for ethnic intimidation and certain offenses committed by reason of the victim's race, color, religion, or national origin.

Institutional Vandalism Yes Ohio Rev. Stat. Ann. § 2927.11—Covers damage to places of worship, their furnishings, or religious artifacts or sacred texts within the place of worship.

OKLAHOMA

PENALTY ENHANCEMENT

21 Okl. Stat. Ann. § 850—"No person shall maliciously and with the specific intent to intimidate or harass another person because of that person's race, color, religion, ancestry, national origin or disability."

INSTITUTIONAL VANDALISM

21 Okl. Stat. Ann. § 1765—Covers willful injury to any house of worship or any part thereof, or property therein.

DATA COLLECTION

21 Okl. Stat. Ann. § 850F—Mandates the development of a standard system for state and local law enforcement agencies to report incidents of crime that are apparently directed against members of racial, ethnic, religious groups, or other groups specified in the section.

OREGON

PENALTY ENHANCEMENT

Ore. Rev. Stat. §§ 166.155, 166.165—Covers intimidation because of the perpetrator's perception of that person's race, color, religion, national origin, or sexual orientation.

INSTITUTIONAL VANDALISM

Ore. Rev. Stat. § 166.075—Defines crime of abuse of venerated objects as the intentional abuse of a place of worship.

DATA COLLECTION

Ore. Rev. Stat. § 181.550—"All law enforcement agencies shall report to the Department of State Police statistics concerning crimes."

LAW ENFORCEMENT

Ore. Rev. Stat. § 181.642—Mandates training on the investigation, identification, and reporting of crimes motivated by prejudice based on the perceived race, color, religion, national origin, sexual orientation, marital status, political affiliation or beliefs, membership or activity in or on behalf of a labor organization or against a labor organization, physical or mental handicap, age, economic or social status, or citizenship of the victim.

PENNSYLVANIA

PENALTY ENHANCEMENT

18 Pa. Stat. Ann. § 2710—Enhances penalty for "[a] person commits the offense of ethnic intimidation if, with malicious intention toward the actual or perceived race, color, religion, national origin, ancestry, mental or physical disability, sexual orientation, gender or gender identity of another individual or group of individuals. . . ."

INSTITUTIONAL VANDALISM

18 Pa. Stat. Ann. § 3307—Covers desecration of places used for religious worship or other religious purposes, schools, and community centers.

18 Pa. Stat. Ann. § 5509—Criminalizes desecration of venerated objects.

Data Collection 71 Pa. Stat. Ann. § 250(I)—Gives power and duty for the State Police to collect information relating to crimes and incidents related to the race, color, religion, or national origin of individuals and groups.

RHODE ISLAND

PENALTY ENHANCEMENT

R.I. Gen. Laws § 12-19-38. Hate Crime Sentencing Act—Enhances the penalty when the defender selects a victim because of hatred toward the actual or perceived disability, religion, color, race, national origin or ancestry, sexual orientation, or gender of that person.

INSTITUTIONAL VANDALISM

R.I. Gen. Laws § 11-44-31—Covers the desecration of places of public assemblage, including places used for religious worship or other religious purposes, and buildings used for educational purposes or as a community meeting place.

DATA COLLECTION

R.I. Gen. Laws § 42-28-46—Provides for the development of a system monitoring the occurrence of and collecting data on crimes motivated by racial, religious, ethnic bigotry, or bias on any other matter defined as a hate crime.

LAW ENFORCEMENT TRAINING

R.I. Gen. Laws § 42-28.2-8.1—The commission on standards and training shall prepare and publish mandatory training standards to provide instruction for police officers in identifying, responding to, and reporting all incidents of "hate crimes."

SOUTH CAROLINA

INSTITUTIONAL VANDALISM

S.C. Code Ann. § 16-11-535—Covers willful injury to any place of worship.

S.C. Code Ann. § 16-11-110(B)—Covers church burning.

SOUTH DAKOTA

PENALTY ENHANCEMENT

S.D. Cod. Laws § 22-19B-1—"No person may maliciously and with the specific intent to intimidate or harass another person because of that person's race, color, religion, ancestry or national origin."

TENNESSEE

PENALTY ENHANCEMENT

Tenn. Code Ann. § 40-35-114—Imposes additional penalties for hate crimes when "the defendant intentionally selects the person against whom the crime is committed or selects the property that is damaged. . . . because of the actor's belief or perception regarding the race, religion, color, disability, sexual orientation, national origin, ancestry of gender of that person or of the owner or occupant of that property."

Tenn. Code Ann. § 39-17-309—Outlaws civil rights intimidation based on the same factors.

INSTITUTIONAL VANDALISM

Tenn. Code Ann. § 40-35-114

TEXAS

PENALTY ENHANCEMENT

Tex. Code Crim. Proc. Art. 42.014—Finding that offense was committed because of bias or prejudice.

Tex. Penal Code §12.47—Authorizes sentencing enhancement on the basis of that finding.

INSTITUTIONAL VANDALISM

Tex. Penal Code § 28.08—Covers graffiti or other markings on place of worship.

Tex. Penal Code § 28.03(f)—Covers damage or destruction to a place of worship.

DATA COLLECTION

Tex. Gov. Code § 411.046—Provides for the establishment and maintenance of a central repository for the collection and analysis of information relating to crimes that are motivated by prejudice, hatred, or advocacy of violence.

UTAH

PENALTY ENHANCEMENT

Utah Code Ann. § 76-3-203.3—Penalty for hate crimes - Civil rights violation. Covers an act which causes the victim to fear for his physical safety or damages the property of that person or another.

VERMONT

PENALTY ENHANCEMENT

13 Vt. Stat. Ann. § 1455—Imposes additional penalties for "a person who commits, causes to be committed or attempts to commit any crime and whose conduct is maliciously motivated by the victim's actual or perceived race, color, religion, national origin, sex, ancestry, age, service in the armed forces of the United States, handicap, sexual orientation or gender identity."

VIRGINIA

PENALTY ENHANCEMENT

Va. Code Ann. § 18.2-57—Imposes additional penalties "if a person intentionally selects the person against whom an assault and battery resulting in bodily injury is committed because of his race, religious conviction, color or national origin."

INSTITUTIONAL VANDALISM

Va. Code Ann. § 18.2.127—Covers willful or malicious injury to places of worship.

Va. Code Ann. § 18.2.138—Covers destruction of property within places of worship.

DATA COLLECTION

Va. Code Ann. § 52-8.5—Covers reporting hate crimes.

WASHINGTON

PENALTY ENHANCEMENT

Wash. Rev. Code § 9A.36.080—"A person is guilty of malicious harassment if he or she maliciously and intentionally commits one of the following acts because of his or her perception of the victim's race, color, religion, ancestry, national origin, gender, sexual orientation, or mental, physical, or sensory handicap."

INSTITUTIONAL VANDALISM

Wash. Rev. Code § 9A.36..080(2)(a)—Covers cross burnings.

Wash. Rev. Code § 9.61.160—Covers threats to bomb or injure places of worship or public assembly.

DATA COLLECTION

Wash. Rev. Code § 36.28A.030—Provides for creation of central repository for the collection and classification of information regarding crimes of bigotry or bias.

LAW ENFORCEMENT TRAINING

Wash. Rev. Code § 43.101.290—Mandates training in identifying, responding to, and reporting crimes of bigotry and bias.

WEST VIRGINIA

PENALTY ENHANCEMENT

W. Va. Code Ann. § 61-6-21—Covers prohibiting violations of an individual's civil rights and makes commission of a crime because of the victim's race, color, religion, ancestry, national origin, political affiliation, or sex an aggravating circumstance in imposing sentence.

WISCONSIN

PENALTY ENHANCEMENT

Wis. Stat. Ann. § 939.645—"If a person does all of the following, the penalties for the underlying crime are increased. . . . (b)Intentionally selects the person against whom the crime under par. (a) is committed or selects the property that is damaged or otherwise affected by the crime under par. (a) in whole or in part because of the actors belief or perception regarding the race, religion, color, disability, sexual orientation, national origin or ancestry of that person or the owner or occupant of that property . . . "

INSTITUTIONAL VANDALISM

Wis. Stat. Ann. § 943.012—Covers criminal damage to or graffiti on religious and other property.

WYOMING

PENALTY ENHANCEMENT

Wyo. Stat. § 6-9-102—Outlaws civil rights violations on the basis of race, color, sex, creed, or national origin.

Source: Congressional Research Service. Available online. URL: http://assets.opencrs.com/rpts/RL33099_20050921.pdf. Accessed on August 22, 2008.

APPENDIX C

HIGHLIGHTS FROM FBI UNIFORM CRIME REPORT SECTION ON HATE CRIME, 2006

The FBI continually collects data regarding criminal offenses, which it dissemintates in its annual Uniform Crime Report. The report includes a section specifically on hate crimes, which records crimes committed against persons, property, or society "that are motivated, in whole or in part, by the offender's bias against a race, religion, sexual orientation, ethnicity/national origin, or disability." The report includes statistics under four groups of tables: Incidents and Offense, Victims, Offenders, and Location Type. Following is a summary of the most recent such report.

BACKGROUND

CONGRESS MANDATES THE COLLECTION OF HATE CRIME DATA

On April 23, 1990, Congress passed the Hate Crime Statistics Act, which required the Attorney General to collect data "about crimes that manifest evidence of prejudice based on race, religion, sexual orientation, or ethnicity." The Attorney General delegated the responsibilities of developing the procedures for implementing, collecting, and managing hate crime data to the Director of the FBI, who in turn assigned the tasks to the Uniform Crime Reporting (UCR) Program. Under the direction of the Attorney General and with the cooperation and assistance of many local and state law enforcement agencies, the UCR Program created a hate crime data collection system to comply with the congressional mandate . . . The UCR Program's first publication on the subject was *Hate Crime Statistics, 1990: A Resource Book*, which was a compilation of hate crime data reported by 11 states that had collected the information under state authority in 1990 and were willing to offer their data as a prototype. . . .

SUBSEQUENT CHANGES TO HATE CRIME DATA COLLECTION

In September 1994, lawmakers amended the Hate Crime Statistics Act to include bias against persons with disabilities by passing the Violent Crime and Law Enforcement Act of 1994. The FBI started gathering data for the additional bias type on January 1, 1997.

The Church Arson Prevention Act, which was signed into law in July 1996, removed the sunset clause from the original statute and mandated that the hate crime data collection become a permanent part of the UCR Program.

* * *

DATA PROVIDED

The hate crime data in this Web publication comprise a subset of information that law enforcement agencies submit to the UCR Program. The types of hate crimes reported to the Program (i.e., the biases that motivated the crimes) are further broken down into more specific categories. As collected for each hate crime incident, the aggregate data in this report include the following: offense type, location, bias motivation, victim type, number of individual victims, number of offenders, and the race of the offenders.

Incidents and offenses—Crimes reported to the FBI involve those motivated by biases based on race, religion, sexual orientation, ethnicity/national origin, and disability.

Victims—The victim of a hate crime may be an individual, a business, an institution, or society as a whole.

Offenders—Law enforcement specifies the number of offenders and, when possible, the race of the offender or offenders as a group.

Location type—Law enforcement may specify one of 25 location designations, e.g., residences or homes, schools or colleges, and parking lots or garages.

Hate crime by jurisdiction—Includes data about hate crimes by state and agency.

NATURE

In 2006, there were 7,722 hate crime incidents reported to the FBI. The incidents involved 9,080 separate offenses. There were 7,720 single-bias incidents that involved 9,076 offenses, 9,642 victims and 7,324 offenders. The two multiple-bias incidents reported in 2006 involved four offenses, 10 victims, and six offenders.

Appendix C

Of the 7,720 single-bias incidents, 51.8 percent were racially motivated; 18.9 percent were motivated by religious bias; 15.5 percent resulted from sexual-orientation bias; 12.7 percent stemmed from ethnicity/national origin bias; and 1 percent were prompted by disability bias. See Table 1.

Of the 9,080 reported hate crime offenses in 2006, 32.1 percent were destruction/damage/vandalism; 27.6 percent were intimidation; 19.1 were

TABLE 1
INCIDENTS, OFFENSES, VICTIMS, AND KNOWN OFFENDERS BY BIAS MOTIVATION, 2006

Bias motivation	Incidents	Offenses	Victims[1]	Known offenders[2]
Total	7,722	9,080	9,652	7,330
Single-Bias Incidents	7,720	9,076	9,642	7,324
Race:	4,000	4,737	5,020	3,957
Anti-White	890	1,008	1,054	1,074
Anti-Black	2,640	3,136	3,332	2,437
Anti-American Indian/Alaskan Native	60	72	75	72
Anti-Asian/Pacific Islander	181	230	239	181
Anti-Multiple Races, Group	229	291	320	193
Religion:	1,462	1,597	1,750	705
Anti-Jewish	967	1,027	1,144	362
Anti-Catholic	76	81	86	44
Anti-Protestant	59	62	65	35
Anti-Islamic	156	191	208	147
Anti-Other Religion	124	140	147	63
Anti-Multiple Religions, Group	73	88	92	49
Anti-Atheism/Agnosticism/etc.	7	8	8	5
Sexual Orientation:	1,195	1,415	1,472	1,380
Anti-Male Homosexual	747	881	913	914
Anti-Female Homosexual	163	192	202	154
Anti-Homosexual	238	293	307	268
Anti-Heterosexual	26	28	29	26
Anti-Bisexual	21	21	21	18
Ethnicity/National Origin:	984	1,233	1,305	1,209
Anti-Hispanic	576	770	819	802
Anti-Other Ethnicity/National Origin	408	463	486	407
Disability:	79	94	95	73
Anti-Physical	17	20	21	17
Anti-Mental	62	74	74	56
Multiple-Bias Incidents[3]	2	4	10	6

[1]The term *victim* may refer to a person, business, institution, or society as a whole.

[2]The term *known offender* does not imply that the identity of the suspect is known, but only that an attribute of the suspect has been identified, which distinguishes him/her from an unknown offender.

[3]In a *multiple-bias incident,* two conditions must be met: (a) more than one offense type must occur in the incident and (b) at least two offense types must be motivated by different biases.

simple assault; 13 percent were aggravated assault; the remaining 8.2 percent of hate crimes were comprised of additional crimes against persons, property, and society. See Table 2.

Law enforcement agencies reported 9,080 known offenders in conjunction with the 7,722 hate crime incidents recorded in 2006. Of the known offenders, 3,593 were linked to crimes against property, 5,449 were associated with crimes against persons, and 38 with crimes against society. The single most reported offense, intimidation, was committed by 2,508 offenders. Table 3 breaks down the known offenders by offense type and race.

Source: FBI. "About Hate Crime Statistics, 2006." Available online. URL: http://www.fbi.gov/ucr/hc2006/index.html. Accessed on August 15, 2008.

TABLE 2
INCIDENTS, OFFENSES, VICTIMS, AND KNOWN OFFENDERS BY OFFENSE TYPE, 2006

Offense type	Incidents	Offenses	Victims[1]	Known offenders[2]
Total	**7,722**	**9,080**	**9,652**	**7,330**
Crimes against persons:	**4,378**	**5,449**	**5,449**	**5,770**
Murder and nonnegligent manslaughter	3	3	3	4
Forcible rape	6	6	6	8
Aggravated assault	860	1,178	1,178	1,606
Simple assault	1,447	1,737	1,737	2,116
Intimidation	2,046	2,508	2,508	2,018
Other[4]	16	17	17	18
Crimes against property:	**3,593**	**3,593**	**4,165**	**1,912**
Robbery	142	142	200	311
Burglary	155	155	177	112
Larceny-theft	261	261	283	182
Motor vehicle theft	25	25	44	17
Arson	41	41	51	30
Destruction/damage/vandalism	2,911	2,911	3,348	1,212
Other[4]	58	58	62	48
Crimes against society[4]	**38**	**38**	**38**	**58**

[1]The actual number of incidents is 7,722. However, the column figures will not add to the total because incidents may include more than one offense type, and these are counted in each appropriate offense type category.

[2]The term *victim* may refer to a person, business, institution, or society as a whole.

[3]The term *known offender* does not imply that the identity of the suspect is known, but only that an attribute of the suspect has been identified, which distinguishes him/her from an unknown offender. The actual number of known offenders is 7,330. However, the column figures will not add to the total because some offenders are responsible for more than one offense type, and they are, therefore, counted more than once in this table.

[4]Includes additional offenses collected in the NIBRS. See Methodology.

TABLE 3
OFFENSES
KNOWN OFFENDER'S RACE BY OFFENSE TYPE, 2006

Offense type	Total offenses	Known offender's race					Unknown offender	
		White	Black	American Indian/Alaskan Native	Asian/ Pacific Islander	Multiple races, group	Unknown race	Unknown offender
Total	**9,080**	**3,710**	**1,026**	**66**	**75**	**247**	**891**	**3,065**
Crimes against persons:	**5,449**	**3,122**	**839**	**53**	**66**	**213**	**390**	**766**
Murder and nonnegligent manslaughter	3	2	0	0	0	0	0	1
Forcible rape	6	4	0	0	0	1	0	1
Aggravated assault	1,178	715	248	12	36	52	50	65
Simple assault	1,737	1,041	368	27	16	101	78	106
Intimidation	2,508	1,356	215	13	14	59	259	592
Other[1]	17	4	8	1	0	0	3	1
Crimes against property:	**3,593**	**573**	**173**	**13**	**8**	**33**	**496**	**2,297**
Robbery	142	47	61	1	2	10	7	14
Burglary	155	27	15	1	1	2	24	85
Larceny-theft	261	58	23	3	0	3	59	115
Motor vehicle theft	25	4	3	0	0	1	6	11
Arson	41	7	2	1	0	0	9	22
Destruction/damage/vandalism	2,911	409	59	6	5	17	385	2,030
Other[1]	58	21	10	1	0	0	6	20
Crimes against society[1]	**38**	**15**	**14**	**0**	**1**	**1**	**5**	**2**

[1]Includes additional offenses collected in the NIBRS. See Methodology.

APPENDIX D

LOCAL LAW ENFORCEMENT HATE CRIMES PREVENTION ACT OF 2007

The following is the full text of the Local Law Enforcement Hate Crimes Prevention Act of 2007 (H.R. 1592), as passed in the House of Representatives on May 3, 2007. Unofficially known as the Matthew Shepard Act, it would expand federal jurisdiction over hate crimes to include those committed because of a person's gender, sexual orientation, gender identity, or disability. Its Senate counterpart (S. 1105) passed as an addition to a defense spending bill in September 2007. This text was withdrawn from the bill in December, however, when it became clear that congressional support for the measure would not be enough to override President Bush's expected veto.

AN ACT

To provide Federal assistance to States, local jurisdictions, and Indian tribes to prosecute hate crimes, and for other purposes.

Be it enacted by the Senate and House of Representatives of the United States of America in Congress assembled,

SECTION 1. SHORT TITLE.

This Act may be cited as the 'Local Law Enforcement Hate Crimes Prevention Act of 2007'.

SEC. 2. DEFINITION OF HATE CRIME.

In this Act—

(1) the term 'crime of violence' has the meaning given that term in section 16, title 18, United States Code;

(2) the term 'hate crime' has the meaning given such term in section 280003(a) of the Violent Crime Control and Law Enforcement Act of 1994 (28 U.S.C. 994 note); and

(3) the term 'local' means a county, city, town, township, parish, village, or other general purpose political subdivision of a State.

SEC. 3. SUPPORT FOR CRIMINAL INVESTIGATIONS AND PROSECUTIONS BY STATE, LOCAL, AND TRIBAL LAW ENFORCEMENT OFFICIALS.

(a) Assistance Other Than Financial Assistance-

(1) IN GENERAL- At the request of State, local, or Tribal law enforcement agency, the Attorney General may provide technical, forensic, prosecutorial, or any other form of assistance in the criminal investigation or prosecution of any crime that—

(A) constitutes a crime of violence;

(B) constitutes a felony under the State, local, or Tribal laws; and

(C) is motivated by prejudice based on the actual or perceived race, color, religion, national origin, gender, sexual orientation, gender identity, or disability of the victim, or is a violation of the State, local, or Tribal hate crime laws.

(2) PRIORITY- In providing assistance under paragraph (1), the Attorney General shall give priority to crimes committed by offenders who have committed crimes in more than one State and to rural jurisdictions that have difficulty covering the extraordinary expenses relating to the investigation or prosecution of the crime.

(b) Grants-

(1) IN GENERAL- The Attorney General may award grants to State, local, and Indian law enforcement agencies for extraordinary expenses associated with the investigation and prosecution of hate crimes .

(2) OFFICE OF JUSTICE PROGRAMS- In implementing the grant program under this subsection, the Office of Justice Programs shall work closely with grantees to ensure that the concerns and needs of all affected parties, including community groups and schools, colleges, and universities, are addressed through the local infrastructure developed under the grants.

(3) APPLICATION-

(A) IN GENERAL- Each State, local, and Indian law enforcement agency that desires a grant under this subsection shall submit an application to the Attorney General at such time, in such manner, and accompanied by or containing such information as the Attorney General shall reasonably require.

(B) DATE FOR SUBMISSION- Applications submitted pursuant to subparagraph (A) shall be submitted during the 60-day period beginning on a date that the Attorney General shall prescribe.

(C) REQUIREMENTS- A State, local, and Indian law enforcement agency applying for a grant under this subsection shall

(i) describe the extraordinary purposes for which the grant is needed;

(ii) certify that the State, local government, or Indian tribe lacks the resources necessary to investigate or prosecute the hate crime;

(iii) demonstrate that, in developing a plan to implement the grant, the State, local, and Indian law enforcement agency has consulted and coordinated with nonprofit, nongovernmental violence recovery service programs that have experience in providing services to victims of hate crimes; and

(iv) certify that any Federal funds received under this subsection will be used to supplement, not supplant, non-Federal funds that would otherwise be available for activities funded under this subsection.

(4) DEADLINE - An application for a grant under this subsection shall be approved or denied by the Attorney General not later than 30 business days after the date on which the Attorney General receives the application.

(5) GRANT AMOUNT - A grant under this subsection shall not exceed $100,000 for any single jurisdiction in any 1-year period.

(6) REPORT - Not later than December 31, 2008, the Attorney General shall submit to Congress a report describing the applications submitted for grants under this subsection, the award of such grants, and the purposes for which the grant amounts were expended.

(7) AUTHORIZATION OF APPROPRIATIONS - There is authorized to be appropriated to carry out this subsection $5,000,000 for each of fiscal years 2008 and 2009.

SEC. 4. GRANT PROGRAM.

(a) Authority To Award Grants - The Office of Justice Programs of the Department of Justice may award grants, in accordance with such regulations as the Attorney General may prescribe, to State, local, or

Tribal programs designed to combat hate crimes committed by juveniles, including programs to train local law enforcement officers in identifying, investigating, prosecuting, and preventing hate crimes .

(b) Authorization of Appropriations - There are authorized to be appropriated such sums as may be necessary to carry out this section.

SEC. 5. AUTHORIZATION FOR ADDITIONAL PERSONNEL TO ASSIST STATE, LOCAL, AND TRIBAL LAW ENFORCEMENT.

There are authorized to be appropriated to the Department of Justice, including the Community Relations Service, for fiscal years 2008, 2009, and 2010 such sums as are necessary to increase the number of personnel to prevent and respond to alleged violations of section 249 of title 18, United States Code, as added by section 7 of this Act.

SEC. 6. PROHIBITION OF CERTAIN HATE CRIME ACTS.

(a) In General - Chapter 13 of title 18, United States Code, is amended by adding at the end the following:

'Sec. 249. Hate crime acts

'(a) In General -

'(1) OFFENSES INVOLVING ACTUAL OR PERCEIVED RACE, COLOR, RELIGION, OR NATIONAL ORIGIN- Whoever, whether or not acting under color of law, willfully causes bodily injury to any person or, through the use of fire, a firearm, or an explosive or incendiary device, attempts to cause bodily injury to any person, because of the actual or perceived race, color, religion, or national origin of any person—

'(A) shall be imprisoned not more than 10 years, fined in accordance with this title, or both; and

'(B) shall be imprisoned for any term of years or for life, fined in accordance with this title, or both, if—

'(i) death results from the offense; or

'(ii) the offense includes kidnaping or an attempt to kidnap, aggravated sexual abuse or an attempt to commit aggravated sexual abuse, or an attempt to kill.

'(2) OFFENSES INVOLVING ACTUAL OR PERCEIVED RELIGION, NATIONAL ORIGIN, GENDER, SEXUAL ORIENTATION, GENDER IDENTITY, OR DISABILITY-

'(A) IN GENERAL- Whoever, whether or not acting under color of law, in any circumstance described in subparagraph (B), willfully causes bodily injury to any person or, through the use of fire, a firearm, or an explosive or incendiary device, attempts to cause bodily injury to any person, because of the actual or perceived religion, national origin, gender, sexual orientation, gender identity or disability of any person—
'(i) shall be imprisoned not more than 10 years, fined in accordance with this title, or both; and
'(ii) shall be imprisoned for any term of years or for life, fined in accordance with this title, or both, if—
'(I) death results from the offense; or
'(II) the offense includes kidnaping or an attempt to kidnap, aggravated sexual abuse or an attempt to commit aggravated sexual abuse, or an attempt to kill.
'(B) CIRCUMSTANCES DESCRIBED- For purposes of subparagraph (A), the circumstances described in this subparagraph are that—
'(i) the conduct described in subparagraph (A) occurs during the course of, or as the result of, the travel of the defendant or the victim—
'(I) across a State line or national border; or
'(II) using a channel, facility, or instrumentality of interstate or foreign commerce;
'(ii) the defendant uses a channel, facility, or instrumentality of interstate or foreign commerce in connection with the conduct described in subparagraph (A);
'(iii) in connection with the conduct described in subparagraph (A), the defendant employs a firearm, explosive or incendiary device, or other weapon that has traveled in interstate or foreign commerce; or
'(iv) the conduct described in subparagraph (A)—
'(I) interferes with commercial or other economic activity in which the victim is engaged at the time of the conduct; or
'(II) otherwise affects interstate or foreign commerce.
'(b) Certification Requirement - No prosecution of any offense described in this subsection may be undertaken by the United States, except under the certification in writing of the Attorney General, the Deputy Attorney General, the Associate Attorney General, or any Assistant Attorney General specially designated by the Attorney General that—

'(1) such certifying individual has reasonable cause to believe that the actual or perceived race, color, religion, national origin, gender, sexual orientation, gender identity, or disability of any person was a motivating factor underlying the alleged conduct of the defendant; and

'(2) such certifying individual has consulted with State or local law enforcement officials regarding the prosecution and determined that—

'(A) the State does not have jurisdiction or does not intend to exercise jurisdiction;

'(B) the State has requested that the Federal Government assume jurisdiction;

'(C) the State does not object to the Federal Government assuming jurisdiction; or

'(D) the verdict or sentence obtained pursuant to State charges left demonstratively unvindicated the Federal interest in eradicating bias-motivated violence.

'(c) Definitions- In this section—

'(1) the term 'explosive or incendiary device' has the meaning given such term in section 232 of this title;

'(2) the term 'firearm' has the meaning given such term in section 921(a) of this title; and

'(3) the term 'gender identity' for the purposes of this chapter means actual or perceived gender-related characteristics.

'(d) Rule of Evidence- In a prosecution for an offense under this section, evidence of expression or associations of the defendant may not be introduced as substantive evidence at trial, unless the evidence specifically relates to that offense. However, nothing in this section affects the rules of evidence governing impeachment of a witness.'

(b) Technical and Conforming Amendment - The table of sections at the beginning of chapter 13 of title 18, United States Code, is amended by adding at the end the following new item:

249. Hate crime acts.

SEC. 7. SEVERABILITY.

If any provision of this Act, an amendment made by this Act, or the application of such provision or amendment to any person or circumstance is held to be unconstitutional, the remainder of this Act, the amendments made by this Act, and the application of the provisions of such to any person or circumstance shall not be affected thereby.

SEC. 8. RULE OF CONSTRUCTION.

Nothing in this Act, or the amendments made by this Act, shall be construed to prohibit any expressive conduct protected from legal prohibition by, or any activities protected by the free speech or free exercise clauses of, the First Amendment to the Constitution.

Passed the House of Representatives May 3, 2007.

Source: "Local Law Enforcement Hate Crimes Prevention Act of 2007 (Engrossed as Agreed to or Passed by House)." THOMAS database, Library of Congress. Available online. URL: http://thomas.loc.gov/home/gpoxmlc110/ h1592_eh.xml. Accessed on November 22, 2007.

APPENDIX E

ADVOCACY AND DEBATE OVER PENDING LEGISLATION, 2007

After a new federal law has been introduced, the House and Senate customarily explore the future impact of the legislation in hearings, while individual senators and representatives advocate their positions in speeches from the floor of the House or Senate, as well as from their official congressional web pages. This section presents a selection of speeches and opinions given by members of Congress in April and May 2007 regarding the Local Law Enforcement Hate Crimes Prevention Act (known as S. 1105 in the Senate and as H.R. 1592 in the House of Representatives).

SENATE SPEECHES SUPPORTING S. 1105 (APRIL 12, 2007)

EDWARD KENNEDY [D-MA]:

Mr. President, hate crimes violate everything our country stands for. They send the poisonous message that certain Americans deserve to be victimized solely because of who they are. These are crimes committed against entire communities, the Nation as a whole and the very ideals upon which our country was founded.

The vast majority of Congress agrees. In 2000, 57 Senators voted in support of this bill. In 2002, 54 Senators voted with us, and, in 2004, we had 65 votes. Today, we are re-introducing this bicameral, bipartisan bill with the support of 39 original cosponsors, and we have the votes to get cloture. We have the votes in the House too. This year, we are going to get it done.

Our legislation is supported by a broad coalition of over 210 law enforcement, civic, religious and civil rights groups, including the International Association of Chiefs of Police, the National Sheriffs Association, the Anti-Defamation League, the Interfaith Alliance, the U.S. Conference of Mayors, the Leadership Conference on Civil Rights, the National District Attorneys Association, and the National Center for Victims of Crime.

Data from the National Crime Victimization Survey are especially disturbing because they indicate that a large number of hate crimes go unreported. The data indicates that an average of 191,000 hate crimes take place every year, but only a small percentage are reported to the police.

We obviously need to strengthen the ability of Federal, State and local governments to investigate and prosecute these vicious and senseless crimes. The existing Federal hate crime statute was passed in 1968, soon after the assassination of Dr. Martin Luther King, Jr. It was such an important step forward at the time, but it is now a generation out of date.

The absence of effective legislation has undoubtedly resulted in the failure to solve many hate-motivated crimes. The recent action of the Justice Department in reopening 40 civil-rights-era murders demonstrates the need for adequate laws. Many of the victims in these cases have been denied justice for decades, and for some, justice will never come.

This bill corrects two major deficiencies in current law—one, the excessive restrictions requiring proof that victims were attacked because they were engaged in certain "federally protected activities," and, two, the limited scope of the law, which covers only hate crimes based on race, religion, or ethnic background, excluding violence committed against persons because of their sexual orientation, gender, gender identity, or disability.

The federally protected activity requirement is outdated, unwise and unnecessary, particularly when we consider the unjust outcomes that result from this requirement. Hate crimes can occur in a variety of circumstances, and citizens are often targeted during routine activities that should be protected.

For example, in June 2003, six Latino teenagers went to a family restaurant on Long Island. They knew one another from their involvement in community activities and were together to celebrate one of their birthdays. As the group entered the restaurant, three men who were leaving the bar assaulted them, pummeling one boy and severing a tendon in his hand with a sharp weapon. During the attack, the men yelled racial slurs and one identified himself as a skinhead.

Two of the men were tried under the current Federal law for committing a hate crime and were acquitted. The jurors said the government failed to prove that the attack took place because the victims were engaged in a federally protected activity—using the restaurant. The result in this case is only one example of the inadequate protection under current law. The bill we introduce today will eliminate the federally protected activity requirement. Under this bill, the defendants who left the courtroom as free men would almost certainly have left in handcuffs through a different door.

The bill also recognizes that hate crimes are also committed against people because of their sexual orientation, their gender, their gender identity, or their disability. It's up to Congress to make sure that tough Federal penalties also apply to those who commit such crimes as well. Passing this bill will send a loud and clear message. All hate crimes will face Federal prosecution. Action is long overdue. . . .

EVAN BAYH [D-IN]:

Mr. President, like acts of terrorism, hate crimes have an impact far greater than the impact on the individual victim. They are crimes against entire communities, the whole Nation, and the ideals of liberty and justice upon which America was founded.

First enacted nearly 40 years ago after the assassination of Martin Luther King, Federal hate crime laws have provided an important basis for prosecuting those who commit violent acts against another due to the person's race, color, religion or national origin.

Current law, however, makes it unnecessarily difficult to investigate and prosecute these and other insidious hate crimes. Consequently, the time has come to remove some of these hurdles and to expand the scope of Federal law so Americans who fall victim to hate crimes can receive protection under Federal law.

That is why I have cosponsored the Local Law Enforcement Hate Crimes Act of 2007, a bipartisan bill with broad political support that has been endorsed by 210 law enforcement, civil rights, civic, and religious organizations.

The bill will strengthen the ability of Federal, State, and local governments to investigate and prosecute hate crimes based on race, ethnic background, religion, gender, sexual orientation, disability, and gender identity.

The bill will also provide grants to help State and local governments meet the extraordinary expenses involved in hate crime cases.

This bill, while adding to Federal authority, properly leaves with the State or local law enforcement officials the primary responsibility of protecting citizens against crimes of violence. The bill authorizes actual Federal prosecutions only when a State does not have jurisdiction, when a State asks the Federal Government to take jurisdiction, or when a State fails to act. It is a Federal back-up for State and local law enforcement.

While State and local governments should continue to have the primary responsibility for investigating and prosecuting hate crimes, an expanded Federal role is necessary to ensure an adequate and fair response in all cases. The Federal Government must have jurisdiction to address those limited, but important cases in which local authorities are either unable or unwilling to investigate and prosecute.

Failure to pass Federal hate crimes legislation would signify our failure as a nation to accord each of our citizens the respect and value they deserve.

According to FBI statistics, 27,432 people were victims of hate-motivated violence over the last three years. That's an average of over 9,100 people per year, with nearly 25 people being victimized every day of the year, based on their race, religion, sexual orientation, ethnic background, or disability. But it is estimated that the vast majority of hate crimes goes unreported. Survey data from the biannual National Crime Victimization Survey suggests that an average of 191,000 hate crime victimizations take place per year.

While hatred and bigotry cannot be eradicated by an act of Congress, as a nation, we must send a strong, clear, moral response to these cowardly acts of violence. I believe that the Federal Government must play a leadership role in confronting criminal acts motivated by prejudice.

All Americans have a stake in responding decisively to violent bigotry. We must pull together to combat ignorance and hatred. The devastation caused by hate crimes impacts the victims, members of his or her family, as well as entire communities, and the Nation as a whole.

I am reminded of the great wisdom of Martin Luther King, "Darkness cannot drive out darkness; only light can do that. Hate cannot drive out hate; only love can do that. Hate multiplies hate, violence multiplies violence, and toughness multiplies toughness in a descending spiral of destruction. The chain reaction of evil—hate begetting hate, wars producing wars—must be broken, or we shall be plunged into the dark abyss of annihilation." *Strength to Love*, 1963.

I urge my colleagues to stand up against ignorance and intolerance and vote for the Local Law Enforcement Hate Crimes Prevention Act.

CHARLES SCHUMER [D-NY]:

Mr. President, I am proud to be a co-sponsor of the Local Law Enforcement Hate Crimes Prevention Act of 2007, and I commend my friend and colleague, Senator Kennedy, for his leadership and determination on this issue. We have tried for the better half of a decade to get this legislation passed, signed, and enacted into law. Today represents our strongest effort to date, and it is long past time that crimes based on hate be recognized and criminalized under Federal law. The need for Federal hate crimes legislation has been apparent for years as hate crimes know no State borders and—in part because their impacts often affect the very fabric of our society—they are a problem that affects all Americans.

This act sends the message that we will not tolerate acts of aggression and violence towards targeted communities or individuals who become victims of violence merely for being themselves. Perpetrators of this type of violence will now be subject to Federal prosecution under this act. Before we had to rely on the States to act, and some simply have failed to do enough to stem this type of criminal behavior. This act recognizes that hate crimes have national consequences and are not mere localized occurrences.

Put simply, a hate crime tends to impact an entire community, as opposed to being limited to the victim or the victim's family. It is a crime against a particular group, and must be treated as such. In essence, there are two crimes—one against the victim, and one against the victim's group or community. Some have asked, "But aren't all crimes based on hate?" No, they are not. Hate crimes are unique because they cut at the very fabric of our national values.

The framework of the Constitution provides a sound basis for our actions today—both the Commerce Clause and the Thirteenth Amendment are implicated by these crimes. The effects of hate crimes do not end at a State's border, but rather transcend those borders. These crimes implicate a citizen's ability to move and travel freely. Additionally, violence based on someone's race, religion, sexual orientation, or the other characteristics noted in the act are reminiscent of the ultimate hate crime—slavery. As such, the Thirteenth Amendment allows for Federal action to remedy this problem. The courts have ruled time and time again that discrimination in housing and discrimination in contractual agreements could be remedied through Federal statutes promulgated under the authority of the Thirteenth Amendment. It matters not what the discrimination is based on, what matters is the discrimination itself. In an attempt to rid the last vestiges of slavery from our society, the courts have allowed the Thirteenth Amendment to be the basis of such legislation.

Let us be very clear, we are not criminalizing speech. Violent acts against an African American, a woman, or a Sikh because of who they are do not constitute free expression. Nor are we criminalizing evil thoughts. We are only criminalizing action—harmful and violent action that cuts against our society and against the very meaning of what it is to be an American. Congress and local law enforcement are not becoming the "thought-police." Rather, we are criminalizing the violent actions of closed-minded and hateful individuals.

In today's society, we see all too frequently violence based on the person's race, religion, sexual orientation, or other characteristics. We must act to address these injustices. This is not about special rights to any particular group. Actually, it is quite the contrary. This is about equal rights. This is about going after those individuals who act on their harmful beliefs. By committing hate crimes, they are attempting to relegate certain people to second-class citizenship. They think they can do this through violence. But they are wrong, and this legislation is a forceful statement that this country will not tolerate this behavior. . . .

Source: The three previous statements were from GovTrack.us. "Statements on Introduced Bills and Joint Resolutions." Available online. URL: http://www.govtrack.us/congress/record.xpd?id=110-s20070412-36&bill=s110-1105#sMonofilemx003Ammx002Fmmx002Fmmx002Fmhomemx002Fmgovtrackmx002Fmdatamx002Fmusmx002Fm110mx002Fmcrmx002Fms20070412-36.xmlElementm8m0m0m. Accessed on November 22, 2007.

SUPPORT AND DISSENT FROM THE HOUSE SUBCOMMITTEE HEARINGS (APRIL 17, 2007)

The House and Senate customarily hold public hearings to explore the future impact of proposed federal legislation, hear testimony from experts and witnesses, and allow those favoring or opposing the law to express their views. The following excerpts were taken from the text of a hearing before the House Subcommittee on Crime, Terrorism, and Homeland Security, April 17, 2007, on the revised hate-crimes bill. Representative Jerrold Nadler of New York served as chairman of the hearing, while Representative John Conyers of Michigan is the bill's primary sponsor. Representative Louie Gohmert of Texas presented the case against the hate-crimes bill.

JERROLD NADLER [D-NY]:

Today's hearing deals with one of the most destructive crimes in our society, crimes committed against victims who have been singled out solely because someone does not like who they are. Whether it is because of the actual or perceived race, color, religion, national origin, sexual orientation, gender, gender identity or disability of the victim, these violent acts often can cause death or bodily injury and are absolutely reprehensible. They target not just an individual but an entire group. These crimes do and are often intended to spread terror among all members of the group, and they are intended not merely to do so, but often to deter members of the group from exercising their constitutional rights, sometimes from simply walking down the wrong street or, indeed, any street. As with most criminal activity, bias crimes are properly investigated and prosecuted at both the Federal and State or local levels, depending on the facts of the case and the needs of the investigation.

. . . The proposed legislation that we are going to be considering would provide real penalties and address the problem as it actually exists. It would deal not just with crimes designed to deprive someone of a narrow list of federally protected rights, but with all hate crimes committed where there is Federal jurisdiction. It also provides assistance for law enforcement back home to help them cope with this problem.

Let us be clear: This is not an issue of free speech. What is covered here are criminal acts in which the victim is actually harmed and is selected because of his or her status. The law routinely looks to the motivation of a crime and treats the more heinous of them differently. Manslaughter is different from premeditated murder, which is different from a contract killing, though the result is the same in all cases. We all know how to make these distinctions and the law does it all the time. The only question for Members is whether they believe that singling out a person for a crime of violence because of his or her race or religion or because of any other trait mentioned in this bill is sufficiently heinous to require strong action by law enforcement.

Do we want to give law enforcement the tools to deal with this very real problem? I, for one, hope the answer is yes. For many years, Congress debated what were known as the Federal lynch laws. These were designed to deal with the widespread practice of lynching primarily African Americans. There was staunch resistance of these laws here in Congress, and their enactment was delayed for decades. It was not a proud moment or, I must say, a series of moments lasting for decades in our Nation's history. We now have the opportunity to do the right thing. I hope we can agree to do so. I thank you. I now yield to the distinguished Ranking Member, Mr. Gohmert, for opening comments.

LOUIE GOHMERT [R-TX]:

A couple of the most often cited cases as a basis for creating new hate crimes laws usually include the case, tragically, where the African American in Texas was dragged to death and another horrible case in Texas where a young man was killed for being a homosexual. In both of those cases, the main perpetrators got the death penalty they deserved.

These and other cases are often cited as reasons for hate crime laws. These are cases in which hate crime laws actually would have made no difference at all.

In the dragging death case, I would personally support punishment where the victim's family in that case could choose the rope or the chain used to drag and then the terrain they want to drag the defendant over to bring about the death penalty. But that is not what this does. In fact, the death penalty is not even an issue here. So it would have had absolutely no effect on some of the cases that are heralded as poster examples.

The new hate crime bill creates a vague, ambiguous Federal offense that sends a message that random, senseless acts of violence, possibly like yesterday at Virginia Tech, are far more preferable in society than the same violent actions with a motive.

Never mind that sociopaths and antisocial personalities who commit random, senseless acts of violence are normally more than likely difficult to be rehabilitated. They will not get punished under this new law. Gang members who commit some of the most senseless and tragic acts of violence, sometimes simply as an initiation ritual, will be punished not under this bill.

This hate crimes bill says to the world that sexual orientation—and not just gender, but gender identity, whatever that vague definition means—are in the same category as those persons who have suffered for the color of their skin or their religion. It says to the world that in the priorities of the majority of the United States Congress, a transvestite with gender identity issues will now be more important to protect than a heterosexual, than college or school students, or even senior citizens and widows with no gender identity issues.

Whatever happened to the idea that we were all created equal and that we were all matter equally in God's eyes? We all deserve equal protection. . . .

JOHN CONYERS [D-MI]:

Well, thank you for giving me enough time to get my breath after that presentation, Mr. Chairman.

As the author of this subject matter, hate crimes, for the last decade, I have never started a hearing with that much opposition to this legislation. But then that is what we are here for, to see if we can talk and reason our way across this understanding that we are not giving anybody superior protection; we are bringing in a group that have been excluded for a long time.

You yourself referred to lynchings, which were tragically one time commonplace in this country. Nearly 4,000 African Americans were killed, lynched, tortured between 1880 and 1930, and during the same period, thereafter, religious groups of Jewish faith, Mormons also, and others were subject to attack. Arab Americans are now coming into that category as well.

As we all understand, hate violence against minority groups of all kinds in this Nation has a long and ignominious history that continues even today. We have seen and we have heard the statistics that Chairman Nadler has referenced, and so to protect against this hate violence, to protect the Nation against hate violence, I have introduced the Hate Crimes Prevention Act for the last decade with ever-increasing support.

The measure before us today has more than 130 cosponsors and will provide assistance to State and local enforcement agencies to amend Federal law to facilitate the investigation and prosecution of violent, bias-motivated crimes. It does not take the original jurisdiction away from the States. This complements some very important support that frequently is needed in some areas for these crimes to be prosecuted.

I am proud that over 230 educational, religious organizations, civic groups, civil rights organizations, virtually every major law enforcement organization in the country has endorsed the proposal that is before us. It is a proposal that is very little different from the one I introduced in the last Congress that passed the House of Representatives.

So, despite the deep impact of hate violence on communities, current law limits Federal jurisdiction over hate crimes to incidents only if the victim is engaged in federally protected activities, and that we propose to modify.

And so, like the Church Arson Prevention Act of 1996 which helped Federal prosecutors combat church arson by addressing unduly rigid jurisdictional requirements under Federal law, State and local authorities currently prosecute the overwhelming majority of hate crimes and will continue to do so under this legislation. The Federal Government will continue to defer to State and local authorities in the vast majority of cases. The Attorney General or high-ranking Justice Department official must approve any prosecutions taken in this sense.

So we come together to reaffirm in even greater numbers and with greater understanding the need for hate crime legislation, and I have every confidence that it will pass in the House of Representatives, and we are hoping to get it through this time in the other body.

Thank you for this opportunity, Mr. Chairman.

Source: The three previous statements were from the Government Printing Office. "Hearing Before the Subcommittee on Crime, Terrorism, and Homeland Security of the Committee on the Judiciary House of Representatives One Hundred Tenth Congress First Session on H.R. 1592." Available online. URL: http://frwebgate.access.gpo.gov/cgi-bin/getdoc. cgi?dbname=110_house_hearings&docid=f:34756.wais. Accessed on July 15, 2008.

DISSENTING VIEWS FROM THE HOUSE JUDICIARY COMMITTEE REPORT (APRIL 30, 2007)

Customarily, after a bill is introduced in Congress, it is referred to an appropriate committee. The committee then reports back to the House of Representatives on the bill's contents and intended effect, and includes both supporting and dissenting views. The following excerpts were taken from House Report 110-113, a report of the House Judiciary Committee covering Local Law Enforcement Hate Crimes Prevention Act of 2007 (H.R. 1592) released on April 30, 2007. It summarizes the views of eight opponents of the hate crimes bill (Lamar Smith, Steve Chabot, Chris Cannon, Ric Keller, Mike Pence, Tom Feeney, Trent Franks, and Jim Jordan). Despite

Hate Crimes

the opposition recorded here, the bill was successfully reported out of committee and passed in the House by a vote of 237-180 on May 3, 2007. It was then referred to the Senate Judiciary Committee, where it remained as of December 2008.

We oppose H.R. 1592 as an unconstitutional threat to religious freedom, freedom of speech, equal justice under law and basic federalism principles.

Justice should be blind to the personal traits of victims. Under the Democrats' hate crime bill, H.R. 1592, criminals who kill a homosexual, transvestite or transsexual will be punished more harshly than criminals who kill a police officer, a member of the military, a child, a senior citizen, or any other person. Hate crimes legislation hands out punishment according to the victim's race, sex, sexual orientation, disability or other protected status.

Our criminal justice system has been built on the ideal of "equal justice for all." If enacted this bill will turn that fundamental principle on its head—justice will depend on whether or not the victim is a member of a protected category: a vicious assault of a homosexual victim will be punished more than the vicious assault of a heterosexual victim. A senseless act of violence, committed with brutal hatred, will be treated as less important than one where a criminal is motivated by hatred of specific categories of people. Justice will no longer be equal but now will turn on the race, sex, sexual orientation, disability or other protected status of the victim. All victims should have equal worth in the eyes of the law, regardless of race or status.

By opening the door to criminal investigations of an offender's thoughts and beliefs about his or her victims, this bill will raise more controversy surrounding a crime. Groups now will seek heightened protections for members of their respective groups, and require even more law enforcement resources to investigate a suspect's mindset.

Even more dangerous, and perhaps unintended, the bill raises the possibility that religious leaders or members of religious groups could be prosecuted criminally based on their speech or protected activities under conspiracy law or section 2 of title 18, which makes criminally liable any person who aids, abets, counsels, commands, induces or procures the commission of the crime, or one who "willfully causes an act to be done" by another. It is easy to imagine a situation in which a prosecutor may seek to link "hateful" speech to causing hateful violent acts. A chilling effect on religious leaders and others who express their beliefs will unfortunately result.

The bill itself is unconstitutional and will be struck down by the courts. No matter how vehemently proponents of the bill try to defend a Federal nexus—there is simply no impact of such crimes on interstate or foreign commerce. The record evidence in support of such a claim is transparent and will be quickly brushed aside by any reviewing court.

Aside from the constitutional infirmities that riddle this bill, the sponsors are seeking to address a problem that is not overwhelming our state or local governments. FBI statistics show that the incidence of hate crimes has actually declined over the last ten years. Of the reported hate crimes in 2005, 6 were murders and 3 were rapes. Only 6 of approximately 15,000 homicides in the nation involved so called "hate crimes." A majority of the crimes reported by the FBI involved "intimidation" with no bodily injury—words or verbal threats against a person. There is zero evidence that States are not fully prosecuting violent crimes involving "hate." Violent crimes are vigorously prosecuted by the States. In fact, 45 States and the District of Columbia already have specific laws punishing hate crimes, and Federal law already punishes violence motivated by race or religion in many contexts.

At the markup, we sought to address these problems with the bill—to restore equal justice under law, to protect the freedom of expression and religious freedom that is so important to our nation, and to ensure that the enumerated powers of the Federal Gvernment are not inappropriately expanded. The majority defeated our attempts to address these problems.

H.R. 1592 RAISES FIRST AMENDMENT CONCERNS AND OPENS THE DOOR TO THE PROSECUTION AND INVESTIGATION OF SPEECH AND RELIGIOUS ACTIVITIES AND GROUPS

The first amendment to the Constitution provides that "Congress shall make no law respecting an establishment of religion or prohibiting the free exercise thereof." America was founded upon the notion that the government should not interfere with the religious practices of its citizens. Constitutional protection for the free exercise of religion is at the core of the American experiment in democracy.

Hate crimes legislation that selectively criminalizes bias-motivated speech or symbolic speech is not likely to survive constitutional review; hate crimes statutes that criminalize bias motivated violence are likely to survive a first amendment challenge.

However, hate crimes legislation can have a chilling effect on speech and first amendment rights by injecting criminal investigations and prosecutions into areas traditionally reserved for protected activity. The line between bias-motivated speech and bias-motivated violence is not so easy to draw.

For example, in prosecuting an individual for a hate crime, it may be necessary to seek testimony relating to the offender's thought process to establish his motivation to attack a person out of hatred of a particular group. Members of an organization or a religious group may be called as witnesses to provide testimony as to ideas that may have influenced the defendant's thoughts or motivation for his crimes, thereby expanding the focus of an investigation to include ideas that may have influenced a person to commit an act of violence. Such groups or religious organizations may be chilled from expressing their ideas out of fear of involvement in the criminal process.

Ultimately, a pastor's sermon concerning religious beliefs and teachings could be considered to cause violence and will be punished or at least investigated. Once the legal framework is in place, political pressure will be placed on prosecutors to investigate pastors or other religious leaders who quote the Bible or express their long-held beliefs on the morality and appropriateness of certain behaviors. Religious teachings and common beliefs will fall under government scrutiny, chilling every American's right to worship in the manner they choose and to express their religious beliefs

Hate crimes laws could be used to target social conservatives and traditional morality. Hate crimes laws have already been used to suppress speech disfavored by cultural elites—indeed this may be their principal effect. Of the 9,430 "hate crimes" recorded by the FBI in 1999, by far the largest group was labeled "intimidation." The "intimidation" category does not even exist for ordinary crimes. This vague concept is already being abused by some local governments, which target speech in favor of traditional morality as "hate speech." In New York, a pastor who had rented billboards and posted biblical quotations on sexual morality had them taken down by city officials, who cited hate-crimes principles as justification. In San Francisco, the city council enacted a resolution urging local broadcast media not to run advertisements by a profamily group, and recently passed a resolution condemning the Catholic Church because of its "hateful" views. No viewpoint should be suppressed simply because someone disagrees with it.

H.R. 1592 IS INCONSISTENT WITH FEDERALISM PRINCIPLES

The bill raises significant federalism concerns and provides protected status to victims based on religion, national origin, gender, sexual orientation, gender identity or disability.

A federal law criminalizing violent actions taken because of the victim's immutable characteristics would be such an act. Such a law criminalizes acts that have long been regulated primarily by the states. Under the Federal system, the Supreme Court has observed, "States possess primary authority for defining and enforcing the criminal law." *Brecht v. Abrahamson*, 507 U. S. 619, 135 (1993) (quoting *Engle v. Isaac*, 456 U.S. 107, 128 (1982)). "Our national government is one of delegated powers alone. Under our Federal system the administration of criminal justice rests with the States except as Congress, acting within the scope of those delegated powers, has created offenses against the United States." *Screws v. United States*, 325 U.S. 91, 109 (1945) (plurality opinion).

The Court has viewed the expansion of Federal criminal laws with great concern due to their alteration of the balance of Federal-State powers. "When Congress criminalizes conduct already denounced as criminal by the States, it effects a change in the sensitive relation between Federal and State criminal jurisdiction."

Congress should not act quickly or without due deliberation before it chooses to further federalize yet another area that generally lies within the competence of the States. Given the principles of federalism that govern the Constitution, Congress should not use its powers until it is confident that hate crimes are a problem that is truly national scope.

H.R. 1592 VIOLATES THE INTERSTATE COMMERCE CLAUSE AND HAS NO SUPPORT UNDER THE THIRTEENTH, FOURTEENTH, AND FIFTEENTH AMENDMENTS

In addition to federalism concerns, the legislation creates Federal jurisdiction on tenuous constitutional grounds, relying on the Commerce Clause, as well as the Thirteenth, Fourteenth, and Fifteenth Amendments.

Interstate Commerce Clause

The Supreme Court, in *United States v. Morrison*, struck down a prohibition on gender-motivated violence, and specifically ruled that Congress has no power under the Commerce Clause or the Fourteenth Amendment over "non-economic, violent criminal conduct" that does not cross state lines.

The Supreme Court's *Morrison* decision followed several other decisions in which the Court clarified the Constitution's restrictions on Congress's exercise of its powers under both the Interstate Commerce Clause and section 5 of the Fourteenth Amendment.

Federal efforts to criminalize hate crimes cannot survive the federalism standards articulated by the Supreme Court. Not only does much of the hate crime problem go beyond what Congress may regulate under the Interstate Commerce Clause, but Congress has yet to perform the extensive fact-finding required to demonstrate that hate crimes are a national problem that requires a Federal solution.

In cases where Congress uses its enforcement powers under section 5 of the Fourteenth Amendment, the Court has said, it must identify conduct that violates Fourteenth Amendment rights, and its must tailor the legislative scheme to remedying or preventing such conduct. To meet these requirements, Congress must conduct fact-finding to demonstrate the concerns that led to the law. For example, the Court observed in *Florida*

Prepaid, a challenge to the Voting Rights Act, Congress developed an "undisputed record of racial discrimination" and upheld the statute under this standard.

In order to create a case for the constitutionality of a law criminalizing hate crimes, Congress must engage in fact-finding. Unfortunately, in their haste to rush this bill through the Committee, the majority has not done any fact finding whatsoever. To meet this standard, the Majority failed to hold adequate hearings concerning the scope of hate crimes in this country, their numbers, and their impact on the economy. Until Congress engages in this sort of legislative spadework, it will not be able to justify its findings in this bill and the factual basis for its action.

Fourteenth and Fifteenth Amendments

The Fourteenth and Fifteenth Amendments do not provide Congress with the claimed authority. The Fifteenth Amendment forbids the Federal Government or a state from denying or abridging the right to vote on the basis of an individual's race, color or previous condition of servitude. The Fourteenth Amendment prohibits the States from denying equal protection of the law, due process or the privileges and immunities of U.S. citizenship. Both of these amendments extend only to state action and do not encompass the actions of private persons. Hate crimes by private persons are outside the scope of these amendments.

Thirteenth Amendment

Section 2 of the Thirteenth Amendment stands on different footing. The amendment proscribes slavery and involuntary servitude without reference to Federal, State or private action. In order to reach private conduct, i.e., individual criminal conduct, Congress would have to find that hate crimes against certain groups constitute a "badge and incidence" of slavery.

Unlike the Fourteenth Amendment, the Court emphasized, the Thirteenth Amendment allows Congress to enact laws that operate upon the acts of individuals, regardless of whether they are sanctioned by state law or not. Section 2 of the amendment "clothed Congress with power to pass all laws necessary and proper for abolishing all badges and incidents of slavery in the United States."

Congress should tread carefully before it chooses to pass a hate crimes statute on the basis of section 2 of the Thirteenth Amendment. Such a law would have to be utterly clear that it is based on the grant of authority to combat slavery. Only vaguely asserting that some hate crimes might be linked to vestiges, badges, or incidents of slavery or segregation would not be enough.

Although there have been few judicial pronouncements on the scope of the Thirteenth Amendment, the *Jones* case was limited to discrimination on the basis of race, specifically discrimination against African-Americans. Efforts to include within a hate crimes prohibition those crimes motivated by national origin, religion, gender, sexual orientation, disability and any other factor other than race would amount to a congressional effort to interpret the Thirteenth Amendment beyond that so far permitted by the Supreme Court. The Court will want to ensure that, in defining badges and incidents of slavery to include hate crimes, Congress has enacted remedial and preventative legislation that seeks to end the true effects of slavery, rather than attempting to re-define the term "slavery" or "involuntary servitude" as it has been interpreted by the Supreme Court.

STATISTICS SHOW THAT HATE CRIMES HAVE DECLINED OVER THE LAST TEN YEARS

FBI statistics show that the incidence of hate crimes has declined over the last ten years. In 1995, 7,947 hate crime incidents were reported. Statistics for the last four years, 2002 through 2005, have shown a decline in the number of hate crimes reported. In 2005, for example, 7,163 hate crimes were reported.

Of the reported hate crimes in 2005, six were murders, three were rapes, and a majority of the crimes were characterized as 'intimidations' as opposed to any involving bodily injury. As an example, for 2005, there were 1,017 violent incidents based on bias for sexual orientation, or approximately four incidents per million of population. In contrast, the national rate of violent crime in 2005 was 1.4 million, or 492 incidents per 1 million of population.

Fifty-six percent of the crimes involved racial bias; 11 percent anti-religion bias; 14 percent national origin bias; and 14 percent sexual orientation bias. Anti-disability and anti-sexual identity bias was less than 1 percent. The Hate Crimes Statistics Act does not require collection of hate crimes statistics for violent crimes alleged to be motivated by "gender identity."

STATE PROSECUTIONS ALREADY ADDRESS VIOLENT CRIMES AND HATE CRIMES

Hate-crimes laws are unnecessary: the underlying offense is already fully and aggressively prosecuted in almost all States. There is zero evidence that States are not fully prosecuting violent crimes involving "hate."

Moreover, 45 States and the District of Columbia already have laws punishing hate crimes, and Federal law already punishes violence motivated by race or religion in many contexts. In the absence of data that States are unable to prosecute or decline to prosecute hate crimes, there is no reason for the Federal assertion of jurisdiction or the diversion of Federal resources to such investigations and prosecutions.

Some of the most notorious hate crimes were prosecuted under state laws, and there is no evidence that States are unable or unwilling to prosecute such crimes. Of the five states with no current hate crime legislation (Georgia, Indiana, Arkansas, South Carolina, and Wyoming), Georgia and Indiana have both tried to pass legislation pertaining to hate crimes in the past two years, and in both cases the legislation has been struck down by the courts.

NEED TO PROTECT MILITARY, CHILDREN, POLICE, ELDERLY, VICTIMS AND WITNESSES

In protecting a limited categories of groups, such as race, religion, sexual orientation, gender or gender identity, the majority rejected our attempts to add other equally meritorious groups such as members of the Armed Forces, law enforcement officers, children, senior citizens, witnesses, pregnant women, and crime victims. We can see no reason to distinguish among these groups—all of them deserve heightened protection against hate-motivated crimes. The majority has made its priorities clear, and has done a disservice to our Armed Forces, police officers, children, senior citizens, pregnant women, witnesses and crime victims.

* * *

Conclusion

As outlined above, H.R. 1592 suffers from numerous problems. The majority's rush to judgment ensures that, even if enacted, the hate crimes statute will be overturned by the courts. That will undermine its stated goal of assisting state and local law enforcement to reduce bias-motivated violence.

Source: Government Printing Office. "House Report 110-113." URL: http://frwebgate.access.gpo.gov/cgi-bin/getdoc.cgi?dbname=110_cong_reports&docid=f:hr113.110.pdf. Accessed on August 15, 2007.

"UNCONSTITUTIONAL LEGISLATION THREATENS FREEDOMS" (RON PAUL, MAY 7, 2007)

Last week, the House of Representatives acted with disdain for the Constitution and individual liberty by passing HR 1592, a bill creating new federal programs to combat so-called "hate crimes." The legislation defines a hate crime as an act of violence committed against an individual because of the victim's race, religion, national origin, gender, sexual orientation, gender identity, or disability. Federal hate crime laws violate the Tenth Amendment's limitations on federal power. Hate crime laws may also violate the First Amendment guaranteed freedom of speech and religion by criminalizing speech federal bureaucrats define as "hateful."

There is no evidence that local governments are failing to apprehend and prosecute criminals motivated by prejudice, in comparison to the apprehension and conviction rates of other crimes. Therefore, new hate crime laws will not significantly reduce crime. Instead of increasing the effectiveness of law enforcement, hate crime laws undermine equal justice under the law by requiring law enforcement and judicial system officers to give priority to investigating and prosecuting hate crimes. Of course, all decent people should condemn criminal acts motivated by prejudice. But why should an assault victim be treated by the legal system as a second-class citizen because his assailant was motivated by greed instead of hate?

HR 1592, like all hate crime laws, imposes a longer sentence on a criminal motivated by hate than on someone who commits the same crime with a different motivation. Increasing sentences because of motivation goes beyond criminalizing acts; it makes it a crime to think certain thoughts. Criminalizing even the vilest hateful thoughts—as opposed to willful criminal acts—is inconsistent with a free society.

HR 1592 could lead to federal censorship of religious or political speech on the grounds that the speech incites hate. Hate crime laws have been used to silence free speech and even the free exercise of religion. For example, a Pennsylvania hate crime law has been used to prosecute peaceful religious demonstrators on the grounds that their public Bible readings could incite violence. One of HR 1592's supporters admitted that this legislation could allow the government to silence a preacher if one of the preacher's parishioners commits a hate crime. More evidence that hate crime laws lead to censorship came recently when one member of Congress suggested that the Federal Communications Commission ban hate speech from the airwaves.

Hate crime laws not only violate the First Amendment, they also violate the Tenth Amendment. Under the United States Constitution, there are only three federal crimes: piracy, treason, and counterfeiting. All other criminal matters are left to the individual states. Any federal legislation dealing with criminal matters not related to these three issues usurps state authority over criminal law and takes a step toward turning the states into mere administrative units of the federal government.

Because federal hate crime laws criminalize thoughts, they are incompatible with a free society. Fortunately, President Bush has pledged to veto HR 1592. Of course, I would vote to uphold the president's veto.

Source: "Ron Paul's Texas Straight Talk." Available online. URL: http://www.house.gov/paul/tst/tst2007/tst050707.htm. Accessed on November 22, 2007.

APPENDIX F

WHITE HOUSE POSITION STATEMENT (MAY 3, 2007)

In this White House document, released on the day that the House of Representatives was voting on the hate crimes bill, the Bush administration lays forth its official view of the proposed legislation.

The Administration favors strong criminal penalties for violent crime, including crime based on personal characteristics, such as race, color, religion, or national origin. However, the Administration believes that H.R. 1592 is unnecessary and constitutionally questionable. <u>If H.R. 1592 were presented to the President, his senior advisors would recommend that he veto the bill.</u>

State and local criminal laws already provide criminal penalties for the violence addressed by the new Federal crime defined in section 7 of H.R. 1592, and many of these laws carry stricter penalties (including mandatory minimums and the death penalty) than the proposed language in H.R. 1592. State and local law enforcement agencies and courts have the capability to enforce those penalties and are doing so effectively. There has been no persuasive demonstration of any need to federalize such a potentially large range of violent crime enforcement, and doing so is inconsistent with the proper allocation of criminal enforcement responsibilities between the different levels of government. In addition, almost every State in the country can actively prosecute hate crimes under the State's own hate crimes law.

H.R. 1592 prohibits willfully causing or attempting to cause bodily injury to any person based upon the victim's race, color, religion, or national origin, gender, sexual orientation, gender identity, or disability. The Administration notes that the bill would leave other classes (such as the elderly, members of the military, police officers, and victims of prior crimes) without similar special status. The Administration believes that all violent crimes are unacceptable, regardless of the victims, and should be punished firmly.

Moreover, the bill's proposed section 249(a)(1) of title 18 of the U.S. Code raises constitutional concerns. Federalization of criminal law concerning the violence prohibited by the bill would be constitutional only if done in the implementation of a power granted to the Federal government, such as the power to protect Federal personnel, to regulate interstate commerce, or to enforce equal protection of the laws. Section 249(a)(1) is not by its terms limited to the exercise of such a power, and it is not at all clear that sufficient factual or legal grounds exist to uphold this provision of H.R. 1592.

Source: The White House, Office of Management and Budget. "Statement of Administration Policy: H.R. 1592, Local Law Enforcement Hate Crimes Prevention Act of 2007." Available online. URL: http://www.whitehouse. gov/omb/legislative/sap/110-1/hr1592sap-h.pdf. Accessed on August 25, 2008.

APPENDIX G

SENATOR OBAMA ON JENA, JUSTICE, AND HATE CRIMES (SEPTEMBER 28, 2007)

Senator Barack Obama delivered the following remarks on hate crime legislation at the annual convocation of Howard University in Washington, D.C., on September 28, 2007, at which event he was given an honorary degree. At this time Obama had been running for the Democratic Party nomination for seven months; although he was raising by far the most money of any candidate, he was still trailing Senator Hillary Clinton in the polls. Howard University was named for General Oliver Howard, commissioner of the Freedman's Bureau, and has played a key role in the modern civil rights movement.

It's a privilege to be a part of today's convocation and an honor to receive this degree from Howard. There are few other universities that have played so central a role in breaking down yesterday's barriers and inching this country closer to the ideals we see inscribed on the monuments throughout this city.

It was Howard that sent the first African American to the United States Senate. It was Howard that graduated the first African American to become governor and the first to become mayor of the largest city in the country. It was here, within the halls of this campus, where Thurgood Marshall huddled with the brilliant minds of his day to craft the arguments in Brown v. Board that ignited a movement that changed the world. And it is because of these victories that a black man named Barack Obama can stand before you today as a candidate for President of the United States of America.

But I am not just running to make history. I'm running because I believe that together, we can change history's course. It's not enough just to look back in wonder of how far we've come—I want us to look ahead with a fierce urgency at how far we have left to go. I believe it's time for this generation to make its own mark—to write our own chapter in the American story. After all, those who came before us did not strike a blow against injustice only so that we would allow injustice to fester in our time. . . .

In a media-driven culture that's more obsessed with who's beating who in Washington and how long Paris Hilton is going to jail, these moments are harder to spot today. But every so often, they do appear. Sometimes it takes a hurricane. And sometimes it takes a travesty of justice like the one we've seen in Jena, Louisiana.

There are some who will make Jena about the fight itself. And it's true that we have to do more as parents to instill in our children that violence is always wrong. It's wrong when it happens on the streets of Chicago and it's wrong when it happens at a schoolyard in Louisiana. Violence is not the answer. Non-violence was the soul of the Civil Rights Movement, and we have to do a better job of teaching our children that virtue.

But we also know that to truly understand Jena, you have to look at what happened both before and after that fight. You have to listen to the hateful slurs that flew through the halls of a school. You have to know the full measure of the damage done by that arson. You have to look at those nooses hanging on that schoolyard tree. And you have to understand how badly our system of justice failed those six boys in the days after that fight—the outrageous charges; the unreasonable and excessive sentences; the public defender who did not call a single witness.

Like Katrina did with poverty, Jena exposed glaring inequities in our justice system that were around long before that schoolyard fight broke out. It reminds us of the fact that we have a system that locks away too many young, first-time, non-violent offenders for the better part of their lives—a decision that's made not by a judge in a courtroom, but by politicians in Washington. It reminds us that we have certain sentences that are based less on the kind of crime you commit than on what you look like and where you come from. It reminds us that we have a Justice Department whose idea of prosecuting civil rights violations is trying to rollback affirmative action programs at our college and universities; a Justice Department whose idea of prosecuting voting rights violations is to look for voting fraud in black and Latino communities where it doesn't exist.

We know these inequities are there. We know they're wrong. And yet they go largely unnoticed until people find the courage to stand up and say they're wrong. Until someone finally says, "It's wrong that Scooter Libby gets no jail time for compromising our national security, but a 21-year-old honor student is still sitting in a Georgia prison for something that wasn't even a felony. That's wrong."

It's not always easy to stand up and say this. I commend those of you here at Howard who have spoken out on Jena 6 or traveled to the rally in Louisiana. I commend those of you who've spoken out on the Genarlow Wilson case. I know it can be lonely protesting this kind of injustice. I know there's not a lot of glamour in it. . . .

I don't want to be standing here and talking about another Jena four years from now because we didn't have the courage to act today. I don't want this to be another issue that ends up being ignored once the cameras are turned off and the headlines disappear. It's time to seek a new dawn of justice in America.

From the day I take office as President, America will have a Justice Department that is truly dedicated to the work it began in the days after Little Rock. I will rid the department of ideologues and political cronies, and for the first time in eight years, the Civil Rights Division will actually be staffed with civil rights lawyers who prosecute civil rights violations, and employment discrimination, and hate crimes. And we'll have a Voting Rights Section that actually defends the right of every American to vote without deception or intimidation. When flyers are placed in our neighborhoods telling people to vote on the wrong day, that won't only be an injustice, it will be a crime.

As President, I will also work every day to ensure that this country has a criminal justice system that inspires trust and confidence in every American, regardless of age, or race, or background. There's no reason that every single person accused of a crime shouldn't have a qualified public attorney to defend them. We'll recruit more public defenders to the profession by forgiving college and law school loans—and I will ask some of the brilliant minds here at Howard to take advantage of that offer. There's also no reason we can't pass a racial profiling law like I did in Illinois, or encourage state to reform the death penalty so that innocent people do not end up on death row.

When I'm President, we will no longer accept the false choice between being tough on crime and vigilant in our pursuit of justice. Dr. King said it's not either-or, it's both-and. We can have a crime policy that's both tough and smart. If you're convicted of a crime involving drugs, of course you should be punished. But let's not make the punishment for crack cocaine that much more severe than the punishment for powder cocaine when the real difference between the two is the skin color of the people using them. Judges think that's wrong. Republicans think that's wrong. Democrats think that's wrong, and yet it's been approved by Republican and Democratic Presidents because no one has been willing to brave the politics and make it right. That will end when I am President.

I think it's time we also took a hard look at the wisdom of locking up some first-time, non-violent drug users for decades. Someone once said that ". . . long minimum sentences for first-time users may not be the best way to occupy jail space and/or heal people from their disease." That someone was George W. Bush—six years ago. I don't say this very often, but I agree with the President. The difference is, he hasn't done anything about it. When I'm President, I will. We will review these sentences to see where we can be smarter on crime and reduce the blind and counterproductive warehousing of non-violent offenders. And we will give first-time, non-violent drug offenders a chance to serve their sentence, where appropriate, in the type of drug rehabilitation programs that have proven to work better than a prison term in changing bad behavior. So let's reform this system. Let's do what's smart. Let's do what's just.

Now, there is no doubt that taking these steps will restore a measure of justice and equality to America. They will also restore a sense of confidence to the American people that the system doesn't just work—it works for everyone.

. . . One of the most inspiring things about the response to Jena was that it did not begin with the actions of any one leader. The call went out to thousands across the internet and black radio and on college campuses like this one. And like the young Americans of another era, you left your homes, and got on buses, and traveled South. It's what happened two years earlier when students here at Howard and Americans from every walk of life took it upon themselves to try and rescue a city that was drowning. It's how real change and true justice have always come about. . . .

Source: BarackObama.com. "Remarks of Senator Barack Obama: Howard University Convocation." Available online. URL: http://www.barackobama.com/2007/09/28/remarks_of_senator_barack_obam_26.php. Accessed on July 29, 2008.

INDEX

Locators in **boldface** indicate main topics. Locators followed by *c* indicate chronology entries. Locators followed by *b* indicate biographical entries. Locators followed by *g* indicate glossary entries.

Index

Index

317

Index

Index

Index

Index